Threshold Dwellers in the Age of Global Pandemic

Threshold Dwellers in the Age of Global Pandemic

EDITED BY
Eleazar S. Fernandez

PICKWICK *Publications* · Eugene, Oregon

THRESHOLD DWELLERS IN THE AGE OF GLOBAL PANDEMIC

Pickwick Publications
An Imprint of Wipf and Stock Publishers
199 W. 8th Ave., Suite 3
Eugene, OR 97401

www.wipfandstock.com

PAPERBACK ISBN: 978-1-6667-0919-3
HARDCOVER ISBN: 978-1-6667-0920-9
EBOOK ISBN: 978-1-6667-0921-6

Cataloguing-in-Publication data:

Names: Fernandez, Eleazar S., editor.

Title: Threshold dwellers in the age of global pandemic / edited by Eleazar S. Fernandez.

Description: Eugene, OR: Pickwick Publications, 2022. | Includes bibliographical references.

Identifiers: ISBN 978-1-6667-0919-3 (paperback). | ISBN 978-1-6667-0920-9 (hardcover). | ISBN 978-1-6667-0921-6 (ebook).

Subjects: LCSH: COVID-19 (Disease)—Religious aspects—Christianity. | Pastoral theology. | Theology. | Ethics. | Theodicy.

Classification: BV4335 T15 2022 (print). | BV4335 (ebook).

05/16/22

To the Frontliners and to Those Who Lost Their Lives
Due to the Pandemic

Contents

Acknowledgments

WITH THE PANDEMIC POSING threat and wreaking havoc, it did not take much time for me to take immediate and concrete steps to respond to its challenge. Given my position at Union Theological Seminary (Philippines), by April of 2020 I was already able to facilitate the public offering of a five-part series of online lectures/seminars to help our communities deal with the onslaught of the pandemic. The online lectures/seminars included the following topics: Psychological Responses in a Time of Pandemic, The COVID-19 Crisis and the Global Economy: Roots and Impacts, Spiritual Practice for Spiritual Caregivers in Time of Pandemic, Healthy Self: Radical Self-Care in the Time of Corona, From Fear to Hope: Contradictions in the Time of the Coronavirus Pandemic. Also, almost every week I posted on Facebook reflections to critique what has been going on and to inspire our people so we can remain resilient in the face of the pandemic. In addition to these timely and concrete steps, without much hesitation, I thought of editing a book on the pandemic.

At first, I thought that it would not take much time to give birth to this project but, as I moved forward, I was confronted with the reality that the completion of the work, as in the case of edited volume, was not completely within my control, and much more so when people are dealing with the stresses that the pandemic has wrought on top of demands from day-to-day work. Contrary to my earlier expectation, the number of meetings and gatherings went up when people began to get used to the online mode of communication. Also, an edited volume that purports to help our people, including the chapter contributors, can only be true to its intent by the way it shows care and concern with people along the way, because the journey is constitutive of the destination. I am glad that, in spite of the challenges that the pandemic posed, the pieces have finally come together.

As in any edited volume, the project cannot move forward without the contributions of essay writers. It is to them first that I would like to express my deep appreciation: Ferdinand A. Anno, Trina Armstrong, Jennifer Awes Freeman, Jonathan Barnes, Ruben L. F. Habito, AHyun Lee, Francisco Lozada Jr., Rodolfo R. Nolasco Jr., Neal D. Presa, Justin Sabia-Tanis, Rey Ty, and Demian Wheeler. Although busy with other concerns, they have been generous in gifting this project with their time and skills.

Before I proceed with acknowledging others, no project is possible without financial support. I would like to mention the common Global Ministries of the United Church of Christ USA and Christian Church (Disciples of Christ) for the support through Dr. Derek Duncan, Area Executive for East Asia and the Pacific. Also, I would like to express my appreciation to individuals who have worked behind the scenes to make this project possible. In particular, I would like to give thanks to Max Brumberg-Kraus, who has taken the greater bulk in editing this work, and to others who have contributed in one way or another, including Daria Day, Kakay M. Pamaran, and Zenaida A. Roy, for her meticulous proofreading work.

As always, I am grateful for my wife, Jo, for her support in my professional life and my publication work. She has been such a great companion in the journey we call life.

June 13, 2021

Written in the rainy days of June, punctuated by staccato sounds of lightning and thunderstorms with the shrill songs of the cicadas in the background.

Contributors

Ferdinand Anno teaches liturgy and religious studies at Union Theological Seminary–Philippines and is currently the director of the school's Doctor of Ministry program. He earned his theological degrees from Leeds University (PhD), Edinburgh University (MTh), and Silliman Divinity School (MDiv). Among his most recent publications are: "Resources for Indigenous Theology: Perspective from the Philippines" (*The Ecumenical Review*, 62:4), "Towards a Liturgical Approach to Re-routing Missions" (Oxford: Regnum, 2010), and "Toward an Indigenous *Podong* Spirituality for the Struggle" (*The Union Seminary Journal*, 2019).

Trina Armstrong is an Associate Professor of Marriage and Family Therapy and Pastoral Theology at Louisville Presbyterian Theological Seminary. Dr. Armstrong is a Licensed Marriage and Family Therapist, Certified Pastoral Counselor, Life Coach, Spiritual Director, and Founder of The Center of Wellness Encounters. She is an ordained Itinerant Elder in the African Methodist Episcopal Church, serving as Associate Minister at DuPage AME Church. Dr. Armstrong has a PhD in Practical Theology and Spiritual Care and Counseling from the Claremont School of Theology, a Master of Divinity from Fuller Theological Seminary, a Master's degree in Psychology from California Southern University, and a Bachelor of Science degree in Information Systems from Golden Gate University.

Jennifer Awes Freeman is Assistant Professor and Program Director of Arts and Theology at United Theological Seminary of the Twin Cities. She came to United in 2018 after teaching at the University of St. Thomas as a Louisville Institute Postdoctoral Fellow. Awes Freeman's publications have examined the role of images and material culture in religious meaning-making during Late Antiquity and the early Middle Ages. Two of her current writing projects are: The Good Shepherd: Image, Meaning, and Power (Baylor University Press), and Erasing God: The Carolingian Reception of the Ashburnham Pentateuch (Boydell & Brewer). One of her most recent articles is: "The Good Shepherd and the Enthroned Ruler," in *The Art of Empire: Christian Art in its Imperial Context* (eds., Lee Jefferson and Robin Jensen, Fortress).

Jonathan Barnes serves as the Director of Higher Education and Communications for Higher Education and Leadership Ministries of the Christian Church (Disciples of Christ). In addition, he serves as affiliate faculty at several institutions, including Christian Theological Seminary, Lexington Theological Seminary, and the University of Indianapolis. He previously served for over a decade in South Africa and Mozambique with Global Ministries (Christian Church [Disciples of Christ] and the United Church of Christ) and the Mennonite Central Committee. He received his PhD in Theology and Development from the University of KwaZulu-Natal, and is the author of *Power and Partnership: A History of the Protestant Mission Movement* (Pickwick Publications, 2013) and co-editor of *Restoring Dignity, Nourishing Hope: Developing Mutuality in Mission* (2016).

Eleazar S. Fernandez is President of Union Theological Seminary, Philippines. He was a Professor of Constructive Theology at United Theological Seminary of the Twin Cities for about three decades. He received his PhD degree from Vanderbilt University. Among his writings are: *Teaching in a World of Violent Extremism* (editor; Pickwick Publications, 2021), *Teaching for a Multifaith World* (editor; Pickwick Publications, 2017), *Teaching for a Culturally Diverse and Racially Just World* (editor; Cascade Books, 2013), *New Overtures: Asian-North American Theology in the 21st Century* (editor, 2012), *Burning Center, Porous Borders* (Wipf and Stock, 2011), *Reimagining the Human* (Chalice, 2004), *Realizing the America of our Hearts* (co-editor with Fumitaka Matsuoka; Chalice, 2003), *A Dream Unfinished: Theological Reflections on America from the Margins* (co-editor with Fernando Segovia; Orbis, 2000), and *Toward a Theology of Struggle* (Orbis, 1994).

Ruben L. F. Habito is Professor of World Religions and Spirituality and Director of Spiritual Formation at Perkins School of Theology, Southern Methodist University, Dallas, Texas. Among his works are: *Zen and the Spiritual Exercises: Paths of Awakening and Transformation* (Orbis, 2013), *The Gospel Among Religions: Christian Ministry, Theology and Spirituality in a Multireligious World* (co-editor; Orbis, 2010), *Vida Zen, Vida Divina: un Dialogo entre Budismo Zen y Cristianismo* (Mexico DF: Editorial Pax, 2008), *Healing Breath: Zen for Buddhists and Christians in a Wounded World*, 3rd edition (Wisdom Publications, 2006), *Experiencing Buddhism: Ways of Wisdom and Compassion* (Orbis, 2005).

AHyun Lee, PhD, LPC, is an Assistant Professor of Pastoral Care at Wesley Seminary in Indiana Wesleyan University. Her scholarly research, clinical and ministerial experiences, and teaching experiences are grounded in interdisciplinary studies in the psychology of religion, self-psychology, psychoanalysis, intercultural studies, feminist and womanist theories, Asian theology, and practical theology. Prof. Lee is an Elder in the United Methodist Church in Wisconsin and a licensed Professional Counselor. Prof. Lee has served several cross-cultural and cross-racial ministries and has completed numerous professional certifications. Her dissertation, "Narrative Therapy, Postcolonial and Transcultural Pastoral Care and Counseling: Perspectives on the Experience of Korean Clergy Women," provided the impetus for ongoing research of interdisciplinary methods in transnational and multicultural counseling in global and postcolonial contexts. Her book *Selves in Between: Offering Care and Forging Bonds with Difference* is forthcoming and will be published by New Book, General Board of Higher Education and Ministry.

Francisco Lozada Jr. is the Charles Fischer Catholic Professor of New Testament and Latinx Studies at Brite Divinity School. He holds a doctorate in New Testament and Early Christianity from Vanderbilt University. He is a past co-chair of the Johannine Literature Section (SBL), past chair of the Program Committee of the Society of Biblical Literature (SBL), and a past member of SBL Council. He is a past president of the Academy of Catholic Hispanic Theologians of the United States, a past steering committee member of the Bible, Indigenous Group of the American Academy of Religion (AAR), and past co-chair of the Latino/a and Latin American Biblical Interpretation Consultation (SBL). He also serves on the board of directors for the Hispanic Summer Program, and mentored several doctoral students with the Hispanic Theological Initiative (HTI). Dr. Lozada's most recent publications are concerned with cultural and ideological interpretation while exploring how the Bible is employed and deployed in ethnic/racial communities.

Rodolfo R. Nolasco Jr. is Professor of Pastoral Theology at Garrett-Evangelical Seminary, Chicago, Illinois, since 2018. He earned his Doctor of Theology degree in Pastoral Psychology from Boston University. Among his writing projects are: *The Contemplative Counselor: A Way of Being* (Fortress, 2011). *Compassionate Presence: A Radical Response to Human Suffering*

(Wipf and Stock, 2016), *God's Beloved Queer: Identity, Spirituality, Practice* (Wipf and Stock, 2019), *Heart Ablaze: Awakening the Queer Spirit* (Church Publishing Inc., forthcoming) and *Depression, Dark Night of the Soul and Joy* (Cascade, forthcoming).

Neal D. Presa is a Presbyterian Church (USA) pastor in Rancho Santa Fe, California, Visiting Professor of Practical Theology at the International Theological Seminary in West Covina, CA, Visiting Professor and Scholar at the Union Theological Seminary in Dasmariñas, Cavite (Philippines), Research Fellow of Practical and Missional Theology at the University of the Free State in Bloemfontein, South Africa, and a Fellow for the Center for Pastor Theologians in Oak Park, Illinois. He was the former Moderator of the 220th General Assembly of the Presbyterian Church (USA). He is the author and editor of six books, including *Liturgical-Missional: Perspectives on a Reformed Ecclesiology* (Wipf and Stock, 2016) and *Our Only Comfort: 52 Reflections on the Heidelberg Catechism* (Westminster John Knox, 2015).

Justin Sabia-Tanis is an Assistant Professor and Program Director for Social Transformation at United Theological Seminary of the Twin Cities. He has degrees from the Graduate Theological Union, Harvard University, and San Francisco Theological Seminary. His career has included pastoral ministry as well as communications work for several national LGBTQ advocacy organizations. He is the author of *Transgender: Ministry, Theology, and Communities of Faith*, which was a finalist for a Lambda Literary Award and a contributor to *Understanding Transgender Identity* (Baker Academic), among others. He has also contributed chapters to the *Queer Bible Commentary* and *Take Back the Word: A Queer Reading of the Bible*.

Rey Ty is a faculty member of the Department of Peace Studies as well as the incoming Director, starting March 16, 2022, of the Institute of Religion, Culture, and Peace—also known as the Religion, Culture, and Peace Lab—both of which of Payap University in Thailand. He has taught in various universities in the USA and in the Philippines. His peer-reviewed academic publications on youth and interfaith peacebuilding, human rights, environmental action, gender, refugees, migrant labor, statelessness, climate change, and other issues are indexed in BASE, ERIC, ORCID, Sch-Hub, Semantic Scholar, and Scopus. Dr. Ty received his Master's degree in Asian Studies (Political Science) from the University of California at Berkeley. Pursuing additional studies, he received his second Master's degree in Political Science (Comparative Politics, Political Theory, International Relations, Southeast Asian Politics) and doctorate degree in

Education (adult and higher education administration; public policy; human resource development; community development; social movement) from Northern Illinois University.

Demian Wheeler is Associate Professor of Philosophical Theology and Religious Studies and Director of Advanced Studies at United Theological Seminary of the Twin Cities. He is the author of *Religion within the Limits of History Alone: Pragmatic Historicism and the Future of Theology* (State University of New York Press, 2020) and the co-editor of *Conceiving an Alternative: Philosophical Resources for an Ecological Civilization* (Process Century, 2019).

Introduction

I NEVER THOUGHT THAT I would witness a global pandemic of this magnitude in my lifetime. I had read books about past epidemics and writings on future pandemics that would be catastrophic, but I had brushed them aside as remote and distant. This is often what we do, enjoying complacency until such time that something unfolds before our own eyes and we are shocked to recognize that the world we have taken for granted has come crashing down. We have been living in a bubble of complacency for quite some time and the coronavirus pandemic has forced us to recognize that fact. It has required just such a crisis of pandemic proportion for us to come to our senses. With the pandemic infecting and claiming many lives on its raging path, even claiming the lives of people we know and care about, what seemed remote and only a matter of statistics has sent tremors into our distraught souls. With the statistics hitting home and becoming more personal, the pandemic has become a reality that can no longer be ignored. It must be faced with courage, and responded to creatively, if we are to not only survive but also thrive.

The COVID-19 virus, commonly called the coronavirus, has wreaked havoc on a global pandemic proportion. In just a few months since it was detected, it has spread rapidly to the far corners of our globalized world, claiming so many lives. In order to slow down the spread of the virus, flatten the curve, and not overwhelm healthcare facilities, many countries have issued quarantine and lockdown orders and individuals have been mandated to observe "shelter-in-place," which means that people should not leave their residences except to get basic essentials, such as food and medicine. Schools, houses of worship, malls and theaters, restaurants, entertainment centers, and others have been closed. Travels, especially international flights, have been closely monitored and severely restricted. Institutions and businesses have been mandated or encouraged to adapt to this unprecedented situation by adjusting work practices, doing online classes and meetings, online worship, and working from home when possible. Those who have been most adversely and disproportionately affected are the working poor and daily wage earners who do not have regular salaries and are most likely not to have the option to work at home. The fallout will surely be beyond the terror that the current pandemic has wrought, which has catastrophic impact on our socio-political and economic life.

It is not a surprise that the coronavirus has occupied our days, for it has occupied our lives. It is not a surprise that it has occupied our lives, for it has threatened and terrorized us with death, not to mention those who are already dying before their time, before and during this pandemic. We cannot and should not be nonchalant in the face of the challenge of the coronavirus: the darkness around us is truly deep. I do not doubt that this pandemic will be a historic landmark in the history of humankind, at the very least it will define discourse and interactions in the next generations until the arrival of another possible event of catastrophic proportion, which only reminds us of our fragility and shared vulnerability.

Given this catastrophic event that is shaping our lives and history, I find it difficult to go on with my normal life without dealing and responding, in whatever way I can, to this catastrophic phenomenon that is threatening life and our way of dwelling. As scholars, teachers of religion, pastors, social activists and change agents, and common citizens who care about our shared plight, what contribution can we offer to make our communities become better equipped to deal with the challenges of the global pandemic? How can we best respond to the threats of pandemic for the sake of our shared flourishing? What can we learn from this global pandemic? What can we learn from it about humanity, our shared and fragile life, and that of our cosmic abode, and about God? What do religion, theology, and practical ministry have to offer so we may thrive, not in spite of, but even in and through the challenges of pandemic? We do not have all the answers and solutions, but we can do our share.

It is in light of the above challenge and my desire to offer or contribute helpful and contextually timely responses that I am proposing a writing project, an edited volume, in which others can contribute based on their fields of expertise, in a way in which a single author cannot. The urgency of responding to the challenge could be addressed as well if various authors contribute their pieces to the topic.

Description of the Book

Excluding the Introduction by the editor, this volume has thirteen chapters. At the very outset, the first three chapters wrestle head on with the issue of the COVID-19 pandemic from theological, historical, and biblical perspectives. They are followed by socio-political critique and ethical responsibility (chapter 4) and an exposition on what it means to be human in the face of the pandemic (chapters 5). The next three chapters (chapters 6–8) offer some practical ways on how we can cope and remain physically, psychologically, and spiritually healthy in the face of the assault of the pandemic. Chapters 9–11 focus on the challenge of what it means to be a church and how to reimagine mission and the place of liturgy with the pandemic in mind. Finally, the last two chapters (chapters 12–13) deal with vision, hope, and pathways toward a post-pandemic world.

Briefs from Essay Contributions

Chapter 1, by Demian Wheeler, "Coronavirus, Pantheistic Naturalism, and the Problem of Evil: A Postpandemic Theology," contends that the COVID-19 pandemic, as a "paradigm evil event," places substantial plausibility constraints on personal theism, a theology that understands God as an agential being with intentionality, conscious awareness, and humanly recognizable goodness. Wheeler then proposes *pantheistic naturalism*, which he claims as a more compelling theological alternative to a personalistic model of divinity. From the point of view of *pantheistic naturalism*, the destructive aspects of existence, such as the coronavirus pandemic, are necessarily included in the divine life and are natural givens that we must cope and contend with spiritually and ethically. Taking the destructive aspects as part of the divine life, pantheistic naturalism invites us to let go of false hopes and accept divinity for what it actually is, namely, a morally inscrutable web in which creation and destruction, life and death, good and evil are ontologically intertwined. Furthermore, pantheistic spirituality also generates a *humanistic* resolve to assume moral responsibility for the state of the world, to recognize that the possibility for social transformation and global health rests squarely with human decision.

From a theological position that exposes the plausibility constraints of the more common personal theism and proposes pantheistic naturalism, especially in light of the COVID-19 pandemic, Jennifer Awes Freeman (chapter 2, "'And Who Is My Neighbor?': Historical Images of Christian Responses to Pandemic") approaches the topic of pandemic from a historical perspective. While pandemics have often incited and exacerbated violence, superstition, and bad theology throughout history, such crises have also proved to be generative, leading to acts of goodwill, generosity, and even self-sacrifice. This chapter surveys the various contexts of the Justinianic Plague of the sixth century, the bubonic plague of the fourteenth and sixteenth centuries, smallpox in the Americas during the early modern period, the 1918 Flu, and the AIDS pandemic. Revisiting how religious thinkers and leaders have responded to these pandemics can help us to reflect critically on our own responses and invite us to embrace opportunities for theological innovation, spiritual care, and social responsibility that are grounded in theology and the history of the church.

Following a historical perspective on the pandemic is a biblical account (chapter 3) by Francisco Lozada Jr., "Contemporary Biblical Interpretations: Reflections amid the COVID-19 Pandemic." In light of the COVID-19 global pandemic, Lozada contends that biblical interpreters need to take seriously the responsibility of interpretation and the ways it can imagine the task and the world anew. COVID-19's compelling message, among others, is to imagine a new relationship to our world and to others through biblical interpretation. Informed by Fernando F. Segovia's presidential address ("Criticism in Critical Times: Reflections on Vision and Task") to the Society of Biblical Literature (November 2014), the chapter—in the first part—reviews his address and employs his line of interpretation (global-systematic approach) as a way to provide reflection on the task of biblical interpretation in light of COVID-19. In the second part, the chapter delineates the impact of COVID-19 on the vulnerable immigrant communities along the US-Mexico southern border and reflects on the task of biblical interpretation moving forward.

Chapter 4, "Ethics, Social Justice, and COVID-19," by Justin Sabia-Tanis, starts with a critical account of how the coronavirus has impacted the United States, which includes a critique of the uneven impact of the virus, especially on the poor and communities of color, and how a health crisis has become a socio-political crisis. After examining some specific impacts of the virus, Sabia-Tanis's chapter explores fundamental ethical questions about social responsibility. He raises such questions as: What is our responsibility for the wellbeing of others and ourselves? What role do leaders play in containing and responding to the crisis, which is local and global in nature? What do our religious and ethical traditions teach us about care, especially for the most vulnerable among us during this time of pandemic? The rest of the chapter is an articulation of his response to the questions raised with a particular emphasis on how religious traditions, when interpreted and practiced rightly, are best suited to respond to the challenge of the pandemic. Instead of using our freedom for our personal purposes, our freedom provides an opportunity to act responsibly for the common good.

In chapter 5, "Reimagining the Human: How Shall We Be for Each Other?," Eleazar S. Fernandez calls our attention to the catastrophic reality that we are facing and what we can learn from it as human beings in our shared global village. Shocking and painful as it is, this global pandemic could be a portal leading us to a new way of being, dwelling, relating, and acting in the world. His chapter seeks to ask as well as to answer foundational questions: Who are we, not only in the limited sense, but in relation to the wider web of life? What is our plight? Who have we become in light of the pandemic? What matters to us the most? How shall we live, which is the philosophical variant of the question, what shall we do? This presupposes that our "being-in-the-world" affects our "doing-in-the-world" and vice versa.

The next three chapters (chapters 6–8), offer some practical thoughts on how we can cope and remain physically, psychologically, and spiritually healthy in the face of the assault of the pandemic. Chapter 6, "COVID-19 and Traumatic Stress," from AHyun Lee and Rolf R. Nolasco Jr. lays out clearly what it wants to deliver. It sees the COVID-19 pandemic as a traumatic event. After defining trauma and presenting types of traumas, the authors claim that the COVID-19 pandemic is a complex and collective trauma. Although at first external, it moves inside and adversely affects our care, connection, and meaning-making systems. When this happens, we are more vulnerable to psychic and collective injury. It affects our whole selves: mental, physical, social, emotional, and spiritual well-being. The pandemic, its death toll, uncertainty of its ending, and the various protocols, such as social distancing, quarantine, isolation, and more, have impacted all areas of life, including human health, medical systems, economy, politics, education. The rest of the chapter deals with how people are coping with the pandemic and suggests some ways to respond to the complex and collective trauma. It ends with suggestions on how to mitigate the hazards of COVID-19 pandemic at the individual and communal level. The chapter's intention is to provide basic help so we can cope, survive, and thrive during this time of pandemic.

As the title of chapter 7 clearly defines, Trina Armstrong offers "Pastoral Care for Grief and Loss in Pandemics." Armstrong introduces her chapter by presenting the havoc and the impact of the pandemic in the lives of people, which has adversely affected those with comorbidities and communities of color. While the most visible markers of the pandemic are infections and death, the pandemic has other markers and has collateral effects that include the spiritual, emotional, financial, physical, and ecological aspects of our lives. They lead to other losses that produces ripple effects of suffering, many of which are untold and unacknowledged and can linger far beyond the immediate impact of the pandemic. Armstrong walks us through the rest of her chapter by articulating the sense of loss that human communities have experienced in the time of pandemic and its primary expression—grief, which includes three expressions: anticipatory, disenfranchised, and complex. Religious communities play an important role in helping individuals and communities make sense or make meaning of this loss. The remaining part of the chapter ends with guidance on how to provide pastoral care in light of the situation, which religious communities are well poised to do because they have the right resources to help address that deep human need.

In chapter 8, "Spirituality in an Age of Pandemics: Breathing with Uncertainty, Isolation, and Pain: Envisioning a Different World," Ruben L. F. Habito assesses and brings to our attention the spiritual sickness that the pandemic has brought to our lives. There are three salient features that have emerged to best describe our state of mind and way of being in this age of global pandemic: uncertainty, isolation, and pain. Uncertainty is in the air which breeds anxiety and can degenerate into fear. In addition to uncertainty, there is also the feeling of isolation. Lastly, with the help of social media, we have become more aware of the pain and suffering around us, especially as the rate of infection and death toll increases. This weighs on us and can lead to pessimism and despair. Habito, however, does not leave us with this precarious situation. Based on the understanding that at the depth of our malady is a spiritual matter, Habito offers spiritual pathways or practices to healing. He makes the point that spiritual practice can make a difference in the way we live through this lingering contagion. The rest of the chapter provides spiritual resources on how we can overcome anxiety and fear, alienation and separation, pessimism and despair that is not just a return to our "normal ways," but come out with a new way of thinking and dwelling.

Dealing with the topic of the church, mission, and worship in relation to the pandemic are chapters 9–11. Jonathan Barns (chapter 9, "Mission and Ministry in the Age of Pandemics") takes on the topic of God's mission and, derivatively, the church's mission and ministry in the age of pandemics, which is simultaneously perennial and contextually timely. Barnes says that the pandemic has brought us to a point in which we are now experiencing a liminal moment, a liminal moment not of our own choosing or making, in which old ways of living, experiencing, and thinking about the world have been upended, and the "what's next" is not clear by sight. In the midst of this uncertainty and confusion, what can we say about mission and ministry? With this question in mind, Barnes offers some general directions as to what this mission may be about, which include (1) embracing our shared humanity and connection to God's wider creation, (2) acknowledging and addressing the great disparities that exist between people, both locally and around the world, (3) and advancing three mission motifs: mission as lament, mission as dialogue, and mission as witness to life. The rest of the chapter articulates these general directions.

After presenting the challenges of the COVID-19 "pandemic" and what he calls the "endemic" of racial, economic, and ecological injustice, Neal Presa (chapter 10, "Being and Doing Church in the Age of Pandemics") puts two confessions of faith of the Reformed theological tradition, particularly the World Alliance of Reformed Churches (WARC)—the *Belhar Confession* (1986) and the *Accra Confession* (2004)—in conversation with two prescient documents from the World Council of Churches (WCC), *Together Towards Life: Mission and Evangelism in Changing Landscapes* (2013) and *The Church: Towards a Common Vision* (2013), which put forward what it means to be a church in the twenty-first century. These convergent documents, contends Presa, have something significant to say on how we understand the church's identity, and how a robust and nimble ecclesiology as set forth in these theological sources strengthen the church's witness in an age of pandemics. More specifically, the two *Confessions* have much to say from global contexts with respect to our health pandemic and racial endemic, while the two WCC documents have much to say on how the church in the global context is living into the witness of the Holy Spirit in communities at the margins of societies.

In chapter 11, "God's Passion and the Gospel of Cocooning Toward Life's Rising: A Resistance Liturgics Perspective," Ferdinand A. Anno attempts to discern the signs and irruptions of God's presence in a situation where humanity seems to have been mercilessly orphaned by the gods. He proposes ways of discerning these signs of divine presence, what this presence means to humanity, and how this presence challenges us to become witnesses of God's radical solidarity with humanity and creation. The discussions and propositions immediately proceed from reflections on the Lenten passion narrative, particularly informed by the Filipino *Pasyon*, and its theology of God's solidarity with humanity and creation. To expound his ideas, Anno appropriates the concept of "life-rite" from ritual studies and the Christian rites to discern how God's presence is sensed and experienced in the creativity of a ritual process with inputs from the God-talk of popular struggles. He contends that struggle for social change, when seen as a rite of passage, reframes, performs, and binds together the story of God's presence and the narrative of the people's struggle to form a subversive narrative of hope.

Rey Ty (chapter 12, "Post-COVID-19 Pandemic Futures: The New Normal, Status Quo Ante, and Peaceful Future") starts by reminding us that the world before the COVID-19 pandemic was already in crisis: the plagues of predatory capitalism, environmental crisis, and climate emergency. The pandemic has only exacerbated and unveiled the deep fractures in our society.

Using Interactive Historical and Contextual Analysis as a theoretical framework for his research, which rests on the assumption that economic, political, and ideological structures of nature and society are intertwined, he names three contending post-pandemic futures that include: the "new normal," "status quo ante" or "back to normal," and the "just, green, and peaceful future." He develops his chapter with these questions: (1) What are the features of the new normal? (2) What are the divergent and competing models of the "back to normal?" (3) What are the elements of the structure of the just, green, and peaceful future that its proponents present? We must take note, says Ty, that these three contending futures are not mutually exclusive. Opting for the just, green, and peaceful future, he claims it as the best viable future in contrast to the "new normal" and the status quo ante. The struggle for a just, green, and peaceful future will not be an easy one, continues Ty, but an uphill struggle in which progressives of all hues must continue to be engaged.

The last chapter by Eleazar S. Fernandez (chapter 13, "Threshold Dwelling to Make Hope and History Rhyme: Reimagining a Post-pandemic World"), serving as a conclusion, calls us to live in active hope, which entails living at the threshold for the purpose of making hope and history rhyme. It challenges us to move beyond cynicism and despair and take the pandemic as an opportunity to give birth to a post-pandemic world that befits us as human beings created in the image of God. In order for us to move forward in the direction of becoming the better versions of ourselves, we need to live ourselves into a new way of thinking, and let us remind ourselves that the road is made by walking.

1

Coronavirus, Pantheistic Naturalism, and the Problem of Evil

A Post-pandemic Theology

—DEMIAN WHEELER

The Dawning of Post-pandemic Theology: The Coronavirus Outbreak as a New Paradigm Evil Event

> The tragedy of where we are today is it didn't have to be this bad.
> . . . The President keeps telling us the virus is going to disappear.
> He keeps waiting for a miracle. Well, I have news for him, no
> miracle is coming. We lead the world in confirmed cases. We
> lead the world in deaths. Our economy is in tatters, with Black,
> Latino, Asian American, and Native American communities
> bearing the brunt of it.
>
> —Joseph R. Biden, 2020 Democratic National Convention Speech

EVIL IS, AND ALWAYS has been, one of religion's most vexing problems. This life is beset by so much sadness and sorrow, desolation and destruction, wantonness and woe—terminal illnesses and horrific twists of fate, senseless violence and inexplicable acts of cruelty, famine and debilitating poverty, unfulfilled longings and irredeemable losses, untimely death and tsunamis that consume everything in their path. All religious traditions must confront the immense challenges (both philosophical and practical) of living in such a pain-ridden and morally ambiguous world. All religious traditions must face the fact that existence involves suffering and that bad things happen (and not just to good people). All religious traditions, in brief, must grapple with the menace of evil—its origins, its meaning, and its alleviation.[1]

However, evil is especially problematic for *theistic* religious traditions such as Judaism, Christianity, and Islam. The theist is burdened with the task of reconciling the existence of an omnipotent and omnibenevolent creator with the sufferings and flaws of creation. In short, why would an all-powerful and all-good deity permit cancer and tornadoes, torture and war?[2]

By my reckoning, the problem of evil is the single greatest threat to classical theism,[3] which, for the sake of simplicity, will be defined as the belief that a conscious, omnipotent, and all-beneficent entity created and providentially governs the world.[4] Evil is at once a logical and an evidential problem. For one thing, numerous critics argue that the following statements are contradictory:

1. God possesses absolute power.

2. The divine character is unambiguously good.

3. Evil exists in great abundance.

These propositions, the argument goes, cannot all be true; the veracity of any two of them implies the falsity of the third.[5] As David Hume famously queried in the eighteenth century: "Is he willing to prevent evil, but not able? Then he is impotent. Is he able, but not willing? Then he is malevolent. Is he both willing and able? Whence then is evil?"[6]

The evidential problem of evil is even more daunting: the world's miseries and catastrophes count as potent *evidence* against the reality of God, at least a supremely powerful and perfectly loving God. Evil, in other words, renders classical theism not only logically inconsistent but also empirically implausible. In his autobiography (posthumously published in 1887), Charles Darwin confessed that the presence of suffering in nature—predation, tragic species extinctions, the eventual annihilation of life on earth, and so on—is elegantly explained by "the view that all organic beings have been developed through variation and natural selection," but is extremely

---

1. Crosby, *Living with Ambiguity*, xi.

2. Davis, "Introduction," ix–x.

3. Needless to say, I am not alone in stressing the enormity of the problem of evil for theistic perspectives. For a couple of present-day examples, see Weisberger, "The Argument from Evil"; Ehrman, *God's Problem*.

4. See Davis, "Introduction," viii–ix.

5. Davis, "Introduction," x. See also Weisberger, "The Argument from Evil," 166–70.

6. Hume, *Dialogues concerning Natural Religion*, 63.

difficult to square with "the existence of a personal God."[7] Human atrocities raise similar issues. As Andrea Weisberger vividly illustrates:

> Where was God? Where was the intelligent designer of the universe when 1.5 million children were turned into smoke by zealous Nazis? Where was the all powerful, all knowing, wholly good being whose very essence is radically opposed to evil, while millions of children were starved to death by Stalin, had their limbs chopped off with machetes in Rwanda, were turned into amputees by the diamond trade in Sierra Leone, and worked to death, even now, by the child slave trade that, by conservative estimates, enslaves 250 million children worldwide? Without divine justice, all of this suffering is gratuitous. How, then, can a wholly good, all-powerful God be believed to exist?[8]

Of course, this is hardly news to adherents of theistic religions. Over the millennia, theists have devoted a lot of intellectual energy to "theodicy," that is, the effort to justify (*dike*) the sovereignty and righteousness of God (*theos*) in the face of evil—"natural evil" as well as "moral evil." Natural evil denotes the destructive calamities of nature. The theist is compelled to ask why an omnipotent and absolutely loving deity would allow starvation and sickness, fires and floods, black holes and the black death. Why did God create a world in which survival is contingent upon organisms preying upon other organisms, a world in which meteoric collisions result in the obliteration of entire species, a world in which genetic disorders and freak accidents wreck the lives of multitudes? To be sure, for many people today, disasters such as these are not consciously intended; they are natural occurrences rather than "acts of God." Nevertheless, theologians often describe them as "evil" because they ravage the environment and wreak untold havoc on humans and other sentient beings.[9] Moral evil, by contrast, *is* caused by conscious agents. Moral evil refers to all the pain and grief that is brought about by human wrongdoing and malice, or what theologians traditionally describe as "sin." Moral evil is the evil that people do—to each other, to nonhuman creatures, and to the planet.[10] And moral evil, like natural evil, begs the theodicy question: where is God? Why does God not intervene to stop genocide, terrorism, rape, police brutality, white supremacy, animal cruelty, rapacious consumerism, and the abduction of children? As Weisberger candidly puts it: "There is an abundance of evil

---

7. Darwin, "Autobiography," 94–96.

8. Weisberger, "The Argument from Evil," 166.

9. See Crosby, *Living with Ambiguity*, 35.

10. Davis, "Introduction," xi; Crosby, *Living with Ambiguity*, x, 33–41.

in our world. If we can prevent it, then we are morally obligated to do so. How much more obligated a perfectly powerful and perfectly good God must be to do the same?"[11]

Historically, theodicies have often been constructed (and deconstructed) in response to what Stephen Davis terms "paradigm evil events," which function as cultural symbols of immense and unspeakable human suffering.[12] For example, the Lisbon earthquake of November 1, 1755, which killed tens of thousands of people, captured the attention of numerous Enlightenment thinkers, from Voltaire to Immanuel Kant. And after World War II, the *Shoah*—the murder of six million Jews by Hitler and the Nazis—became *the* paradigm evil event with which every theology had to reckon. Many, if not most, theologians since the mid-twentieth century have sensed that "the Holocaust," to quote Rabbi Irving Greenberg, "poses the most radical counter-testimony to both Judaism and Christianity."[13]

I want to suggest that humanity now stands on the precipice of a new paradigm evil event. I am speaking of COVID-19, a novel coronavirus (SARS-CoV-2) that originated in China in December 2019 and subsequently set off a worldwide pandemic. At the time of writing, there have been 102,399,513 confirmed cases of the coronavirus, and the global death toll is north of two million.[14] In the United States, 25,921,703 people have contracted the disease, 438,035 of whom have perished[15] (Minnesota, my home state, accounts for 6,202 of those casualties).[16] The University of Washington's Institute for Health Metrics and Evaluation expects that the number of fatalities in America will surpass five hundred thousand by March 2021, just one year after the virus sent the country into lockdown.[17] Such projections are grim, to say the least. Then there is the economic, social, and personal fallout from the pandemic: the rise in unemployment and homelessness, the overtaxing of our healthcare systems and frontline workers, the fear of a recession and chronic financial hardship, the intensification of political and ideological polarization, the closing of schools, businesses, and houses of worship, the worsening of addictions, depression, and other underlying medical conditions. Tragically, the list could be extended indefinitely.

11. Weisberger, "The Argument from Evil," 179.
12. Davis, "Introduction," xiii.
13. Greenberg, "Cloud of Smoke, Pillar of Fire," 11.
14. WHO, "WHO Coronavirus (COVID-19) Dashboard."
15. CDC, "COVID Data Tracker."
16. Minnesota Department of Health, "Situation Update for COVID-19."
17. IHME, "Cumulative Deaths."

In the introduction to this anthology, Eleazar Fernandez notes that the coronavirus may be a "landmark" in the history of human civilization.[18] I concur unreservedly. And I suspect that it may also be a landmark in the history of theological reflection, becoming a new paradigm evil event against which future theodicies will be measured. Sadly, President Biden is right: COVID-19 is a horrendous tragedy, the worst pandemic in more than one hundred years, and no miracle appears to be coming. How will theologians come to terms with this disconcerting empirical fact? We may very well witness the dawning of "post-pandemic theology," just as post-Holocaust theology arose out of the ashes of Auschwitz.[19] That prediction probably seems premature, but my reasoning is twofold.

First, the pandemic is a palpable and looming example of so-called surd evil.[20] Surd evil is superfluous and gratuitous evil, undeserved and unjustified evil, evil that is incapable of being tamed, diluted, or explained away. It is, in the words of Elizabeth Johnson, "an irrational force that cannot be made to fit meaningfully into a divine plan for the world."[21] Like the *Shoah* and other paradigm evil events throughout the ages, the carnage unleashed by the coronavirus is catastrophic, soul-crushing, and utterly confounding, pressing hard upon our most deeply-held religious convictions and demanding theological resolution. Jewish theologian David Blumenthal talks about "the irruption of the holocaust into modern consciousness" and the troubling questions it raises: "How *can* one speak of beauty or meaning with six million ghosts hovering in the background? How *can* one write poetry or paint in the shadow of the holocaust? How *can* one do theology in the presence of one million burning children?" Blumenthal declares that the modern Jew must acknowledge the brokenness and fragmentation of theological discourse in the post-Holocaust era, facing God "without flinching." Writing theology after the Holocaust is "living in a nightmare, with its sudden turns, its flashbacks."[22] My hunch is that theology written in the aftermath of the coronavirus will also have a nightmarish and ruptured quality, its reasoned speech shattered by the millions of lives and livelihoods lost to the pandemic, its faith in divine goodness haunted by the memories of loved ones left to die alone and afraid in nursing homes and hospital beds. As Fernandez ominously remarks, "the darkness around us is truly deep," a grim reminder of our "shared vulnerability." COVID-19 has "threatened

---

18. See Fernandez, "Introduction," 2, above.
19. See, e.g., Rubenstein, *After Auschwitz*.
20. See Davis, "Introduction," xi.
21. Johnson, *Quest for the Living God*, 51.
22. Blumenthal, *Facing the Abusing God*, 8–9, 235.

and terrorized us with death" and, as such, will shape our thinking and theologizing for generations to come.[23] A post-pandemic theology will emerge, and it will be a theology of trauma.

Second, the coronavirus outbreak is paradigmatic inasmuch as it blurs the distinction between natural evil and moral evil; it is complexly and inextricably both. Obviously, COVID-19 is a product of blind evolutionary processes, an infectious disease that spreads without intention or conscious awareness. But many of its devastations are, to a significant degree, the result of *human* shortcomings, missteps, and transgressions—egregious political blunders, preexisting social inequalities, the willful decision by both citizens and states to prioritize personal freedoms and individual rights over the common good.

In America, the mishandling of the pandemic by the federal government, and the incompetence of the Trump administration in particular, have been well documented.[24] Donald Trump himself misled the American public by downplaying the severity of the crisis, denigrated and politicized mask-wearing and other preventive measures, spurned the expertise of scientists, refused to heed WHO and CDC guidelines, received and passed along alternative "data" on COVID-19,[25] and touted baseless claims of election fraud as coronavirus cases reached record highs throughout the country. New research from the Harvard T. H. Chan School of Public Health cites additional failures, from the failure to prevent entry of the virus into the United States from Europe to the failure to mitigate exposure and transmission in the workplace. The study's conclusion is both severe and direct:

> All cases and deaths cannot be prevented—that clearly is not possible with a novel pandemic—but the evidence suggests that ineffective national policies and responses, especially as compared to those of other wealthy nations or compared to the intricate preparation and planning by previous administrations of both parties, have been driving the terrible toll of COVID-19 and its inequities in the US. This country—and its political leaders, who bear responsibility—can and must do better.[26]

Also cited here is the pandemic's "disproportionate impact" on Black, Latinx, and Native American populations, which are "already made vulnerable by racism and dangerous jobs, inadequate wages, and unaffordable

23. See Fernandez, "Introduction," 2, above.
24. See Aratani, "Oversight Report"; Shear et al., "Inside Trump's Failure."
25. See Armus, "Deborah Birx."
26. Hanage et al., "COVID-19," 1003.

housing."[27] Indeed, due to economic and social determinants such as poverty, insufficient access to healthcare and testing, and employment in essential fields, communities of color are experiencing higher rates of infection, hospitalization, and mortality. As the CDC soberly reports, "long-standing systemic health and social inequities have put many people from racial and ethnic minority groups at increased risk of getting sick and dying from COVID-19."[28]

In short, the coronavirus pandemic is as much a political disaster as it is a natural disaster. Yes, it is a respiratory illness and a global health emergency. But it is also a moral failure of epic proportions, an abysmal breakdown of national leadership, and a consequence of economic disparities, systemic racism, white supremacy, and other pervasive and pernicious social injustices. It is a paradigm evil event for which we are at least partially responsible.

My essay will begin to explore the *theological* implications of this new paradigm evil event. I will advance a bold and perhaps unsettling thesis: most theodicies—including philosophically erudite theodicies like process theism—fail to offer an adequate solution to the "dysteleological surplus"[29] that is the coronavirus. The inconvenient truth is that COVID-19, no different than the Holocaust and the Lisbon earthquake, places substantial plausibility constraints on any theology that views God as a personal being with intentionality, conscious awareness, and humanly recognizable goodness. I will then put forward *theistic naturalism* as a more compelling alternative to agential models of divinity and the various theodicies that are deployed to safeguard them from what John Roth calls the "slaughter-bench" of history.[30] More specifically, I will argue for a *pan*theistic naturalism, reimagining God as a metaphor for the whole of nature, nature in all its mystery, wildness, plurality, and ambiguity. According to pantheism, the destructive aspects of the world are necessarily included within the divine life, and the salvation of humanity is not the center of the divine economy. Indeed, human interests are not any more significant to God than viral ones. Thus, pantheists tend to see evil less as a theoretical problem and more as a pragmatic one. Plagues

27. Hanage et al., "COVID-19," 1001–3.

28. CDC, "Health Equity Considerations." See also Golden, "Coronavirus in African Americans"; Oppel et al., "The Fullest Look Yet."

29. "Dysteleological surplus" is Hick's evocative name for surd evil. He elaborates: "Such suffering remains unjust and inexplicable, haphazard and cruelly excessive. The mystery of dysteleological suffering is a real mystery, impenetrable to the rationalizing human mind. It challenges Christian faith with its utterly baffling, alien, destructive meaninglessness." See Hick, *Evil and the God of Love*, 371.

30. Roth, "A Theodicy of Protest," 7.

are not enigmas that need to be harmonized with an anthropomorphic deity and an anthropocentric creation. Rather, they are natural realities, divine forces, that we have to cope and contend with. A pantheist theodicy, to a large extent, amounts to an antitheodicy.

I will conclude by considering how we ought to live spiritually and ethically in light of this austere vision of God, using the coronavirus outbreak as a case study. Pantheism, I will propose, is an invitation to let go of false hopes and wishful thinking and just accept reality, accept divinity, for what it actually is, namely, a morally inscrutable mixture of creation and destruction, life and death, good and evil. For the pantheist, the spiritual calling in a time of pandemic is to assume our rightful place within the vast expanse of nature and to religiously orient ourselves to the ambiguous "all" that God "is"—praising its beauties, fearing its terrors, celebrating its blessings, revering its mysteries, lamenting its wastes, protesting its injustices, augmenting its goods, and facing its tragedies with honesty, authenticity, courage, and, most importantly, compassion. This pantheistic spirituality also generates a *humanistic* resolve to assume moral responsibility for the state of the world, to recognize that the possibility for ethical improvement, social transformation, prophetic resistance, ecological resilience, and global health rests squarely with human decision.

The Futility of Theodicy: Plagues and the Limits of Anthropomorphic Theologies

> Committed as he is to affirming the untrammeled power and goodness of God, the theist . . . needs to perform cognitive backflips to explain God's inaction in the face of war, oppression, hurricanes, famine, plagues, and corporate capitalism.[31]

The coronavirus is certainly not the first public health crisis to elicit deep theological questioning and searching. In her contribution to this anthology, medieval historian Jennifer Awes Freeman expertly surveys the history of Christian responses to pandemics, from the plague of Justinian that spread throughout the Mediterranean world in the early middle ages, to the black death that eradicated a sizeable segment of the population in Afroeurasia during the fourteenth century, to the smallpox virus that traveled across the Atlantic with European colonizers and ravaged Native American communities, to the AIDS epidemic that has claimed more than thirty-five

---

31. Rubenstein, *Pantheologies*, 176.

million lives over the past four decades.[32] Eerily, 2019 marked the centennial of the great influenza pandemic, which swept across the planet from 1918 to 1919 and killed nearly twenty-five million people (less conservative estimates place the number of casualties much higher). Donald Crosby describes the misery in graphic detail:

> The people of entire villages perished in Alaska and southern Africa, and populations in a number of towns elsewhere in the world were also wiped out. Mass graves had to be dug in some places to bury the dead. Individuals with no prior symptoms would be suddenly stricken with the disease, experience pervasive weakening of their bodies within hours, and die the next day. Initially mild cases of the flu would often turn quickly into vicious cases of pneumonia. People would desperately gasp for air as fluid filled their lungs, and bloody froth would issue from their mouths and noses before they expired. . . . Wives, husbands, children, brothers, sisters, other family members, friends, colleagues, and neighbors were cut down by the disease and bemoaned by those who survived.[33]

The Spanish flu, as it is commonly known, along with COVID-19 and other plagues, are random, unintentional forces of nature that disrupt and devastate with no regard for human concerns or desires (although as I tried to show in the previous section, their disruptions and devastations are very often exacerbated by human ignorance, socioeconomic inequities, and moral and political deficiencies). Such systemic natural evils remind us of our fragility, our susceptibility to sickness and sudden death, and our relative insignificance in the grand scheme of things.[34] And in my view, they also constitute powerful counterevidence against theism—at least overly anthropomorphic forms of theism.

Classical theists typically endorse some iteration of what Paul Tillich termed "supranaturalism," which conceives of divinity personalistically—i.e., as a purposive, eternal, all-powerful being with consciousness, agency, and benevolent intentions, a determinate entity who possesses a will, a loving and morally perfect character, a providential awareness of history, and an ability to act and intervene in the world.[35] The supranaturalist, in Tillich's

32. See Awes Freeman's chapter, "'And Who Is My Neighbor?': Historical Images of Christian Responses to Pandemic," below.

33. Crosby, *Living with Ambiguity*, 33–34.

34. Crosby, *Living with Ambiguity*, 33–37.

35. See Wildman, "Ground-of-Being Theologies," 616, 628–29; Wildman, *Science and Religious Anthropology*, 19–25.

words, "separates God as a being, the highest being, from all other beings, alongside and above which he has his existence. In this position he has brought the universe into being at a certain moment (five thousand or five billion years ago), governs it according to a plan, directs it toward an end, interferes with its ordinary processes in order to overcome resistance and to fulfil his purpose, and will bring it to consummation in a final catastrophe."[36] The spiritual and theological benefits of personal theism are undeniable, imagining ultimate reality as a gracious, compassionate, and caring deity, a deity who created the heavens and the earth and yet loves us, forgives us, and knows us by name. This is a God who heals the sick, liberates the oppressed, and resurrects the dead. This is a God who gets involved in our lives and hears and answers our prayers. This is a God who inspires majestic architecture and beautiful works of art. This is a God who instills cosmic optimism and eschatological hope, ensuring us that life is meaningful and that history is going somewhere. In brief, this is a God who is scaled to our deepest human longings—and is powerful enough to satisfy them.

But with benefits come costs. And for some theologians (myself included), supranaturalism is simply too high a price to pay for whatever comforts and assurances personal theism offers. Its greatest asset is also its greatest deficit: anthropomorphism. That is, personalistic variants of theism model God on the agential and intentional capacities of human persons, a model that makes divinity relatable and relevant to our wants and needs, but that also bumps up against big history, multiverse theories, quantum mechanics, evolutionary biology, ecology, the sociology of knowledge, and more recent advances in the cognitive sciences—to say nothing of the projection analyses of religion put forward by Ludwig Feuerbach, Karl Marx, Friedrich Nietzsche, Sigmund Freud, Emile Durkheim, and many other thinkers since the nineteenth century.[37] However religiously appealing, excessively anthropomorphic theologies are becoming harder to defend in a post-Copernicus, post-Darwin, post-Einstein world.

And I would hazard that they will be hard to defend in a post-COVID world. The reality of suffering in nature (e.g., pandemics and their aftershocks) puts enormous pressure on anthropomorphic views of God, and the classical doctrines of omnipotence, omniscience, and omnibenevolence in particular. One of the most formidable burdens facing personal theism is the need to relieve the cognitive dissonance that is generated by the contraindicating evidence of evil, to manage the contradiction between the belief in humanly recognizable divine goodness and the experience of

36. Tillich, *Systematic Theology*, 6.
37. Wildman, "Incongruous Goodness," 269–72.

pain and grief, loss and tragedy. Above all, the theist must grapple with, and attempt to refute, what Wesley Wildman dubs *the argument from neglect*.[38] Human parents who fail to intervene and protect their children when misjudgment or mischievousness or malice threatens to harm them are deemed negligent—sometimes criminally so. Should we not hold God, our heavenly parent, to the same standard? How could our all-controlling, all-knowing, and all-loving father just stand by as lives are destroyed by violence and virulent diseases? Is this not divine negligence?[39]

Maybe not. Maybe it is a punishment for sin. Maybe it is a part of a bigger and mysterious divine plan. Maybe it is a temporary state of affairs that will be made right in the end, in some blissful, beatific, suffering-free afterlife. Maybe it is an illusion, a mere privation of the good. Or maybe it is a necessary condition for the good. Under that scenario, evil is seen as an unavoidable (and unfortunate) side effect of living in the best of all possible worlds—for example, a world with moral virtue and free will, a world in which finite creatures are capable of building character and freely entering into a genuine, uncoerced relationship with their creator.[40]

None of these theodicies, in my estimation, justifies suffering or satisfactorily explains God's putative negligence. Consider the "Irenaean" answer to the problem of evil.[41] One of the leading defenders of this theodicy, John Hick, hypothesizes that evil exists to cultivate moral and spiritual maturity—or "soul-making." Without danger, deprivation, hardship, and anguish,

---

38. Wildman, "Incongruous Goodness," 277–78.

39. For a forceful articulation of the argument from neglect, see Jones, *Is God a White Racist?* Jones's basic thesis is that there is unrelieved tension between black theology, which is premised on the existence of a liberating God, and black history, which is marred by immense and ongoing oppression: slavery, segregation, mass incarceration, poverty and economic disenfranchisement, police brutality, redlining, voter suppression, and so on. Jones does not mince words: "The excessive amount of black suffering and its enormity, both of which are admitted by calling the black situation oppressive, make it risky if not foolhardy to affirm that God is at work for the liberation of blacks. Must not the black theologian first explain how their plight came about in the first place in the face of God's alleged activity in their behalf?" (75). In other words, the dearth of liberation calls into question the reality of God the liberator. Theodicy, therefore, is the proper prolegomenon to any theology of liberation. Why does this allegedly liberating God seem to neglect the oppressed? Is God really on the side of the poor and the downtrodden? Given the lived experiences of people of color, how do we know that God is not a white racist?

40. See Wildman, "Incongruous Goodness," 268, 272, 283–87, 290–94; Weisberger, "The Argument from Evil," 171–79.

41. The Irenaean position is so named because it takes its primary inspiration from the second-century Christian apologist and church father, Irenaeus. See Hick, *Evil and the God of Love*, part III.

there would be no bravery, charity, empathy, or persistence.[42] But such a view drastically underestimates the tragic nature and sheer excess of evil. The stubborn reality is that most people suffer and die without developing into morally and spiritually superior beings. In actuality, pain and trauma very often lead to the exact opposite, to ethical compromises and the loss of faith. And when it comes to paradigm evil events, soul-*breaking* seems to far outpace soul-making; Hitler's gas chambers produced more victims than saints. Hick, as John Roth rightly criticizes, "sees the world too much as a schoolroom when it is actually more like a dangerous alley. How is the Holocaust compatible with the plan of person-perfecting that he describes? How does Auschwitz fit the claim that divine intent ensures evolutionary progress where human character is concerned? In the Holocaust, persons were ruined and destroyed more than they were made or perfected. Auschwitz is waste, the very antithesis of providential design and purpose in God's economy."[43] Besides, what kind of God would allow the excruciating deaths of so many merely to promote the religious growth of a few?[44]

An even more common theodicy is the free-will defense.[45] The free-will defense postulates that genuine freedom entails a voluntary self-limitation on divine omnipotence, which, in turn, opens up the possibility of evil. Desiring to relate to human beings as persons rather than automatons, God chooses to show restraint, permitting evil in order to allow moral and spiritual agency to flourish.[46] But surely an omnipotent and omnibenevolent God both *could* and *should* make exceptions from time to time. After all, wise and caring parents do not let their offspring do whatever they want, but seek a *balance* between letting be and stepping in, between giving them the liberty to learn and protecting them from danger (whether self-inflicted or externally caused).[47] If I am able to prevent my son Shailer from making a life-altering mistake or hurting another person or getting run over by an intoxicated driver, then I am ethically required to do so, even if such parental interference requires that I coerce him and constrain his will. Likewise, are there not certain situations in which an all-beneficent and all-seeing God would be morally compelled to intervene and overrule human autonomy? Would not a freedom-preserving

42. See Hick, "A Irenaean Theodicy."

43. See Roth's critique in Hick, "A Irenaean Theodicy," 62–63.

44. Weisberger, "The Argument from Evil," 174–76.

45. For a recent and fairly vigorous argument for the free-will defense, see Davis, "Free Will and Evil."

46. Crosby, *Living with Ambiguity*, 13; Griffin, "Creation and the Problem of Evil," 117.

47. Wildman, "Incongruous Goodness," 278, 290.

God be obliged to prevent Hitler from robbing nine million human beings of *their* freedom? If so, then interpreting God's nonintervention as neglect, as a sin of omission, seems entirely reasonable.

Moreover, even if a free but fallen world is preferable to a sinless but predestined world, does there need to be *this much* affliction and agony? Even if *some* wickedness is an inevitable byproduct of free will, could we at least do without concentration camps, animal cruelty, crippling accidents, sex trafficking, and nuclear weapons? And how do free-will theists account for natural evils, evils that are not the result of human volition: parasitism, mass extinctions, childhood leukemia, disease-transmitting mosquitoes, tidal waves that obliterate entire villages? To wax philosophical, I am unconvinced that freedom is incompatible with a world with *less* evil, a world without gratuitous misery and suffering in nature. And I am convinced that such a world would be better than the one we currently have.[48] Which is the best of all possible worlds: a world with carnivores or a world with vegetarians only, a world with an unchecked Hitler or a world without Auschwitz, a world with pandemics or a world with just epidemics? Presumably, an almighty deity *could* have created a world with a significant amount of liberty and autonomy, while still occasionally intervening to stop *heinous and excessive* evils. And a morally perfect creator would be *obligated* to do this. Yet heinous and excessive evils abound, God is suspiciously absent, and the question of divine negligence looms large. Frankly, I question the absolute and unambiguous benevolence of a deity who allows rampant evils for the sake of certain goods (e.g., freedom or character-building).[49] As David Ray Griffin unnervingly asks: "Can we consider perfectly good and loving an omnipotent being who, having the power to prevent such acts, does not do so?"[50]

Given these difficulties, champions of free-will and soul-making theodicies (and personal theists in general) frequently appeal to mystery and eschatology. Some evils are incomprehensible, but God is in charge, has a plan, and will never give us more than we can handle; billions have suffered without justification and died without peace, but a new heaven and a new earth is coming, a time when mourning, crying, pain, and death will be no more and soul-making will be complete; the Lisbon earthquake, Auschwitz, and COVID-19 feel excessive and dysteleological, but God's ways are not our ways, and we trust that everything happens for a

48. Weisberger, "The Argument from Evil," 176–79. See also Wildman, "Incongruous Goodness," 285.

49. Crosby, *Living with Ambiguity*, 15.

50. Griffin, "Creation and the Problem of Evil," 118.

reason—or at least that all things will work together for good. Though sometimes offering hope, meaning, and consolation, these sorts of theodical moves seem hollow and desperate, retreating to ignorance, sentimentalism, wishful thinking, confessionalism, special pleading, superstition, escapism, and leaps of faith. Worse, they run the risk of trivializing suffering and evil. To assert or imply that the Holocaust served a greater purpose or that the coronavirus will not matter in the eschatological long run is to disregard their wastes and their tragic, irrational character. I call this *the argument from negligibility*. Genocides, natural disasters, and plagues are not interludes in some grand salvation history. Rather, they are true catastrophes and irredeemable losses—surd evils. We should grieve them, not avoid them, and we owe it to their victims and survivors not to whitewash them with empty promises of a divine blueprint or a future eschaton. In the end, assurances of a final redemption in the by and by make too light of suffering in the here and now. And they fail the theodicy test, because they never adequately explain why God would allow suffering in the first place—especially agonizing and needless suffering.[51]

In short, anthropomorphic and agential concepts of God, particularly ones that conceive of divinity as an omnipotent, infinitely wise, and all-caring being, buckle under the weight of the problem of evil. Wildman sums it up well:

> Determinate-entity theism of many kinds requires God to be a compassionate entity with personal knowledge of suffering, the power to act in history and nature, and all the while to be perfectly good in ways that human beings can grasp. This places determinate-entity theism in the middle of a host of daunting theoretical difficulties. . . . The problem, in a nutshell, is that this idea of God is an admirable but finally ineffective attempt to deal with the empirical gap between life as we experience it and the goodness we long to affirm in God as ultimate reality.[52]

Many of us believe in a loving and protective divine parent *precisely because* we suffer. However, experiences of suffering, especially intense, unrelieved, and meaningless suffering, also create cognitive dissonance and grate against theistic belief, leaving us to feel exposed, confused, and abandoned—in a word, neglected.[53] And most, if not all, of the theodicies that are implemented to prop up classical theism and justify God's negligence

51. See Roth's critique in Davis, "Free Will and Evil," 97–101.
52. Wildman, "Incongruous Goodness," 292–93.
53. Wildman, "Incongruous Goodness," 278.

in the face of evil are tenuous and profoundly unsatisfying—intellectually, existentially, and spiritually.

A number of theologians today realize that solving the problem of evil requires more revisionary theological measures. One strategy, which is especially prevalent among liberal Christians and other religious progressives, is to jettison the traditional doctrine of omnipotence. These "limited-deity theisms" come in several varieties,[54] the most philosophically sophisticated of which is *process theism*.

Grounded in Alfred North Whitehead's "philosophy of organism,"[55] process theism rejects the all-controlling, interventionist, *creatio-ex-nihilo* God of classical theology. The process God is not even the ultimate reality, but a divine agent who is both subject to "creativity" and affected by the world. God is one "actual entity" among others within the evolving processes of reality, albeit an entity with a very special role to play. To be precise, God is the supreme being who maximizes value in the cosmos and lures the creative advance toward complexity, novelty, justice, and aesthetic harmony. For David Ray Griffin and other process theists, God is not the intelligent designer who made the world out of nothing, but the divine poet who brings order out of chaos. In a Whiteheadian perspective, the relationship between God and creation is reciprocal rather than unilateral; the future is open rather than settled; divine power is persuasive rather than coercive; and self-determination is inherent to the nature of things rather than bestowed by a creator. Accordingly, colliding meteors and deadly pandemics are not divinely permitted byproducts of the best of all possible worlds, but emergent products of a chaotic, contingent, and indeterminate world, a world that God influences but does not entirely control. These disasters are precisely that: disasters. They are the unrelenting facts of existence. They are realities that God endures and works to assuage, not side effects that God allows for the sake of moral virtue or free will. It is not that God *does not* intervene to prevent a meteor from slamming into the earth or keep a pandemic from decimating humanity; it is that God *cannot*. It is not that God is self-limited by choice (which, to repeat, raises the question of divine negligence); it is that

---

54. A more "evangelical" variety of limited-deity theism is open and relational theology. See especially Oord, *The Uncontrolling Love of God*. As a limited-deity theist, Oord boldly claims that God *cannot* unilaterally prevent genuine evil. But his "essential kenosis" model of open and relational theism is located in between classical free-will theism, which asserts that God voluntarily self-limits, and process theism, which asserts that God is externally constrained by the ontological principles that govern the cosmos. According to Oord, God is limited neither by divine decisions nor by outside forces, but by God's necessarily kenotic and agapeic nature. In other words, the power and providence of God are limited by the uncontrolling love of God.

55. See Whitehead, *Process and Reality*.

God is *metaphysically* limited by a universe that is essentially relational and spontaneous, a universe that eventually brought forth creatures with increasingly greater agency and autonomy. Even the supreme divine being is unable to remove evil and guarantee salvation, because power is always shared, and freedom is not something that God creates or can override.[56]

And yet, although omnipotence is a theological mistake,[57] *omnibenevolence* is still defensible,[58] as God tenderly and patiently leads the world "by his vision of truth, beauty, and goodness."[59] Thus, process theists can preserve an all-compassionate and all-loving deity without having to proclaim that all is well despite appearances or perform the mental gymnastics that are required to explain why God neglects to stop hurricanes and holocausts. They can unblinkingly acknowledge the moral ambiguities of the cosmic process, while still maintaining that God is perfectly good. They can accept plagues as the threats and ineradicable tragedies that they are, while continuing to find refuge in a God whose intentions and aims are always redemptive, a God who makes the most of whatever happens and saves whatever can be saved.[60] Life is full of pointless and unpreventable suffering, but God, as Whitehead assures, "uses what in the temporal world is mere wreckage."[61]

I appreciate process theology and understand its intellectual and spiritual appeal. In fact, the theological stance I will develop in the following section—pantheistic naturalism—germinates (in part) from the "empirical" lineage within Whiteheadian thought. Nevertheless, most process theodicies, in my judgment, are profoundly flawed. While solving the problem of divine neglect, the notion of a limited-but-omnibenevolent deity creates other theodical problems. For instance, there is *the argument from incompetence.*[62] Depriving divinity of omnipotence and ultimacy enables process theologians to proclaim that God is not a neglectful or absentee ruler, but a conscientious and co-suffering activist, trying the divine hardest to bring about beauty and joy in a chaotic world, a world that is violent and sometimes hostile to human longings and interests. But one might wonder whether such a God is competent, much less deserving of attention and

56. Griffin, "Creation and the Problem of Evil," 108–25. See also Griffin, *God, Power, and Evil.*

57. See Hartshorne, *Omnipotence and Other Theological Mistakes.*

58. See Griffin, "Creation and the Problem of Evil," 119.

59. Whitehead, *Process and Reality*, 346.

60. Wildman, "Incongruous Goodness," 272–75; Wildman, *Effing the Ineffable,* 36–42.

61. Whitehead, *Process and Reality*, 346.

62. See Wildman, "Incongruous Goodness," 278–79.

worship. Nature teems with pain, injustice, and senseless misery, and human history shows scant evidence of real moral progress. So, just how influential is the process God? Perhaps it is cogent, and even heartening, to believe that God is *struggling* to call forth a better reality, a reality without genocides and pandemics (or at least with less of them). Yet nearly ten thousand Jews per day died during the Holocaust, and coronavirus cases just surpassed twenty million in India. God may intend otherwise, but the road to hell is paved with good (divine) intentions. God may be doing all that God can, but God's best is scarcely enough. There is a fine line between a persuasive God and a pathetic God, a God that is frequently (usually?) overmatched by evil. As Roth harshly intones, the process God is a "weak God," a "God on a leash," a God that is "too small" to inspire awe and veneration.[63]

Wildman perceptively points out that the argument from incompetence renders process theology ineffectual, not incoherent; the idea of a deity who suffers but is not powerful enough to prevent suffering is simply not as religiously useful and attractive as process theologians profess.[64] However, the philosophical foundations of a process theodicy are also a bit shaky. Shakiest of all is the doctrine of divine omnibenevolence, which is hard to sustain in a Whiteheadian outlook. I dub this *the argument from ambiguity*. In order to maximize harmony in the universe, the process God must somehow balance all the possibilities for value in each occasion of experience. But as Donald Crosby astutely detects, such balancing and harmonization necessarily involves sacrificing potential goods for the sake of others, since values inevitably conflict with one another (for example, what is beneficial for the coronavirus is bad for human civilization and vice versa). Thus, the "goodness" of any divine aim is really perspectival and relative, which means that even the supremely benevolent entity in the cosmos cannot be *unambiguously* benevolent.[65]

The argument from incompetence and the argument from ambiguity are ultimately symptoms of an underlying problem, the same problem that dogs most classical forms of theism: anthropomorphism. The God that process theists seek to justify is a subject with consciousness, feeling, personality, agency, and a perfect moral character. But given our experience of suffering in nature, and bearing in mind our knowledge of the immensity of the universe, the biodiversity of the earth, the relatively recent appearance of *Homo sapiens*, and the universal human penchant for "anthropomorphic

---

63. See Roth's critique in Griffin, "Creation and the Problem of Evil," 125–28.

64. Wildman, "Incongruous Goodness," 279.

65. Crosby, *Living with Ambiguity*, 15–19.

promiscuity,"[66] how plausible is the existence of a person-like, people-friendly, and purpose-driven God? As much as I respect the Whiteheadian heritage and even identify with certain strands of it, the limited-but-omnibenevolent God of process theology is very difficult to substantiate empirically, at least if conceptualized as a literal being (later I will suggest that subordinate deities might be repurposed as symbols or "sacred conventions"). And linking divine activity solely with worldly events that are supportive of human wellbeing or morally good in a humanly perceptible way strikes me as arbitrary and anthropocentric.

That conclusion probably seems atheistic. On the contrary, I simply think that the menace of evil (among other things) demands a more credible (read: less anthropomorphic) concept of God. To state the matter as starkly as possible, theodicy is an exercise in futility, particularly when the *theos* is conceived in overly personalistic terms. Plagues and other dysteleological surds cast serious doubt on the reality of an agential deity—both the classical version and the process version. For that reason, I take an alternate theological route, a position I label *pantheistic naturalism*. Pantheistic naturalism is a road less traveled in philosophical theology, venturing into spiritual territory that is underexplored and sparsely populated. But in my view, it leads to a more promising post-pandemic destination, reimagining divinity non-anthropomorphically and, in so doing, eliminating the need for theodical justifications. Pantheistic naturalism is, in effect, an antitheodicy.

God Is the Whirlwind: Pantheism, Religious Naturalism, and the Ground of Being

> Why is it necessary (and how is it possible?) to have a God one trusts and approves of? I say this not as someone who has known only the Father God, but as someone who has known the world: its droughts and floods, its extremes of climate, its strange combination of tender bounty and indifference, and the uneasiness of human society with its descents into savagery. However certain one may be that one is loved by some presence in the universe . . . that same presence will kill us all in turn, will visit our lovers with sudden devastating illnesses, will freeze our

---

66. F. LeRon Shults coined the term "anthropomorphic promiscuity" to designate the "suite of evolved cognitive tendencies" that "fosters the attribution of intentionality in general (and personification in particular) to non-living entities, forces, or patterns, thereby contributing to the emergence of god-beliefs." Shults, *Practicing Safe Sects*, 20–31; quote on 21.

crops, will age our friends, and will never for one moment stand between us and any person who wishes us harm.[67]

The Hebrew Bible recounts the story of Job, an upright and blameless man undergoing unspeakable trauma and desperately searching for an answer to an age-old question: Why must we suffer? Why do bad things happen to good people? Why is there so much injustice in the world? Job dares to interrogate God:

> Therefore I will not restrain my mouth; I will speak in the anguish of my spirit; I will complain in the bitterness of my soul. . . . I loathe my life. . . . Let me alone, for my days are a breath. What are human beings, that you make so much of them, that you set your mind on them, visit them every morning, test them every moment? Will you not look away from me for a while, let me alone until I swallow my spittle? If I sin, what do I do to you, you watcher of humanity? Why have you made me your target? Why have I become a burden to you? (Job 7:11–21)

In the midst of despair, grieving, and remonstration, Job gradually learns some important lessons—theological, cosmological, and otherwise. First of all, Job discovers that the creator is overwhelmingly powerful and even has a destructive side.[68] Job encounters a God who is awesome and formidable, unfathomable and capricious, morally inassimilable and unscaled to human interests. This is a God who stretches out the heavens and tramples the waves of the sea. This is a God who multiplies wounds and crushes with a tempest (9:1–20). There is no refuge from the divine terror; Job has no choice but to submit and protest: "See, he will kill me; I have no hope; but I will defend my ways to his face" (13:15).

Job also comes to realize that anthropocentrism is a myth, and that the creation is grander than we can possibly imagine. Later on in the book, God famously addresses Job from a whirlwind, revealing that we are not the measure of all things, that we are but a speck in a wild and infinite universe. As Judith Plaskow comments, in chapters 38–41 we find "a description of the intrinsic value of nature apart from human purposes, a paean to the wonders of a strange and mysterious creation that preexists human beings and that has its own order and meaning." God is teaching Job that the world is not founded on human standards of fairness and

---

67. Madsen, "If God Is God She Is not Nice," 104.
68. See Wildman, *God Is*, 1–8.

justice. Rather, "the world is about other things entirely: creativity, beauty, diversity, power, energy."[69]

The message of Job is straightforward yet profound: shit happens; life is long on suffering and short on reasons; people do not always get what they deserve; the cosmos does not revolve around human beings or human concerns; and God is inscrutable, mighty, fierce, and untamable, transcending our moral expectations. The pantheistic naturalist readily embraces this ancient wisdom, but with one crucial caveat: creator and creation are really one and the same. In the provocative words of Margaret Atwood: "God is not the voice in the whirlwind. God *is* the whirlwind."[70]

But let me back up and first define pantheistic naturalism. We begin with pantheism. Etymologically, pantheism simply denotes that all (*pan*) is divine (*theos*). In the pantheist's theological lexicon, the terms "God," "nature," "cosmos," "ultimate reality," "the universe," and "the whole" are practically interchangeable. Pantheism, therefore, differs from pan*en*theism, which claims that all is *in* God.[71] For panentheists (e.g., most process theologians), God and the world are inseparable but distinct; the divine is present within yet more than nature. By contrast, the fundamental theological intuition of the pantheist is that all *is* God. God and the world are *indistinct*; the divine is *coincidental with* nature.[72] Pantheists follow Baruch Spinoza in speaking of "God *or* nature"—*Deus sive Natura*. To quote Mary-Jane Rubenstein: "The universe we are in—and which, in turn, is in us—is what we *mean* when we say the word 'God'; conversely, 'God' is nothing other than the creative work of creation itself."[73]

There are many types of pantheism. The particular type defended here is a species of *religious naturalism*. Essentially, religious naturalism is a spiritually evocative form of naturalism that is oriented to the mystery, splendor, and transcendent depths of nature. All naturalists are metaphysical monists, regarding nature as self-subsistent and all-encompassing. The natural order is "outsideless," so to speak: whatever is—including humankind and its sundry creations—is in and of *this* world, the only world there is. Hence, for the naturalist, there are no supernatural realms or entities of any sort, no immortal souls or otherworldly planes of existence, no agential deities with awareness and intentionality. For the *religious* naturalist, however, the rejection of supernaturalism does not entail the rejection of

---

69. Christ and Plaskow, *Goddess and God in the World*, 188–89.

70. Quoted in Rue, *Religion Is Not about God*, 366.

71. Keller, *On the Mystery*, 53.

72. Frankenberry, "Classical Theism," 29.

73. Rubenstein, *Pantheologies*, 2.

religion. Religious naturalism heralds the promise of a *naturalistic religiosity*, deeming nature both ultimately real *and* ultimately important, both exhaustive of reality *and* worthy of reverence. *Nature itself* is sacred. *Nature itself* is the most fitting object of ultimate concern and commitment. *Nature itself* is the ground of all being and value. *Nature itself* is our home. *Nature itself* is the source of our deepest spiritual feelings—awe, wonder, appreciation, belonging, terror, humility.[74]

Some strains of religious naturalism are nontheistic, while others have a decidedly theistic cast.[75] The theists in the family are not quite ready to give up on God, not only sacralizing but also *deifying* the world. Unlike their more atheistic relatives, who reject theism as "hopelessly anthropomorphic,"[76] theologically inclined religious naturalists opt to de-anthropomorphize, de-personify, and de-supernaturalize divinity, considering "God" an appropriate (if not unproblematic) symbol for nature. But they debate amongst themselves about whether God should be symbolically identified with a particular aspect of nature (e.g., "the personality evolving activities of the universe"[77] or "the source of human good"[78]) or with the ambiguous whole of nature. The *pan*theistic naturalist takes the latter view, equating divinity with *all* things, with nature in its entirety. God is not just *within* the world; God *is* the world.

Pantheistic naturalism, then, is a theological variant of religious naturalism that divinizes the totality of nature. To be very clear, pantheistic naturalists do not believe that nature is divinely ensouled or suffused by a divine mind, spirit, or consciousness. On the contrary, "God" is simply another metaphor for nature in all its mystery, plurality, ambiguity, vastness, materiality, impermanence, and wonder-working power. Hence, on one level, pantheistic naturalism is a hermeneutics, even a theopoetics, of nature. The pantheist maxim "all is God" is a way of seeing and taking the world. As Charles Milligan explains: "Pantheism is a theism, not in the sense of Personal Theism . . . but in the sense that it beholds reality in a worshipful as well as analytic mood, and expresses that in gratitude and devotion."[79]

74. The literature on religious naturalism is vast. See Crosby, *A Religion of Nature*; Goodenough, *The Sacred Depths of Nature*; Hogue, *The Promise of Religious Naturalism*; Rue, *Nature Is Enough*; Stone, *Religious Naturalism Today*; Wildman, "Religious Naturalism."

75. For a comparative analysis of different varieties of religious naturalism, see Demian Wheeler, "*Deus sive Natura*."

76. Crosby, *A Religion of Nature*, 9.

77. Mathews, *The Growth of the Idea of God*, 192–234.

78. Wieman, *The Source of Human Good*.

79. Milligan, "The Pantheistic Motif," 599.

Metaphysically, pantheistic naturalism is perhaps best described as a *ground-of-being process theology*.[80] On the one hand, pantheistic naturalism is adjacent to certain modalities of ground-of being theism. The basic instinct of Paul Tillich and other ground-of-being theologians is that determinate-entity theologies—theologies that portray God as a personal, conscious, intentional agent with plans and powers to act in the world—are susceptible to idolatry and anthropomorphic distortion.[81] Pantheistic naturalists find Tillich persuasive, contending that God is not *a* being—whether classical theism's supernatural creator, who brought the universe into existence and presides over it, or even process theism's "fellow-sufferer who understands."[82] Rather, God, as Tillich said, is "the creative ground of everything that has be-ing." God is "the infinite and unconditional power of being or, in the most radical abstraction, . . . being-itself."[83]

But pantheistic naturalism is a ground-of-being theism with a White-headian twist. More specifically, pantheistic naturalism is a variety of "empirical" process theology, a subtradition within Whiteheadianism that stretches back to the "Chicago school" theologians of the mid-twentieth century.[84] Among other things, the empirical Whiteheadians push process theology away from personalism and panentheism, denying the reality of a divine being that has agency and life-enhancing aims for the world and is somehow more than the creative transformation of the universe. Whereas process theists like Griffin follow Whitehead in distinguishing God from "creativity" (the Whiteheadian equivalent of "being itself"),[85] process empiricists like Henry Nelson Wieman argue that "God *is* creativity."[86] God is not so much *in* process as God *is* process.

Of special importance here is Bernard Loomer, a Whiteheadian empiricist who, in the twilight of his career, drifted toward pantheism. Typical of the empirical process theologians, Loomer embraced a spiritually fecund naturalism, declaring that "the qualities of profound religious encounters and the resources for living an abundantly meaningful life . . . are to be experienced within the concrete realities of this world."[87] He also bristled

---

80. See Wheeler, "Bernard Loomer."

81. Wildman, "Ground-of-Being Theologies," 613, 617n6.

82. Whitehead, *Process and Reality*, 351.

83. Tillich, *Systematic Theology*, 2, 7.

84. For a fuller treatment of the empirical option in Whiteheadian philosophy and theology and its divergence from more conventional iterations of process theism, see Wheeler, "Seizing a Whiteheadian Alternative."

85. See Cobb, *A Christian Natural Theology*, 115–20.

86. Wieman, "Reply to Cherbonnier," 281.

87. Loomer, "The Size of God," 29.

against anthropomorphism and naturalized divinity: "God" is a symbol of nature, not an "enduring concrete individual with a sustained subjective life." But Loomer went a step further than most process empiricists and divinized the *entirety* of nature's processes—not only its creative processes, but its destructive ones as well. If naturalists are right, and "the one world, the experienceable world with its possibilities, is all the reality accessible to us," then God is either a part of the world or synonymous with it. Loomer chose the latter option, the pantheist option: the divine symbolizes "the world in *all* the dimensions of its being." God, he ventured, is "the concrete, interconnected *totality* of this struggling, imperfect, unfinished, and evolving societal web." Thus, Loomer completely collapsed the Whiteheadian distinctions between creativity, divinity, and cosmos. God is none other than "the creative advance of the world in its adventure" or "the organic restlessness of the whole body of creation."[88]

Pantheistic naturalism leans heavily on Loomer and sets forth a radically immanental theology that naturalizes Tillich's ground (being itself = the processes within nature that make and unmake all actualities and potentialities) and divinizes Whitehead's world (God = the entirety of nature in its becoming and relationality). God *is* nature. And the nature that God "is" is both the grandeur of creation and the élan of creativity, both the whole of finite things and the whence of that whole.[89] Mary-Jane Rubenstein notes that critics of pantheism usually object that associating the divine with the material world diminishes the former and adds nothing to the latter. But what if *hyle* (matter) and *kosmos* (world) are virtually god-like—vital and vibrant, animate and emergent, dynamic and self-organizing? What if materiality, rather than deriving from an outside force or an external principle, "generates, regulates, and even regenerates itself"? What if the universe is "an open, evolving, and interpoietic multiplicity of open, evolving, and interpoietic multiplicities"—or in the words of Friedrich Nietzsche, "a monster of energy, without beginning, without end . . . eternally changing . . . the eternally self-creating, the eternally self-destroying"? Might not *this* world be deserving of divinization—or at least deserving of the same kind of awe, respect, gratitude, fear, love, reverence, and devotion traditionally reserved for God?[90] To make the same point in a Loomerian key, the world deified by pantheism is not a deterministic machine engineered by a cosmic watchmaker, but the processual and relational web that creates, and is created by, whatever is. "The

88. Loomer, "The Size of God," 20, 41–42; emphases added.

89. At this juncture, pantheistic naturalists depart from Tillich, who wanted to maintain the distance between the whole of finite things and their "infinite ground." See Tillich, *Systematic Theology*, 2, 7.

90. Rubenstein, *Pantheologies*, 27, 68, 98–99, 105–6, 184–85.

world is God," writes Loomer, "because it is the source and preserver of all meaning" and "because it contains and yet enshrouds the ultimate mystery inherent within existence itself."[91] This is why pantheists join together what the vast majority of theists put asunder. In a pantheistic theology, "God" and "nature," "creator" and "creature," "sacred" and "profane," "ultimate reality" and "the universe," "the power of being" and "the interconnected web of life" coincide. They are different names for *Deus sive Natura*, the source, end, and totality of everything that is or will ever be.

The pantheistic naturalist is hardly the popular kid on the playground of theologians. According to Wildman, the ground-of-being model of ultimate reality (of which pantheistic naturalism is one expression) is usually found at the mystical and apophatic "undersides" of religious and philosophical traditions.[92] And pantheism is almost universally denounced and demonized. Even though pantheistic intimations and insights abound in the history of religion,[93] "pantheist" is an epithet that just about everyone seeks to avoid. As Rubenstein observes, "pantheism is primarily a polemical term, used most often to dismiss or even ridicule a position one determines to be distasteful." Even more portentously, pantheism engenders fear and disgust, treated as a "monstrosity" that demolishes sacrosanct binaries—most fundamentally, the binary between God and world.[94] Only a very small minority of theologians today explicitly identify as pantheists, a sign perhaps that "the panic over pantheism" lingers in contemporary theological discourse.

Be that as it may, notwithstanding its unpopularity, pantheism—and pantheistic naturalism in particular—has much to offer theology, *especially in a time of pandemic*. My own brand of pantheism has been worked out in some detail elsewhere,[95] and I will not rehearse these arguments here. Instead, I wish to devote the remainder of the present essay to the question of suffering, zeroing in on the ways in which pantheistic naturalism understands and responds to evil—specifically surd evils such as COVID-19. Predictably, I will draw on sympathetic religious naturalists like Bernard Loomer, Wesley Wildman, and Donald Crosby. But I will also look to a host of other thinkers, from Jewish and Christian post-Holocaust theologians like Richard Rubenstein, Judith Plaskow, and John Roth (all of whom exhibit ground-of-being

---

91. Loomer, "The Size of God," 29, 31–32, 42.

92. Wildman, "Ground-of-Being Theologies," 612–13, 615, 618–19. See also Wildman, *Religious Philosophy as Multidisciplinary Comparative Inquiry*, 294–304.

93. See Harrison, *Elements of Pantheism*, 13–38.

94. Rubenstein, *Pantheologies*, xx–xxi.

95. Wheeler, "*Deus sive Natura*," 113–16; Wheeler, "The Spirituality of Size." See also Wheeler, *Religion within the Limits of History Alone*, ch. 8.

sensibilities) to pantheist-leaning feminist philosophers like Nancy Franken-berry, Grace Jantzen, and Mary-Jane Rubenstein.

Divine Ambiguity, Theocosmocentric Spirituality, and Human Responsibility: The Piety and Praxis of Pantheistic Naturalism

> In any pluralistic metaphysic, the problems that evil presents are practical, not speculative.[96]

The first, and most obvious, point to make is that God is not all-good. Why? Because the world that the pantheist deifies is not all-good. On the contrary, the world is a *coincidentia oppositorum*, a morally ambiguous web in which order and chaos, creation and destruction, life and death, beauty and trag-edy, emergence and extinction, value and disvalue, pleasure and pain are ontologically entangled and interdependent. As Crosby illustrates:

> We would not be here were it not for the vast extinctions in evolutionary history that preceded us. Our solar system would not exist without the cataclysmic explosion of a supernova star. Many of earth's wonders have resulted from stupendous earth-quakes, floods, storms, and fires. . . . Gravity mercifully holds us to the surface of the earth, but it can also kill us. . . . When we eat, we usually destroy some previously living thing.[97]

The ambiguity of nature also implies that "good" and "evil" are intertwined and perspectival.[98] To cite Crosby again: "It is good for predators to find their prey . . . because predation is necessary to preserve their lives and the lives of their progeny. But the process of being killed and eaten is evil from the perspective of the ones being preyed upon and from the standpoint of their progeny, now left defenseless and unprotected. Both perspectives are real or aspects of the real."[99]

Acknowledging the ambiguity of existence is unlikely to result in heresy charges. After all, what is theodicy if not the effort to square a beneficent (and/or omnipotent) creator with an utterly ambiguous creation, a creation rife with injustices, cruelties, defects, sorrows, absurdities, disappointments, and unthinkable catastrophes? But that is precisely the reason pantheism is

96. James, *A Pluralistic Universe*, 124.

97. Crosby, "A Case for Religion of Nature," 499

98. Crosby, *Living with Ambiguity*, ix, 22–33, 36, 74–77, 79–90. See also Crosby, *A Religion of Nature*, 85–87, 124, 132–45.

99. Crosby, *Living with Ambiguity*, 27, 36.

so controversial, so monstrous: it *equates* rather than reconciles God with the ambiguities of the world. One of the more sobering, and perhaps distressing, implications of a pantheist theology is the renunciation of divine omnibenevolence, of an unambiguously good and morally perfect God. A deity that is identical with the *whole* of reality is inescapably ambiguous. As Loomer realized, if God *is* nature, then the divine life necessarily includes the *diversity* of natural forces—even the "noncreative and destructive" ones. In other words, a *pan*theistic God encompasses *all* things—"all the evil, wastes, destructiveness, regressions, ugliness, horror, disorder, complacency, dullness, and meaninglessness, as well as their opposites."[100]

Loomer blasted other process thinkers for imagining a kind of quasi-dualistic struggle between good and evil. Whitehead, for instance, ontologically separated "God" and "creativity," positing "an aesthetic form of persuasiveness that is pitted against the coercive and inertial powers of the world." Loomer harshly judged that such an "unambiguous structure or character" is empirically untenable. Wieman improved upon Whitehead by urging that "the being of God is not other than the being of the world." But even the doggedly empiricist Wieman identified God with only one type of natural process, namely, the process that brings about the increase of good and gives rise to new values and qualitative meanings. Similar to Whitehead's "divine eros," Wieman's "creative event" is defined by moral perfection and unqualified goodness. And by Loomer's lights, neither is concretely real. Omnibenevolent deities are "bloodless," "clean-cut," and "orderly" abstractions, evasions of "the unmanageable vitalities of concrete life." Nature is intrinsically—metaphysically—ambiguous, manifesting creative transformation *as well as* destruction, advances into novelty *as well as* brute repetition, appetitions toward the good *as well as* passions for greater evil. Why associate God only with the former?[101]

The ambiguity of God is a predominant motif of ground-of-being theologies in general. Tillich claimed that the holy "originally lies below the alternative of the good and the evil" and "can appear as creative and as destructive," as "both divine and demonic."[102] Indeed, to describe divinity as "the ground of being" is to proclaim that God is the source of *all* events, patterns, and potentialities whatsoever, regardless of whether human beings would classify them as good or evil (or neutral). As Wildman contends, God's nature is expressed and unveiled in the interconnections, possibilities, and axiological structures of the universe, some of which make for life and

100. Loomer, "The Size of God," 40, 42.
101. Loomer, "The Size of God," 21, 40, 43, 48–51.
102. Tillich, *Dynamics of Faith*, 14–18.

flourishing and others of which lead to senseless suffering and annihilation.[103] Most theists desire a deity whose character is different from, or at least less ambiguous than, the entirety of nature. The ground-of-being theist, by contrast, accents the *correspondence* between the divine character and the worldly character, hypothesizing that "the moral ambiguity of reality is a natural outcome deriving from the character of ultimacy itself."[104] The world that is disclosed through human experience and opened up by scientific inquiry is emergently ordered yet terrifying, wild, capricious, violent, and unimaginably vast, evincing little, if any, evidence of anthropocentric meaning, cosmic purpose, or divine impeccability. And the ultimate that is glimpsed, dimly and inchoately, in the depth dimensions of the world is utterly ambiguous, at once supportive of and indifferent to our longings and concerns. The ground of all being is also "the abyss of infinite darkness."[105] In the stirring words of Wildman:

> Aristotle had it half right when he conceived God as the principle of natural order that knits together the natural purposes of every living creature into bodily, moral, social, and intellectual harmonies. The half he underplayed is that ultimacy is also the morally impenetrable chaos of mass feeding, the blind chance of random symbiotic events, and the heartless opportunism of viral parasitism. We can narrate one side of this great natural truth about the depths of nature and convince ourselves that we are telling the whole story. We can invent theodicies and other conceptual deflections to manage the painful cognitive dissonance that results. . . . But the whole story of ultimacy . . . is still there to be told. For nature manifests abysmal depths that pass understanding, that absorb mindlessly and hunt mercilessly, that defy moral taming and remain oblivious to the predictable interests of social orders. The apophatic mystics of all traditions have seen this.[106]

Post-Holocaust theologians have also seen this—perhaps more clearly than anyone else. As Roth inveighs, believing in an unambiguously good and all-loving deity is an enormous strain "in the presence of the Holocaust's burning children." History's "slaughter-bench" is just too bloody and

103. Wildman, "Incongruous Goodness," 281–82.

104. Wildman, "Ground-of-Being Theologies," 618.

105. Wildman, "Ground-of-Being Theologies," 612–13; Wildman, *Science and Religious Anthropology*, 19–25, 194–98, 200–206; Wildman, "The Ambiguous Heritage," 54, 60–61.

106. Wildman, *Science and Religious Anthropology*, 204.

brutal, life's "waste" too immense and intense, to deny God's complicity in evil and less-than-perfect moral character.[107]

The Jewish "death-of-God" theologian, Richard Rubenstein, is even more radical, writing about the pervasive sense of divine absence brought on by the *Shoah*, by the extermination of six million Jews (including more than one million children) in Nazi Germany. The Holocaust effectively killed the God of traditional Judaism, the transcendent, righteous, almighty, and omniscient God who rules over the world, acts in history, enters into covenants, rewards obedience, punishes disobedience, and elects Israel as the divinely chosen nation. In other words, "the sovereign Lord of covenant and election" is dead (i.e., no longer credible or culturally meaningful), and no theodicy is robust enough to vindicate the justice of God in the face of the death camps. What contemporary Judaism needs is "a view of God quite different from the biblical and rabbinic mainstream," a theology that is actually believable after Auschwitz. And similar to Loomer and Wildman, Rubenstein lays out a post-theistic, even quasi-pantheistic, ground-of-being theology that stresses the *continuity* between God and the cosmos in its multiplicity and ambiguous wholeness. Drinking from the wells of Lurianic Kabbalism, Hegelian idealism, and nature paganism, Rubenstein speaks of God as the "Holy Nothingness," as the ineffable "*En-Sof*," as the "aboriginal *Urgrund*," as the "ground, content, and final destiny of all things," as the divine "Mother" who creates from her very own substance, as "the dark unnamable Abyss out of which the empirical world has come." This is a form of "mysticism and dialectic pantheism," an immanental and nondualistic theological perspective that closes the gap between divinity, humanity, and nature: there is nothing outside of "the all-embracing, universal totality we name as God," according to Rubenstein. Here, he draws inspiration from Sumerian mythology, where Nammu is portrayed not as the goddess *of* the sea but as the goddess who *is* the sea. Rubenstein offers up an evocative analogy:

> God is the ocean and we the waves. Each wave has its moment when it is identifiable as a somewhat separate entity. Nevertheless, no wave is entirely distinct from the ocean, which is its substantial ground. Furthermore, because the waves are surface manifestations of the ocean, our knowledge of the ocean is largely dependent upon the way the ocean manifests itself in the waves.[108]

Indeed, one of the things we know about waves is that they create *and* destroy. Might this signal that creativity and destruction are inherent

---

107. Roth, "A Theodicy of Protest," 6–7, 31–33.
108. Rubenstein, *After Auschwitz*, 299.

in the "oceanic substratum" as well, in the depths of divinity itself? Rubenstein answers in the affirmative, gesturing toward "the inseparability of the creative and the destructive in the divine activity." The *entire* drama of creation—its ebbs and flows, its makings and unmakings, its joys and sorrows—is the deepest expression of the divine life. The prophet Isaiah stumbled upon this great truth when he affirmed that God alone is the creator of both good and evil, as did "the wise pagans of the ancient Mediterranean," who intuited that the earth is not just a Mother, but a *cannibal* Mother. She who births the world out of her own womb, out of her very essence, will eventually consume her children. We are the fruit *and the food* of the gods, destined to return to the divine source from whence we came. Or to revisit the aforementioned metaphor, we will recede back into the sea and "give way to other waves," a humbling reminder that "death is the final price we pay for life and love."[109]

Wrestling with the problem of evil, and the horrors of the Holocaust in particular, also opened Judith Plaskow's eyes to "the frightening and overwhelming side of God." Plaskow, similar to Rubenstein, is a Jewish ground-of-being theologian who conceives of divinity as the source and ultimate horizon of the world in its totality, "the power of life, death, and regeneration in the universe." Although technically a panentheist rather than a pantheist, she strongly resonates with the character Shug in Alice Walker's novel *The Color Purple*, who declares that "God is everything. . . . Everything that is or ever was or ever will be."[110] And if God truly is *everything*, or at least the creative energy that underlies, animates, and sustains everything, then "the negative, destructive, and terrifying aspects of creation are also part of God." Most theologies simply leave out too much, dissociating (and protecting) God from the unpleasant and dreadful parts of existence, the parts that engulf, consume, and annihilate, the parts that are indifferent to human plans, purposes, and aspirations.

And so do most *feminist* theologies. Plaskow is a leading voice in second-wave Jewish feminism, but she upbraids fellow feminists for ignoring divine ambiguity. With a nod to Catherine Madsen,[111] Plaskow complains that the God of feminist theology is too "nice," too "sanitized," too "controllable"—too unambiguous. Feminist accounts of divinity tend to restrict God to so-called feminine characteristics (nurturing, caretaking, healing, etc.), inadequately attending to the divisive and demonic features of our experience and to the universal human capacity for cruelty and injustice. And they

109. Rubenstein, *After Auschwitz*, 157–76, 247–65, 293–306.

110. Quoted in Christ and Plaskow, *Goddess and God in the World*, 121.

111. See Madsen, "If God Is God She Is not Nice."

cordon off God from a huge chunk of reality, from the unpredictability and ferocity of the world. Carol Christ, for example, advances a process-relational feminist theology that understands divinity as a non-omnipotent but omniamorous Goddess, an intelligent, personal, and loving consciousness that is embodied in all being and is luring every actual entity toward the best possible future. On Plaskow's reading, faith in such a deity amounts to little more than wish fulfillment. "There are signs of love and care written into the structures of the world," she allows, "but there is also evidence of neglect and violence." To exclude the latter from the divine life is to sever an entire side of existence from the sacred and to contradict the notion that God is the ground of *all* being. Reminiscent of Loomer and Wildman, Plaskow theologically prioritizes inclusiveness and wholeness over perfection, preferring a concept of God that embraces nature in all its messiness and complexity to one that overemphasizes divine goodness. To be sure, God is not purely evil either. Rather, God is *ambiguous*, unbound by our moral categories. God is the creative source of *everything* that exists—the good, the bad, and the ugly. For Plaskow, this sensibility is quintessentially Jewish, lying at the heart of scripture and rabbinic traditions. Both Tanakh and Talmud hold up a mirror to the ambiguities of nature (and *human* nature) and refuse to "disconnect God from the contradictory whole of reality." Plaskow, like Rubenstein, regularly quotes Isaiah 45:7: "I form light and create darkness, I make weal and create woe—I, the Lord do all these things."[112]

Why would anyone want, much less worship, a morally ambiguous God? Let me acknowledge upfront that the model of divinity sketched out above is unlikely to attract throngs of converts. Many find the austerity of ground-of-being theology spiritually useless and ethically indigestible,[113] and the pantheist divinization of "nature red in tooth and claw" is a nonstarter for the majority of theologians. But there are upsides, too. Above all, ground-of-being theism, and pantheism in particular, furnishes an intellectually elegant, existentially satisfying, and theologically honest response to the problem of evil—a quality that seems especially desirable in the aftermath of a devastating pandemic. Stated in the most general terms, the pantheistic naturalist views good and evil as ontologically co-primal; suffering and destruction are woven into the very fabric of (ultimate) reality, into the abysmal depths of the divine totality—*Deus sive Natura*.[114] However bleak, this theological viewpoint, I submit, possesses five

---

112. Christ and Plaskow, *Goddess and God in the World*, 118–30, 171–87, 231–38; Plaskow, *The Coming of Lilith*, 134–37.

113. See Wildman, *In Our Own Image*, 208–12.

114. See Wildman, "Incongruous Goodness," 294.

cardinal virtues, virtues that enjoy heightened relevance and urgency in our emerging post-coronavirus landscape: (1) a quadrilaterally supported doctrine of divine ambiguity; (2) a theocosmocentrism; (3) a nondualistic and pluralistic pantheology; (4) a spirituality of size; and (5) an antitheodicy of protest and humanistic praxis.

First, pantheistic naturalists find support for a morally ambiguous God in reason and experience as well as in scripture and tradition. Understandably, the perfectly loving and righteous character of God is a nonnegotiable for many theists.[115] But such faith commitments make God and nature more hospitable and humanly congenial than we know and feel them to be. Wildman powerfully argues that belief in an omnibenevolent creator is strained, even contradicted, by the unrelenting facts of existence and our ordinary experiences of life, both of which reveal that the creation is a morally neutral environment for the interplay of numerous processes—some safe, beautiful, and life-giving, others dangerous, awful, and death-delivering. Process theology is much more rationally intelligible and experientially credible, granting that the creative advance is marked by destruction, tragedy, and ambiguity. Yet even Whiteheadians associate *God* with human-scaled goodness and confine divine activity to morally palatable trajectories in the cosmos, skipping over the rest of reality "in a kind of half-hearted and half-spoken Manichaeism."[116] As Loomer concludes, the unambiguous deity of process theology is "a high abstraction from the world of events," devoid of a concrete and empirical referent.[117]

What is more, the myopic focus on divine goodness often leads theologians to either miss or dismiss *scriptural and historical* sources that testify to the ambiguity of the sacred. The God of the Bible is good, but not all the time. I already mentioned the calamities that Yahweh (or was it Satan?) unleashed on Job. This same deity also commanded Abraham to bind and kill Isaac (Gen 22:1–19), devoured the sons of Aaron for offering the wrong kind of sacrifice (Lev 10:1–3), and warned the Israelites not to come too

---

115. Griffin, for example, asserts that the idea of a morally ambiguous God violates "the very nature of religion." See his critique in Roth, "A Theodicy of Protest," 26. Griffin is mistaken, however. As Wildman keenly observes, excessively personalistic strains of Western theism, and the attending notion of humanly relevant divine goodness, have a history. They are "post-Reformation" cultural constructions that are "deeply linked to the 'turn to the subject' in modern philosophy and theology." In actual fact, theistically minded people in most times and places "tended and still tend to see God behind all life events, both the satisfying and the tragic, both the comforting and the discomfiting, both the welcome and the terrifying." Wildman, *Effing the Ineffable*, 31, 45–47; quote on 46.

116. Wildman, "Incongruous Goodness," 273–77.

117. Loomer, "The Size of God," 38, 49.

close to the base of Sinai lest they die (Exod 19:12–13).[118] The Apocalypse of John foretells the coming of the "King of kings and Lord of lords," who will ride into history upon a white horse, bearing a sharp sword, wearing a robe dipped in blood, and striking down the nations with the fury and wrath of the Almighty (Rev 19:11–21).[119]

Throughout the history of theology, a smattering of thinkers has dared to explore the abysmal, demonic side of divinity. As I have already intimated, every religious tradition, including Christianity and Judaism, has its mystics who posit some sort of God beyond the god(s) of theism and whose core intuition is that whatever is ultimate and sacred is unspeakable, incomprehensible, and morally inscrutable. Even the fathers of the Protestant Reformation, Martin Luther and John Calvin, recognized the ominousness and horribleness of divine power. Luther, for his part, wrote extensively about the grace and forgiveness of God. But, according to Rudolf Otto, he also encountered a God who "is more terrible and frightful than the Devil," a God who is a "consuming, devouring fire." Luther, Otto comments, "knows depths and abysses in the Godhead that make his heart despond."[120]

Instead of ignoring or downplaying these biblical passages and traditions of theological interpretation, the pantheistic naturalist views them as religiously indispensable and even revelatory. The plenary witness of scripture and the iconoclastic wisdom encoded in the history of religion are a window onto the ambiguity and mystery of existence. The difficult and disturbing parts of our religious heritages—for example, the Bible's "texts of terror"[121]—mythically point to facets of reality (human as well as divine) that we need to confront and perhaps change.[122] And they quell the nearly ubiquitous human inclination to anthropomorphize, domesticate, and defang God. As Wildman effuses, humans try to tame the "wildness" and "fierceness" of divinity, forgetting that God is "overwhelmingly awesome," "crushingly powerful," and "unaccountable to any moral standards."[123] Biblical narratives and historical theologies that picture God as ultimately and unequivocally good are, at best, partially true, because God is, and is the source of, *all* goods—even goods that are bad for humans. First John contains one of the greatest hyperboles in all of scripture: "God is love" (4:8). But the author misses the mark entirely in professing that "God is light and

---

118. Plaskow, *The Coming of Lilith*, 135.

119. Wildman, *God Is*, 2–3.

120. Otto, *The Idea of the Holy*, 98–99.

121. See Trible, *Texts of Terror*.

122. Christ and Plaskow, *Goddess and God in the World*, 180.

123. Wildman, *God Is*, 4–8.

in him there is no darkness at all" (1:5). This is why pantheistic naturalism approaches the Bible and the tradition in the same way it approaches life itself: holistically, attempting to account for as much of the data as possible. Embracing the contradictory whole of our religious inheritances enables us to come to grips with the darker dimensions of divinity, with the God that is both the creative ground of all loves and the divine destroyer who may rip us apart—and, yes, rain down plagues upon us (see Ezek 38:22). God is a shepherd who comforts and restores and bestows goodness and mercy (Ps 23). But God is also a threatening bear with its claw to our throats (Hos 13:8).[124] Or to put it more pantheistically, the ambiguities of our scriptures and religious histories symbolically orient us to a *world* that is ambiguous, a world where pandemics and other evils serve as constant reminders that human beings are not the center of the universe.

This brings us to the second cardinal virtue of pantheistic naturalism: theocosmocentrism. One of the primary benefits of making the mysterious and ambiguous whole of nature the proper object of religious orientation is the tempering of anthropocentrism. In other words, the emphasis on divine wholeness shines the theological spotlight on human littleness. The world that the pantheist divinizes is mind-bogglingly immense and ancient, complex and diverse. *Homo sapiens* is merely one species among millions, in a galaxy that is one among billions. And if that is not humbling enough, 99.998 percent of the historical development of the cosmos already occurred before human persons and their personal gods even arrived on the scene. In that sense, pantheistic naturalism is narrative theology writ large—*really* large. Human history (and the history of religion) is a *very* recent chapter in a much bigger and older story, which stretches from the big bang, to the birth of the first stars, to the formation of our solar system and our home planet, to the emergence of life, sentience, consciousness, and culture. For the pantheistic naturalist, this "epic of evolution" functions as a kind of science-based and non-anthropocentric creation myth, a myth that situates, relativizes, and decentralizes humanity within the infinitely broader rhythms of nature.[125]

Assuming our rightful place within the vast expanse of nature requires accepting that everything is not about us (much less about me and my tribe). We are not the *axis mundi* or the apex of evolution. Rather, we are star-born, earth-formed, extinction-bound organisms, a spectacular but miniscule, contingent, and finite part of the interdependent web of all

124. Wildman, *God Is*, 4–6.

125. Hogue, "Religion without God," 3; Rue, *Religion Is not about God*, 21–27; Loomer, "The Size of God," 21.

being, of the interlocking natural systems (atomic, molecular, biochemical, anatomical, ecological, geological) apart from which human existence is inconceivable[126]—in a word, what the pantheist means by "God." Pantheistic naturalism, therefore, undercuts our anthropocentric proclivities and pretentions, allowing *Deus sive Natura* to take center stage. Loomer bemoans that most theology "is written under the assumption that man is the peak of creation and that what creation is about is . . . humankind: as though all the rest of nature were the backdrop against which we act out our silly little lives." The pantheistic naturalist assumes the converse: "nature is the measure, and not man."[127]

This "theocosmocentric" outlook, as it were, is precisely what theologians and religious communities need in a time of pandemic. In my judgment, one of the major takeaways from the COVID-19 outbreak is that the world (aka God) does not revolve around humanity. Wieman is surely correct to call God (aka the world) the source of human good.[128] But God is also the source of viral good! To quote Mary-Jane Rubenstein: "In the absence of . . . an anthropomorphic creator and his anthropocentric creation . . . there is no assurance that human interests are any more significant than bovine, mineral, or bacterial interests. Rather than being absolute terms, good and evil become as perspectival as anything else."[129] If the past two years have taught us anything, it is that the world is largely indifferent to our wants and needs—our cultural and economic stability, our personal and social comforts, our physical and psychological health. For the pantheistic naturalist, the theological implication is plain: God is not reducible to humanly recognizable goodness and does not conform to our moral expectations, to what we think is right and fair and just. To presume otherwise (e.g., to believe that God is for humanity and against the coronavirus) is to deny reality and, worse, to court idolatry, to absolutize ourselves, overestimate our importance, and arrogantly assume that human salvation is the divine priority.

In such a time as this, it is helpful to remember that there are more things in heaven and earth than are dreamt of in our theologies and soteriologies. In such a time as this, it is helpful to remember that we are transcended by, related to, and dependent on an environment that supports us, but is sometimes inimical to our plans and projects, our wishes and wellbeing. In such a time as this, it is helpful to remember that humans are not the

126. Rue, *Religion Is not about God*, 21–27.

127. Loomer, "Meland on God," 143.

128. See Wieman, *The Source of Human Good*.

129. Rubenstein, *Pantheologies*, 178–79.

lords of creation or even masters of our own fate. In such a time as this, it is helpful to remember that *Homo sapiens* is relatively inconsequential in the infinite order of nature, that "the universe," in the eloquent words of Andrew Irvine, "was and will be devoid of human worries and delights for all but a tiny sliver of its temporal extension."[130] In such a time as this, it is helpful to remember that divine actions are not centered on human flourishing, and that God is a terrifying and terrible mystery, not a pleasant and omnibenevolent being. Indeed, Job learned all of these lessons eons ago. But it is time to relearn them. It is time to humble ourselves in the sight of the world and stop pretending that we are more significant than we actually are. It is time to lean into our finitude and vulnerability, accept our earthly origins and destiny, and put our confrontation with the coronavirus in the perspective of a much larger natural community.[131] It is time to realize that a God that is disconnected from the whole, from the ambiguous totality of *all* things, is a God that is too small for a post-pandemic age.

Of course, that is exactly what pantheistic naturalists espouse: God is connected to, even synonymous with, the ambiguous totality of all things. Such "pantheological thinking," to borrow Mary-Jane-Rubenstein's delicious designation, is the third cardinal virtue of pantheistic naturalism. More than anything else, the pantheist, or pantheologian, is unabashedly and radically *antidualistic*, naturalizing God and God-ing nature; God and nature are not two realities, but one. In so doing, pantheism combines what most theologians try to keep separate, attributing to God characteristics that the West typically associates with nature: physicality, change, contingency, corporality, immanence. For pantheists, God *is* nature in its material, processual, indeterminate, embodied, and this-worldly wholeness.[132]

Pantheism's trait-mixing, boundary-crossing ways are frequently the object of scorn, vitriol, and mockery—and, according to Rubenstein, the very reason why pantheists are branded as heretics, seducers, and purveyors of preposterous and grotesque conflations. However, for the committed pantheist, pantheology is, or at least has the potential to become, *a theology of liberation*. Here, I take a cue from Grace Jantzen, who proposes that pantheism is able to underwrite a feminist philosophy of religion, destabilizing the "raced and gendered ontic distinctions" endemic to Western metaphysics. By collapsing the dichotomy between spirit and matter and identifying the divine with the world, the pantheist deconstructs what John Dewey

---

130. Irvine, "Liberation Theology in Late Modernity," 936.

131. See Crosby, *Living with Ambiguity*, 87, 105.

132. Rubenstein, *Pantheologies*, xx, 1–10, 47.

once called "the whole brood and nest of dualisms."[133] Pantheism, in other words, untangles and cuts through the thicket of oppressive and hierarchically ordered bifurcations that are upheld by the Greco-Roman-Abrahamic opposition of creator and created, God and world: male over female, light over darkness, good over evil, activity over passivity, mind over body, reason over passion, humans over every other organism.[134] Like Rubenstein, I find Jantzen's proposal intriguing and compelling—and post-pandemically useful. Symbolically recoding God *as* the universe in its materiality, mutuality, and multiplicity carries profound repercussions for feminist, LGBTQ, antiracist, postcolonial, and ecological theologians who wish to subvert the myriad privileges that are secured by the anthropomorphic, immaterial, omnipotent, and masculine God of classical Western theism. We project a pantheistic deity, Rubenstein and Jantzen contend, "for the sake of our threatened planet, in the face of our waning biodiversity, and in solidarity with those living and nonliving beings whom the Father-aligned continue to master, colonize, denigrate, and destroy"—and, I would add, in order to disrupt the binary logic of supremacy, mastery, and domination that has led to the disproportionate impact of COVID-19 on African Americans and other people of color. Pantheist projections also reinforce an important, albeit difficult, truth: if neither divinity nor humanity is dualistically other than animality or vegetality or minerality, then people and viruses are not ontologically distinct. Rather, they are interrelated and sacred parts of the one nature that there is, of the entangled web that pantheists insist on divinizing.[135] Or to put it (pan)theologically, they are children of God.

Rubenstein hazards that a pantheist God is a *queer* God, a "mixed-up, chimeric" God that crosses divisions, blurs boundaries, and unsettles dualities. For that reason, God is *plural*, not singular. Rehabilitating and reimagining the "pluralistic pantheism" of William James, Rubenstein claims that *pan* denotes "all things," not "the All," an "un-totalizable" totality, not a "smoothed-out whole." In other words, the one nature that there is, *Deus sive Natura*, "is irreducibly many in its oneness." Pluralism reminds pantheists that the cosmos they divinize, the divinity they cosmicize, is more of a multiverse than a universe, "a proliferation of multiplicities" as opposed to "a vast, undifferentiated identity." Accordingly, pantheism, when construed pluralistically, spills over into a kind of *polytheism*.[136] To deify

133. Dewey, *Reconstruction in Philosophy*, xxxi.

134. Jantzen, *Becoming Divine*.

135. Rubenstein, *Pantheologies*, xx, 1–20; quote on 12.

136. For my own spin on a polytheistic pantheism, see Wheeler, "The Spirituality of Size," part III.

the *multiversal* universe, the manifold unfoldings of the world, is to affirm "endless, particular loci of divinity." So conceived, the divine life is not just incarnational but *pancarnational*. Deity is incarnate not just in a single human body, but in and as the embodied and material manyness of nature itself. God is "a mobile and multiply-located concatenation of pan-species intra-carnation." The upshot of a polytheistic and pancarnational theology, of a pantheology, is that God looks no more like a person than "a dingo, an ocean, or the electromagnetic force." If the *theos* is truly *pan*, if God is the "stubbornly un-totalized run of all things," then everything whatsoever is a site of divinity—even the coronavirus.[137]

To be sure, none of this implies that we ought to love or worship the coronavirus. COVID-19 is divine, but it is not good—from *our* vantage point, anyway. As I argued in the opening section, the pandemic is a natural and moral evil. And as I will argue shortly, we ought to *protest* and work to *transform* natural and moral evils. What I think a pantheology, or a pluralistic naturalism, does entail is that the coronavirus, no less than human persons, "participates in the ongoing creation, destruction, and re-worlding of worlds," in the "messy multiplicity" that pantheists call "God." To be a pantheist is to be awakened to the holiness, indeed the divinity, of all things. But pantheism does not require us to *like* or *serve* all things. Viruses, no different from anything else in the cosmos (a photon, an asteroid, a butterfly, a frontline worker), are emergent manifestations of the ground of all being, ambiguous expressions of "the monstrous many-one that God-or-nature 'is.'" However, this does not mean that viruses are good for us or worthy of our devotion. Goodness and even godness are perspectival, not absolute.[138]

So, should we prevent the spread of COVID-19 and try to end the pandemic? Yes. Should we recognize the coronavirus as a part of the creative-destructive processes of sacred nature? Yes. It is a both/and. When God is trying to kill us, we need to fight back! But pantheism asks us to fight back reverently and humbly, contemplatively and relationally. We resist knowing that resistance is very often futile. We defend ourselves against hostile forces both great and small while acknowledging that our enemies are also our kin. We struggle to survive and thrive in full awareness of the existence and value of other interests and the relativity and ambiguity of our own. To quote Rubenstein: "Pantheologically, we are not only surrounded but also constituted by nonhuman persons who can feel, hurt, rejoice, and who for those reasons deserve our respect and care—or at the very least our thoughtful deliberation whenever we decide to override the intentions of some assemblages (say,

---

137. Rubenstein, *Pantheologies*, 21–28, 41, 57–58, 146–47, 172–73, 182, 190.
138. Rubenstein, *Pantheologies*, 56–57, 173, 179–82.

those of termites, their nests, mounds, shelter tubes, and gut bacteria) with others (say, those of a concrete foundation for a wood-frame house; its feline, canine, and human inhabitants; and *their* gut bacteria)."[139]

Divinizing the plurality and precarity of this virus-strewn, plague-ridden world (as opposed to limiting the meaning of the symbol "God" to the parts of reality that conduce to human wellbeing) inspires a particular suite of religious affections and attitudes. On my reading, pantheology breaks open *a spirituality of size*, a spiritual posture befitting of a post-pandemic civilization.[140] This is the fourth cardinal virtue of pantheistic naturalism.

To begin with, to the pantheistic naturalist, size matters—at least spiritually. In Loomer's thought, "size" is the capacity to take in "the volume of life," to "deal with the tensions involved in deep ambiguities."[141] A *spirituality* of size requires opening oneself to the size of *God*, to as much of the universe, as much of the divine, as one can bear.[142] Indeed, the spiritual kernel of pantheistic naturalism is that the bigness of God carries more weight than the goodness of God. That is to say, the religious value of nature lies in its magnitude, antiquity, and totality and not just in its support for human flourishing.

A spirituality of size is also attuned to the *mystery* of God. Pantheistic naturalism is a naturalistic breed of mystical theology, encountering and conceiving nature as a *mysterium tremendum et fascinans*, as a *via negativa*, as a cloud of unknowing. Pantheistic naturalists certainly believe that the world reveals itself to us through science, art, religion, and other modes of human inquiry. In the end, however, revelation is always partial. *Deus sive Natura* is the ultimate horizon that continually recedes from our rational advances, the divine darkness that exceeds our limited notions of truth, beauty, and goodness. And its mysterious ways—its axiological depths and aesthetic marvels, its exuding creativity and mindless destruction, its ordered regularity and unpredictable contingencies, its plural particulars and relational networks, its unimaginable vastness and sheer isness—arouse profound spiritual feelings of astonishment and humility, reverence and gratitude, dependence and creatureliness, trepidation and silence.

Thus, pantheists are not anonymous atheists; they are nature mystics. Referring to nature as "God" is not just window dressing or a superfluous bit

---

139. Rubenstein, *Pantheologies*, 182.

140. For more on the religious and spiritual qualities of pantheistic naturalism, see Wheeler, "The Spirituality of Size," part II.

141. Loomer, "S-I-Z-E," 6; Loomer, "Response to David R. Griffin," 368.

142. See Lee, "Loomer on Deity," 63, 70–73.

of semantics.[143] Rather, nature is God because it really exhibits divine characteristics: mystery, transcendence, sovereignty, ineffability, sublimity, everlastingness, overwhelming power—"size," in the fullest sense of the term. Nature is God because it is metaphysically ultimate and religiously ultimate, the ontological ground that creates, sustains, and destroys all things and the holy ground that deserves our utmost attention, fidelity, and devotion. For many critics, a world-God—an impersonal and immanental God—is not much different from a non-existent God. For the pantheist, however, the difference is subtle but significant. As Loomer pronounces, pantheists "deify this interconnected web of existence" for both philosophical and pragmatic reasons, namely, in order to convey that the world is "an adequate object of worship," has "an absolute claim on our loyalty," demands "a priority within the ordering of our commitments," embodies "a richness of resources for the living of life at its depths," and enshrouds "a transcendent and inexhaustible meaning that forever eludes our grasp."[144] Admittedly, pantheism will leave some theologians cold. Regardless, it is not simply "a euphemism for atheism," as Schopenhauer famously charged.[145]

Without a doubt, the pantheist *is* atheistic with respect to the God of personal theism. However, much like Einstein, pantheistic naturalists make lots of room for a "cosmic religious sense," for a "rapturous amazement" at the order of the cosmos. Einstein rightly realized that such awestruck veneration unveils the "vanity" of anthropomorphic and anthropocentric religion, of theological doctrines that are modeled and centered on human beings.[146] A pantheistic God, by contrast, is a "big" God, a God that is sized to the grandeur and multiplicity of nature, not to the aims of humankind. As such, *Deus sive Natura* functions as an idol-smashing "relativizer," an "ultimate point of reference" that exposes our limits and checks our tendency to deny those limits.[147] In other words, pantheism evokes what Rudolf Otto called "creature-consciousness," reminding us that we are but dust and ashes.[148] Or as Plaskow eloquently expresses it, humanity assumes its place as "a tiny node in the great fabric of existence," no more important or special than a blade of grass or a distant star (or a viral infection, for that matter). We are not the epicenter of reality, but a small, vulnerable, and contingent part of an inconceivably large, diverse, and wondrous whole—"the astounding variety

143. See Frankenberry, "Classical Theism," 44.

144. Loomer, "The Size of God," 41–42.

145. Rubenstein, *Pantheologies*, 13.

146. Rubenstein, *Pantheologies*, 152–54, 184.

147. See Kaufman, *In Face of Mystery*, ix–xv, 3–17, 32–44, 301–40.

148. Otto, *The Idea of the Holy*, 10, 20.

and intricacy of our world and the universe beyond, of innumerable life forms (animate and inanimate) in their particularity and their relation to each other."[149] Of course, a big God is also an ambiguous God, which means that pantheism's religious affect is an "*ambivalent* wonder," to borrow Mary-Jane Rubenstein's haunting phrase. "The wonderer," she effuses, "undergoes a complicated dance of attraction and revulsion, admiration and horror, love and fear"—a kind of "horrified awe."[150]

The last two years have been more horrifying than awesome. From my perspective, it has been one long and painful confrontation with the size of God, with the mystery and ambiguity of God. The God of the coronavirus is the God of the whirlwind—the God that does not fit into our anthropomorphic boxes, is not scaled to our religious hopes, and will not abide by our moral expectations. Many, maybe most, people of faith will find the big God of pantheistic naturalism spiritually unbearable. But for others, the spiritual fruits of divine bigness are both nourishing and liberating. And a time of pandemic is a time for gathering the harvest.

The natural piety that emerges from a pantheist theology is humble, iconoclastic, and truth-telling. To perceive and experience the size of God is to face our mortality vis-à-vis a nature that is infinite and always bats last. The proper religious attitude is one of surrender and deference to the real, and the spiritual vocation is to cultivate courage, acceptance, and authenticity in the presence of life's ambiguities, tragedies, and perpetual perishings. Stated otherwise, a spirituality of size is an invitation to replace romanticism with realism, to relinquish omnibenevolent deities, overreaching teleologies, optimistic cosmologies, and other reassuring fantasies and just embrace reality, embrace divinity, for what it actually is: an intricate and precarious web that is at once creative and destructive, life-producing and death-dealing. Released from the burden of having to believe in and vindicate an anthropomorphic God, a God who is either unwilling or unable to stop catastrophes from occurring, the pantheist is free to sanctify and venerate whatever is. To quote Plaskow: "If God is not a personal being with benign or malign consciousness, then it is possible to let go of anger and to stand in awe before the mysterious complexity of the world and the boundless creative energy that births its myriad forms and to accept the reality that all is a mixture of good and evil."[151]

To my mind, the spirituality of size is best captured by Wildman. By Wildman's lights, ground-of-being theologians (including pantheists like

---

149. Christ and Plaskow, *Goddess and God in the World*, 186–87, 276–77.

150. Rubenstein, *Pantheologies*, 185; emphasis added.

151. Christ and Plaskow, *Goddess and God in the World*, 237.

Loomer, Rubenstein, and myself) are *pietistic realists*. They reject the comforts (and the existence) of person-shaped ultimate realities and all-good subordinate deities, refuse to "associate God only with human-scaled and human-focused goodness," and privilege plausibility over religious appeal, "making the most of the latter given what the former allows." And yet ground-of-being theology "is the very breath of spiritual life for some people." As Wildman baldly encapsulates it, "suchness is the rule here: the world just is a . . . morally perilous blend of pleasure and pain, which we blithely or desperately inscribe onto the ambiguous cosmos as the play of good and evil. In this case the spiritual calling is to surrender to suchness with no deflections, to worship what is—no flirting with delusion."[152] Wildman is actually quite sympathetic to detractors who find this view religiously unusable and morally intolerable. It is, after all, "not easily assimilated into our humanly configured cultural worlds" or "our anthropocentric ways of thinking." At the same time, he asserts that ground-of-being theologies support an "authenticity-based spiritual quest" that resists wishful thinking and accepts "the world as it is without evasion or dreaming." The endpoint of such a quest is enlightenment, where "reality is taken for what it is," and the truth about ultimacy "sears our souls," "awakens us again and again from our anthropomorphic theological slumbering," and "drives us to love that which destroys even as it creates."[153]

In short, pantheists, and ground-of-being theists in general, seek to religiously orient themselves to the size of God, to the whole of reality in all its mystery, plurality, and ambiguity. In so doing, they nurture a spirituality of suchness, realism, acceptance, and deference, surrendering themselves to life as it most truly is, "without reserve" and "without illusions and . . . limitations to human interests and longings." They discern sacred depth in the way things are and proclaim that all things without exception, including those patterns and processes that bring forth destruction, tragedy, and suffering (yes, even COVID-19), are divinely grounded and testify to the divine glory.[154] And pantheistic naturalists, I would hazard, push these spiritual intuitions as far as they will go by completely collapsing the God-world distinction.

A spirituality of size, therefore, puts a high premium on *honesty*. On that score, pantheistic naturalism shares Roth's strong allergy to sentimentalism. Roth is spot-on, in my view: nearly all theodicies are too good to be true. Imagining that the universe is controlled (or lured) by the love of

---

152. Wildman, *In Our Own Image*, 173.

153. Wildman, *Effing the Ineffable*, 39–49, 60–61, 212–13.

154. Wildman, *Effing the Ineffable*, 41–42, 47–48, 62.

God, or that the tragedies of the world amount to naught in comparison with the glory to come, or that freedom somehow justifies all the pain and anguish we experience, underestimates just how horrendous, scarring, wasteful, absurd, omnipresent, gratuitous, and primordial suffering really is. Similar to Roth, pantheistic naturalists want nothing to do with pie-in-the-sky panaceas, eschatological happy endings, illusory wish fulfillments, unambiguously benevolent gods, heavenly escape hatches, evil-excusing divine plans, or overpromising and overly hopeful theologies that expect all things to work together for good or stubbornly insist that everything is (or will be) alright despite the overwhelming evidence to the contrary.[155] Instead, they opt to confront reality's harshest facts truthfully, unblinkingly, and plaintively, accepting that existence is shadowed by cruelty and calamity, death and disaster, extinction and entropy, privation and plague. It just is. Pantheistic naturalists, as I will suggest below, are *not* ultra-pessimists, holding plenty of space for joy, celebration, and even hope. But they *are* truth-tellers. That is, they are brutally honest about the world's suffering—and what it entails theologically. The pragmatist William James would classify them as "sick souls," as tough-minded empiricists for whom "life and its negation are beaten up inextricably together."[156] As James elaborates elsewhere, sick souls find religious optimism too saccharine and idyllic. And they ask frank and uncomfortable questions:

> Is the last word sweet? Is all "yes, yes" in the universe? Doesn't the fact of "no" stand at the very core of life? Doesn't the very "seriousness" that we attribute to life mean that ineluctable noes and losses form a part of it, that there are genuine sacrifices somewhere, and that something permanently drastic and bitter always remains at the bottom of its cup?[157]

Roth says that a post-Holocaust age is "a time for sick souls."[158] So is a post-pandemic age. Sick bodies tend to breed sick souls, after all.

To be clear, a spirituality of size, suchness, surrender, and soul-sick realism does not necessarily terminate in a passive resignation to the evils and tragedies of life. Pantheists are habitually accused of cutting the nerve of religious commitment and ethical obligation. Opponents of pantheism suspect that divinizing and accepting the ambiguous totality of reality is a slippery slope leading to a submissive acquiescence to the way things are, a veneration

---

155. Roth, "A Theodicy of Protest." See also Crosby, *Living with Ambiguity*, 108.

156. James, *The Varieties of Religious Experience*, 139.

157. James, *Pragmatism*, 141.

158. Roth, "A Theodicy of Protest," 19.

of brute power, and a "romantic love of evil."[159] Frankenberry summarizes the critique well: "How are we to establish any priorities in the ordering of values and commitments if nature as a whole is considered divine and known to contain evil as well as good, destruction as much as creation?"[160]

But surely relativizing the human good (cosmologically, theologically, and spiritually) is not the same as abandoning religion and ethics. And honestly acknowledging, even reverencing, the ambiguity of ultimate reality, of God or nature, is not the same as romanticizing or legitimizing evil.[161] Far from encouraging submission to the status quo or undercutting the impetus for moral action and social change, pantheistic naturalism offers a fundamentally pragmatic, religiously healing, and ethically empowering response to the problem of evil—*an antitheodicy of protest and humanistic praxis*. This is the fifth, and final, cardinal virtue of pantheistic naturalism.

Let me start off with a basic, but crucial, observation: pantheism affirms that all things are *God*, not that all things are *good*. Consequently, evil is still a problem in a pantheist model. But as Mary-Jane Rubenstein avers, it is a *practical* problem rather than a theoretical or conceptual problem. The pantheistic naturalist is just as troubled and outraged by oppression, violence, injustice, and sickness as the personal theist. However, for the pantheistic naturalist, oppression, violence, injustice, and sickness are not philosophical conundrums that need to be reconciled with an anthropomorphic God (whether omnipotent, omnibenevolent, or both), much less inevitabilities that demand fatalistic and quietistic endorsement. On the contrary, they are concrete realities, natural givens, that we empirially negotiate and attempt to overcome.[162] Hence, pantheistic naturalism understands evil *naturalistically and pragmatically*. Why do we suffer and inflict suffering upon others? Because nature is precarious and comprised of finite beings with competing interests. Why do we die? Because death is an intrinsic part of life, a result of nonnegotiable physical laws. What should we do? Take responsibility for the messes we make, embrace our fragility and finitude, acknowledge that we are not the center of the universe or in complete control of things, and try to make the world a better place.[163]

But do not pantheistic naturalists *deify* the totality of reality? Indeed, they do. And is this not tantamount to excusing slavery, war, patriarchy, genocide, and disease? By no means! Undeniably, pantheism declares that

---

159. For example, see Shaw, "The Romantic Love of Evil."

160. Frankenberry, "Classical Theism," 39.

161. See Roth, "A Theodicy of Protest," 17.

162. See Crosby, *Living with Ambiguity*, 53.

163. Rubenstein, *Pantheologies*, 15–16, 174–79; Crosby, *Living with Ambiguity*, 106.

everything whatsoever participates in "multiple, ongoing processes of cosmic makings and unravelings," in the ambiguous many-one that God "is." But to divinize all things is not to bless all things. To venerate the whole is not to forsake the good. To some extent, slavery, war, patriarchy, genocide, and disease are *more*, not less, problematic in a pantheistic outlook, since the pantheist rejects the existence of an otherworldly problem-solver.[164]

Accordingly, pantheistic naturalism calls for the renunciation of the *speculative* problem of evil, not the problem of evil *per se*. In other words, it renounces *theodicy*. As both Rubenstein and Plaskow astutely discern, explaining (or explaining away) dysteleological surds such as COVID-19 becomes necessary *only if* one believes that "good" and "evil" are self-evident, stable, and transcendental categories, that God is an anthropomorphically benevolent and all-powerful person who has intentions and rules over history, and that nature revolves around human beings and their felicity.[165] However, exonerating God is no longer necessary if these theistic beliefs are jettisoned. In fact, for pantheists, asking why God permits evil is a category mistake. Theodicy rests on the premise that the *theos* is a being with purposive agency, conscious awareness, and human-measured goodness. But that premise is false, according to pantheistic naturalism. To put it sternly, there is no personal God to exculpate. In that sense, pantheistic naturalism is an *antitheodicy*. Rather than laboring to account for divine inaction, to rationalize God's unwillingness or inability to bring an end to holocausts and horrific pandemics, pantheistic naturalists aim to cope with suffering and, wherever possible, to contest it and make it otherwise.[166] As Crosby assures, "we can work to eradicate those evils that can be eradicated and seek ways to accept with humility, courage, and composure those that cannot."[167]

Admittedly, a lot of theologians will regard pantheism's antitheodicy as defeatism. But pantheistic naturalists experience it as *freedom*. They are free to let go of cognitive dissonance. They are free to part ways with a God who never shows up, a God who is either neglectful or incompetent. And they are free to liberate themselves from the burdensome conclusions of theism. To quote Rubenstein: "insofar as God does *not* intervene—even in the face of unprecedented levels of global suffering and cruelty—we can only be led to conclude that God must condone or even will, say, the escalating refugee crisis, phallo-nuclear brinkmanship, the normalization of sexual violence, the extinction of thousands of species for the sake of capitalist comfort, the

---

164. Rubenstein, *Pantheologies*, 174–76, 183.

165. Plaskow, *The Coming of Lilith*, 135; Rubenstein, *Pantheologies*, 15–16.

166. Rubenstein, *Pantheologies*, 177–78.

167. Crosby, *Living with Ambiguity*, 101.

unbridled resurgence of anti-black racism, and industrial agriculture's obliteration of untold scores of nonhuman animals."[168] Pantheistic naturalism bids theologians to stop justifying these evils and start ameliorating them, to look for practical solutions, not intellectual ones. As Jantzen warns, engaging in theodicy is not only unproductive but also distracting, diverting time and energy away from the struggle against suffering and victimization.[169]

And yet, some theodicies *do* aid in the struggle against suffering and victimization—most notably, the various "theodicies of protest" taken up by post-Holocaust theologians over the last century. Pantheistic naturalism welcomes, even invites, a theodicy of protest. A theodicy of protest, I propose, allows the pantheistic naturalist to relate to the ambiguities of life, to the ambiguities of *Deus sive Natura*, in a religiously healthy and ethically energizing way.

According to Roth, a theodicy of protest is actually a kind of antitheodicy, giving up on the quest to defend divine omnibenevolence; God's righteousness and moral purity are simply indefensible in the face of reality's injustices and excessive tragedies. Life's wastes—its sudden deaths, its mass destructions, its irretrievable losses, its unrighted wrongs, its unspeakable abuses, its unanswered prayers—are unjustifiable, which implies that "God is going to be much less than perfectly justified." Rather than overstressing God's love or rushing too quickly to hope and eschatological victories, protesting theodicies approach divinity with Job-like defiance, grieving and quarreling with God over the suffering that permanently scars existence. Even if humanity is largely responsible for the inhumanity of the *Shoah*, human freedom "does not remove God from the dock." The God of Genesis declared the creation good, but a world created by a benevolent creator should be better. A theodicy of protest puts God on trial, and the verdict is guilty. "History itself is God's indictment," intones Roth. And sadness, lamentation, and anger are appropriate religious responses to "God's wasteful complicity in evil."[170] As David Blumenthal testifies:

> We will try to accept God as God is; we will protest our innocence, as our ancestors and great thinkers have done. And we will accuse God of acting unjustly, as fully and as directly as we can, as our greatest poets and sages have done. We cannot forgive God and concentrate on God's goodness. Rather, we will try to accept God—the bad along with the good—*and* we will

168. Rubenstein, *Pantheologies*, 174.
169. Jantzen, *Becoming Divine*, 259–64.
170. Roth, "A Theodicy of Protest," 1–20, 36.

speak our lament. We will mourn the bad, and we will regret that things were, and are, not different than they are.[171]

Of course, pantheistic naturalists are unable to adopt a theodicy of protest without qualification. For instance, in addition to protest, pantheistic naturalism encourages gratitude, exultation, and rejoicing for the manifold graces bestowed by nature. The pantheistic naturalist sings a doxology for the gift of family and friendship, for the beauty and bounty of the earth, for the stupefying splendor of the universe and its endless forms most wonderful, for the natural community of creatures in which we participate, for the human capacity for decency, love, compassion, altruism, heroism, and moral idealism, for the breakthroughs of medical science, for the miracle of consciousness and the blessing of life itself.[172] That being said, I concur with Roth: *complete* joy is not in the offing.[173] Evil's stain is just too deep, COVID's devastation too immeasurable. An ambiguous God calls for a *tragicomic* religiosity, for hymns of adulation *and* dirges of dissent. As Roth expounds:

> Worship cannot have vitality without praise and thanksgiving. But honesty is no less important to its life. In worship one professes and celebrates God's goodness to the extent that such goodness is experienced and thereby anticipated. Other things have been experienced, too, and they rightly produce lamentation and rage, heartbreak and melancholy. *God, why did you create this world? Why do you let injustice and suffering so often have their ways? Why did you form men and women in your image?* Those questions belong in post-Holocaust sanctuaries.[174]

Needless to say, those questions also belong in post-pandemic sanctuaries—although, for the pantheistic naturalist, they are chiefly *religious* questions, not philosophical questions. Unlike Roth, pantheistic naturalism does not conceptualize divinity as a sovereign and omnipotent entity, as the "the master of the universe" or "the One for whom everything is possible."[175] And if the divine is not an agential and intentional being, then God is not *literally* culpable or blameworthy.[176] Be that as it may, when construed as *mythmaking, liturgics,* and *theological metaphor,* interrogating and even

---

171. Blumenthal, *Facing the Abusing God*, 267.
172. Crosby, *Living with Ambiguity*, 80–81, 88–89, 101, 111.
173. Roth, "A Theodicy of Protest," 32.
174. Roth, "A Theodicy of Protest," 36.
175. Roth, "A Theodicy of Protest," 4, 8, 13–14.
176. See Crosby, *Living with Ambiguity*, 107.

blaming God for the calamities that befall us—How long, O Lord?—may serve as potent vehicles for reckoning with evil, struggling against despair, and orienting ourselves to the ambiguity of ultimate reality. Thus, in a pantheistic framework, a theodicy of protest is less a philosophy of religion than *a form of healing*, an instrument for bringing forth salvation and liberation, existential catharsis and communal wellbeing.

That nicely illustrates an overarching principle of pantheistic naturalism: what is false at the level of philosophical conceptuality can still be meaningful at the level of religious poetry—and transformative at the level of ritual practice.[177] Tillich, Wildman, Plaskow, and other liberal theologians are right: there is truth in broken symbols.[178] Although untrue in a literal sense, religious symbols and stories (e.g., the personalistic language and imagery of the Bible) are capable of metaphorically communicating profound insights into the nature of reality, into the complexities of the human condition and the vicissitudes of existence.[179] For that reason, the pantheistic naturalist deliteralizes rather than discards the symbolic dimensions of religion.

My iteration of pantheistic naturalism even finds a place for anthropomorphic gods. To repeat, theological personalism is inadequate as a metaphysics of divinity. However, pantheistic naturalism retains personal deities (e.g., divine liberators) as "imaginative constructions" or "sacred conventions,"[180] as religiously compelling human creations that "shield us from the searing light of ultimate reality"[181] and enable us to symbolically and selectively engage the divine totality, the mysterious and ambiguous whole of God or nature. Pantheistic naturalists live and theologize in the real world, while calling on gods and other fictional characters to help them imagine and instantiate "otherwise worlds,"[182] anti-racist and post-pandemic worlds.

In fact, drawing inspiration from Richard Rubenstein, I would go so far as to suggest that gods, symbols, narratives, parables, icons, laws, traditions, liturgies, rites, and artworks are even *more* necessary in "the time of the death of God." In Rubenstein's eloquent words: "If it is no longer possible to believe in the God who has the power to annul the tragedies of existence, the need religiously to share that existence remains." Religion, after all, is not primarily a system of doctrines, but a historical repository of myths, rituals, customs,

---

177. See Wildman, "Ground-of-Being Theologies," 623–24.

178. See Neville, *The Truth of Broken Symbols*.

179. Christ and Plaskow, *Goddess and God in the World*, 279–85.

180. See Kaufman, *In Face of Mystery*, parts I and IV; Dean, *The American Spiritual Culture*, 70–86.

181. Wildman, *Effing the Ineffable*, 210.

182. See Rubenstein, *Pantheologies*, 186–87.

and shared memories and experiences. These inherited traditions and embodied practices are the means through which human beings make meaning and find solace, consecrate the good and oppose the bad, mark important events, and cope with death, ambiguity, and crisis—individual as well as collective. And in the midst of grief and trauma, holocaust and plague, we turn to religion not to overcome our predicament, but to bear it—together.[183] Our imprecatory psalms and divine tribunals, our prayers of lament, rituals of mourning, and theodicies of protest, may not provide accurate information about the nature of God, but they do help us contend with the God of nature. In that sense, the contributions that practical, pastoral, liturgical, and moral theologians make to the problem of evil—and to life in a time of pandemic— are even more indispensable than those of philosophical, dogmatic, systematic, and constructive theologians.

So, we get by with a little help from our friends—human and divine, real and imaginary. But there is no escaping the fact that it is *up to us* to muster the strength to carry on, to find the courage to be. And it is also up to us to bring morality and ethics into existence. It is up to us to opt for the poor and liberate the oppressed. It is up to us to preserve our democracy. It is up to us to build an ecological civilization. It is up to us to bend the moral arc of the universe toward justice. It is up to us to end the COVID-19 nightmare and prepare for the next pandemic. It is up to us to transform the social and economic conditions that put communities of color at greater risk of infection, hospitalization, and death. For pantheistic naturalists, there is no omnibenevolent divine entity who will lure us toward truth, beauty, and goodness, much less a *deus ex machina* who will swoop in and save the day.[184] Rather, *we* are the ones we have been waiting for. Plaskow hits the nail on the head, in my estimation: it is *our* task as human beings, as beings who have the power to distinguish right from wrong, good from evil, to choose life (cf. Deut 30:19)—to ally ourselves with voices of compassion and to "create a society in which everyone shares the earth's resources without depleting or destroying them."[185] In other words, we must *be* the change we want to see in the world. Or as Catherine Madsen more pantheistically enunciates it: "We must try to become what we wish God was."[186]

Accordingly, pantheistic naturalism fosters a religiously and ethically galvanizing *humanism*, a praxis of human empowerment. Pantheism's

---

183. Rubenstein, *After Auschwitz*, 173–74, 256, 261, 264; quote on 174. See also Crosby, *Living with Ambiguity*, 91.

184. Rubenstein, *Pantheologies*, 175.

185. Christ and Plaskow, *Goddess and God in the World*, 180.

186. Madsen, "If God Is God She Is Not Nice," 105.

decriers (e.g., process theists) worry that the deification of ultimate reality (the ground and totality of all things) means that human efforts toward peace, justice, liberation, and healing are not mirrored or sponsored by God. But pantheists are not too worried. As Frankenberry maintains:

> Nature is often indifferent to human desires and deaf to our moral urgencies, a sign, perhaps, of the remorselessness of the divine nature, but a fact that should be no more disturbing to our religious and ethical sensibilities than the discovery that the Sermon on the Mount contains no urban renewal program, or that the Buddha's injunction to practice compassion provides no guidelines for the Human Genome Project. Ethics, like government, represents the human, historical gift to life on this planet. Both come in better and worse forms, and neither needs the backing of natural law or divine command.[187]

Pantheism actually *promotes* morality and social ethics. I side with Wildman here: authentically embracing reality for what it is and humbly acknowledging the ambiguous character of divinity generates a Nietzschean determination to become morally accountable for the wellbeing of humanity and the earth.[188] Ethical progress, political change, environmental sustainability, and world health are *human* obligations, and spiritual maturity means accepting these awesome responsibilities as sacred duties. Roth also insists that approaching the tragedies of life in a spirit of "quarrelsome protest" often gives way to compassion and moral commitment.[189] I agree wholeheartedly. Antitheodicy and divine ambiguity are a summons to face paradigm evil events with unflinching honesty, loving kindness, and prophetic ire, encouraging us to relieve and reduce suffering, to enter into solidarity with the victimized, and to repent for our sins—both what we have done and what we have left undone. Rather than theologically justifying the genocidal madness of the Holocaust and the fatal mismanagement of the COVID-19 outbreak, the pantheistic naturalist exclaims: "never again!"

My intention is not to champion works righteousness. Pantheistic naturalism is only semi-Pelagian, because the very capacity to discover viruses and develop vaccines and deliver victims is nature's gift to us, God's gift to us. And *pantheism itself* is not without ethical ramifications and directives. Divinizing the multiplicities and material particularities of nature heightens our sense of belonging and connection to all things and inculcates an

---

187. Frankenberry, "Classical Theism," 40.
188. Wildman, *Effing the Ineffable*, 48–49.
189. See Roth, "A Theodicy of Protest," 17, 35–37.

"entangled empathy."[190] As Loomer argues, even if the cosmos is not created or guided by an all-loving divine being, love is an acknowledgement of our essential interrelatedness.[191] Plaskow concurs:

> As creatures who have self-consciousness, who, in our better moments, are able to glimpse and appreciate our place in the larger whole, we have a deep ethical obligation to act in the interests of that whole and of the individuals and human and biotic communities within it. . . . There is no commander who issues orders from outside the web of creation, but there are obligations inherent in the interconnectedness of things that link our own self-interest to the preservation and prospering of all life.[192]

The world divinized by the pantheist also evinces deep pockets of value as well as purposes and passions that aim at cooperation and mutual enhancement. According to Loomer, while reality is devoid of a discernable moral *telos*, "there persists a restlessness or a tropism not only to live, but to live well and to live better (Whitehead)."[193]

Pantheistic naturalists even carve out space for a kind of *melioristic* hope. A mainstay of classical American pragmatism, meliorism steers a middle course between optimism and pessimism, treating salvation as possible rather than inevitable, as partial rather than absolute. Our pluralistic universe, says William James, possesses *some* of the conditions for life's betterment.[194] Or as Frankenberry avows: "The ambiguous nature . . . of historical experience gives no destiny. It permits something more—an open future, of possibly greater unity. This does not secure our projects from shipwreck nor does it promise that unity is anything other than a contingent emergent."[195] Hence, for the meliorist, triumph over a pandemic is a real if fragile possibility, never certain or complete and always conditional, contradictory, and costly.

Thus, the cosmos is, in some measure, supportive of human flourishing. At the end of the day, however, *we* are the deciders. It is we who must decide which side of the divine nature to engage. As Wildman provocatively concludes:

---

190. Rubenstein, *Pantheologies*, 185.

191. Loomer, "The Size of God," 33.

192. Christ and Plaskow, *Goddess and God in the World*, 186–87.

193. Loomer, "The Size of God," 42–43, 51.

194. James, *Pragmatism*, 136–41.

195. Frankenberry, "Taking Measure of 'The Size of God,'" 83.

Can we choose purposelessness, violence, and cruelty? Yes, and God awaits us along that path as self-destruction and nihility. Should we choose to create meaning, nurture children, and spread justice? If we do, the possibility is a divinely grounded one. Does God care which way we choose? God is not in the caring business, on this view. The divine particularity is expressed in the structured possibilities and interconnections of worldly existence; wanting and choosing is the human role.[196]

And yet, even if moral advancement and historical progress and herd immunity depend on human decision, humility must have the final word. Like Jacob, we wrestle with God, with the ambiguous angels of nature, and refuse to let go until we receive a blessing. But we will not always prevail, and even when we do, we will walk away with a limp. Or to use a less biblical metaphor, our ethical, sociopolitical, and medical endeavors are Sisyphean struggles.[197] We push. We promote the potentialities of life for all creatures, human and nonhuman. We opt for grace, kindness, and mercy. We seek reparations and reconciliation. We support one another, especially the most vulnerable, in times of crisis and grief. We proclaim that **Black Lives Matter**. We care for the sick. We vaccinate. We brace ourselves for pandemics to come. Yet we know full well that the boulder will roll back down the hill. Disasters will strike. Setbacks will happen. Answers will elude us. Coronaviruses, and social viruses like white supremacy, will continue to rob us of breath. And all of us will die, some tragically and prematurely. So, we persist, but we persist *humbly*. We protest and fight against evil and suffering without banking on ultimate victories, final resolutions, teleological endpoints, eschatological guarantees, or presumptions of cosmic significance. We try to change the world without assuming that everything can or should be changed. We construct sacred conventions without neglecting to revere the sacred mystery of the whole. We deify creativity without failing to recognize that the creator is also the destroyer. We choose the good without pretending that human goodness is the point of existence, the center of the universe, or the nature of ultimate reality. We work to recover from COVID-19 without forgetting that human persons and deadly diseases are interrelated and interdependent parts of *Deus sive Natura*, the source, end, and totality of all that is and ever shall be. Therein lies the piety—and the praxis—of pantheistic naturalism.

---

196. Wildman, "Incongruous Goodness," 282.

197. See Pinn, *Humanism*, 1–9, 147–51.

Bibliography

Aratani, Lori. "Oversight Report Calls Trump Administration Response to the Pandemic a 'Failure.'" *The Washington Post*, October 30, 2020. https://www.washingtonpost.com/local/trafficandcommuting/trump-coronavirus-response-failure/2020/10/29/cb58e066-1a15-11eb-82db-60b15c874105_story.html.

Armus, Teo. "Deborah Birx Said Trump Was Being Given 'Parallel Data' on COVID-19." *The Washington Post*, January 25, 2021. https://www.washingtonpost.com/nation/2021/01/25/deborah-birx-interview-trump-covid/.

Blumenthal, David R. *Facing the Abusing God: A Theology of Protest*. Louisville: Westminster John Knox, 1993.

Centers for Disease Control and Prevention. "COVID Data Tracker." https://covid.cdc.gov/covid-data-tracker/#cases_casesper100klast7days.

———. "Health Equity Considerations and Racial and Ethnic Minority Groups." https://www.cdc.gov/coronavirus/2019-ncov/community/health-equity/race-ethnicity.html.

Christ, Carol P., and Judith Plaskow. *Goddess and God in the World: Conversations in Embodied Theology*. Minneapolis: Fortress, 2016.

Cobb, John B. *A Christian Natural Theology: Based on the Thought of Alfred North Whitehead*. 2nd ed. Louisville: Westminster John Knox, 2007.

Crosby, Donald A. "A Case for Religion of Nature." *Journal for the Study of Religion, Nature, and Culture* 1.4 (2007) 489–502.

———. *Living with Ambiguity: Religious Naturalism and the Menace of Evil*. Albany: State University of New York Press, 2008.

———. *A Religion of Nature*. Albany: State University of New York Press, 2002.

Darwin, Charles. "Autobiography." In *The Portable Atheist: Essential Readings for the Nonbeliever*, edited by Christopher Hitchens, 93–96. Philadelphia: Da Capo, 2007.

Davis, Stephen T. "Free Will and Evil." In *Encountering Evil: Live Options in Theodicy*, edited by Stephen T. Davis, 73–107. Louisville: Westminster John Knox, 2001.

———. "Introduction." In *Encountering Evil: Live Options in Theodicy*, edited by Stephen T. Davis, vii–xiii. Louisville: Westminster John Knox, 2001.

Dean, William. *The American Spiritual Culture: And the Invention of Jazz, Football, and the Movies*. New York: Continuum, 2002.

Dewey, John. *Reconstruction in Philosophy*. Enlarged ed. Boston: Beacon, 1957.

Ehrman, Bart D. *God's Problem: How the Bible Fails to Answer Our Most Important Question—Why We Suffer*. New York: HarperOne, 2008.

Frankenberry, Nancy. "Classical Theism, Panentheism, and Pantheism: On the Relation between God Construction and Gender Construction." *Zygon* 28.1 (1993) 29–46.

———. "Taking Measure of 'the Size of God.'" In *The Size of God: The Theology of Bernard Loomer in Context*, edited by William Dean and Larry E. Axel, 77–84. Macon, GA: Mercer University Press, 1987.

Golden, Sherita Hill. "Coronavirus in African Americans and Other People of Color." *Johns Hopkins Medicine*, April 20, 2020. https://www.hopkinsmedicine.org/health/conditions-and-diseases/coronavirus/covid19-racial-disparities.

Goodenough, Ursula. *The Sacred Depths of Nature*. New York: Oxford University Press, 1998.

Greenberg, Irving. "Cloud of Smoke, Pillar of Fire: Judaism, Christianity, and Modernity after the Holocaust." In *Auschwitz: Beginning of a New Era?*, edited by Eva Fleischner, 7–55. New York: Ktav, 1977.

Griffin, David Ray. "Creation and the Problem of Evil." In *Encountering Evil: Live Options in Theodicy*, edited by Stephen T. Davis, 108–44. Louisville: Westminster John Knox, 2001.

———. *God, Power, and Evil: A Process Theodicy*. Lanham, MD: University Press of America, 1991.

Hanage, William P., et al. "COVID-19: US Federal Accountability for Entry, Spread, and Inequities—Lessons for the Future." *European Journal of Epidemiology* 35 (2020) 995–1006.

Harrison, Paul. *Elements of Pantheism: Understanding the Divinity in Nature and the Universe*. Boston: Element, 1999.

Hartshorne, Charles. *Omnipotence and Other Theological Mistakes*. Albany: State University of New York Press, 1984.

Hick, John. *Evil and the God of Love*. New York: Harper and Row, 1966.

———. "A Irenaean Theodicy." In *Encountering Evil: Live Options in Theodicy*, edited by Stephen T. Davis, 38–72. Louisville: Westminster John Knox, 2001.

Hogue, Michael S. *The Promise of Religious Naturalism*. Lanham, MD: Rowman and Littlefield, 2010.

———. "Religion without God: The Way of Religious Naturalism." *The Fourth R* 27.3 (2014) 3–6, 15–16.

Hume, David. *Dialogues concerning Natural Religion*. Indianapolis: Hackett, 1998.

IHME. "Cumulative Deaths." https://covid19.healthdata.org/united-states-of-america?view=cumulative-deaths&tab=trend.

Irvine, Andrew B. "Liberation Theology in Late Modernity: An Argument for a Symbolic Approach." *Journal of the American Academy of Religion* 78.4 (2010) 921–60.

James, William. *A Pluralistic Universe*. New York: Longmans, Green, and Co., 1909.

———. *Pragmatism: A New Name for Some Old Ways of Thinking*. Cambridge: Harvard University Press, 1978.

———. *The Varieties of Religious Experience: A Study in Human Nature*. New York: Penguin, 1902.

Jantzen, Grace M. *Becoming Divine: Towards a Feminist Philosophy of Religion*. Bloomington: Indiana University Press, 1999.

Johnson, Elizabeth A. *Quest for the Living God: Mapping Frontiers in the Theology of God*. New York: Continuum, 2007.

Jones, William R. *Is God a White Racist? A Preamble to Black Theology*. Boston: Beacon, 1998.

Kaufman, Gordon D. *In Face of Mystery: A Constructive Theology*. Cambridge: Harvard University Press, 1993.

Keller, Catherine. *On the Mystery: Discerning God in Process*. Minneapolis: Fortress, 2008.

Lee, Bernard J. "Loomer on Deity: A Long Night's Journey into Day." In *The Size of God: The Theology of Bernard Loomer in Context*, edited by William Dean and Larry E. Axel, 63–76. Macon, GA: Mercer University Press, 1987.

Loomer, Bernard. "Meland on God." *American Journal of Theology and Philosophy* 5.2–3 (1984) 138–43.

————. "Response to David R. Griffin." *Encounter* 36 (1975) 361–69.

————. "S-I-Z-E." *Criterion* 13 (1974) 5–8.

————. "The Size of God." In *The Size of God: The Theology of Bernard Loomer in Context*, edited by William Dean and Larry E. Axel, 20–51. Macon, GA: Mercer University Press, 1987.

Madsen, Catherine. "If God Is God She Is Not Nice." *Journal of Feminist Studies in Religion* 5.1 (1989) 103–5.

Mathews, Shailer. *The Growth of the Idea of God*. New York: Macmillan, 1931.

Milligan, Charles S. "The Pantheistic Motif in American Religious Thought." In *Religion and Philosophy in the United States of America*, edited by Peter Freese, 582–602. Essen: Die Blaue Eule, 1987.

Minnesota Department of Health. "Situation Update for COVID-19." https://www.health.state.mn.us/diseases/coronavirus/situation.html.

Neville, Robert Cummings. *The Truth of Broken Symbols*. Albany: State University of New York Press, 1996.

Oord, Thomas Jay. *The Uncontrolling Love of God: An Open and Relational Account of Providence*. Downers Grove, IL: IVP Academic, 2015.

Oppel, Richard A., Jr., et al. "The Fullest Look yet at the Racial Inequity of Coronavirus." *The New York Times*, July 5, 2020. https://www.nytimes.com/interactive/2020/07/05/us/coronavirus-latinos-african-americans-cdc-data.html.

Otto, Rudolf. *The Idea of the Holy: An Inquiry into the Non-Rational Factor in the Idea of the Divine and Its Relation to the Rational*. Translated by John W. Harvey. 2nd ed. London: Oxford University Press, 1950.

Pinn, Anthony B. *Humanism: Essays on Race, Religion, and Popular Culture*. London: Bloomsbury, 2015.

Plaskow, Judith. *The Coming of Lilith: Essays on Feminism, Judaism, and Sexual Ethics, 1972–2003*. Boston: Beacon, 2005.

Roth, John K. "A Theodicy of Protest." In *Encountering Evil: Live Options in Theodicy*, edited by Stephen T. Davis, 1–37. Louisville: Westminster John Knox, 2001.

Rubenstein, Mary-Jane. *Pantheologies: Gods, Worlds, Monsters*. New York: Columbia University Press, 2018.

Rubenstein, Richard L. *After Auschwitz: History, Theology, and Contemporary Judaism*. 2nd ed. Baltimore: Johns Hopkins University Press, 1992.

Rue, Loyal. *Nature Is Enough: Religious Naturalism and the Meaning of Life*. Albany: State University of New York Press, 2011.

————. *Religion Is Not about God: How Spiritual Traditions Nurture Our Biological Nature and What to Expect When They Fail*. New Brunswick, NJ: Rutgers University Press, 2005.

Shaw, Marvin C. "The Romantic Love of Evil: Loomer's Proposal of a Reorientation in Religious Naturalism." *American Journal of Theology and Philosophy* 10.1 (1989) 33–42.

Shear, Michael D., et al. "Inside Trump's Failure: The Rush to Abandon Leadership Role on the Virus." *The New York Times*, July 18, 2020. https://www.nytimes.com/2020/07/18/us/politics/trump-coronavirus-response-failure-leadership.html.

Shults, F. LeRon. *Practicing Safe Sects: Religious Reproduction in Scientific and Philosophical Perspective*. Boston: Brill, 2018.

Stone, Jerome A. *Religious Naturalism Today: The Rebirth of a Forgotten Alternative*. Albany: State University of New York Press, 2008.

Tillich, Paul. *Dynamics of Faith*. New York: HarperOne, 1957.

————. *Systematic Theology*. Vol. 2. Chicago: University of Chicago Press, 1957.

Trible, Phyllis. *Texts of Terror: Literary-Feminist Readings of Biblical Narratives.* Philadelphia: Fortress, 1984.

Weisberger, Andrea M. "The Argument from Evil." In *The Cambridge Companion to Atheism,* edited by Michael Martin, 166–81. Cambridge: Cambridge University Press, 2007.

Wheeler, Demian. "Bernard Loomer as a Bridge between Whitehead and Tillich: Towards a Ground-of-Being Process Theology." *Bulletin of the North American Paul Tillich Society* 46.1 (2018) 22–29.

———. *"Deus sive Natura*: Pantheism as a Variety of Religious Naturalism." In *The Routledge Handbook of Religious Naturalism,* edited by Donald A. Crosby and Jerome A. Stone, 106–17. London: Routledge, 2018.

———. *Religion within the Limits of History Alone: Pragmatic Historicism and the Future of Theology.* Albany: State University of New York Press, 2020.

———. "Seizing a Whiteheadian Alternative: A Retrieval of the Empirical Option in Process Thought." In *Conceiving an Alternative: Philosophical Resources for an Ecological Civilization,* edited by Demian Wheeler and David E. Conner, 115–47. Anoka, MN: Process Century, 2019.

———. "The Spirituality of Size: The Religious Qualities of Pantheistic God Metaphors." *American Journal of Theology and Philosophy* 42.1 (2021) 8–31.

Whitehead, Alfred North. *Process and Reality: An Essay in Cosmology.* Edited by David Ray Griffin and Donald W. Sherburne. Corrected ed. New York: Free, 1978.

Wieman, Henry Nelson. "Reply to Cherbonnier." In *The Empirical Theology of Henry Nelson Wieman,* edited by Robert W. Bretall. New York: Macmillan, 1963.

———. *The Source of Human Good.* Atlanta: Scholars, 1995.

Wildman, Wesley J. "The Ambiguous Heritage and Perpetual Promise of Liberal Theology." *American Journal of Theology and Philosophy* 32.1 (2011) 43–61.

———. *Effing the Ineffable: Existential Mumblings at the Limits of Language.* Albany: State University of New York Press, 2018.

———. *God Is . . . : Meditations on the Mystery of Life, the Purity of Grace, the Bliss of Surrender, and the God beyond God.* Eugene, OR: Cascade Books, 2019.

———. "Ground-of-Being Theologies." In *The Oxford Handbook of Religion and Science,* edited by Philip Clayton, 612–32. Oxford: Oxford University Press, 2006.

———. *In Our Own Image: Anthropomorphism, Apophaticism, and Ultimacy.* Oxford: Oxford University Press, 2017.

———. "Incongruous Goodness, Perilous Beauty, Disconcerting Truth: Ultimate Reality and Suffering in Nature." In *Physics and Cosmology: Scientific Perspectives on the Problem of Natural Evil,* edited by Robert J. Russell et al., 267–94. Vatican City: Vatican Observatory, 2007.

———. "Religious Naturalism: What It Can Be, and What It Need Not Be." *Philosophy, Theology, and the Sciences* 1.1 (2014) 36–58.

———. *Religious Philosophy as Multidisciplinary Comparative Inquiry: Envisioning a Future for the Philosophy of Religion.* Albany: State University of New York Press, 2010.

———. *Science and Religious Anthropology: A Spiritually Evocative Naturalist Interpretation of Human Life.* Farnham: Ashgate, 2009.

World Health Organization. "WHO Coronavirus (COVID-19) Dashboard." https://covid19.who.int/.

2

"And Who Is My Neighbor?"

Historical Images of Christian Responses to Pandemic

—JENNIFER AWES FREEMAN

"YOU REMEMBER, BELOVED, THAT man who was wounded by the robbers, and half dead by the way," Augustine of Hippo preached from his bishop's chair, "how he was strengthened, by receiving oil and wine for his wounds. His error indeed was already pardoned, and yet his weakness is in process of healing in the inn. The inn, if you recognize it, is the Church." Many of Augustine's congregants, standing before him some five yards away, would have been able to make eye contact with their bishop as he went on to explain that the church is likened to an inn because humans are but travelers in this life.[1] This sermon, preached in Carthage on Sunday, September 23rd, 417 CE, is characteristic of Augustine's concern with spiritual healing and unity in the church.[2] He often preached and wrote on the parable of the Good Samaritan (Luke 10:25–37), emphasizing the church as a place of recovery—for saints and sinners alike.[3] He conceived of Christ as the

1. Augustine of Hippo, *Sermon* 131.6, adapted from MacMullen's translation of *Sermons on Selected Lessons of the New Testament*, 864. On Augustine as a preacher, see Brown, *Augustine of Hippo*, 250–58; Burns and Jensen, *Christianity in Roman Africa*, 271–72, 284–86; and from Augustine himself, *On Christian Teaching*.

2. This unity was important during the theological controversies of the fourth and fifth centuries, and for Augustine especially around the time of this sermon, which was concurrent with the Pelagian controversy that would be officially condemned in 418. See, e.g., Augustine of Hippo's works: *Contra duos epistolas Pelagianorum*; *Contra Iulianum haeresis Pelagianae defensorem*; *De gestis Pelagi*. See also Dupont, *Gratia in Augustine's Sermones*.

3. See also Augustine of Hippo, *Quaestiones euangeliorum libri duo* 2.19; *In Iohannis euangelium tractatus CXXIV* 41.13; *Enarrationes in Psalmos* (101–150) 125.15. My

Good Samaritan and the two denarii paid to the innkeeper as "the love of God and the love of our neighbor."[4] Augustine's metaphor of the church as an inn, akin to a hostel or hospital, also reflected the historical relationship between medical care and the early Christian church. The emergence of the hospital in the mid-fourth century CE owed its origins to the medical charity of the first three centuries of Christianity, as well as monastic infirmaries, which, in addition to the monks or nuns, served the poor at no cost.[5] While early Christianity embraced the medical knowledge of the Greco-Roman culture into which it entered, Christian medicine and hospitality were based equally—if not more—in ancient Egyptian and Jewish models of social welfare than in Greco-Roman philanthropy, paying special attention to the poor, widows, orphans, the sick, and the imprisoned.[6] This, along with the concentration of early Christian communities in urban centers, meant that Christianity, its resources, and teachings were at the frontline of disease and pandemic in much of the premodern world.

Although crises caused by disease and pandemics generate acts of goodwill, generosity, and self-sacrifice, they also often incite or exacerbate violence, superstition, and bad theology. Revisiting how religious thinkers and leaders have responded to pandemic can help us reflect critically on our responses to the ongoing coronavirus pandemic and invite us to embrace opportunities for theological innovation, spiritual care, and social responsibility that are historically grounded. In what follows, a selection of such episodes highlight the intermingling of the political and the religious, bouts of violence and anti-Judaism, the role of public and private, the importance of repentance and reconciliation, the desire to find spiritual meaning in suffering, and the enduring question, "who is my neighbor?"

The Judgment of God and the Justinianic Plague

In 541 CE, the city of Constantinople was a thriving metropolis of some five hundred thousand residents. Strategically located on the Bosporus strait, which connects the Sea of Marmara and the Black Sea, sixth-century Constantinople was a major cultural and economic force. It was the city's role as a trade center that led to its contraction of the plague by the spring

---

sincere thanks goes to Patout Burns for bringing these passages to my attention.

4. Augustine of Hippo, *Enarrationes in Psalmos* (101–150) 125.15.11.

5. Ferngren, *Medicine and Healthcare in Early Christianity*, 125–30; Risse, *Mending Bodies, Saving Souls*, 94–105. On the impact of early hospitals, see Horden, "The Earliest Hospitals," 361–89.

6. Risse, *Mending Bodies, Saving Souls*, 73.

of 542 from ships delivering grain from Egypt.[7] Based on contemporaneous descriptions, it is almost certain that the disease was *Yersinia pestis*, also known as the bubonic plague.[8]

The Byzantine historian Procopius of Caesarea (ca. 500–570 CE) captured the physical and psychological devastation caused by the plague in his writings. The disease seemed to move through the population without rhyme or reason, as Procopius observes, "about this calamity there is no way to find any justification, to give a rational account, or even to cope with it mentally, except by referring it to God."[9] According to Procopius, some victims fell sick suddenly upon experiencing waking or sleeping visions of demons striking their bodies.[10] For others, the disease began as an apparently benign fever, only to escalate dramatically, such that bubonic swellings developed in the next day or two. Procopius notes that victims then experienced a variety of symptoms, including comas, dementia, and hysteria.[11] Still others died of starvation—whether from refusing to eat, being left unattended, or because of the "true famine [that] was careering about in a city that nevertheless abounded in all goods."[12] Just as the spread of the disease seemed to defy reason—not being bound by weather, region, or social location—so too did death and survival seem to be arbitrary.

As the death toll rose, there were not enough people to bury the dead, nor were there sufficient burial sites to accommodate so many bodies, and so the emperor Justinian (ca. 482–565 CE) dedicated some soldiers and imperial funds to address the issue. Once all of the graves were full, they took to digging ditches, but soon had to resort to even more drastic measures: "They climbed up the towers of the fortified structure, the one in Sykai, tore off the roofs, and tossed the bodies there in a tangled heap . . . and then they covered them again with their roofs. A foul stench would waft there to the city and bring even more grief to its people."[13] A grim picture is painted of a city that had quickly become a shell of its former self. Perhaps these towers, packed with the rotting dead, struck the surviving inhabitants of Constantinople as a kind of morbid inversion of the heavenly, expansive interior of the recently rebuilt cathedral of Hagia Sophia.

7. Gregory, *A History of Byzantium*, 120. The plague likely originated in central Africa. See, e.g., Sarris, "Bubonic Plague in Byzantium."

8. E.g., Evagrius, *Ecclesiastical History*, 4.29, and Procopius, *The Wars of Justinian*, 2.22–23, discussed below.

9. Procopius, *The Wars of Justinian*, 2.22.2–3 (120).

10. Procopius, *The Wars of Justinian*, 2.22.10 (121).

11. Procopius, *The Wars of Justinian*, 2.22.18–21 (121).

12. Procopius, *The Wars of Justinian*, 2.23.19 (124).

13. Procopius, *The Wars of Justinian*, 2.23.9–11 (123).

Procopius laments that, "All the customs of burial were overlooked at that time"[14]—there were no processions or singing, only a never-ending pile of bodies. Still, Procopius notes with interest, some political factions that had formerly opposed one another came together to perform funeral rites and bury those who did not belong to their faction.[15]

In the Liturgy of St. John Chrysostom, which originated in Hagia Sophia and by the end of Justinian's reign had become the standard liturgy in the east, Christians prayed for, "A Christian ending to our life: painless, blameless, and peaceful; and a good defense before the dread judgment seat of Christ."[16] The possibility of a sudden death by the plague, which threatened a pious and peaceful transition, motivated some to repentance and even religious fervor. Procopius criticizes those who "became religious to an extreme degree," but then upon recovering from the disease reverted to their old ways.[17] Procopius seems to scoff, "One would not, therefore, utter a falsehood if he were to assert that this disease, whether by some chance or providence, carefully picked out the worst people and let them live."[18]

This particular instance of the plague lasted for four months in Constantinople, according to Procopius, with the death toll rising to five thousand a day, and even as high as ten thousand in a single day.[19] Within a year, the plague spread around the Mediterranean to wreak havoc throughout Byzantium, Africa, Spain, Italy, Gaul, and even the British Isles. The bishop Gregory of Tours (538–94 CE) recorded the 543 appearance of the plague in Gaul in *The History of the Franks*, in which he also tells several stories of miraculous protection through intercessory prayers and relics.[20] The last epidemic Gregory records is that of 590, which took the life of Pope Pelagius II. Gregory of Tours preserves one of the sermons of Pelagius's

14. Procopius, *The Wars of Justinian*, 2.23.12 (123).

15. Procopius, *The Wars of Justinian*, 2.23.9–11 (123).

16. Chrysostom, *The Divine Liturgy*, 58–59.

17. Procopius, *The Wars of Justinian*, 2.23.14 (124).

18. Procopius, *The Wars of Justinian*, 2.23.16 (124). In his unpublished works known as *The Secret History*, Procopius writes frankly and critically about the emperor, revealing that he clearly considers Justinian to be one of these "worst people." Procopius explains that the "continuous series of catastrophes" of wars, flooding, earthquakes, and the plague during Justinian's reign were interpreted by himself and some of his contemporaries as either a divine judgment on Justinian and the empire, or as evidence of Justinian's demonic villainy. Procopius does not make much of the fact that Justinian recovered from the plague himself but notes only the rumor that the emperor had died and the resulting conspiracies. Procopius, *The Secret History*, 2.18 (76–77), 1.4 (15).

19. Procopius, *The Wars of Justinian*, 2.23.12–13 (123).

20. Gregory of Tours, *The History of the Franks*, 199–200. Discussed in Little, "Life and Afterlife of the First Plague Pandemic," 10.

successor, who came to be known as Gregory the Great. In April 590, he preached repentance to Rome in the face of sudden death, concluding his message with instructions for a city-wide procession that would include everyone from the community.[21] After praying the psalms for three days, the various groups were to begin at seven different churches throughout Rome, all processing "with prayers and lamentations" to converge on "the basilica of the blessed Virgin Mary," that is, Santa Maria Maggiore, at the center of the city.[22] Thus, the soon-to-be pope and his flock physically covered the city in penitential prayer. And, according to tradition, their prayers of *Kyrie eleison* were heard: as they crossed the Tiber, the Archangel Michael appeared atop Hadrian's mausoleum and sheathed his flaming sword, which was understood to symbolize the end of the plague.[23] The event is memorialized to this day in a large bronze statue of a sword-wielding angel on top of the building.[24]

Ultimately, the so-called Plague of Justinian took the lives of somewhere between thirty and fifty million people, that is, about a third of the empire's entire population. The plague would return in a roughly fifteen-year cycle for the next two centuries, such that every generation was touched by it in some way.

Ars Moriendi: Dying Well during the Black Death[25]

> Disease was sent forth; the quivering spear of the Almighty was aimed everywhere and infected the whole human race with its pitiless wounds. . . . Mourn, mourn, you peoples, and call upon the mercy of God.[26]

21. Gregory of Tours, *The History of the Franks*, 10.1 (545).

22. Gregory of Tours, *The History of the Franks*,10.1 (546).

23. Gregory of Tours, *The History of the Franks*, 546n16; James of Voragine, *Golden Legend*, 2:202, discussed in Little, "Life and Afterlife of the First Plague Pandemic," 31.

24. The current statue dates to the eighteenth century; it replaced a sixteenth-century statue, which itself had replaced earlier statues dating at least to the thirteenth century. Little, "Life and Afterlife of the First Plague Pandemic," 32.

25. It is not lost on this writer that the phrase "Black Death" or "Black Plague" has taken on new additional meaning in the context of the concurrent coronavirus pandemic and the uprisings in response to police brutality, both of which are disproportionately taking the lives of people of color. See Taylor, "The Black Plague."

26. Gabriele de' Mussis, "1. The Arrival of the Plague," in Horrox, *The Black Death*, 16. Significant literary treatments of the plague include the Pardoner's Tale in Geoffrey Chaucer's *Canterbury Tales*, lines 1–20, 199–222, and Giovanni Boccaccio's *Decameron*, in which sheltering during the Black Death is the premise for characters telling the hundred tales.

Thus, the Italian chronicler Gabriele de' Mussis (ca. 1280–1356 CE) conceptualized the plague of the fourteenth century as an act of divine wrath. In the 1330s, the disease had begun to spread through central Asia, arriving on the northern coast of the Black Sea by 1346.[27] From there it continued westward across the Mediterranean to Italy and then northward, entering Scandinavia by the middle of 1350 and moving eastward to arrive in Moscow during the subsequent year, for a deadly duration of barely five years. An estimated "60–80 percent of Europeans were infected and 75–90 percent of those people died: by those figures, the disease killed somewhere between 45 and 72 percent of the population."[28] A second wave hit about a decade later, which primarily took the lives of children, followed by a third wave another decade later; the plague would continue to reemerge sporadically for another four centuries, though not to the degree of that initial wave. Population levels in Europe would not be regained until the mid-sixteenth century.[29]

Medieval doctors speculated that the plague was spread through corrupted or infected air, which led to attempts at prevention by surrounding oneself with aromatic vapors by burning wood or spices or by carrying something fragrant.[30] Various other causes of the plague were speculated—including astrological influences[31] and earthquakes.[32] While medieval doctors did not identify the rat flea as the vector of the plague, they knew that a contagious agent was operating.[33] Plague tracts instructed their readers to avoid "over-indulgence in food or drink, and also avoid baths and everything

27. See, e.g., Hymes, "Epilogue." The plague did not come to be known as the "Black Death" until much later. It is also important to note that the story—often repeated by academics—that the Mongol army engaged in germ warfare by launching bodies of their dead into a city in Crimea is both inaccurate and potentially xenophobic. Hoffman, *An Environmental History of Medieval Europe*, 289. The bubonic plague is transmitted primarily through the bites of the rat flea or the human louse; the more rare and deadly (and therefore literally shorter-lived) pneumonic plague can be spread through water droplets or bodily fluids; the third and very rare form of the plague is the septicemic, which can be transmitted through exposure to a cough or direct contact with infected tissue. On the entry of the plague into Europe, see, e.g., Ditrich, "The Transmission of the Black Death," 25–39.

28. Hoffman, *An Environmental History of Medieval Europe*, 291.

29. Hoffman, *An Environmental History of Medieval Europe*, 292.

30. See the plague tracts of Bengt Knutsson and John Jacobus. Horrox, *The Black Death*, 173–77. The later development of the plague hood with its distinct bird-like beak filled with aromatics was based on the same principle.

31. As speculated by Geoffrey de Meaux. Horrox, *The Black Death*, 167–72.

32. Horrox, *The Black Death*, 177–82.

33. Medieval doctors also distinguished between the bubonic and pneumonic manifestations of the plague, the latter of which was even more deadly.

that might rarefy the body."[34] Recommended treatments included blood-letting, herbal ointments, and other medicines.[35]

The various potential physical causes of disease were not mutually exclusive from spiritual causes.[36] As in previous generations, plague was understood to be an expression of God's judgment and punishment; therefore, repentance and turning to God were the best ways to stop the spread of the disease.[37] The threat of plague inspired a range of religious responses, most of which were motivated by reconciliation with God—to either abate judgment or at the very least to prepare the faithful for a good death. Public penitential processions and masses were organized in the hope for the success that Gregory the Great's procession had accomplished in the sixth century.[38] Similarly, many were inspired to go on pilgrimage either in anticipation of plague or as thanksgiving for surviving it.[39] The Virgin Mary was often called upon to intercede with her Son on behalf of the faithful,[40] as were numerous saints, including St. Sebastian, the

34. "62. The Treatise of John of Burgundy, 1365," in Horrox, *The Black Death*, 186.

35. "62. The Treatise of John of Burgundy, 1365," in Horrox, *The Black Death*, 188–93.

36. E.g., "63. A Fifteenth-century Treatise on the Pestilence," Horrox, *The Black Death*, 193. "It should be known to all Christians that pestilence, and every other manifestation of God's vengeance arises because of sin. . . . If I am asked what is the cause of pestilence, what is its physical cause and by what means can someone save himself from it, I answer to the first question that sin is the cause, as set forth above. To the second question I say that it arises from the sea." Among the many alleged spiritual causes for punishment via plague was that of "indecent clothing," that is, ornate and impractical fashions that included numerous slashes, buttons, and so on. Tait, *Chronica Johannis*, 88–89, 166–68; Haydon, *Eulogium Historiarum sive Temporis*, 3:230–31; Horrox, *The Black Death*, 133–34. Accordingly, sumptuary laws were issued in England in 1363. Horrox, *The Black Death*, 340–42.

37. Horrox, *The Black Death*, 95.

38. E.g., William of Edendon, "33. A Voice in Rama," in Horrox, *The Black Death*, 115–17.

39. E.g., Robert de Stretton, "50. Pilgrimage to Merevale, 1361," in Horrox, *The Black Death*, 148–49.

40. As in this prayer preserved in a late medieval Book of Hours, "Star of Heaven, who nourished the Lord and rooted up the plague of death which our first parents planted; may that star now deign to counter the constellations whose strife brings the people the ulcers of a terrible death. O glorious star of the sea, save us from the plague." The prayer poetically links the death incurred by the original sin with that of the Black Death, and thus by invoking the Virgin Mary perhaps also plays into the long-established antithesis between Eve (sin) and Mary (redemption). The Eve/Mary antithesis appears over two-hundred times in theological works from the fifth to thirteenth centuries. Wordsworth, *Horae Eboracensis*, 69; Horrox, *The Black Death*, 124; Flood, *Representations of Eve*, 14.

third-century martyr, whose arrow wounds served as visual echoes of the buboes and pustules caused by the bubonic plague.[41]

One of the more visible and extreme penitential movements was that of the flagellants, who consisted of "men and women alike, many barefoot, others wearing hairshirts or smeared with ashes. As they processed with lamentations and tears, and with loose hair, they beat themselves with cruel whips until the blood ran."[42] As the flagellants marched, they often recited the thirteenth-century *Stabat mater*, which celebrated Mary's contemplation of her dead son's sufferings.[43] Although the pope had participated in their processions at Avignon,[44] the flagellants were eventually outlawed by Pope Clement VI in 1349 because of their resistance to church authority and the anti-Judaism they incited.

Many Christians blamed the Jews for the plague, which led to pogroms throughout Europe.[45] For example, Heinrich Truchess von Diessenhoven, who had been a chaplain of Pope John XXII, described with some relish persecutions against the Jews that took place in 1348–49. According to him, "all the Jews between Cologne and Austria were burnt and killed" for allegedly poisoning wells and rivers and therefore infecting the population with the plague.[46] Local authorities extracted confessions from the accused through torture before executing them.[47] He notes a particularly gruesome account in which, "On 4 January the people of Constance shut up the Jews in two of their own houses, and then burnt 330 of them in the fields at sunset on 3 March. . . . They were burnt shut up in a house which had been especially built for that purpose."[48] He also records that in some instances the infants of Jewish

41. E.g., "40. A Prayer Made to St. Sebastian against the Mortality Which Flourished in 1349," in Horrox, *The Black Death*, 125–26.

42. "5. The Plague at Avignon," in Horrox, *The Black Death*, 44.

43. Horrox, *The Black Death*, 97, 150–54.

44. "5. The Plague at Avignon," in Horrox, *The Black Death*, 44.

45. In 1215, the Fourth Lateran Council had ordained that Jews and Muslims wear special dress to distinguish themselves from Christians (Canon 68). On antisemitism and the medieval persecution of the Jews, see, e.g., Chazan, *Reassessing Jewish Life in Medieval Europe*. On the Christian representation of Jews in medieval art, see Strickland, *Saracens, Demons, and Jews*; Merback, *Beyond the Yellow Badge*. For firsthand primary source representations of Jewish experience in the Middle Ages, see Marcus, *The Jew in the Medieval World*, and more recently Sienna, *A Rainbow Thread*.

46. Heinrich Truchess von Diessenhoven, "69. The Persecution of the Jews," in Horrox, *The Black Death*, 208; Boehmer, *Fontes Rerum Germanicarum*, 38–71.

47. Heinrich Truchess von Diessenhoven, "69. The Persecution of the Jews," in Horrox, *The Black Death*, 209.

48. See, e.g., d'Oron, "70. Measures Taken against the Jews in Lausanne," in Horrox, *The Black Death*, 210–11; and "71. Examination of the Jews Captured in Savoy," in

parents who had been killed were then taken and baptized. Documentary sources like these—of which there are many—reveal the complicity and even verve with which local Christian populations organized and dedicated their resources to torturing and murdering Jews.

In 1348, Pope Clement VI reissued the papal bull *Sicut Judeis*, which forbade the persecution of the Jews.[49] But it remained an issue. Six months later, in a letter dating to January of 1349, the authorities in Cologne wrote to those in Strasbourg to follow up on numerous letters inquiring about accusations against the Jewish population. After expressing concern that massacres could lead to revolts in major cities, the authors of the letter write,

> we are still of the opinion that this mortality and its attendant circumstances are caused by divine vengeance and nothing else. Accordingly we intend to forbid any harassment of the Jews in our city because of these flying rumours, but to defend them faithfully and keep them safe, as our predecessors did—and we are convinced that you ought to do the same.[50]

Despite the official position of the Catholic Church and of many local authorities, anti-Jewish violence and persecution, which had gained momentum during the Black Death, would continue in Europe for centuries.

Generally speaking, death was a familiar and accepted part of life in the Middle Ages, however, the dramatic increase in death rates caused by plague in the fourteenth and fifteenth centuries contributed to a fear of sudden death and thus to increased efforts to prepare for a good death. Contemplation of mortality was prompted visually through various themes and media, which can collectively be categorized as *memento mori*, that is, "remember you must die" or "remember death." A popular iteration of this is a tale known as the Three Living and the Three Dead, in which three young men, finely dressed, go out hunting and encounter three dead men similarly riding horses, but in various states of decomposition.[51] Then, "A

Horrox, *The Black Death*, 212–19.

49. The first iteration of this bull had been issued in the early twelfth century in response to violence against the Jews during the First Crusade. In his subsequent message to prelates and clergy, the pope acknowledges that, "Our Savior chose to be born of Jewish stock," before listing the popes before him who had similarly codified the protection of the Jews. He argues that "it cannot be true that the Jews, by such a heinous crime, are the cause or occasion of the plague, because throughout many parts of the world the same plague, by the hidden judgement of God, has afflicted and afflicts the Jews themselves and many other races who have never lived alongside them." Clement VI, "73. Mandate of Clement VI concerning the Jews," in Horrox, *The Black Death*, 221–22.

50. "72. Letter from Cologne to Strassburg," in Horrox, *The Black Death*, 220.

51. The Three Living and the Three Dead was already widespread by the thirteenth

dialogue ensues in which the living express mortification, while the mortified admonish them to improve their ways, and to ponder the transience and essential baseness of the human condition."[52] Visual depictions of the legend are found throughout Europe in the wall paintings of parish churches and illuminated manuscripts.[53]

Medieval Christians kept death physically and psychologically close through small personal objects, such as jewelry, decorated with *memento mori*. These objects often juxtaposed the vanity of earthly pursuits with the inevitability of death—contrasting precious materials and craftsmanship with images of skulls and inscriptions that instruct the owner to contemplate death. This tension is explicit in an ivory rosary, produced in Germany in the early sixteenth century (Fig. 2.1).[54]

Figure 2.1: Rosary, ca. 1500–25, German, The Metropolitan Museum of Art, New York, Gift of J. Pierpont Morgan, 1917.

---

century, recorded in some sixty versions. Another popular theme was the Danse Macabre, or Dance of Death, which similarly served as an allegory of the universality and inevitability of death.

52. Binski, *Medieval Death*, 134.

53. Binski, *Medieval Death*, 135.

54. On this object, see, e.g., Perkinson, *The Ivory Mirror*, 50–52; Scholten, "Scale, Prayer and Play," 200–201.

About twenty-four inches long, this reduced rosary (or chaplet) consists of eight segments, the middle six for saying *Aves*, which display bust portraits of upper-class men and women carved in ivory and set into leafy frames of gilded silver. The backsides of the second and fifth portraits each reveal an image of a skeleton accompanied by an inscribed banner, "think to die" and "I am what you will be," respectively.[55] The two terminal *Paternoster* beads are heads carved in the round; their faces are split directly down the middle with one side presenting the decaying face of a deceased man and the other side a skull. The visual interplay between the portraits and the skeletons—fittingly rendered in ivory—materializes the tension between the living and their inevitable death, the goal of which is to inspire devotion and self-examination.

If death was especially imminent, one may have turned to a pamphlet of the *Ars moriendi* ("the art of dying"), which was a popular handbook written in the early fifteenth century, now preserved in over three hundred Latin and vernacular versions.[56] Although it emerged from the sacrament of Last Rites, the handbook was designed to facilitate a good death with or without clergy.[57] Its text led the dying person through three major tools for self-examination and preparation: the five temptations (unbelief, despair, impatience, pride, avarice) and countering inspirations; a series of questions regarding one's spiritual state with a focus on contrition and repentance; and a series of prayers to be prayed with or on behalf of the dying person.[58]

The Black Death took the lives of some two hundred million people in Afro-Eurasia, and its economic, cultural, and religious impact would last for generations. In fact, civic quarantine policies, iterations of which are being enforced today, were developed around the Mediterranean during the Black Death.[59] But perhaps even more enduring than the effect that the plague had on day-to-day operations was its impact on late medieval religious practices

55. *COGITA MORI* and *SV VOTERIS* (i.e., *SV[M] QUOD ERIS*), respectively. Levin, *Images of Love and Death*, 117. The second phrase alternatively been transcribed as SV e VOT[IS] ERIS, and translated as "you will be of prayer itself."

56. See, e.g., O'Connor, *The Art of Dying Well*; Beaty, *The Craft of Dying*.

57. "A good death could be the guarantor of the future in two senses: the material and the social world of the deceased, their sphere of personal obligation and possessions, could be put in order by the due process of the will—increasingly important and elaborate form of document—and the soul's future could be cared for." Binski, *Medieval Death*, 33. On the shortage of priests during the plague, see Horrox, *The Black Death*, 271–74.

58. Binski, *Medieval Death*, 39–43.

59. In fact, "quarantine" comes from the Italian word *quaranta*, referencing the forty days that ships suspected of carrying plague were required to anchor before entering a harbor. Hoffman, *An Environmental History of Medieval Europe*, 298.

by bringing mortality and the condition of the soul to the forefront of the collective imagination. In the words of the *Ars moriendi*, "To know how to die is to have a heart and soul ever ready to go Godwards."[60]

The Responsibility of the Christian: Martin Luther's Response to Plague

The reformer Martin Luther (1483–1546) was no stranger to the plague, having lost several friends, family members, and acquaintances to it throughout his life.[61] In August of 1527, the plague spread to Wittenberg, causing many citizens to flee the city. Johann Hess, who was a pastor some two hundred miles away in Breslau, had written to Luther on several occasions requesting Luther's perspective on "whether it is proper for a Christian to run away from a deadly plague."[62] Luther eventually responded in an open letter, which was published by Hans Lufft and widely circulated as a pamphlet. The guiding principle of the letter is love for one's neighbor.

Luther begins his answer to Johann Hess with what are arguably the most clear-cut cases: those in which people are bound by official duties to remain during a plague.[63] In order to "care and provide for the soul in time of death," Luther instructs his fellow pastors to encourage their congregants "to attend church and listen to the sermon so that they learn through God's word how to live and how to die."[64] They should also go to confession, take communion weekly or every other week, make a will, and reconcile with their neighbors.[65] If there are sufficient clergy to attend to the needs of the sick, Luther explains, it is advisable for some of the clergy to leave the area so as to limit unnecessary infection. Similarly, public officials may only be excused from their obligations if they secure acceptable substitutes. From these offices he shifts to the mutual responsibility of the master-servant relationship, the care of children, and for other personal obligations: just as state and church officials should not abandon their posts without leaving sufficient staffing,

---

60. *Ars moriendi*, ch. 1, in Horrox, *The Black Death*, 346.

61. Luther's contemporary Ulrich Zwingli also wrote on the plague. Zwingli himself had almost died in 1519 during a plague outbreak, which killed almost half the population of Zurich. Around that time Zwingli composed the poem known as "Plague Hymn." In it, Zwingli expresses surrender to the divine will, "Thy vessel am I; To make or break altogether." Zwingli, *Early Writings*, 56.

62. Luther, *Luther's Works*, 43:119.

63. Luther, *Luther's Works*, 43:121.

64. Luther, *Luther's Works*, 43:134.

65. Luther, *Luther's Works*, 43:134.

"no one should dare leave his neighbor unless there are others who will take care of the sick in their stead and nurse them."[66] This is no small statement, considering how contagious and deadly the plague was.

When a person is not bound by formal responsibilities and relationships, Luther discerns that "they have an equal choice either to flee or to remain."[67] Here Luther the pastor surveys several biblical examples to affirm that the impulse to care for, protect, or save one's life is not only natural but in a sense is also commanded by God (e.g., 1 Cor 12:21–26). To those who interpret pestilence as God's judgment and therefore something they should succumb to, Luther argues that, "We must pray against every form of evil and guard against it to the best of our ability in order not to act contrary to God."[68] We owe it to ourselves, and, perhaps more importantly, to our neighbors, to do what we can to remain healthy and curb the spread of sickness. Furthermore, plague may be understood not only as punishment, but also as a test of faith and love, to which the Christian is called to submit to and serve their neighbor.[69]

Luther believed that, "all the epidemics, like any plague, are spread among the people by evil spirits who poison the air or exhale a pestilential breath which puts a deadly poison into the flesh."[70] Similarly, Luther explains that the devil stirs up "abhorrence, fear, and loathing" and "horror and repugnance in the presence of a sick person."[71] The devil does so not only because it delights in our despair but also in order to prevent us from helping our neighbor and ultimately from serving Christ. Luther provides the reader with a scripted rebuttal to the devil that contrasts the death and the destruction of the devil with the life and healing power of Christ.

Some of Luther's comments regarding sinful responses to the plague read like they could have been plucked from contemporary critiques on social media of those who do not take precautions against the spread of COVID-19 seriously:

> They disdain the use of medicines; they do not avoid places and persons infected by the plague, but lightheartedly make sport of it and wish to prove how independent they are. They say that it is God's punishment; if he wants to protect them he can do so without medicines or our carefulness. This is not trusting God

66. Luther, *Luther's Works*, 43:122.
67. Luther, *Luther's Works*, 43:123.
68. Luther, *Luther's Works*, 43:125.
69. Luther, *Luther's Works*, 43:127.
70. Luther, *Luther's Works*, 43:127.
71. Luther, *Luther's Works*, 43:127.

but tempting him. God has created medicines and provided us with intelligence to guard and take good care of the body so that we can live in good health.[72]

He continues:

> It is even more shameful for a person to pay no heed to his own body and to fail to protect it against the plague the best he is able, and then to infect and poison others who might have remained alive if he had taken care of his body as he should have. He is thus responsible before God for his neighbor's death and is a murderer many times over.[73]

In other words, care for the neighbor extends well beyond tending to the sick on a one-on-one capacity; it also means using resources responsibly with an eye toward potential impact on the larger community.

The importance of caring for family members and neighbors was also related to the fact that hospitals were not widespread in the early sixteenth century. Luther remarks that, "It would be well, where there is such an efficient government in cities and states, to maintain municipal homes and hospitals staffed with people to take care of the sick."[74] Similarly, he makes practical recommendations about cemeteries, including burial outside of the city, as was the custom of Jews, pagans, and Christians in antiquity. Not only is it more sanitary, the reformer explains, but a secluded, quiet cemetery also creates an atmosphere of respect and honor for the deceased.[75]

Luther himself had been faced with the choice of fleeing a plague on more than one occasion. In 1527, he chose to stay in Wittenberg even after John Frederick, the elector of Saxony, had ordered him to flee.[76] Luther did more than merely remain in Wittenberg: he actively ministered to and cared for the sick, even going so far as opening his home to them.[77] As he wrote to Johann Hess, anyone who "forsakes [their neighbor] and leaves him to his misfortune, becomes a murderer in the sight of God, as St. John states in his epistles, 'Whoever does not love his brother is a murderer.'"[78]

72. Luther, *Luther's Works*, 43:131.

73. Luther, *Luther's Works*, 43:131.

74. Luther, *Luther's Works*, 43:126.

75. Luther, *Luther's Works*, 43:136–37.

76. Luther, *Luther's Works*, 43:115.

77. He did so on more than one occasion, as for example in 1539 when he temporarily took in four orphaned children, whose parents had died from the plague. *D. Martin Luthers Werke: Kritische Gesamtausgbe*, Briefe, 8, 3398, Oct. 26, 1539, in Roper, *Martin Luther*, 293.

78. Luther, *Luther's Works*, 43:126; 1 John 3:15.

Luther's firsthand experiences of the gruesome and deadly effects of the plague render his later application of the word "plague" to the Jews all the more vile.[79] While Luther had been optimistic about the conversion of the Jews earlier in his career, by the late 1530s and early 1540s he had abandoned hope of their conversion and actively worked to have them expelled from the region.[80] Three years before his death, Luther wrote the venomous treatise *On the Jews and Their Lies*, in which the reformer calls for the violent oppression and persecution of the Jews, including the destruction of synagogues and schools.[81] Luther declares, "they are a heavy burden, *a plague, a pestilence*, a sheer misfortune for our country," and again, "Such a desperate, thoroughly evil, poisonous, and devilish lot are these Jews, who for these fourteen hundred years have been and still are *our plague, our pestilence*, and our misfortune."[82] In decrying Jews as "devilish," Luther fixates on their mouths, which he alleges pray for the death and suffering of Christians and curse Jesus' name.[83] Luther speculates, "If I were to eat, drink, or talk with such a devilish mouth, I would eat or drink myself full of devils by the dish or by the cupful, just as I surely make myself a cohort of all the devils that dwell in the Jews and that deride the precious blood of Christ."[84] Although Luther does not explicitly blame the Jews for the plague, his association of their mouths with the devil echoes his perspective on the spread of the plague by "evil spirits who poison the air or exhale a pestilential breath which puts a deadly poison into the flesh."[85]

It is difficult to overstate the significance of Martin Luther as a historical figure and theological thinker. The pamphlet and the treatise discussed in this section give a sense of the complexity of Luther's legacy in western Christianity. In his response to Johann Hess, as well as in his own actions during the plague in Wittenberg, Luther demonstrated his rational and pastoral approach to crisis, rooted in the belief that, "Service to God is indeed

79. Conversely, it is interesting that after Luther's death the phrase, "Living I was your plague, dying I will be your death, O Pope," was associated with numerous images of Luther. D. *Martin Luthers Werke: Kritische Gesamtausgbe*, Tischreden 3, 3543A, 390:17, in Roper, *Martin Luther: Renegade and Prophet*, 372.

80. On Martin Luther's anti-Judaism, see Kaufmann, *Luther's Jews*; Kaufmann, "Luther and the Jews."

81. Although it was known and circulated leading up to World War II, the degree of this treatise's influence on German antisemitism has been debated among scholars. See, e.g., Michael, *Holy Hatred*, 105–51.

82. Luther, *Luther's Works*, 47:265, 275; emphasis added.

83. Luther, *Luther's Works*, 47:275.

84. Luther, *Luther's Works*, 47:275.

85. Luther, *Luther's Works*, 43:127.

service to our neighbor."[86] It should go without saying that his treatment of the Jews is reprehensible and in absolute contradiction to his own core teachings and interpretations of Christian Scriptures. Luther, in all of his potential, his pastoral ability, and his destructive prejudice is instructive to us in our current moment. May we also scrutinize our own prejudices and fears that may manifest and respond to Luther's call to love our neighbor—that is, every person—whether by tending to the sick, wearing masks in public, or donating money, resources, and time.

Dying of "Improvement": Smallpox in North America[87]

The impact of disease on belief and cosmology can be observed in the encounters between European settlers and colonizers and Indigenous populations in the Americas. One of the most devastating diseases of this period was that of smallpox, which took the lives of millions of people, with many Native American communities being completely eradicated or significantly depleted, thereby radically shaping the course of American history.[88] European colonizers brought with them several novel diseases to the Americas, which, because of a lack of corresponding antibodies in the population, resulted in almost universal infection and high mortality rates among Native Americans.[89] While colonial texts ascribed the spread of diseases like the smallpox to God's judgment and the alleged ineptitude of Indigenous people, the historical record shows that Indigenous populations incorporated new

---

86. Luther, *Luther's Works*, 43:129.

87. This section title is a reference to the anecdote often told by Dr. Carlos Montezuma in which a sick person died even though his doctor had continually reported him as improving. Thus, one of his friends remarked that, "he died of improvement." Andrew J. Blackbird, "The Indian Problem: From the Indian's Standpoint," in Peyer, *American Indian Nonfiction*, 244–45. While smallpox spread accidentally, there were also numerous accusations of Euro-Americans engaging in biological warfare against Native Americans via "smallpox blankets" and similar items. E.g., Fenn, "Biological Warfare in Eighteenth-Century America." On fraudulent accounts, see Brown, "Did the US Army Distribute Smallpox Blankets to Indians?" My deep thanks to Marie Balsley Taylor who gave helpful feedback on this section; any shortcomings are of course my own.

88. The indelible mark left by the smallpox pandemic has gained new significance in light of the current coronavirus pandemic, and in fact a film is in production at the writing of this essay (and scheduled for a winter 2020 release) that tells the story of the smallpox pandemic in the eighteenth century. *Creatures* is produced by KK Productions, directed by Kristian Kerry, and cast with all Native American actors and is shot on location at the Blackfeet Reservation in Montana.

89. On this phenomenon, see Crosby, *Ecological Imperialism*; Crosby, "Virgin Soil Epidemics," 289–99. Paul Kelton nuances and pushes back against the "virgin soil" thesis in *Cherokee Medicine, Colonial Germs*.

diseases into their cosmologies and their medicine practitioners developed effective treatments and rituals, including quarantine.[90]

Declared eradicated by the World Health Organization in 1980,[91] smallpox (*variola virus*) was an acute viral infection of the lymphatic system, which was contracted through the upper respiratory system, either through respiratory secretions or through contact with infected scab material transmitted, for example, by bed linens.[92] That is, close contact was required for the disease to spread. After a twelve-day incubation period, patients experienced headache, high fevers, and muscle pain; five days later a painful rash developed and worsened over the next two weeks, particularly on the face, hands, arms, and feet. Pustules crusted and sloughed off, hence the "pocks," and further infections of the skin could occur. Complications could include pneumonia, abscesses, septic joints, and conjunctivitis, which could lead to blindness. In severe cases, internal hemorrhaging caused death even before the initial rash appeared.[93]

Smallpox was likely first brought to the Americas in the early sixteenth century by Spanish conquistadors to the West Indies. The disease quickly spread and decimated the Indigenous populations, which led to an increased importation of African slaves, some of whom brought more smallpox cases to the region. Ultimately, the epidemic took the lives of at least three million people between 1550 and 1850 and enabled the Spanish conquest of the Aztecs and Incas, as well as several other civilizations in Central and South America.[94] Smallpox was introduced to North America in the early seventeenth century by French, Dutch, and English colonists, beginning in ports and spreading inland. Again, smallpox devastated Native American tribes, including the vast majority of the Massachusett, an Algonquian-speaking nation who were among some of the first to encounter English settlers in the Boston area. Many of the Massachusett would become the earliest converts in part because their community had been so decimated by disease. In other words, disease and conversion often went hand in hand. In 1721—a century after the first wave of disease, the minister Cotton Mather introduced inoculation, which he had learned from his African slaves, to the Massachusetts Bay Colony.[95] As vaccination was increasingly practiced in the late eighteenth

---

90. As argued by Kelton, *Cherokee Medicine, Colonial Germs*.

91. Fenner et al., *Smallpox and Its Eradication*.

92. Patterson and Runge, "Smallpox and the Native American," 216–17.

93. Patterson and Runge, "Smallpox and the Native American," 217.

94. Patterson and Runge, "Smallpox and the Native American," 217–18.

95. On the eighteenth-century American reception of African medicine, see Wisecup, "African Medical Knowledge."

and early nineteenth centuries among colonists, and especially the army, Native American populations remained largely unprotected.

Broadly speaking, European Christians saw disease as evidence of divine work—most commonly that of judgment. In the context of the "New World, the Europeans conveniently and consistently conceived of disease among Indigenous tribes as a God-ordained phenomenon that punished them and affirmed colonization. During the conquest of the Aztecs in the early sixteenth century, Francisco de Aguilar observed, "When the Christians were exhausted from war God saw fit to send the Indians smallpox, and there was a great pestilence."[96] A century later, Governor John Winthrop—who had likely read accounts of the Spanish conquest[97]—stated of the outbreak in the Massachusetts Bay Colony, "But for the natives in these parts, God hath so pursued them, as for 300 miles space the greatest part of them are swept away by the smallpox which still continues among them. So as God hath thereby cleared our title to this place."[98] Meanwhile, many tribes associated European disease with European religion, as in the case of the Huron, who observed many of their people dying from smallpox after having been baptized by the Jesuits.[99]

In 1832, the US Congress passed the Indian Vaccination Act. While it resulted in the vaccination of some forty to fifty thousand American Indians, the program excluded some tribes, such as the Mandan Indians and other Upper Missouri River tribes, for political reasons.[100] In fact, the program was also used to "enable Indian removal, to permit relocation of Native Americans to reservations, to consolidate and compact reservation communities, to expedite westward expansion of the United States, and to protect Indian nations viewed as friendly or economically important."[101] In short, the treatment of

---

96. de Aguilar, "Eighth Jornada," 198.

97. Kelton, *Cherokee Medicine, Colonial Germs*, 10.

98. Winthrop to D'Ewes, July 21, 1634, in Winthrop, *Winthrop* 3:171–72, quoted in Kelton, *Cherokee Medicine, Colonial Germs*, 5. Winthrop's perspective on the epidemic is treated at length in Silva, *Miraculous Plagues*.

99. For further discussion of how tribes conceptualized European disease, see, e.g., Stephen Greenblatt's essay "Invisible Bullets," in Greenblatt, *Shakespearean Negotiations*, 21–65, esp. 36–39.

100. Pearson, "Lewis Cass and the Politics of Disease," 17–23. Even those tribes that were part of vaccination efforts were often the secondary focus of an such stated missions. For example, eight hundred dollars of the program's initial twelve thousand dollars was used to offset the costs of a federal cartographic and geological survey of Ojibwe country. Pearson, "Lewis Cass and the Politics of Disease," 17.

101. Pearson, "Lewis Cass and the Politics of Disease," 9.

disease and the diagnosis of disease among Native people were almost always tied to land removal, which was not the case for settlers.[102]

In 1887, an Ottawa leader who went by the name Andrew J. Blackbird (Mack-e-te-be-nessy, ca. 1810–1900) published a history and grammar of the Ottawa and Ojibwe people in Michigan. He describes how the Ottawa population had been "greatly reduced in numbers" because of "the smallpox which they brought from Montreal during the French war with Great Britain" (ca. 1760).[103] Blackbird writes that the Ottawa were sold a small box that they were told contained something supernatural that "would do them great good, and their people!" and they were given instructions not to open it until they returned to their country.[104] They opened it to discover a series of nested boxes, smaller and smaller, culminating in a one-inch box in which they found "nothing but mouldy particles."[105] Soon sickness spread throughout the community, taking the lives of entire families and even their great doctors. The "mouldy particles" that Blackbird describes may have actually been the infectious matter used in smallpox inoculations, which could be accomplished by blowing or inserting powdered smallpox scabs into the nose.[106] That is, it is difficult to know whether these materials were given to the Ottawa with ill-intent or as a medical resource.[107]

Just as Native American tribes had long-established medical practices, they had also incorporated disease into their cosmologies well before contact with Europeans and the diseases they brought with them.[108] For

102. The separate and inferior medical treatment of Indigenous people continues to be a reality today. See for example, St. Pierre, *Madonna Swan*.

103. Blackbird, *History of the Ottawa and Chippewa Indians of Michigan*, 9. N.B. Chippewa is an anglicization of Ojibwe.

104. Blackbird, *History of the Ottawa and Chippewa Indians of Michigan*, 9.

105. Blackbird, *History of the Ottawa and Chippewa Indians of Michigan*, 10.

106. "The practice of smallpox inoculation is dated to the eleventh century in China and was known in Africa and the Middle East. Translations of Chinese medical treatises were a major means of promoting smallpox inoculations in eighteenth-century Europe and the Americas." Jaskoski, "'A Terrible Sickness among Them,'" in *Early Native American Writing*, 144. Cutaneous inoculation was the most popular and was milder. Patterson and Runge, "Smallpox and the Native American," 220. See also Silva, *Miraculous Plagues*, 142–79.

107. E.g., Fenn, "Biological Warfare in Eighteenth-Century America." On fraudulent accounts, see Brown, "Did the U.S. Army Distribute Smallpox Blankets to Indians?"

108. In the study of the smallpox epidemic in early America, scholars have too often uncritically accepted colonial accounts, which "created a powerful narrative that gave germs agency in the destruction of the Native peoples, blamed the victims for the incompetent response to those germs, and thereby exonerated colonizers from responsibility." At the same time, there is actually evidence that Native "leaders incorporated smallpox into their cosmology, constructed rituals to deal with threatened or actual

instance, the Cherokee believed that they lived in tension with a world of visible creatures and invisible spirits, the latter of which had both creative and destructive powers.[109] As described in Cherokee myths and ceremonies—albeit often imperfectly preserved through colonial texts, Cherokee cosmology emphasized the importance of respecting both creatures and spirits, which was expressed in prayers and rituals, in order to maintain balance.[110] Disease could be caused by disrespected spirits and animal guardians, as well as by the lonely deceased, who sought companionship with their living kinsmen. Those who intentionally practiced bad medicine could also cause sickness and even death.[111] In short, the Cherokee understood sickness and mortality as a consequence of their actions, which had repercussions in the spiritual and physical realms.

Cherokee practitioners of medicine—of any gender—were respected leaders in the community, who approached medicine as a collective endeavor that included the dynamic spirit world. They consulted dreams and omens to make their diagnoses; treatment could include medicines, prayers, and powerful or purifying materials such as crystals, fire, water, and various plants.[112] The communal approach to health is reflected in the importance of the major ceremonies that were celebrated in conjunction with different points of the seasonal cycle.[113] Smallpox was unlike any other disease they had encountered, but Cherokees—who were first exposed to it in the 1690s—were still able to draw "on their preexisting cosmological knowledge and explained outbreaks of smallpox as a consequence of disrespect shown to the spirit world."[114] That said, such an interpretation of the epidemic was not mutually exclusive with identifying European colonizers and traders as the proximate source of transmission.[115] Contrary to colonial interpretations, which perceived Native medical practitioners

---

epidemics of the disease, and gave constructive advice to their followers about avoiding exposure." Kelton, *Cherokee Medicine, Colonial Germs*, 10.

109. Kelton, *Cherokee Medicine, Colonial Germs*, 68–70.

110. Mooney, *The Sacred Formulas of the Cherokees*; Mooney, *History, Myths, and Sacred Formulas of the Cherokees*.

111. See, e.g., Kelton, "Avoiding the Smallpox Spirits"; Fogelson, "An Analysis of Cherokee Sorcery and Witchcraft."

112. Kelton, *Cherokee Medicine, Colonial Germs*, 72–76; Irwin, "Cherokee Healing," 237–57.

113. Discussed in Kelton, *Cherokee Medicine, Colonial Germs*, 76–81.

114. Kelton, *Cherokee Medicine, Colonial Germs*, 81.

115. E.g., Moore to [Trustees], September 14, 1739, *Colonial Records of the State of Georgia*, 5:229; Ogelthorpe to Verelst, October 19, 1739, CRG 22.2:244–49; discussed in Kelton, *Cherokee Medicine, Colonial Germs*, 85–87.

to be inept and superstitious, Cherokees employed their medical knowledge, which included quarantine, cool baths, and medicines, to treat their smallpox patients.[116] They also developed two new rituals: a preventative "physic dance" and a "smallpox ceremony."[117] Over the course of the seven-day smallpox ceremony, individuals partook from a communal medicine pot and restricted their movements, only leaving their homes to acquire food and then avoiding main travel routes. The priest prayed on behalf of the community and distributed medicine to them. While the smallpox ceremony included common ritual elements like sacrifice, divination, and meal, it seems that it did not include a dance element, and instead was characterized by a stillness akin to mourning.[118]

Native American communities and European settlers and colonizers alike attempted to make spiritual sense of disease, including the smallpox, even as they treated it medically. The Cherokee "smallpox ceremony" brought together spiritual, communal, and medical elements, reflective of the Cherokee belief in their ability and responsibility to bring balance to the world around them.

The Pale Horse and the Spanish Lady: The 1918 Flu in America

> I looked and there was a pale green horse! Its rider's name was Death, and Hades followed with him; they were given authority over a fourth of the earth, to kill with sword, famine, and pestilence, and by the wild animals of the earth. (Rev 6:8)[119]

---

116. Kelton, *Cherokee Medicine, Colonial Germs*, 87–91.

117. As recorded in the writings of the Protestant missionary Daniel Butrick (1789–1851). Anderson et al., *The Payne-Butrick Papers*, 2:144, 168; Kelton, *Cherokee Medicine, Colonial Germs*, 91–97.

118. Summarized in Kelton, *Cherokee Medicine, Colonial Germs*, 91–97.

119. Twenty years after surviving the influenza pandemic, the novelist Katherine Anne Porter wrote a collection of short novels entitled *Pale Horse, Pale Rider* (1939), which drew its title from an African-American spiritual of the same name, which in turn was based on Revelation 6:8. Porter based the main character of the title story on her own experience surviving the pandemic; the character Miranda wakes up after being hospitalized some time to learn that the beloved lieutenant Adam who had cared for her had himself died of the flu a month earlier. The story concludes, "No more war, no more plague, only the dazed silence that follows the ceasing of the heavy guns; noiseless houses with the shades drawn, empty streets, the dead cold light of tomorrow. Now there would be time for everything." Porter, *Pale Horse. Pale Rider*, 264. On the role of memory in this story, see Davis, "The Forgotten Apocalypse."

As World War I was drawing to an end in 1918, the world continued to battle a vicious viral enemy,[120] which would infect a third of the world's population and take the lives of an estimated fifty to one hundred million people worldwide, with more than five hundred thousand deaths in the United States. Commonly known as the "Spanish flu," this deadly strain of the H1N1 virus attacked the patient's lungs, which caused an overstimulation of the immune system, which in turn often resulted in the destruction of lung cells and hemorrhaging and mucous production that could lead to suffocation. Other symptoms included severe fever, headache, chills, nausea, and explosive diarrhea or vomiting. It was given the nickname "Spanish flu"—and sometimes the "Spanish Lady"—because Spain, which was neutral during the Great War, had a freer press that enabled its newspapers to cover the outbreak early on, while other countries, such as Britain, enforced censorship in an effort to curb fear and panic.[121] These efforts to protect morale contributed to the spread of the disease, as it was transmitted at large events like bond drives and celebrations of the Armistice.

The origin of the pandemic is debated but hypotheses have included France, China, and Kansas, the latter of which was the location of the military base where some of the first cases of the influenza pandemic were recorded in the United States.[122] In March 1918, five hundred soldiers were hospitalized at Fort Riley in a single week. There were three main waves of the pandemic: first, the spring of 1918; second, from September 1918 to February 1919, which was the deadliest; and finally, the remainder of 1919. The quick spread and high mortality rate left many children orphaned, parents lost multiple children at a time, and community resources were exhausted, as there were not enough medical staff, nor enough coffins for the increasing body count. This strain of the flu was particularly devastating as it seemed to target those in their 20s and 30s who were otherwise healthy. It took the lives of many famous people, including Max Weber, Gustav Klimt, and Egon Schiele; famous survivors included Franz Kafka, Walt Disney, King Alfonso XIII of Spain, and President Woodrow Wilson, whose resulting impairment is speculated to

---

120. Steve Coll has rightly noted that "war metaphors fail to capture the natural and intimate character of a severe and contagious illness, and how its effect on individual behavior can often be subtle and difficult to measure." Coll, "Woodrow Wilson's Case of the Flu."

121. Arnold, *Pandemic 1918*, 10–11. It is generally agreed upon that the "Spanish flu" is a misnomer; more accurate alternatives include the 1918 Flu or the Great Influenza.

122. Regarding the potential origin and early spread, see Oxford et al., "Who's That Lady?," 1351–52; Barry, "The Site of Origin of the 1918 Influenza."

have negatively impacted the Versailles Treaty in 1919, and therefore arguably contributed to the causes of World War II.[123]

As in any era experiencing deadly disease, there were a variety of religious responses to the influenza pandemic and the panic and devastation it left in its wake; a handful of such responses, as documented in American newspapers and thus demonstrably part of public consciousness, will be addressed briefly here. Twelve thousand people died in America during the month of September 1918, leading to the order at the end of that month for the closure of churches and other public places throughout the country. During the closures, communities continued to pray earnestly for the end of the pandemic; sermons and prayers were published in some newspapers[124] and several denominations organized national days of prayer, as well as outdoor services.[125] Pastors delivered supplementary materials for devotion through the mail and in at least one case, with the help of Boy Scouts.[126] On one Sunday in the middle of October, the *Los Angeles Times* printed a collection of messages and sermons from various local religious leaders from Jewish, Presbyterian, Catholic, Lutheran, Baptist, Methodist, and Universalist communities. While some of the messages communicate quotidian information like updates on building renovations, most exhort their readers regarding sin, love, and the faithfulness of God. One Baptist minister reminds his readers of Job, who worshiped God in the midst of his suffering. Many of the leaders couch their comments in the years of trials caused by the First World War, with another Baptist minister declaring that, "The religion of the cross is not a sentimental, nauseating religion, but the only religion that is worthy of the boys in France, who have learned the meaning of the cross

123. Barro et al., "The Coronavirus and the Great Influenza Pandemic," 3, discussed in Coll, "Woodrow Wilson's Case of the Flu," and Barry, *The Great Influenza*.

124. E.g., "Prayer for Epidemic Period," *Washington Post*, Oct. 12, 1918, p. 6; "All Dressed Up and No Place to Go," *Milwaukee Sentinel*, Oct. 13, 1918, p. 1, in Navarro and Markel, *The American Influenza Pandemic of 1918–1919*.

125. E.g., "Presbyterians Set Day of Prayer to Check Influenza," *Dallas Evening Journal*, Oct. 31, 1918, p. 1; "Pastors Send Messages to Church Members," *Dallas Morning News*, Oct. 19, 1918, p. 17, in Navarro and Markel, *The American Influenza Pandemic of 1918–1919*. In Los Angeles, for example, a call for organized prayer suggested that "at the hour of family worship in the morning, time be given to petitioning God for his especial blessing; that at twelve o'clock all businesses stop for five minutes of prayer, and that the evening be made an at-home evening with God, and spend it in prayer and devotions." "Issue Call to Prayer," *Los Angeles Times*, Nov. 2, 1918, p. 1, in Navarro and Markel, *The American Influenza Pandemic of 1918–1919*.

126. "Go to Church on Your Own Today: Pastors of Many Flocks, Barred from Their Houses of Worship by the Influenza Closing Order, Present Their Pulpit Messages through the Columns of the 'Times,'" *Los Angeles Times*, Oct. 13, 1918, p. 1, in Navarro and Markel, *The American Influenza Pandemic of 1918–1919*.

in the Gethsemane and the Calvary of war. Only such a religion will enlist and enroll the manhood of America."[127] Rev. Herbert Smith of Immanuel Presbyterian and Rabbi Edgar F. Magnin of Temple B'nai B'rith both encourage their congregants to buy Liberty Bonds as an expression of devotion to God and country. Rabbi Magnin pleads, "If our boys are giving their bodies and their souls to the cause can we not at least give our souls?"[128] Most of the messages do not make explicit mention of the influenza pandemic—even though it was the very reason they were printing their sermons instead of delivering them at their respective pulpits.

While there were some religious leaders—like Rabbi Samuel Thurman in St. Louis[129]—who publicly affirmed the quarantine order, there were many others who protested the closing of religious buildings, citing that other businesses, including "saloons," remained open, and more importantly that such closures impeded ministry efforts, as well as intercessory prayers on behalf of the troops overseas.[130] During the peak of the pandemic in the fall of 1918, for instance, the Rev. Randolph H. McKim of the Episcopal Church, published a letter to the editor in *The Evening Star*, in which he argued that the continued closure of churches was a "deprival of rights."[131] Having served as a young man in the Confederate Army as a private under "Stonewall" Jackson, McKim invokes the soldiers abroad, speculating, "What will our boys at the front say if we acquiesce in an order which forbids us to come together to pray God to bless them and give them victory, and which proclaims to the world that this great Christian country has stepped down to a materialistic platform?"[132] He goes on to call for a "great tidal wave of holy indignation" and condemns the order as a "deliberate assault on the Christian privileges of our people."[133] During the month of October, 195,000 people died of the flu in America.

---

127. "Go to Church on Your Own Today," *Los Angeles Times*, Oct. 13, 1918, p. 6.

128. "Go to Church on Your Own Today," *Los Angeles Times*, Oct. 13, 1918, p. 6.

129. "Rabbi Thurman Applauds St. Louis Flu Quarantine," *St. Louis Globe Democrat*, Nov. 2, 1019, p. 5, in Navarro and Markel, *The American Influenza Pandemic of 1918–1919*.

130. E.g., "Dr. Slack to Hold Church Services," *New Orleans States*, Oct. 13, 1918, p. 4; Elsie Coates Nelson, "Closing the Churches and Keeping Open the Saloons," *Baltimore Sun*, Oct. 16, 1918, p. 6, in Navarro and Markel, *The American Influenza Pandemic of 1918–1919*.

131. Randolph H. McKim, "Closing of the Churches," *The Evening Star* (Washington, DC), Oct. 26, 1918, p. 7, in Navarro and Markel, *The American Influenza Pandemic of 1918–1919*.

132. McKim, "Closing of the Churches," 7.

133. McKim, "Closing of the Churches," 7.

Amidst the stories of chaos, grief, and insurmountable loss on personal and national scales, there are also stories of compassion, self-sacrifice, and sharing of resources. Images of hope are found in the women of the Beth Israel congregation in Portland, Oregon who made masks for the public,[134] the community of Turkish and Albanian Muslims in Maine who purchased a large burial plot for flu victims,[135] and Archbishop Hanna of San Francisco, who gave the Red Cross the use of forty church buildings and hundreds of priests and nuns.[136]

Seeing Christ in Suffering: An Image of the AIDS Crisis

In March 1983, *The Bay Area Reporter*—"the region's most widely read gay newspaper"—published its first AIDS obituary.[137] The brief write-up gave a detailed account of the physical condition of Jim Gresham, age thirty-five, who had suffered from an AIDS-related skin cancer (Kaposi's sarcoma) and a parasite that had prevented him from digesting food for the last several months of his life.[138] It would be the first of thousands of such obituaries.[139]

On the other side of the country, in the same year, a young gay Jesuit priest was asked to celebrate the first Mass for people with HIV/AIDS in New York City. Thereafter, Father William Hart McNichols began volunteering as a chaplain for AIDS hospice patients at St. Vincent's Hospital in Greenwich Village.[140] The first HIV/AIDS cases had been recorded in New

134. "Improvement of Influenza Cases," *Oregon Daily Journal*, Oct. 26, 1918, p. 3, in Navarro and Markel, *The American Influenza Pandemic of 1918–1919*.

135. Ghanea Bassiri, *A History of Islam in America*, 185. As did their co-religionists in other regions throughout America. On immigration during the pandemic, Kraut, "Immigration, Ethnicity, and the Pandemic."

136. Crosby, *America's Forgotten Pandemic*, 24.

137. Risse, *Mending Bodies, Saving Souls*, 620.

138. See "Friends Gather to Remember Jim Gresham."

139. But, "Instead of being banished once more to the closets with formal obituaries, the dead were often sketched in intimate terms, their lives portrayed as meaningful and symbolic of a stigmatized community determined to overcome another crisis." Risse, *Mending Bodies, Saving Souls*, 620. Contrarily, conceiving of AIDS as a "plague" caused further discrimination against gay people. See Bright, *Plague Making and the AIDS Epidemic*.

140. McNichols came out in 1983 when he was asked to write an article about being gay and a priest. He was invited to do so anonymously, but chose to publish under his own name—after receiving permission from his supervisor. O'Loughlin, "The Cost of AIDS Ministry to a Gay Priest." He later came out on a national scale, when he was profiled in an article for *Time Magazine* in 2002 to comment on the Catholic Church sex abuse scandal. In it, McNichols defended gay priests from being scapegoated. He would leave the Jesuit order in that same year, but continues to this day to serve as a

York City three years earlier during the fall of 1980, although the disease would not be given its current name—human immunodeficiency virus infection (HIV) and acquired immune deficiency syndrome (AIDS)—until July 1982.[141] In the years since, AIDS has taken the lives of some thirty-five million people worldwide and millions more are now able to live with HIV thanks to developments in treatment. At the writing of this essay, *The New York Times* has recently reported that HIV cases are on the rise worldwide (along with tuberculosis and malaria) due to global health resources being diverted to address the coronavirus pandemic.[142]

Father McNichols had his work cut out for him. Given the predominantly negative and damaging treatment of gay men by the Christian church, many of the early HIV/AIDS patients did not want to see a chaplain—let alone a Catholic priest. For this reason, "Father Bill," as he prefers to be called, intentionally dressed in a suit coat instead of clerical garments for his rounds at the hospital. In the early years of the crisis, there was little to be done to ease the physical suffering of patients, making the emotional, spiritual, and practical support all the more significant. Over the next seven years at St. Vincent's, McNichols counseled, befriended, mourned with, and administered sacraments to countless AIDS patients—who were primarily young gay men—and their partners, friends, and families.

In an interview, McNichols described the first room he walked into at the beginning of his ministry, in which an emaciated young man lay in bed, flanked by his boyfriend and mother who were lovingly feeding him orange juice in tiny sips through a straw. McNichols recalled that the scene immediately struck him as a crucifixion with the mother and boyfriend akin to the Virgin Mary and the disciple John and the suffering young man between them as Christ.[143] McNichols had originally come to

---

Catholic priest. Ripley, "Inside the Church's Closet."

141. Dr. Lawrence Mass, a gay physician who was a regular contributor to gay press in the 1980s, was the first to write on the emerging pandemic in an article published in *New York Native* in July 1981. He later wrote a letter to the editor of the New York Times regarding the comparison of Jews and people with AIDS. Mass, "AIDS and the Holocaust," BR62.

142. Fear of contracting the coronavirus and lockdowns are also preventing access to treatment for HIV/AIDS patients. Mandavilli, "'The Biggest Monster' Is Spreading." While the present essay has focused on a small slice of the pictures of the AIDS pandemic in America, of AIDS/HIV in Africa, Cristobal Silva writes, "my analysis suggests that Western epidemiologies of AIDS/HIV in Africa call on a long tradition of colonial tropes, and bring pressure to bear on national and territorial boundaries by translating modern political geographies into nineteenth-century images of the continent." Silva, *Miraculous Plagues*, 184.

143. O'Loughlin, "The Cost of AIDS Ministry to a Gay Priest." In 2016, Christopher Summa made a documentary, *The Boy Who Found Gold*, about Father William Hart

New York to be an artist and earned an MFA there at the Pratt Institute. He naturally turned to artmaking to process what he was experiencing as a chaplain and toward the end of his time at the hospital, he drew a crucifixion scene in pen and ink (Fig. 2.2).

Figure 2.2: *AIDS Crucifixion*, © William Hart McNichols, 1987.
http://frbillmcnichols-sacredimages.com.

Set against the New York City skyline, Jesus' crucified body, clad only in a pair of white briefs, is covered in lesions characteristic of Kaposi's sarcoma. Instead of the sign that traditionally reads some variation of *Iesus Nazarenus Rex Iudoreum*, Latin for "Jesus the Nazarene, King of the Jews" and abbreviated as INRI, the sign atop the cross bears a series of derogatory labels, "AIDS, homosexual, faggot, pervert, sodomite." A banner seems to issue forth from Jesus' mouth, functioning as the speech scrolls commonly found in medieval artwork; its text quotes Luke 23:34, "Father, forgive them! They

McNichols' art and life.

know not what they do." Jesus is surrounded by four figures, who are iden-
tifiable according to common iconographic motifs in the western Christian
tradition. To the left of the cross, a young man consoles a woman draped
in a starry shawl; they are recognizable as the Virgin Mary and the beloved
disciple John, who are almost always depicted at the crucifixion (cf. John
19:26–27). Another woman crouches at the foot of the cross, wrapping her
right arm around its base such that her hand grasps the right leg of Jesus.
Thus, we can read her as Mary Magdalene, who all four gospels place at the
crucifixion. That she is depicted with tears streaming down her face as she
holds her loose hair in her other hand is a reference to the tradition of Mary
Magdalene being conflated with the unnamed "sinful woman" of Luke 7,
who washed Jesus' feet with her tears and hair and anointed them with
oil.[144] To the right of the cross, just behind the crouching woman, a man in
a suit angrily wields a Bible at the crucified man. This figure is in the place
commonly occupied by John the Baptist, who heralded Jesus, "Behold the
Lamb of God, who takes away the sin of the world" (John 1:29). In medieval
crucifixion images, John the Baptist often points to Jesus and sometimes is
accompanied by the text of John 1:29 in a speech scroll. The Bible-wielding
man in McNichols' image is himself a perversion of John the forerunner:
instead of recognizing the crucified man as Jesus, the man instead attempts
to use the word of God as a weapon against him. The image thus suggests
that the Christians who ridicule and persecute gay AIDS patients in fact fail
to recognize them as the very image of God.

Over the years, McNichols has created several other images featuring
AIDS patients—often in the figure of Christ.[145] Joan Blanchfield, who was a
nurse at St. Vincent's and had worked on the hospice team with McNichols,
recalled in an interview her appreciation for the way he incorporated the
physical markers of AIDS into his artworks. She recalled being especially
moved by a crucifixion painting he gave the hospital in which Christ was
covered with Kaposi's lesions, which she connected to one of her patients, "I
could see him suffering as Christ suffered."[146]

144. Ehrman, *Peter, Paul, and Mary Magdalene*, 189. Gregory the Great, "Homily 33."

145. E.g., "Francis 'Neath the Bitter Tree," "St. Aloysius Gonzaga: Patron of People
with HIV-AIDS and Caregivers," and "The Epiphany: Wisemen Bring Gifts to the
Child." McNichols also made artworks that, although they did not explicitly feature
AIDS patients, were inspired by and dedicated to them. "The Stations of the Cross of a
Person with AIDS" (1989) consists of fifteen images that focus exclusively on the hands
of Jesus. McNichols wrote an accompanying text in which he shares "the insight his
experiences have given him into the way persons with AIDS share in the sufferings of
Christ. He enables his readers to stand, as it were, at the foot of the bed just as the loyal
disciples once stood at the foot of the cross on Calvary." Hunthausen, "Introduction."

146. O'Loughlin, "The Cost of AIDS Ministry to a Gay Priest."

After being sent to the emergency room with stress-induced, debilitating back spasms, McNichols moved to Albuquerque, New Mexico, in 1990 to study as an iconographer under Friar Robert Lentz, OFM. Shortly thereafter he painted (or "wrote") the icon "Mother of God, Light in All Darkness," which depicts Mary holding the Christ child, who in turn holds a candle in one hand as he protects its flame with his other. McNichols made the image as a prayer for people with HIV/AIDS and wrote the following text to accompany it:

> Mother of God, Light in All Darkness,
> shelter Him our flame of hope with your tender hands.
> And in our times of dread and nightmares,
> let Him be our dream of comfort.
> And in our times of physical pain and suffering,
> let Him be our healer.
> And in our times of separation from God and one another,
> let Him be our communion.
> Amen.[147]

In his early seventies now, "Father Bill" continues his vocation as an iconographer and serves at a Catholic church in Albuquerque. He has kept the names of all of the patients he served and continues to pray for them, especially on All Souls' Day. Regarding healing, Father William McNichols once remarked:

> When the Friars would wash the bandages covering St Francis' wounds, they would use the water mixed with his blood to heal sick animals and people. This is hope for us that our wounds can even now or eventually be used for the healing of others too. I believe most of our ancient and contemporary Prophets, who have been publicly mocked or martyred in various ways, prove that this is so.[148]

Conclusion

As a historian, I have dedicated my professional life to learning about and from history, mindful of George Santayana's often paraphrased warning,

---

147. McNichols, "Mother of God, Light in All Darkness.".
148. McNichols, "For St. Francis Day."

"Those who cannot remember the past are condemned to repeat it."[149] To which I would add the words of the fictional sailor Ishmael, "these marvels (like all marvels) are mere repetitions of the ages; so that for the millionth time we say amen with Solomon—Verily there is nothing new under the sun."[150] Similarly, Annie Dillard, with her characteristic humor and eloquence, writes:

> There is no one here but us chickens, and so it has always been: a people busy and powerful, knowledgeable, ambivalent, important, fearful, and self-aware; a people who scheme, promote, deceive, and conquer; who prayed for their loved ones, and long to flee misery and skip death. It is a weakening and discoloring idea, that rustic people knew God personally once upon a time—or even knew selflessness or courage or literature—but that it is too late for us . . . There never was a more holy age than ours, and never a less.[151]

And so, there is a kind of strange comradery and uncanny comfort in knowing that we are not alone—not only in the present moment as we "distance together," but also historically, as surveyed briefly in this essay. Humanity has endured pandemics and plagues for countless generations before us. We can look to the prayers and good works of this historical "cloud of witnesses" for inspiration and fortitude. But let us also take heed and learn from the mistakes that previous generations enacted during times of pandemic—their prejudice and superstition, acts of violence, and betrayals of their neighbors. Let us do better together.

Bibliography

Augustine of Hippo. *On Christian Teaching*. Translated by R. P. H. Green. Oxford: Oxford University Press, 2008.

———. "Sermons on Selected Lessons of the New Testament." In *Saint Augustine: Sermon on the Mount, Harmony of the Gospels, Homilies on the Gospels*, edited by Philip Schaff, translated by R. G. MacMullen. A Select Library of the Nicene and Post-Nicene Fathers of the Christian Church, First Series 6. New York: Christian Literature, 1888.

Anderson, William L., et al., eds. *The Payne-Butrick Papers*. 2 vols. Lincoln: University of Nebraska Press, 2010.

149. Santayana, *The Life of Reason*, 172.

150. Melville, *Moby-Dick*, 213. Coincidentally, Ahab goes on in this passage to relay an account of a sea monster given by the Byzantine historian Procopius, whose work was addressed in the first section of this essay.

151. Dillard, *For the Time Being*, 86.

Arnold, Catharine. *Pandemic 1918: Eyewitness Accounts from the Greatest Medical Holocaust in Modern History*. New York: Macmillan, 2018.

Barro, Robert J., et al., eds. "The Coronavirus and the Great Influenza Pandemic: Lessons from the 'Spanish Flu' for the Coronavirus's Potential Effects on Mortality and Economic Activity." https://www.nber.org/system/files/working_papers/w26866/w26866.pdf.

Barry, John M. *The Great Influenza: The Story of the Deadliest Pandemic in History*. New York: Penguin, 2005.

———. "The Site of Origin of the 1918 Influenza and Its Public Health Implications." *Journal of Translational Medicine* 2.1 (2004). https://doi.org/10.1186/1479-5876-2-3.

Beaty, Nancy Lee. *The Craft of Dying: A Study in the Literary Tradition of the Ars Moriendi in England*. New Haven: Yale University Press, 1970.

Binski, Paul. *Medieval Death: Ritual and Representation*. London: British Museum, 1996.

Blackbird, Andrew J. *History of the Ottawa and Chippewa Indians of Michigan: A Grammar on Their Language, and Personal and Family History of the Author*. Ypsilanti, MI: Ypsilanti Job, 1887.

Bright, Gina M. *Plague Making and the AIDS Epidemic: A Story of Discrimination*. New York: Palgrave Macmillan, 2012.

Boehmer, Johann Friederich, ed. *Fontes Rerum Germanicarum*. Vol. 4. Stuttgart: Cotta, 1843.

Brown, Peter. *Augustine of Hippo: A Biography*. Berkeley: University of California Press, 1969.

Brown, Thomas. "Did the U.S. Army Distribute Smallpox Blankets to Indians? Fabrication and Falsification in Ward Churchill's Genocide Rhetoric." *Plagiary: Cross-Disciplinary Studies in Plagiarism, Fabrication, and Falsification* 1 (2006) 100–129.

Burns, J. Patout, Jr., and Robin M. Jensen. *Christianity in Roman Africa: The Development of Its Practices and Beliefs*. Grand Rapids: Eerdmans, 2014.

Butrick, Daniel. *The Payne-Butrick Papers*. Edited by William L. Anderson et al. Lincoln: University of Nebraska Press, 2010.

Candler, Allen, et al., eds. *Colonial Records of the State of Georgia*. Athens: University of Georgia Press, 1906.

Chazan, Robert. *Reassessing Jewish Life in Medieval Europe*. New York: Cambridge University Press, 2010.

Chrysostom, John. *The Divine Liturgy according to St. John Chrysostom*. 2nd ed. South Canaan, PA: St. Tikhon's Seminary Press, 1977.

Coll, Steve. "Woodrow Wilson's Case of the Flu, and How Pandemics Change History." *The New Yorker*, April 17, 2020. https://www.newyorker.com/news/daily-comment/woodrow-wilsons-case-of-the-flu-and-how-pandemics-change-history.

Crosby, Alfred W. *America's Forgotten Pandemic: The Influenza of 1918*. New York: Cambridge University Press, 2003.

———. *Ecological Imperialism: The Biological Expansion of Europe, 900–1900*. New York: Cambridge University Press, 1986.

———. "Virgin Soil Epidemics as a Factor in the Aboriginal Depopulation in America." *William and Mary Quarterly* 33.2 (1976) 289–99.

Davis, David A. "The Forgotten Apocalypse: Katherine Anne Porter's 'Pale Horse, Pale Rider,' Traumatic Memory, and the Influenza Pandemic of 1918." *The Southern Literary Journal* 43.2 (2011) 55–74.

de Aguilar, Francisco. "Eighth Jornada." In *Victors and Vanquished: Spanish and Nahua Views of Conquest*, edited by Stuart B. Schwartz, 198. New York: Macmillan, 2000.

Dillard, Annie. *For the Time Being*. New York: Vintage, 2000.

Ditrich, Hans. "The Transmission of the Black Death to Western Europe: A Critical Review of the Existing Evidence." *Mediterranean Historical Review* 32.1 (2017) 25–39.

Dupont, Anthony. *Gratia in Augustine's Sermones ad Populum during the Pelagian Controversy*. Leiden: Brill, 2013.

Ehrman, Bart D. *Peter, Paul, and Mary Magdalene: The Followers of Jesus in History and Legend*. Oxford: Oxford University Press, 2006.

Fenn, Elizabeth A. "Biological Warfare in Eighteenth-Century America: Beyond Jeffrey Amherst." *The Journal of American History* 86.4 (2000) 1552–80.

Fenner, F., et al. *Smallpox and Its Eradication*. Geneva: World Health Organization, 1988.

Ferngren, Gary B. *Medicine and Healthcare in Early Christianity*. Baltimore: Johns Hopkins University Press, 2009.

Flood, John. *Representations of Eve in Antiquity and the English Middle Ages*. New York: Routledge, 2011.

Fogelson, Raymond D. "An Analysis of Cherokee Sorcery and Witchcraft." In *Four Centuries of Southern Indians*, edited by Charles M. Hudson, 113–31. Athens: University of Georgia Press, 1975.

"Friends Gather to Remember Jim Gresham: AIDS Victim 'Pulled the Plug.'" *The Bay Area Reporter*, March 24, 1983. http://obit.glbthistory.org/olo/display.jsp?name=19830324_Gresham_Jim.

GhaneaBassiri, Kambiz. *A History of Islam in America: From the New World to the New World Order*. New York: Cambridge University Press, 2010.

Greenblatt, Stephen. *Shakespearean Negotiations: The Circulation of Social Energy in Renaissance England*. Berkeley: University of California Press, 1988.

Gregory, Timothy E. *A History of Byzantium*. 2nd ed. Oxford: Wiley-Blackwell, 2010.

Gregory the Great. "Homily 33." https://sites.google.com/site/aquinasstudybible/home/luke-commentary/gregory-the-great-homily-33-on-the-gospels.

Gregory of Tours. *The History of the Franks*. Translated by Lewis Thorpe. New York: Penguin, 1974.

Haeser, Heinrich, ed. *Archive für die gesammte Medicin*. Jena: Mauke, 1841.

Haydon, F. S., ed. *Eulogium Historiarum sive Temporis*. 3 vols. London: Longman, Brown, Green, Longmans, and Roberts, 1858–63.

Hoffman, Richard C. *An Environmental History of Medieval Europe*. New York: Cambridge University Press, 2014.

Horden, Peregrine. "The Earliest Hospitals in Byzantium, Western Europe, and Islam." *Journal of Interdisciplinary History* 35.3 (2005) 361–89.

Horrox, Rosemary. *The Black Death*. Manchester Medieval Sources Series. Manchester, NY: Manchester University Press, 1994.

Hunthausen, Raymond C. "Introduction: Stations of the Cross." *William Hart McNichols Blog*. http://frbillmcnichols-sacredimages.com/blogs/stations-of-the-cross.html.

Hymes, Robert. "Epilogue: A Hypothesis on the East Asian Beginnings of the *Yersinia pestis* Polytomy." In *Pandemic Disease in the Medieval World: Rethinking the Black Death,* edited by Monica H. Green, 285–308. The Medieval Globe 1. Kalamazoo, MI: Arc Medieval, 2014.

Irwin, Lee. "Cherokee Healing: Myth, Dreams, and Medicine." *American Indian Quarterly* 16 (1992) 237–57.

Jaskoski, Helen, ed. *Early Native American Writing: New Critical Essays.* New York: Cambridge University Press, 1996.

Kaufmann, Thomas. *Luther's Jews: A Journey into Anti-Semitism.* Oxford: Oxford University Press, 2017.

———. "Luther and the Jews." In *Jews, Judaism, and the Reformation in Sixteenth-Century Germany,* edited by Dean Phillip Bell and Stephen G. Burnett, 69–104. Leiden: Brill, 2006.

Kelton, Paul. "Avoiding the Smallpox Spirits: Colonial Epidemics and Southeastern Indian Survival." *Ethnohistory* 51 (2004) 45–71.

———. *Cherokee Medicine, Colonial Germs: An Indigenous Nation's Fight against Smallpox, 1518–1824.* Norman: University of Oklahoma Press, 2015.

Kraut, Alan M. "Immigration, Ethnicity, and the Pandemic." *Public Health Reports* 125 (2010) 123–33.

Levin, William R. ed. *Images of Love and Death in Late Medieval and Renaissance Art.* Ann Arbor: University of Michigan Museum of Art, 1975.

Little, Lester K. "Life and Afterlife of the First Plague Pandemic." In *Plague and the End of Antiquity,* edited by Lester K. Little, 3–32. Cambridge: Cambridge University Press, 2006.

Luther, Martin. *Luther's Works.* Vol. 43, *Devotional Writings II.* Edited by Gustav Weincke and Helmut T. Lehmann. Philadelphia: Fortress, 1968.

———. *Luther's Works.* Vol. 47, *The Christian in Society IV.* Edited by Franklin Sherman and Helmut T. Lehmann. Philadelphia: Fortress, 1971.

Mandavilli, Apoorva. "'The Biggest Monster' Is Spreading: And It's not the Coronavirus." *The New York Times,* August 3, 2020. https://www.nytimes.com/2020/08/03/health/coronavirus-tuberculosis-aids-malaria.html.

Marcus, Jacob Rader. *The Jew in the Medieval World: A Sourcebook, 315–1791.* Edited by Marc Saperstein. Rev. ed. Cincinnati: Hebrew Union College Press, 1999.

Mass, Lawrence D. "AIDS and the Holocaust." *New York Times,* October 23, 1988.

McNichols, William. "For St. Francis Day: 'The Epiphany: Wisemen Bring Gifts to the Child.'" *William Hart McNichols Blog,* October 2017. http://frbillmcnichols-sacredimages.com/blogs/for-st-francis-day-the-epiphany-wisemen-bring-gifts-to-the-child-.html.

———. "Mother of God, Light in All Darkness." *William Hart McNichols Blog,* World AIDS Day 2018. http://frbillmcnichols-sacredimages.com/blogs/mother-of-god-light-in-all-darkness.html.

Melville, Herman. *Moby-Dick; or, The Whale.* Berkeley: University of California Press, 1983.

Merback, Mitchell B., ed. *Beyond the Yellow Badge: Anti-Judaism and Antisemitism in Medieval and Early Modern Visual Culture.* Boston: Brill, 2007.

Michael, Robert. *Holy Hatred: Christianity, Antisemitism, and the Holocaust.* New York: Palgrave Macmillan, 2006.

Mooney, James. *History, Myths, and Sacred Formulas of the Cherokees.* Asheville, NC: Historical Images, 1992.

———. *The Sacred Formulas of the Cherokees.* In *Seventh Annual Report of the Bureau of Ethnology, 1885–1886,* 301–97. Washington, DC: Government Printing Office, 1891.

Navarro, J. Alex, and Howard Markel, eds. *The American Influenza Pandemic of 1918–1919: A Digital Encyclopedia.* 2nd ed. University of Michigan Center for the History of Medicine and Michigan Publishing, University of Michigan Library, 2016. https://www.influenzaarchive.org/.

O'Connor, Mary Catherine. *The Art of Dying Well: The Development of the Arts Moriendi.* New York: Columbia University Press, 1942.

O'Loughlin, Michael. "The Cost of AIDS Ministry to a Gay Priest." *Plague: Untold Stories of AIDS & the Catholic Church* (Podcast). https://www.americamagazine. org/faith/2019/12/20/meet-gay-priest-who-served-aids-patients-mass-prayers-and-art.

Oxford, J. S, et al. "Who's That Lady?" *Nature Medicine* 5.12 (1999) 1351–52.

Patterson, Kristine B., and Thomas Runge. "Smallpox and the Native American." *The American Journal of the Medical Sciences* 323.4 (2002) 216–17.

Pearson, J. Diane. "Lewis Cass and the Politics of Disease: The Indian Vaccination Act of 1832." *Wicazo Sa Review* 18.2 (2003) 17–23.

Perkinson, Stephen. *The Ivory Mirror: The Art of Mortality in Renaissance Europe.* Brunswick, ME: Bowdoin College Museum of Art, 2017.

Peyer, Bernd. *American Indian Nonfiction: An Anthology of Writings, 1760s–1930s.* Norman: University of Oklahoma Press, 2007.

Porter, Katherine Anne. *Pale Horse, Pale Rider: Three Short Novels.* New York: Harcourt, Brace, and Co., 1939.

Procopius. *The Secret History.* Translated by G. A. Williamson and Peter Sarris. Rev. ed. New York: Penguin, 2007.

———. *The Wars of Justinian.* Translated by H. B. Dewing. Revised by Anthony Kaldellis. Indianapolis: Hackett, 2014.

Ripley, Amanda. "Inside the Church's Closet." *Time,* May 12, 2002. http://content.time. com/time/magazine/article/0,9171,237034-1,00.html.

Risse, Guenter B. *Mending Bodies, Saving Souls: A History of Hospitals.* New York: Oxford University Press, 1999.

Roper, Lyndal. *Martin Luther: Renegade and Prophet.* New York: Random House, 2016.

St. Pierre, Mark. *Madonna Swan: A Lakota Woman's Story.* Norman: University of Oklahoma Press, 1991.

Santayana, George. *The Life of Reason: Introduction and Reason in the Common Sense, Vol. II, Book I: The Works of George Santayana.* Edited by Marianne Wokeck and Martin A. Coleman. Cambridge: Massachusetts Institute of Technology Press, 2011.

Sarris, Peter. "Bubonic Plague in Byzantium: The Evidence of Non-literary Sources." In *Plague and the End of Antiquity: The Pandemic of 541–750,* edited by Lester K. Little, 119–34. Cambridge: Cambridge University Press, 2007.

Scholten, Frits. "Scale, Prayer, and Play." In *Small Wonders: Late-Gothic Boxwood Micro-Carvings from the Low Countries,* edited by Frits Scholten, 171–210. Amsterdam: Rijksmuseum, 2016.

Schwartz, Stuart B. *Victors and Vanquished: Spanish and Nahua Views of Conquest*. New York: Macmillan, 2000.

Sienna, Noam. *A Rainbow Thread: An Anthology of Queer Jewish Texts from the First Century to 1969*. Philadelphia: Print-O-Craft, 2019.

Silva, Cristobal. *Miraculous Plagues: An Epidemiology of Early New England Narrative*. New York: Oxford University Press, 2011.

Simonsohn, Shlomo, ed. *The Apostolic See and the Jews*. Vol. I, *Documents: 492–1404*. Studies and Texts 94. Toronto: Pontifical Institute of Medieval Studies, 1988.

Strickland, Debra Higgs. *Saracens, Demons, and Jews: Making Monsters in Medieval Art*. Princeton: Princeton University Press, 2003.

Sudhoff, Karl. "Pestschriften aus den ersten 150 Jahren nach der Epidimie des 'schwarzen Todes'1348: III." *Archiv für Geschichte der medizing* 5 (1912) 62–69.

Tait, James, ed. *Chronica Johannis de Reading et Anonymi Cantuariensis, 1346–1367*. Manchester: Manchester University Press, 1914.

Taylor, Keeanga-Yamahtta. "The Black Plague." *The New Yorker*, April 16, 2020. https://www.newyorker.com/news/our-columnists/the-black-plague.

Wisecup, Kelly. "African Medical Knowledge, the Plain Style, and Satire in the 1721 Boston Controversy." *Early American Literature* 46.1 (2011) 25–50.

Wordsworth, Christopher, ed. *Horae Eboracensis: The Prymer or Hours of the Blessed Virgin Mary*. London: Quaritch, 1920.

Zwingli, Ulrich. *Early Writings*. Edited by Samuel Macauley Jackson. 1912. Reprint, Eugene, OR: Wipf & Stock, 1999.

3

Contemporary Biblical Interpretations

Reflections amid the COVID-19 Pandemic

—Francisco Lozada Jr.

THERE IS NO QUESTION that Latinx and African Americans and many vulnerable communities are enduring the effects of the pandemic at a level disproportionately higher than "white" Americans.[1] As many epidemiologists and health public officials have highlighted, Latino/a/xs (henceforth Latinx) and African-American residents of the United States are three times more likely to get infected by COVID-19, and also twice as likely to die from it compared to white residents.[2] As of this writing, the scenario has not changed much. At the same time this pandemic is spreading across the nation and globe, the "virus" of racialization—which really never left after 1619 with the legacy of slavery, or even earlier with the arrival of Spanish nativism in 1492—poked its head up again and played out with fatal effects on African Americans, immigrants in the nation, and asylum seekers (and children) at the southern borderlands of the United States.[3] With the convergence of these events, not to mention the nativist exceptionalism espoused by the previous administration, what is the state and the future of doing biblical studies? How do we teach academic biblical studies, how do we interpret, what are the boundaries of doing

1. See CDC, "Disparities in Incidence of COVID-19." See also CDC, "Health Equity Considerations."

2. See Oppel et al., "The Fullest Look Yet."

3. See an opinion piece by Guttentag and Bertozzi, "Trump Is Using the Pandemic." To support this piece, see U.S. Customs and Border Protection, "Nationwide Enforcement Encounters."

biblical interpretation, and what is the state of theological and religious studies education? These and other questions are what this essay aims to reflect upon in this time of uncertainty. This essay does not claim it has all the answers, but it imagines what biblical interpretation might look like and what its future prospects might be. As the effects of globalization that emerged in the 1990s became more pronounced in society, including academia, rules of interpretation were challenged: What is a text, what is the role of the reader? As the pandemic reveals the fault lines in our economic, social, and political arenas, showing structural inequities affecting the vulnerable, fault lines are also present in the field of biblical interpretation as in the field's distance from the lived experience of the vulnerable through our study of the ancient texts and contexts, interpretation strategies, and the inclusion of readers.[4]

What follows is a modest attempt to reflect critically on doing contemporary biblical interpretation amid a global pandemic, particularly at an early moment in the virus's deadly spread. To embark on this critical reflection, this essay will (1) revisit Fernando F. Segovia's presidential address, "Criticism in Critical Times: Reflections on Vision and Task," at the Annual Meeting of the Society of Biblical Literature, in which he called on the Academy to take seriously the world in front of the text (global) in doing biblical interpretation; and (2) from there, delineate the effects of COVID-19 on vulnerable communities and how it influences the role of interpretation amid this global situation. COVID-19 calls for introspection. To turn away from this crisis and continue to work as if this pandemic has no effect on how we interpret would be a misstep. In other words, in these uncertain times, what should be biblical studies' priorities for promoting and defending the human rights of the vulnerable?

Critical Reading of "Criticism in Critical Times: Reflections on Vision and Task"

In Segovia's Society of Biblical Literature presidential address, the primary interest is what he is calling the academy to reflect on. The address does

---

4. This is not a new argument. Liberation theologians, feminists, and minoritized scholars and their allies of all stripes have argued for a preferential option for the poor, women and children, the oppressed, the minoritized, and the vulnerable. What is different is a new crisis, a pandemic, that exposes even more the structural forces that divide communities and dehumanize the vulnerable. In the United States, the overt (heightened) weaponization of the pandemic against the vulnerable, such as providing misinformation and fear-mongering keeps vulnerable from seeking proper health care and/or saving their lives.

not follow the traditional review of an essay, searching out its merits and questions left unanswered. The essay is prescient given that it calls critics to take seriously the times, such as the COVID-19 pandemic, which now serve as the context in which we critics do interpretation—whether they pertain to the material world of the ancient Mediterranean basin, ancient Jewish literature, early Christian literature, or other writings that fill in the spaces of the ancient world.

The essay is structured in five main parts, which will all be examined here with an eye toward what Segovia is calling on the academy to consider. Prior to the first part, he begins laying out his agenda. For Segovia, it is important that one reflects upon the historical, geopolitical, and spatial dimensions of one's production of meaning. All three dimensions are framed by key moments that mark important occasions in the past and present. The address was delivered on November 22, 2014 in San Diego. He uses this time and place as a moment to reflect critically on the significance of the historical, geopolitical, and spatial dimension that serve as the backdrop/foreground of our interpretations. For instance, historically, Segovia is fully aware that within the last one hundred years, the global arena was immersed in a Great War (1914–18), Second World War (1939–45), Cold War (1947–89/91), First Gulf War (1990–91), Second Gulf War (2003–11), and the Islamic State—the latter three events under the patrol of the North Atlantic Treaty Organization (NATO) (7). As is in these past events, the power to intimidate, to impress, to comply, and to create fear remain with us today, not existing in the shadows but illuminating every aspect of our world as critics. What is more, historically speaking, Segovia also reflects on his role as the first president from outside the West; he was born in Cuba and sees his reading of the times from an outsider-insider point of view. Segovia's reflection on these key historical events also presupposes that we, as critics today, are doing critical study of the biblical text not in a suspended state but rather one completely immersed in a world of a pandemic closely coinciding with the anniversary of the 1918 Spanish flu.

The second dimension that Segovia reflects on is the geopolitical context leading up to his address. In this part, Segovia highlights that the power relations between the Two-Thirds World and the One-Third World (his term) is also marked by the emergence of the Two-Thirds World term sixty years ago. The term first appears in 1952 by Alfred Sauvy as "*le tiers monde*" in *L'Observateur*; the close of the first Indochina War (1956–54) and the beginning of the Second Indochina War (1954–75), and the Bandung (Indonesia) Conference aiming to bring together capitalist and socialist reforms (8). All of these events led Segovia to reflect on his role as one out of the Two-Thirds World or now the Global South (Cuba) and one where he also speaks as an outsider-insider. As I see it, Segovia's reflection calls attention to the fact that the primary referent of critical analysis cannot remain in the Global North, but rather it (the text) must be studied from every possible angle, including the Global South. The same approach must be used with the pandemic. This pandemic must be examined from every possible angle, not simply from the perspective of the powerful and privileged.

The third and final dimension Segovia examines is the spatial dimension. Segovia is speaking about borders, migrations, nations, and Others. Calling attention to another key moment of the past, Segovia travels back fifty years to examine the relationship between the United States and Latin America and the Caribbean (1963–65). He points to the assassination of John Fitzgerald Kennedy (1963), marking the start of the sixties, and the passing of the 1964 Civil Rights Act. At the same time, the Brazilian democratically elected government of President João Goulart was overthrown and the 1965 Immigration and Nationality Acts opened the doors to groups of peoples other than western and northern Europeans. These three events called his attention to the spatial location of his presidential address, San Diego. This city on the border signifies the continual struggle (and contradictions, I might add) between Latin America and the Caribbean that remains to this day between the haves and have-nots. Segovia speaks from this spatial dimension as a first-generation immigrant, a political refugee, and a now minoritized member of the United States. His attention to the spatial dimension, along with the other two, leads him to the critical times of 2014. More significantly, his drawing on these events brings to bear the present, namely, living amid a pandemic with the growing ossification of borders and the unearthing of the economic and "white" privilege that can find refuge during this pandemic while the minoritized and vulnerable communities across the globe are left to die.

Before discussing his outlook on doing criticism in critical times, Segovia spends a moment in the first part examining what various presidential addresses in the Academy looked like one hundred years ago. The aim is to examine how these presidents involved the world of politics in their addresses.

A. The first part, "Presidential Preoccupations in Critical Times of Yesteryear," focuses on those Academy presidents during the years of the First World War—marking the one-hundred-year anniversary of his own presidential address. Segovia briefly discusses the five presidents between 1914 and 1918, and their institutional identities, and their topics. He highlights the last one, James A. Montgomery, Professor of Hebrew and Aramaic at the University of Pennsylvania and the Philadelphia

School of Divinity, and his topic, "Present Tasks of American Biblical Scholarship," as the only one who calls attention to the geopolitical state of affairs of the Great War. However, Segovia argues that the way he uses this state of affairs provides context for his address rather than letting the context speak through his discourse. In short, the Great War serves as background rather than the "object of discourse" (12). For Segovia, the function of criticism must bring together the world of politics with the world of criticism. This view, I argue, is vital today. The pandemic must also continue not as a backdrop to contemporary biblical interpretation but rather it (the pandemic) must serve to ask, "what we do, how we do it, and why it is worth doing."[5]

B. The second part, "The Function of Criticism as Problematic," looks at the role of the intellectual. Segovia's point of departure for this inquiry is Edward Said's "Representations of the Intellectual." What Said's essay identifies after drawing from a broad global perspective are two poles of the role of the intellectual. The first, represented by Antonio Gramsci, is the intellectual speaking inside the Academy with other elite experts. The second, represented by Julien Benda, is the intellectual addressing the world. In the latter position Said situates himself with some revision, challenging foundational positions that maintain the status quo, being a voice for the marginalized and vulnerable. For Segovia, situating himself closer to Benda's and Said's revised and expanded position, the intellectual cannot stay silent about the surrounding political world. And when they do engage it, it must not be done in an abstract way, but a concrete way. Given this pandemic, the intellectual cannot pretend (as many political leaders have done) that people are not being infected and/or dying; rather, they must engage this situation and critically reflect on how the current situation impacts their object of study as well as their interpretations.

C. In the third part of Segovia's address, "Critical Analysis of the Global State of Affairs," he calls on his fellow critics to engage the current state of affairs; in fact, it is critical to do so given the severe times in this post-Cold war period (1989/91 to the present). Segovia, drawing on several geopolitical scholars, delimits the contours of what he means by "our times." What he describes, no different from where we are in these times with the pandemic, is a state of affairs in total disarray as a result of corporatism and the implementation of "shock capitalism" and its policies of deregulation, privatization, and fewer government

---

5. See Appleby et al., *Telling the Truth about History*, 9.

social safety nets. Such a geopolitical state of affairs has caused (and continues to cause) political leaders to search for a solution to stabilize markets and social movements. Segovia sees three geopolitical discourses that signify this instability: global economics, the climate, and global migration. Drawing on other scholars, Segovia examines these three discourses in a framework called the "Post Global South." Segovia suggests that the Global South, as a result of globalization, has put forward certain economic policies that have left the vulnerable bearing the worst economically as a result of neoliberal policies creating a greater split between the haves and have-nots.

Members of the current "Post Global South" are fully aware of the negative results of globalization—they are displaced economically and forced to migrate to the Global North, now visible in many rural and urban locales across the United States, for example. For Segovia, the voices of the "Post Global South" should be the focus of our criticism—those voices suffering from the result of globalization and its neoliberal policies. In short, he is calling for inclusion and the prevention of disenfranchisement on behalf of the poor. Both the climate situation and the migration issues impacting the globe mutually reinforce a world split between those who benefit and those who bear the brunt of certain neoliberal policies. What is important in this brief discussion of the current state of affairs for Segovia is that it is the responsibility of the Academy to be quite informed of the geopolitical issues of the day, since the context surely is one that scholars cannot ignore. The same can be said today with the pandemic. The neoliberal policies that have been pushed by certain economic scholars today favoring policies of a so-called "free" market are showing the cracks in our system, especially when the poor, ethnic/racial marginalized, migrant workers are ironically called "essential," but only "essential" in order for the wealthy to maintain their high standard of living.

D. With the delimitation of the crises presented, Segovia introduces his theoretical agenda in the fourth part, "A Theoretical Framework for Engaging Our Times." He begins by discussing the global studies scholars who inform his thinking and social theory framework. Drawing on the work of Steven Seidman in social theory and the Global South and the importance of engaging the world from the optic of the South, Segovia's framework is colored by this optic. At the same time, Segovia is informed by the work of Boaventura de Sousa Santos, namely, his "epistemologies of the South." He is working with the position that *how* one sees, for example, globalization, will differ tremendously depending on *where* one sees it from. Three premises delineate de Sousa Santos' epistemology: first, the Global South sees the world from a much broader perspective than the West; second, diversity sees no limits; and third, all epistemologies must welcome such diversity to establish a vision of utopia for the future. Segovia embraces these three premises as part of his theoretical framework. To engage the global state of affairs, we must do so not from the perspective of the Global North but from one such as the Global South, that welcomes all knowledges and can view the oppressive structures of the world. For Segovia, the most vulnerable communities call for such an embodiment of these premises. As biblical scholars or critics, for Segovia, global studies must be brought to bear upon biblical studies in all its expressions—particularly one from the perspective of the Global South. Hence, this pandemic must be seen not from the point of view of the privileged, but rather from the vulnerable, immigrant communities, and minoritized peoples. The Global South perspective provides an inclusive vision of the future where all are counted for, valued, and considered as significant and essential people.

E. In the final part, "Imagining an Interpretive Project for Our Times," Segovia proposes a new model of interpretation that he calls "global systemic." The objective of the paradigm is twofold: (1) engagement with each crisis at hand, and (2) engagement of the crisis using theories both from the North and the South. The scope of the paradigm for critics would not only engage the world in front of texts, it would also examine the world behind the texts and its contexts of antiquity. It would also expand to the interpretation of these texts and contexts by critics and the contexts they interpret from then and now. The lens of this "global systemic" approach is wide that brings together and crisscrosses other paradigms of interpretation (history, literary, sociocultural, ideological, cultural, and religious) with the global systematic paradigm. For Segovia, critics must also embrace this global systemic paradigm of interpretation from a religious-theological diverse perspective, one that involves all across geographical space.

In closing, Segovia draws on George Orwell (1984) and Pablo Neruda (*Canción de gesta [Epic Song]*) as examples of authors who intersect politics and their task as writers. Like them, Segovia calls on critics to bring scholarship and the political together in our world; for Segovia, humanity demands it in our critical times. Thus, humanity demands that biblical critics confront the pandemic that cuts across the globe. It is a crisis that cuts across race, economics, politics, modern medicine, health care, education, access to technology, and a host of other factors. And it should cut across texts and contexts in antiquity, interpretations, and the readers and readings of these texts and contexts. In what follows, I choose to examine this latter aspect, taking on Segovia's charge to intersect politics with the social context of readers and readings, envisioning what is needed to move forward in our discipline amid the COVID-19 pandemic.

II. Reflections amid the COVID-19 Pandemic

In the second part of this essay, I intend to focus on a particular issue that has to do with the vulnerable communities (i.e., the poor, ethnic/racial communities, and immigrant communities) that have suffered disproportionally from the dire effects of this pandemic in the US, urban and rural, and along the southern border, and how this pandemic context, in front of the reader, bears upon contemporary biblical interpretation. As Segovia has clearly suggested, humanity calls upon critics of the biblical text to bring together biblical criticism and the global scene. To take on his charge, the remaining part of this chapter seeks to outline the scene that is confronting vulnerable communities. Subsequently, the chapter sketches out what it might look like now when one engages biblical studies amid this pandemic, particularly along the lines of texts and contexts in antiquity, interpretations of these texts and contexts, and the readers and readings of these texts and contexts. This pandemic is a chance to rethink everything anew, including the field of biblical interpretation and our connection to the vulnerable.

Reading of Context: Vulnerable Communities

Before moving forward, it is important to disclose that given the limited time that this pandemic has been circulating despite its powerful and fatal effect on many, the below reflection is crucial to initiate a conversation to understand the pandemic's effects among vulnerable communities: the poor, racialized minorities, immigrant communities, farmworkers, and Native Americans. And given my limitation of physical proximity to many of these communities, especially along the southern borderlands, my recourse is dependent on Zoom meetings,[6] reports by the media, and other mediums, and as the Director of the Borderlands Center at Brite Divinity

---

6. Dr. Irasema Coronado (see n7 below) and I hosted a webinar on April 17, 2020, titled, "Theologizing in an Age of COVID-19: Responsibility to the Most Vulnerable."

School directing a grant sponsored by the Henry Luce Foundation's Theology Program to provide funds to such vulnerable communities. This essay cannot provide a complete picture; rather, it is a glimpse into their worlds and situations, but also an appeal (deliberative) to not forget the vulnerable—regardless of their legal status.

In the midst of COVID-19 (coronavirus), many vulnerable (economically disenfranchised) and immigrant communities (the undocumented, mixed status families, and detained children, individuals, and families), particularly along the southern US borderlands, have been gravely and disproportionally impacted both physically and economically.[7] These vulnerable and immigrant communities are responsible for harvesting the US's food, processing meat in packing facilities, or are engaged in various service or retail industries, such as housekeepers, babysitters, those caring for the elderly, hotel maids, landscapers, and food preparers for restaurants, and are at greater risk of infection of COVID-19, and thus losing their jobs and, in many cases, being detained in or deported out of the country and possibly bringing the virus with them. These jobs were precarious anyway, with no sick leave, paid vacation, or health insurance. These communities are in urgent need of financial assistance for housing, food security, keeping up with bills, and paying for rent. When these communities do not work, they do not get paid. They do not qualify for unemployment benefits (particularly the undocumented). Many of these folks cannot work from home; nor do their children have the technological tools or the bandwidth to connect with their schools and teachers. And if you are sexually minoritized, the challenge of finding a safe home or place to rest during the "shelter-in-place" orders can be very difficult.[8]

The impact of COVID-19 has also put organizational and financial strain on those community members and leaders running shelters and humanitarian aid programs to migrants and food pantries. With the recent closure of the borders by the federal government, the situation has made it even more difficult for migrants, particularly asylum seekers, to move through US ports of entry and instead seek more dangerous routes back and forth into the US.[9] These nonprofits offer all sorts of aid, such as water gallons for migrants journeying through the desert, food packs, medical kits, clothing, international phone service, consulate information, Spanish

7. I am also grateful in this section for the in-depth consultation I received from Dr. Irasema Coronado, Director and Professor of Transborder Studies, Arizona State University.

8. See Cobb, "Transgender People Face Discrimination"; Valencia, "The Challenges of the Pandemic for Queer Youth."

9. See n3 above.

language interpretation, and, more, a place to wash hands or to receive hand sanitizers. These nonprofits are also in urgent need of financial assistance to continue to provide critical services in urban and rural centers as well as along the border. With donations (financial and materials) down and volunteers adhering to shelter-in-place policies, these community members are stretched economically to stay afloat.

Urgent attention to basic needs and critical services to the vulnerable community and immigrant communities is essential. The impact of COVID-19 on the various immigrants' communities described above is only just starting to throw dire health, employment, and psychological consequences at them. Those, particularly women, who go out to the fields, meat facilities, or housekeeping jobs, have no safe place to leave their children. What is more, many families do not have the wherewithal to help school children with their homework. Parents have limited knowledge of how to use computers and might not speak English. Without health insurance, particularly if undocumented, many will die. These vulnerable and immigrant communities are facing social and financial pressures. Many will lose their jobs (if they have not already) and many nonprofits will be forced to cease humanitarian aid to them. It is a catastrophe in the making.

What is more, the pandemic is causing migrants to be taken out of detention centers due to the large amounts gathered in the same place. They need transportation and meals but also funds for legal assistance to help with their cases. At the same time, this attention to those within this country (United States) does not preclude looking on the other side of the border. Attention is also necessary for both sides of the US-Mexico border that serve migrants and asylum seekers of all ages (including infants, pregnant women, children, youth and aging adults) and who are primarily fleeing violence in their home countries of Guatemala, El Salvador, and Honduras. Currently, these populations are living in dire conditions in Juárez as a result of MPP (Remain in Mexico Policy) and are at high risk of murder, kidnapping and extortion while they wait for their US asylum petitions to be processed. If it is not safe for "Americans" to travel across the border, why would it be safe for returned asylum seekers, especially children? The shelters and service providers aim to provide humanitarian aid, education for children and youth, legal services and advocacy, trauma services, and vocational training for migrant populations in Juárez.

It is important to understand that with this pandemic has come an attempt to rewrite immigration laws and asylum policies.[10] It is not

---

10. The rewriting of immigration law and policies during the Trump presidency can be found at National Immigrant Justice Center, "Asylum Seekers & Refugees."

uncommon for the state to use crisis moments such as this pandemic—as with the terrorist attacks of 9/11 and Hurricane Katrina—to engage in the implementation of neo-liberal economic policies and political rewriting of immigration laws and policies under the mandate of protecting the United States' wealth and homeland—to keep the public charge (infected migrants using public programs) out of the country.[11]

Given this dire reality, how does one engage biblical interpretation? Still in the initial stages of reflection, allow me to explore this question amid this pandemic. At the center of these reflections is the conviction that biblical interpretation must be brought together with critical times of today espoused above by Segovia. I add: Do the traditional ways of interpretation fail to keep up with the reality of the lived experience of humanity?

Biblical Interpretation

Segovia's essay refers to three areas of biblical criticism: (1) readings of texts and contexts in antiquity, (2) interpretations of these texts and contexts, and (3) and the readers and readings of these texts and contexts. What might these areas look like amid the pandemic?

Readings of Texts and Contexts in Antiquity

As in any period where there is a global or national crisis, the situation brings forth a heightened sense of attention to the object of study. There is no question that various texts (the world reflected in the stories of the New Testament) will be examined that thematize issues that have surfaced in or been made more visible by the pandemic and its dire results toward the vulnerable, such as touch, the spirit/breath, the "essential/non-essentials," healing, food, fever, gender, children, family, poverty, and body. The list can go on. These are the flesh of the issues. The bones are the issues of power, colonialism, empire, patriarchy, racialization, neo-liberal economics, and status/class. Both the flesh and the bones of these issues are represented in the world of the writings of the New Testament.

If one were to look at the Gospel of Luke, for instance, there is no question that the theme of outsiders such as the poor, women, and

---

11. See Klein, *The Shock Doctrine*. Naomi Klein persuasively argues that the wealthiest and powerful follow a pattern of rewriting the economic, social, and political policies following wars, ecological disasters, and change of governments. Guttentag and Bertozzi, "Trump Is Using the Pandemic." To support this piece, see U.S. Customs and Border Protection, "Nationwide Enforcement Encounters."

disabled, is strongly represented throughout.[12] Luke, perhaps more than the other Gospels, emphasizes the compassion of God upon the people who are treated as social and religious outsiders and thematizes the reversal of value judgements that favors the vulnerable over the powerful. The vulnerable have been "Othered" by the empire and authorities that govern their lives. The clearest example of this is with the birth of Jesus (2:1–14). Set in the background of Roman Empire, Jesus's birth is voiced among the ordinary or lowly shepherds instead of the powerful of the day, he is born in a "manger" with swaddling clothes, and he has no place to shelter. All of these details link Jesus not with the powerful but with the "poor" and outsiders—the vulnerable of society. The Gospel also draws on the Hebrew scriptures (Isa 61:1–2) to again connect Jesus' work and ministry with the announcement of good news to the poor, the recovery of sight to the blind, and the setting free of those who are oppressed (Luke 4:18–19). This is the Gospel where Jesus tells the story of the good Samaritan (10:35–37)— someone seen as an outsider—who is the hero of the story. This point of view is carried later in the plot when Jesus heals ten lepers and it is the Samaritan who gave Jesus thanks that the text emphasizes (17:11–19). And finally, Luke concludes with more compassion toward outsiders when he promises Zacchaeus—a tax collector and a despised outsider—the gift of salvation for his concern for the poor (19:1–10).

Just a cursory examination of the Gospel shows Luke calling attention to the theme of outsiders. Jesus engages in the practice of healing those who are sick, such as lepers, the hearing, speaking, and seeing impaired, disabled, and those with mental challenges. It calls attention and calls for further examination of the social and economic stratification of the ancient world. What is present here is a disaster: apartheid making visible the privileges of the haves or insiders and the plight of the have-nots or outsiders in a way that creates physical and visible borders between the characters in the story of Luke—not unlike today between the wealthy and the disposable vulnerable along the southern borderlands, including Native Americans.

Behind texts is a world, a Roman Empire, that has not only ousted the poor, those considered shameful (Samaritans), and even those with "highly contagious diseases" (cf. Luke 17:11–19), it is an empire that participates in a shock approach (conquering nations and even lowly threats to the

12. I come to the gospels as ideological-literary-cultural expressions within a colonial framework. By no means am I employing Luke as a scriptural warrant for my argument, nor am I corresponding the situation the vulnerable are experiencing today with the vulnerable in antiquity. The gospels, like many texts, are dialogue partners for understanding the present. Given that the gospels are significant (sacred and revelatory for Christians) for human history, they must be engaged.

empire such as Jesus) with the goal of keeping the vast majority of the people in the region who are poor (estimated at 90 percent) and vulnerable confused and at the margins—out of the center of society.[13] The Roman Empire's path is one that speaks directly to their view of the sickness—the vulnerable—pulling their world into a binary so that they can exploit them further. For sure, the privileged world of the Roman Empire has striking parallels (though not the same) with the pandemic world today. There are also some theological parallels where people with money see themselves as blessed and exceptional and those with little seeing their lives as fate or the Divine's displeasure in them. In other words, as some have suggested today, these vulnerable communities failed to take personal responsibility for their health rather than seeing that the health crisis is a collective matter.[14] Such heightened attention to the various issues brought on by this pandemic compared to the text and contexts of antiquity does not (at least for me) aim to find some sort of solution, but rather aims for resilience to endure this pandemic and prepare for the next one.

Interpretations of Texts and Contexts

Segovia's global-systemic paradigm calls attention to the erasing and remaking of the world—whether it is ancient or modern. Amid this pandemic, interpretation is rooted in vulnerable communities. In these communities, one has the vantage point to see how power operates to divide and conquer and how we interpret or reconstruct contexts. No matter what method or approach one engages in the field of biblical interpretation, the goal is to understand how power such as wealth and privilege operate in the making and interpreting of texts and contexts. And given this pandemic, how interpretation participates in the making and analysis of the vulnerable is vital in seeing them as equal to all others. As interpreters, particularly those not viewed as belonging to the vulnerable, that task of interpretation is not to decide what their priorities ought to be (as tempting this might be), but rather to make visible the realities of living as vulnerable people and empowering them to choose.

Interpretation of texts and contexts is not immune to the viruses of objectivity, positivism, and universalism. These three Enlightenment ideas remain present in the methods and approaches of biblical interpretation.

13. See Friesen, "Poverty in Pauline Studies." See also Stambaugh and Balch, "The Ancient Economy."

14. See an excellent essay on the pandemic by Young, "How the Pandemic Defeated America."

The issue is that these ideas see the past independently from the present (the past is written from the present) and that what knowledge is constructed through these ideas applies to all.[15] Interpretation of texts and contexts from a global-systematic paradigm—as I see it—calls for a reading of the world (ancient and modern) that exposes its political power across space and readers. For instance, in Rev 21:4–5, "[He] will wipe every tear from their eyes. Death will be no more; mourning and crying and pain will be no more, for the first things have passed away. And the one seated on the throne said, 'See, I am making all things new.' Also, he said, 'Write this, for these words are trustworthy and true.'"[16] This text surely projects a God who is in control of the present and future. Yet, at the same time, it fails to expose the power systems that cause suffering. As Revelation suggests, not all empires are what they appeared to be—and I would add even those empires espoused by the notion of manifest destiny. They are corrupt and self-interested, and it is the job of people (believers) to renounce it and challenge it on behalf of the vulnerable. A global-systematic paradigm is not simply about "who exercises power" but also "how does it happen?"[17]

What the pandemic has revealed in the last nine months since its arrival in the world (roughly January 2020) is that interpretation of the biblical text would benefit by connecting to the social needs of the vulnerable, through beneficial partnerships, engaging with the people and their issues locally, nationally, and globally. Put them at the center of analysis. Interpretation must not only be read from the center or the majoritized but rather from the perspective of the vulnerable; it must also be read from every possible angle (north, south, east, west). The myth is that the only way anything is worthy of reading, hence universal, is if it is shaped in the United States and succeeds in other lands. To do so is another version of "American" exceptionalism.

Interpreters of texts and contexts are marked by a *filiopietism*, that is, the belief that the methods and approaches have already been discovered and the task of interpreters is merely to pass them on, including the results of knowledge from interpretations, to future interpreters (hence, the history of scholarship in each dissertation). The task of changing how one interprets is difficult. We are socialized or fixed to see interpretation as one way. However, the pandemic calls on us both to reconfigure the existing field, and to rethink how it is practiced and taught. Like the virus moving freely among

---

15. See Appleby et al., *Telling the Truth about History*. See also Trouillot, *Silencing the Past*.

16. See n12 above. My approach applies here too.

17. See Trouillot, *Silencing the Past*, 28.

persons, communities, and borders, interpreters can move freely among disciplinary areas that are linked to other programs and centers. But unlike the virus, interpreters of texts and contexts must move beyond the status quo, disconnected with the vulnerable. Otherwise the discipline is on the path of disappearing and irrelevant as it is today in the political-pandemic issues. A field that attaches itself to abstract knowledge has come to be seen as non-essential and unimportant. The vulnerable communities suffering with COVID-19 have exposed the isomorphism (emulating one another or thing) of the discipline. It also exposes the epidemic of inequality, the privileged, and the superiority of the majoritized over the minoritized. Unlike the apocalyptic stories in the biblical text where people escape to avoid the present, the vulnerable have no escape. Interpretation of texts and contexts must not be for the present only, it must also be done for the future—the laying down of ideas for justice for future generations.

Readers and Readings of Texts and Contexts

Whereas the immediate above sub-section focused on the process of interpretation, the actors of interpretation or interpreters also play a role. A global-systematic paradigm of interpretation is a call not to exclude readers or readings of texts and contexts but rather to include a broad, diverse representation—including socioeconomic diversity—of the nation and globe. The history of biblical interpretation has functioned to exclude non-normative voices, using a certain type of reader and a certain type of reading as a measuring rod to exclude other voices. As the COVID-19 pandemic has shown, this approach of exclusion remains in how the vulnerable are seen and treated. They are the "non-essential" people of our society considered highly contagious and seen as the deplorable poor.

The diversification of readers and readings from all angles of the globe, particularly from the positionality of the vulnerable, generates new interpretations that may have been overlooked by the tradition. These new readers and readings are able to question the underlying or normative assumptions of the field, and they can expose the power dynamics at play within the stories of the text.

For instance, the portrayal of Paul in Galatians is one of exceptionalism. He believes he speaks with the authority of God (apostolic authority) and sees his opponents not with a different point of view but as enemies of and a "virus" to the community that he established. What Paul has established is missionary exceptionalism, destined by God, and sowing the seeds for later missionary endeavors across the globe. If today's readers and readings also see themselves as unique and superior, this notion also will influence the way they behave toward the rest of the world and the vulnerable. For instance, the nativist slogan "Make America Great Again" is based on such exceptionalism, aiming to "return" the United States as unique and superior to all other nations, while seeing poverty, inequality, injustice, migrants, and minorities as a "plague" contaminating the nation. This viewpoint influences how supporters of this ideology treats the vulnerable, particularly in the age of COVID-19 as seen above. The derision of the vulnerable as unhealthy, more likely contagious, makes it easier to avoid engaging the vulnerable on both sides of the border.

How governments and institutions should respond to this pandemic is not simply a medical question, it is also a question of ethics, justice, and politics. Interpretation in an age of COVID-19 calls for responsibility—responsibility that is not "subcontracted" to other scholars in the academic field and arts, but responsibility that we interpreters must embrace in making the voices of the vulnerable heard.

Conclusion

These initial reflections or meta-critical analyses of biblical interpretation amid COVID-19 are still developing. But to interpret and employ criticism as if the pandemic is in the past tense or unrelated to the field of biblical studies in all its expressions would be another disaster unto itself. Segovia's presidential address several years ago is a call to take seriously the global arena and how we interpret texts and contexts. This pandemic is not a local or national issue, it is a global crisis, with the vulnerable like those who are poor and racially marginalized in the United States bearing the brunt of the pandemic.

If anything, the pandemic, along with the dehumanization of migrants (children and families) at the southern border, has exposed the fault lines of the economic, health, and social disparities in the United States and across the globe—much as the Black Lives Matter movement highlights the racial inequities in our society. These fault lines are also present in the field of biblical interpretation and in religious and theological studies. We are not immune. The field cannot lose itself, focusing on building ourselves (à la Tower of Babel) rather than building on the same plane for and communicating with the people—the most vulnerable. The field—generally speaking—cannot mirror the former Trump administration and disconnect from the vulnerable. The field must take responsibility for what we do and how it affects the Other. Segovia's presidential address is a call to respond to the global-systematic issues such as globalization, climate change, immigration, and now, the pandemic.

Bibliography

Appleby, Joyce, et al. *Telling the Truth about History*. New York: Norton, 1994.

Centers for Disease Control and Prevention. "Disparities in Incidence of COVID-19 among Underrepresented Racial/Ethnic Groups in Counties Identified as Hotspots During June 5–18, 2020 — 22 States, February–June 2020." https://www.cdc.gov/mmwr/volumes/69/wr/mm6933e1.htm.

——. "Health Equity Considerations and Racial and Ethnic Minority Groups." https://www.cdc.gov/coronavirus/2019-ncov/community/health-equity/race-ethnicity.html.

Cobb, Julia Symmers. "Transgender People Face Discrimination, Violence amid Latin American Quarantines." *Reuters*, May 5, 2020. https://www.reuters.com/article/us-health-coronavirus-latam-lgbt-idUSKBN22H2PT.

Friesen, Steve J. "Poverty in Pauline Studies: Beyond the So-called New Consensus." *Journal for the Study of New Testament* 26 (2004) 323–61.

Guttentag Lucas, and Stefano M. Bertozzi. "Trump Is Using the Pandemic to Flout Immigration Laws: Refugees and Unaccompanied Children Are the Targets of Summary Border Expulsions." *New York Times*, May 11, 2020. https://www.nytimes.com/2020/05/11/opinion/trump-coronavirus-immigration.html.

Klein, Naomi. *The Shock Doctrine: The Rise of Disaster Capitalism*. New York: Picador, 2007.

Lozada, Francisco, Jr. "Upcoming Event Page." https://www.flozada.com/upcoming-even-page.

National Immigrant Justice Center. "Asylum Seekers & Refugees." https://immigrantjustice.org/issues/asylum-seekers-refugees.

Oppel, Richard A., Jr., et al. "The Fullest Look yet at the Racial Inequality of Coronavirus." *New York Times*, July 5, 2020. https://www.nytimes.com/interactive/2020/07/05/us/coronavirus-latinos-african-americans-cdc-data.html?referringSource=article Share.

Segovia, Fernando F. "Criticism in Critical Times: Reflections on Vision and Task." *Journal of Biblical Literature* 134 (2015) 6–29. http://dx.doi.org/10.15699/jbl.1341.2015.0002.

Stambaugh, John E., and David L. Balch. "The Ancient Economy." In *The New Testament in Its Social Environment*, edited by Wayne A. Meeks, 63–81. Philadelphia: Westminster, 1986.

Trouillot, Michel-Rolph. *Silencing the Past: Power and the Production of History*. Boston: Beacon, 2015.

U.S. Customs and Border Protection. "Nationwide Enforcement Encounters: Title 8 Enforcement Actions and Title 42 Expulsions 2022." https://www.cbp.gov/newsroom/stats/cbp-enforcement-statistics/title-8-and-title-42-statistics.

Valencia, Misha. "The Challenges of the Pandemic for Queer Youth." *New York Times*, June 29, 2020. https://www.nytimes.com/2020/06/29/well/family/LGBTQ-youth-teenagers-pandemic-coronavirus.html?referringSource=articleShare.

Young, Ed. "How the Pandemic Defeated America." *The Atlantic*, August 4, 2020. https://www.theatlantic.com/magazine/archive/2020/09/coronavirus-american-failure/614191/.

4

Ethics, Social Justice, and COVID-19

—Justin Sabia-Tanis

In many ways, viruses are the ultimate equalizer. Social status makes no difference to these micro-organisms: we are all vulnerable to them and the illnesses, even death, that they bring. And yet, it is abundantly clear that they do not impact all members of society equally. Privilege can and does shelter some from contact with disease and provides resources that may mitigate its effects. Particularly in the deeply stratified United States, where health care remains largely controlled by one's ability to pay, some are, in fact, significantly more likely to fall prey to infection and suffer more severe consequences.

Mark Urquiza's obituary in *The Arizona Republic* stated in stark language, "Mark, like so many others, should not have died from COVID-19. His death is due to the carelessness of the politicians who continue to jeopardize the health of brown bodies through a clear lack of leadership, refusal to acknowledge the severity of this crisis, and inability and unwillingness to give clear and decisive direction on how to minimize risk."[1] His daughter Kristin Urquiza penned these words and has continued to speak out—most notably at the Democratic National Convention in the summer of 2020—to raise awareness of the toll that COVID-19 continues to take in American lives, most particularly among people of color. The novel coronavirus has challenged us in many ways, including raising abundant moral and ethical questions. Many of the most critical issues are encapsulated in Urquiza's statements: the responsibilities of leaders to inform and protect the public and the ongoing health crises faced by communities of color that have been deeply exacerbated by the pandemic. We must, of course, add to these the

1. "Mark Urquiza—Obituary."

vital questions of medical ethics when there are simply not enough resources to treat all who need care and the challenges of saving lives in a country where the degree of access to medical services depends far too heavily on the ability to pay, rather than the level of medical need.

Epidemics reveal not only vectors of disease but fractures in society, making visible those who are often unseen and neglected. These divisions have significant impacts on public health and complicate efforts to prevent and treat illness. Our collective failure to address issues of poverty, homelessness, affordable nutrition, educational inequality, and disability have created a society which is overall less healthy and therefore more susceptible to disease than it could or should be. Moreover, efforts to halt the spread of the disease have highlighted additional ruptures among us that have manifested along political lines, such as the rights of the individual to autonomous action versus the responsibilities of the individual to the contribute to the collective wellbeing.

In this chapter, after we examine some specifics about the impact of the virus on the United States, we will explore with fundamental ethical questions of social responsibility—what is our responsibility for the wellbeing of others and ourselves? What role do leaders play in containing and responding to crises which are both global and local in nature? What do our religious and ethical traditions teach us about our care for the most vulnerable among us during this pandemic?

Social Justice and the Pandemic

The United States, despite its outsized share of global economic might and health care resources, has been particularly hard hit by the COVID-19 pandemic. This is true in both real numbers of infected patients and deaths, as well as in per capita numbers.[2] The Trump Administration has downplayed the coronavirus and its impact, claiming repeatedly and falsely that the disease is under control. Political scientist Steven Levitsky noted a commonality among right-wing populist leaders, including those in the United States: "Very often they rail against intellectuals and experts of nearly all types." The leaders, Levitsky said, "claim to have a kind of common-sense wisdom that the experts lack. This doesn't work very well versus COVID-19."[3] Countries with populist leaders, like the United States and Brazil, have higher rates of infection, in large part because of

2. Indeed, one of the challenges of editing this chapter is that the numbers continue to increase dramatically and need revisions because the rise in cases is so meteoric.

3. Leonhardt and Leatherby, "Where the Virus Is Growing Most."

this disregard of medical and scientific experts in favor of the political leader's opinion when forming public health policy.

There are three key factors in addition to populism that particularly impact the ability of the United States to stem the novel coronavirus: economic inequality, systemic racism, and for-profit private health care. It is because of the unique manifestation of these issues in the United States that we will focus primarily on this country. However, it is certainly true that the impact of this virus has been global and that many of these ethical issues are present in other countries as well.

The pandemic's economic effects have been widespread and profound. The United States has vastly greater levels of income inequality than any country with a comparable economy, with more than half of the nation's income going to the top 20 percent of US households prior to 2019.[4] For these wealthiest Americans, 2020 under the coronavirus has been a time of economic expansion. The Institute for Policy Studies reports that "In the 12 weeks between March 18 and June 11, the combined wealth of all U.S. billionaires increased by more than $637 billion, the equivalent of more than 13 percent of all Black wealth."[5] On July 22, 2020, Amazon Chief Executive Jeff Bezos saw his net worth rise by thirteen billion dollars, the largest one-day net increase ever recorded.[6]

Unfortunately, the opposite is true for most Americans, who lived with economic uncertainty prior to the pandemic. Since its onset, the United States has seen huge increases in unemployment, leading to housing, food, and health insecurities, all of which contribute to greater vulnerability to disease and increased need for health care.[7] According to the United States Census's Household Pulse Survey, from August to September, 24 percent of Americans expected someone in their household to lose their income in the next four weeks, 32 percent said they were very or somewhat likely to face eviction or foreclosure in the next two months, and 10 percent report that there was sometimes or often not enough food to eat during the last seven days.[8] Some states reported significantly higher numbers than these national averages. Food banks have been inundated and leaders expect the need for their services to continue to rise.[9]

4. Schaeffer, "6 Facts about Economic Inequality in the U.S."
5. Asante-Muhammad et al., "White Supremacy Is the Preexisting Condition."
6. Kelly, "The Rich Are Getting Richer."
7. Bhargava and Sun Lee, "Food Insecurity and Health Care Utilization."
8. US Census Bureau, "Measuring Household Experiences."
9. Arango and Kenneally, "Just Because I Have a Car."

While the number of Americans who are currently unemployed has decreased from a high of eighteen million who temporarily lost their jobs in April, the number of workers whose jobs have been permanently lost has been increasing.[10] While these impacts are wide ranging across the country, communities of color and women have been hardest hit. Each of these are serious issues of social injustice in and of themselves, but they also increase America's vulnerability to the continued spread of the disease and form substantial barriers to treatment for those who are infected. While the virus itself does not discriminate based on socioeconomic status, race, ethnicity or nationality, the distinctions that we draw among ourselves as a society create vulnerabilities in which some are more likely to be harmed than others. That very inequality then, in turn, increases the risks for all of us as the virus runs more rapidly and thoroughly through the population.

We have long known that poverty plays a critical role in health, in direct ways, such as the inability to obtain medical care due to its cost, and indirect ones, like a lack of access to nutritious food. Again, this is particularly pronounced in the United States, in which health care is extremely expensive in comparison with other countries,[11] putting comprehensive health care out of the reach of many Americans, even despite the advances of the Affordable Care Act. This sets up a vicious cycle in which poverty leads to poorer health outcomes which in turn lead to deepening poverty.

In this destructive cycle, patients are unable to afford the medications their doctors prescribe, including treatments for heart disease, diabetes, kidney disease, and other serious ailments. Patients are also unable to follow up with medical professionals or may simply be forced to avoid expensive treatment altogether. This in turn leads to poorer health, which results in missed work and lost wages, lowering incomes even more, making it even harder to afford effective medical care. Multiple studies note that poverty is the strongest indicator of lifespan. Tom Boyce, MD, chief of the Division of Developmental Medicine at the University of California San Francisco Medical Center comments, "Socioeconomic status is the most powerful predictor of disease, disorder, injury and mortality we have . . . . Impoverished adults live seven to eight years less than those who have incomes four or more times the federal poverty level, which is $11,770 for a one-person household."[12] In addition, in a pandemic in which multiple family members may contract the disease simultaneously, all of these factors can be increased exponentially, with familial loss of income, directly through illness or death,

---

10. Koeze, "6 Months after Coronavirus Shutdowns."
11. Anderson et al., "It's Still the Prices, Stupid."
12. Goodman and Conway, "Poor Health."

and indirectly when family members need to take time off of work to care for the sick, dying, or grieving.

Because systemic racism suppresses economic opportunities in communities of color, lowering average earning power and denying equal education, people of color are more likely to be impoverished and to experience poorer health outcomes in general. Leading into the pandemic, Black households earned 70 percent of the income of white households in the United States,[13] and held one-fifth as much liquifiable wealth as white families, meaning that their reserves to weather an economic crisis are far fewer.[14] While poverty rates had been decreasing prior to the pandemic, Black and Latinx households nonetheless saw rates several times that of their white and Asian counterparts.[15]

Poverty is not the only force that leads to disparities in health outcomes, however. Racism plays a destructive role that leads more directly to poorer health in communities of color. Rates of infection, hospitalization and death due to the coronavirus are significantly higher in Black, Latinx, and Native populations in the United States, and somewhat higher among Asian Americans.[16] Data on COVID-19 rates by racial demographics was not released by the federal government until May 2020, making it difficult to track the impact early in the epidemic, but the picture became clear quickly. Dr. Marcella Nunez-Smith, who heads the Equity Research and Innovation Center at Yale School of Medicine, notes, "I've been at health equity research for a couple of decades now. Those of us in the field, sadly, expected this. We know that these racial ethnic disparities in COVID-19 are the result of pre-pandemic realities. It's a legacy of structural discrimination that has limited access to health and wealth for people of color."[17] This history has exacerbated the rates of chronic diseases, such as diabetes and heart disease, while limiting access to preventive care, diagnosis and treatment. The stress of living in a racist society itself takes a toll, as do systemic barriers to effective and compassionate health care, notes Dr. William F. Marshall III, writing for the Mayo Clinic.[18] All of these factors, Marshall argues, create situations in which people of color are disproportionately impacted by COVID-19 even when their income is the same or higher than whites in adjacent neighborhoods.

13. Gould and Wilson, "Black Workers," 7.
14. Gould and Wilson, "Black Workers," 8.
15. US Census Bureau, "Poverty Rates."
16. CDC, "COVID-19 Hospitalization and Death by Race/Ethnicity."
17. Godoy, "What Do Coronavirus Racial Disparities Look Like?"
18. Marshall, "Coronavirus Infection by Race."

Therefore, when a pandemic which is particularly deadly for those with underlying health conditions, such as COVID-19, strikes, it is overwhelming likely that it will hit the poor much harder than the wealthy. That is exactly what has happened. In the early days of the pandemic, we saw that the rich and famous had access to testing and advanced medical care for the novel coronavirus, while the average American did not. This means that wealthier and more prominent Americans can make decisions about their exposure, risks, and medical treatment while the vast majority remained uncertain and unknowing.

Workers in higher income brackets have had significantly more choices about their risk exposure to COVID-19, having both the capacity to choose to not work in order to self-quarantine or to be able to work remotely and preserve their jobs. Whites, people with higher education, and those who work in management or professional occupations are much more likely to have been able to work remotely during the pandemic than people of color, those in manual or agricultural labor and those without college degrees.[19] Workers in the lowest income brackets are the most in need of steady employment, facing significant pressure to remain in the in-person workforce with its concomitant risks, not only to meet their immediate financial needs but to maintain their employment at all. For many Americans, employment is tied to health insurance access,[20] without which very few can afford medical care. Thus, those who are better off have kept their jobs and health insurance, while those with middle- and lower-income have fared worse.

Moreover, those in the lowest income categories (along with selected higher income earners, such as doctors and managers) have been most likely to be deemed "essential workers," whose work then bears a much higher risk of exposure to COVID-19. Overall, they are much more likely to be living in poverty, to be women and people of color than the general population.[21] These workers include home health aides providing health care services to seniors and those with disabilities, who are themselves more likely to suffer serious consequences if infected. Home health care workers and personal aides are among the most economically disenfranchised in our country; these workers are almost exclusively female (85 percent) and people of color.[22]

19. Dey et al., "Ability to Work from Home."

20. KFF, "Health Insurance Coverage of the Total Population." Employer provided health coverage is the single largest source of insurance for Americans.

21. Kinder, "Essential but Undervalued."

22. Himmelstein and Venkataramani, "Economic Vulnerability."

Other critical workers include those at meatpacking plants, groceries stores, liquor stores and similar services. The Centers for Disease Control (CDC) estimate that 9 percent of the nation's meatpacking workers, for example, have been infected with COVID-19,[23] working in close quarters for long shifts creating prolonged exposure to other workers.[24] Of those infected at meat packing plants, 87 percent of the infected are people of color, even though they make up only 61 percent of plant workers.[25]

Many essential workers lack access to personal protective equipment (PPEs) even while they are required to come to work. If these workers consider the risks to themselves and their loved ones too great, their only choice is to withdraw from the workplace. This, then, leads them into greater financial instability and decreased access to medical care if they do become infected, as noted earlier. Those with lower incomes are also more likely to be living in more dense neighborhoods, sharing housing with others, and taking public transportation, all of which increase the likelihood of coming in contact with an infected person.[26] Lower income workers are far less likely to have paid sick leave, putting additional pressures on them to go to work even when they or a family member are ill, increasing the risks for everyone at their workplace. When self-quarantining becomes economically unfeasible, this, of course, contributes to the spread of the virus.

The closing of schools and moving to distance learning also impacts those who are caring for young children. A survey by the Urban Institute and the Robert Wood Johnson Foundation found that in one-third of families (33.3 percent), a family member had to stay home from work in order to care for minor children; this was more difficult for lower-income and Hispanic families.[27] Thirty-one percent of the parents in their study reported that they had to cut back on food purchase for their families since the pandemic began.[28] According to the US Census Bureau, women are three times more likely than men to be taking time off from work,[29] while an analysis of US Labor Department statistic reported in October 2020 discovered that women were leaving their jobs at four times the rate men are.[30] This can have a long-term effect on women's employment opportunities and leadership:

23. Lucas, "CDC Says."

24. CDC, "Communities, Schools, Workplaces, & Events."

25. Pitt, "CDC."

26. Marshall, "Coronavirus Infection by Race."

27. Gonzalez et al., "Almost Half of Adults."

28. Gonzalez et al., "Parents Are Struggling."

29. US Census Bureau, "Parents Juggle Work and Child Care."

30. Schneider, "Enough Already."

McKinsey & Company note that in the past, women and men left their jobs at comparable rates; that is no longer the case.[31]

These issues are compounded by deliberate interference with public health measures. In multiple states, elected officials have sued one another to block mask-mandates and emergency orders.[32] In Michigan, militias protested at the State Capitol in May, brandishing weapons and leading state legislators to wear bulletproof vests,[33] while in October, the Federal Bureau of Investigation foiled plotters intending to kidnap Michigan's governor and try her for treason for her use of executive powers to contain the virus.[34] All of these situations created substantive distractions from a focus on public health and welfare—rather than considering what offers the greatest protection for Americans from a deadly virus, elected officials and armed groups of citizens argued over who has the authority to mandate that protection.

Public officials have a responsibility to protect the wellbeing of those they represent and serve. In the case of a pandemic, this includes using scientifically based analyses of risk factors to maximize public safety. It means providing reliable information, adequate resources for testing and health care, ensuring appropriate protections for health care workers, and supporting research into treatment and prevention.[35] The US Congress and state legislatures have spent trillions of dollars to offset the economic consequences of the pandemic, to increase access to testing and treatment for COVID-19, and to assist pharmaceutical companies in developing a vaccine. These show our *capacity* to improve conditions for Americans of all income brackets, but a lack of political will to do so outside of this crisis. These efforts have been subjected to partisan politicking and intra-governmental fighting, which drain resources, capacity, and attention from that which will save lives. In addition, legislatures and executives have been cutting public health budgets for many years, despite the significant improvement in overall health directly attributed to public health services.[36]

The same concerns are true about individual citizens' actions. For example, in Minnesota, the Centers for Disease Control and state public health agencies had to halt work on a survey to determine the extent of coronavirus infection in rural areas in September. After health care teams reported multiple instances of being subjected to racist slurs, and one team was blocked

31. Coury et al., "Women in the Workplace."
32. Goodwyn, "Texas Governor Faces Lawsuit"; Romo, "Governor Drops Lawsuit."
33. Romo, "Governor Drops Lawsuit."
34. Bogel-Burroughs, "What We Know."
35. WHO, *Pandemic Influenza Preparedness and Response.*
36. Carroll and Frakt, "It Saves Lives."

and threatened by armed neighbors, the state and federal health care workers ended the survey without obtaining the data they needed.[37] Media reports noted, "Insults came at doorways, from angry people approaching the surveyors or just people walking their dogs on the other sides of the streets, said Stephanie Yendell, a state senior epidemiology supervisor."[38] Not only is racism itself a moral wrong, but the decision of some residents to prioritize racist behavior over public health needs endangers other Midwesterners, since the data that was to be collected would have helped officials make decisions that would contain the spread of the disease.

Finally, once illness hits, stigma interferes with efforts to prevent and treat the disease. Those who are stigmatized are less likely to be tested for a virus because the act of testing exposes them to acts of prejudice or violence. They are therefore less likely to know their health status, to pursue treatment or disclose their status or concerns to a health care provider, which significantly interfere with public health measures. There has been an increase in violence, harassment, and discrimination against Asian Americans as a result of COVID-19,[39] surely exacerbated by President Trump and other elected officials using disparate terms, such as "Kung Flu" to describe the disease. More than two thousand hate-motivated incidents were reported during a three-month window from March to June 2020, according to news reports.[40]

Religious Responses to COVID-19

Religious leaders across the world have drawn upon their ethical and spiritual traditions as sources of both guidance and comfort for the faithful, while adapting to lockdowns, increased illness and death, and the other hardships imposed by the pandemic. Religious observations, including Passover, Easter, and Ramadan, were altered by leaders to protect the faithful and obey laws set by municipal leaders. For example, the Orthodox Union sent out detailed instructions about variances that were allowable during the celebration of Passover that deviated from custom to follow the more central precept of Judaism of protecting human life.[41] Faith leaders,

---

37. Pietsch, "Coronavirus Survey Halted."

38. Olson, "COVID-19 Surveys Halted."

39. Anti-Defamation League, "Reports of Anti-Asian Assaults"; Ruiz et al., "Many Blacks."

40. Donaghue, "2,120 Hate Incidents."

41. Orthodox Union, "Orthodox Union Guidance Regarding COVID-19."

too, have been among the many who have lost their lives, leading to disruptions in denominations and congregations.[42]

By April 2020, 91 percent of respondents to a Pew survey reported that their faith communities were meeting online; almost a quarter of those surveyed stated that their faith had actually strengthened during the pandemic (24 percent), while only a small fraction (2 percent) reported that their faith had weakened.[43] As in many other crises humanity faces, spirituality offers meaning in the midst of hardship and opportunities to serve others. Religious groups offered prayers and meditations that speak directly to the experience of the virus. The Buddhist magazine *Tricycle* reported that use of meditation apps increased 25 percent in March 2020 alone.[44]

Pope Francis pointed the faithful to focus on those with the greatest need. On Good Friday, in April 2020, speaking alone to a camera in a deserted St. Peter's Square at the Vatican in Rome, the pontiff preached,

> The pandemic of Coronavirus has abruptly roused us from the greatest danger individuals and humanity have always been susceptible to: the delusion of omnipotence. A Jewish rabbi has written that we have the opportunity to celebrate a very special paschal exodus this year, that "from the exile of consciousness".[45] It took merely the smallest and most formless element of nature, a virus, to remind us that we are mortal, that military power and technology are not sufficient to save us. . . .
>
> Let us devote the unlimited resources committed to weapons to the goals that we now realize are most necessary and urgent: health, hygiene, food, the fight against poverty, stewardship of creation. Let us leave to the next generation a world poorer in goods and money, if need be, but richer in its humanity.[46]

Reminding us of our fragility, Pope Francis called upon the faithful not only to care for those who are in need, but to remember the central elements of Christian faith. This is, he points out, an opportunity to build a world more closely aligned with God's vision, a concept we will return to in the conclusion. He stresses that we ourselves are not as omnipotent but place our lives

42. Carrega and Brown, "'Sorrowful.'"

43. Gecewicz, "Few Americans."

44. The Editors, "Buddhist Response to COVID-19."

45. Pope Francis is quoting Rabbi Yaakov Yitzhak Biderman, as cited in Goshen-Gottstein, "Coronavirus." T. Rabbi Biderman's message, as well as the blog post in which it is quoted, calls for a return to religion as a source of meaning and guidance in the midst of the pandemic.

46. Francis, "I Have Plans for Your Welfare, Not for Your Woe," cited in Vatican News, "Pope Celebrates Passion of the Lord."

in the hands of God, who bestows on us the responsibility to care for others in the face of this overwhelming health crisis.

Hindu leaders point to the *dharma*—the right way of living and our religious obligations—that differs for us depending on our specific responsibilities. Psychologist Kavita Pallod Sekhsaria notes in an article on the pandemic in the *Hindu-American*, "our *dharma* today is to first and foremost follow the guidelines being put out by our local, state, and federal governments to protect ourselves, our families, and our communities on small and large scales, despite the sacrifices entailed."[47] Others, however, serve in health care and essential services; for these people, Sekhsaria points out *dharma* requires them to put themselves in harm's way, to move closer to those infected, rather than farther away. In this way of viewing ethics, right action depends on our vocations and responsibilities. Most of us should follow social distancing and quarantining guidelines, even if these require sacrifices of us, while others, who are called into essential services, choose ethically to move into danger to save and protect the lives of others.

Rabbi Deborah Waxman, President of the Jewish Reconstructionist Communities and of the Reconstructionist Rabbinical College, also spoke out early in the epidemic, similarly pointing her readers to core religious values that can guide us in right action:

> The first lesson, I think, is a deep exploration of the Jewish mandate for *piku'akh nefesh*, saving a life, which overrides any other law or requirement. This mandate provides a Jewish rationale for social distancing. We must retreat from intensive physical interaction in order to "flatten the curve," slow the virus' spread and prevent the overwhelming of our health care system . . .
>
> We need to practice compassion on ourselves in these challenging times and with the people we love, and we need to practice compassion with people we do not know. Many of the people most deeply at risk of being infected are already vulnerable due to age, disability, or poverty. Judaism teaches that we must care for the widow, the orphan, the poor—those on the fringes of society. As this crisis unfolds, we must give thought to ensuring that people on the edge do not fall off it. Give funds to your local food banks and investigate safe ways to volunteer. Lobby your congresspeople for increased access to nutrition assistance, paid sick leave, a moratorium on evictions.[48]

47. Sekhsaria "How Hindu Spiritual Practices Can Help."
48. Waxman, "When the Threat Is Random."

Waxman points out that the ethical requirements of religion point us towards the right public health decisions—to preserve life, we must follow the guidelines that will protect us from infection. This is intertwined with an abiding and central focus on the needs of those who are vulnerable and experiencing hardship. Religious faith compels us to act responsibly and compassionately in concrete and discernable ways that alleviate suffering due to economic and racial injustice.

However, these views are complicated by a perception, and reality, of religious observation as a source of spread of the disease through worship services, funerals, and other events in faith communities. There have been significant, ongoing tensions between government leaders and Orthodox Jewish communities in New York over mandates requiring masks and banning large gatherings. Jewish leaders have expressed serious concern that they have been targeted for enforcement of these rules in ways that other groups have not, while government officials cite significantly higher rates of COVID transmission in these communities.[49]

Early in the pandemic, news organizations highlighted the arrest of several religious leaders who insisted on holding in-person worship services, despite state emergency orders banning them. When Tony Spell, pastor of Life Tabernacle Church was arrested in Louisiana, CNN reported, "When asked why he will not follow the governor's mandate, he said, 'We have a mandate from the word of the Lord to assemble together. The first amendment says that Congress shall make no law prohibiting the exercise of religion.'"[50] Churches across the country have sued state and local governments over emergency lockdown orders that ban public gatherings and have shut down worship services.[51] Christians have claimed that they cannot contract COVID-19 because they are "covered in Jesus' blood," or that "the blood of Jesus cures every disease."[52] There is evidence that higher rates of religiosity are correlated with smaller declines in mobility during the pandemic, showing decreased adherence to stay-at-home orders in communities with high religious participation.[53]

In an article on the American Psychological Association website highlighting impacts of religion during a pandemic, Bryan Goodman

49. Stack, "Backlash Grows in Orthodox Jewish Areas."

50. Burke, "Second Pastor Charged with Violating Public Orders."

51. Khurana, "The Right to Worship." This is but one of many examples.

52. Goodyear, "Ohio Pastor Calls on Governor."

53. Hill et al., "The Blood of Christ Compels Them." State officials can track levels of compliance with stay-at-home orders using cell phone data to identify patterns of mobility that increase or decrease. The lower the levels of mobility, the greater the likelihood that people are isolating.

points to the phenomenon of "religious deferral" as a potential detriment of religious belief.[54] That is, if we shift responsibility from our own choices to God—"it's all in God's hands"—then we may fail to take appropriate actions that we can control and protect ourselves and others. Frank Aldoff of the Berkley Center for Religion, Peace & World Affairs points to the high levels of individuality and self-centeredness in some streams of American religion that can offset collective caring for society and for those in need.[55] Thus, an understanding that God protects us from disease can deter people from taking appropriate precautions; when combined with a stress on the needs of the individual over the community (or the individual community over the wider society), this can lead believers to act in ways that endanger both themselves and others.

Yet this, too, is not the whole story. Most communities of faith have cancelled in-person worship and practices, while finding alternatives for connection and service, and encouraging adherence to public health measures. Faith groups have pushed back on others who remain open. For example, in an article on "Practicing Islam in the Time of COVID-19," the authors write:

> The decision of mosques to remain open boggles the mind because they proclaim to be following prophet Muhammad (peace be upon him), who unequivocally taught the opposite. Indeed, one of the five higher objectives (*maqasid*) of the *Sharia* is the preservation of life. Therefore, Muslims are mandated to take all steps to prevent harm. This would obviously include taking all steps to prevent the spread of diseases.[56]

Religious organizations already make up a sizeable percentage of donors to charitable causes in the United States and religious affiliation is positively associated with increased levels of philanthropic giving.[57] In response to the hardships created by the pandemic, many communities of faith have increased their giving, expanding food pantries and making additional donations to social service providers and charities. Many of these initiatives, however, focus on meeting immediate needs, rather than systemic changes, which will clearly be needed to fully recover from this pandemic.

54. Goodman, "Faith in a Time of Crisis."

55. Aldoff, "Religion during and after Coronavirus."

56. Kutty and Kutty, "Practicing Islam."

57. The Editors, "New Report."

Who Is My Neighbor?

Let us consider a core teaching of faith and ethics—treating our neighbors as ourselves—and how, then, this principle and other religious beliefs may offer us an opportunity to envision a world which effectively addresses the social justice issues that both led to and resulted from the coronavirus pandemic.

Almost all the religions on earth espouse some form of treating others as we wish to be treated, the Golden Rule. This precept is a fundamental building block of many spiritual practices and theological constructs. Efforts to halt the spread of COVID-19 require us to take actions—self-quarantining, wearing masks, handwashing, and social distancing—that work primarily to protect others from the possibility that we may infect them. They are not so much self-protective measures as they are "neighbor-protecting" ones. As almost all medical experts have pointed out, these steps can effectively contain the virus. Dr. Anthony Fauci, one of the most respected voices on the subject, notes, "A risk for you is not just isolated to you, because if you get infected, you are part—innocently or inadvertently—of propagating a dynamic process of the pandemic."[58]

But the pandemic has tested our essential altruism and willingness to abide by the moral teaching about our responsibility to our neighbors. The same article that features the above quote from Dr. Fauci also notes House Speaker Nancy Pelosi's calling President Donald Trump a coward for his unwillingness to wear a mask. For his part, Trump has mocked those who do wear masks. As commentator Amanda Hess noted in the New York Times about the use of face masks,

> It is the pandemic's defining symbol, a visual stand-in for the coronavirus itself. In America, the medical mask used to be confined to hospital dramas and operating rooms, but now the bare face is what registers as a choice. The mask is a public health device, but it has also revealed itself as a mask in the more traditional sense: a tool in a social ritual, a fetish object that signifies a person's politics, gender expression and relationship to truth itself.[59]

A mask can function as a talisman as well as a practical means of disease prevention, while the lack of a mask can communicate the wearer's feeling that protection is unnecessary.

---

58. Axelrod, "Pelosi."

59. Hess, "The Medical Mask Becomes a Protest Symbol."

In a grocery store recently, I witnessed a common spectacle: a customer forcefully sharing his opinions at the checkout: how useless he feels masks are, how they infringe on his freedoms, and so on. Yet, from an ethical standpoint, our freedoms create the opportunity to act in love for our neighbors, rather than simply allow us to serve our own purposes. Dietrich Bonhoeffer wrote,

> To act out of concrete responsibility means to act in freedom—to decide, to act, and to answer for the consequences of this particular action myself without the support of other people or principles. Responsibility presupposes ultimate freedom in assessing a given situation, in choosing, and in acting. Responsible action is neither determined from the outset nor defined once and for all; instead, it is born in the given situation.[60]

Freedom is not merely a stand for individualism but the mechanism by which we can care for others and treat our neighbors as ourselves. Thus, in our current situation in which we do have some control over the spread of the novel coronavirus to others—as health care experts are continually pointing out—our freedoms allow us to take responsibility for the wellbeing of others. We are not constrained without choices that enable us to care for others as we would want to be treated by them. Rather, it is in many ways completely in our hands—both literally and figuratively—whether we chose to protect those around us.

Moreover, cultivating this sense of responsibility for others can have significant spiritual benefits for individuals and society. In an article on virtue ethics and the pandemic, the authors point to the value of using our freedoms to align our will with that which is good; they then reason,

> Once we embrace the virtues of generosity, courage and prudence and want that our will is directed towards acting in a way that is *virtuous*, then even imposed restrictions, wearing masks when going outside and keeping social distancing do not look as immoral actions anymore (that diminish pleasure and inflict pain) or as a threat to our freedom, but rather as the virtuously right actions we should pursue. Our freedom is no more threatened by limitations, but augmented and dignified in the moment in which our second-order will *wants* to willingly respect the restrictions and the recommendations because this is *what a virtuous person does* in such circumstances.[61]

---

60. Bonhoeffer, *Ethics*, 221.
61. Bellazzi and Boyneburgk, "COVID-19 Calls for Virtue Ethics," 8.

Our dignity is enhanced and our spirits cultivated when we act virtuously; in this case, in ways in that support the aims of public health and treat our neighbor as ourselves. Our individual wellbeing is furthered when we look to the health of others as our own will.

Indeed, a focus on individualism can hinder our response to disease. The COVID-19 pandemic has highlighted the interconnected nature of today's world: we see clearly that borders and status pose no barriers to disease and that the actions of individuals affect others. The choices each of us make have repercussions beyond ourselves; the ways in which we have neglected others also impacts us. That means that we are best served by thinking broadly and caring widely. This then raises ethical questions of those who fail to take public safety measures. The use of freedom to behave irresponsibly or act solely or predominantly for an individual's comfort at the cost of societal protections has wider ramifications. If individuals choose not to wear masks or socially distance, for example, this can lead to the consequence of greater rates of infection and the overwhelming of medical services. This, in turn, can then infringe on personal freedoms because the individual loses the option of turning to those medical providers in time of need. The choice to act for self alone may have unintended, damaging consequences.

Because this pandemic exposes individuals and groups to the virus in disproportional ways in our society, as previously outlined, those who are privileged to have lower risks bear an increased ethical responsibility to protect those who must face more pronounced dangers, such as health care providers, essential workers, those with chronic illnesses, and the elderly. I would argue that the greater the control we have over the virus's transmission and our own exposure to it, the deeper the level of responsibility we bear for acting in ways that care for our neighbor. Similarly, the greater the knowledge that we have about the virus's transmission, the stronger the imperative that we use that information to promote the common good, both through our own actions and those of our society.

Focusing on the need and wellbeing of others, beyond our own individual desires, is one of the great gifts offered to us by religious practices. Thus, taking actions to protect our neighbors becomes an act of faithfulness, in obedience to God's will for the thriving of humanity.

Opportunities for Faithful Reworkings of the World

Our vulnerability to illness reminds us of our mortality and the importance of human life; pandemics can encourage a revaluation of our collective priorities just as individual sickness can cause us to reflect on meaning in our own lives, as evidenced by reports of spiritual deepening during this crisis. Epidemics also speak to us of the urgency and moral necessity to safeguard human rights for all people: they point out the need for a foundational level of health care, nutrition, education, and financial stability. This situation should lead us to challenge a system that allows and encourages those who profit from illness and exploit the economic vulnerabilities of others. Not only are we called to treat our neighbors as ourselves in our personal actions toward others during a health crisis, this is also a tremendous opportunity for us to reshape the world and address the inequities which led to a worsening of this pandemic and caused hardship in so many ways in our world.

Moreover, we know that we have the economic capacity to create a more equitable world and that the benefits of such a society improve the health and wellbeing of all of us. Womanist ethicist Emilie Townes wrote, prior to the pandemic, of the United States: "It is disingenuous to refuse to admit the tremendous power and influence we have on a global scale and also to recognize the awesome responsibility that comes with this. We have the power to do incredible good—and we have done so—and must continue to grow this side of who we are as a nation larger and stronger on the global scale and here at home. We fail to do so at our own peril."[62] There has been tremendous good done in response to the coronavirus pandemic and, as Townes notes, we need a commitment to grow that side of ourselves. There are tremendous benefits that we can accrue as a country if we commit ourselves to ending the poverty, systemic racism, and unaffordable heath systems that have spurred the growth of the pandemic in the United States.

Rev. Dr. William Barber II, co-chair of the Poor People's Campaign and initiator of Moral Mondays, calls upon us to:

> Take a collective oath that we won't be silent anymore. When we get a handle on this virus, we won't return to our apathy that has for far too long ignored the moral crisis of poverty and the racial disparities that mark American inequality.
>
> Take time in this moment to let it change your insight forever, so that from now on we can see how connected we are, how frail we are, and how easily our lives can be disrupted. Take time to meditate on our interrelated humanity. This virus can infect anyone, black, white, or brown, rich or poor, gay or straight, etc. We should see every issue like this.

---

62. Townes, *Womanist Ethics and the Cultural Production of Evil*, 163.

As we are making every effort to mitigate the spread of the virus, we should make the determined commitment to stop the spread of poverty, racism and xenophobia, the climate crisis, and lies.[63]

The economic and social disruptions caused by the coronavirus create space to re-envision our communities and society. The health disparities and economic injustices outlined in this chapter are preventable and correctable and addressing them will protect individuals and communities from disease, despair, and hardship in the future. Not only can we see the negative effects of income inequality, for example, but this crisis has also shown us the positive benefits of providing economic relief to American households and small businesses. While much of the economic stimulus bills also benefitted the rich and large corporations, future efforts can be more targeted to those in need and more efficient at reaching vulnerable households and businesses.[64]

Yet to be truly effective and just, these cannot be only short-term measures in response to the early waves of the pandemic. Liz Theoharis, Director of the Kairos Center for Religions, Rights, and Social Justice at Union Theological Seminary and co-chair of the Poor People's Campaign, writes,

We must take extreme measures to respond to this crisis. But the lesson from our sacred traditions is that these measures, where they align with the basic demands of justice, cannot be temporary. Plague in the Bible is not a storm weathered before a return to normalcy. It's a call to come together in new ways in order to survive, hold the powerful responsible for their unjust policies and the lies they've told to cover up injustice, and rebuild on foundations of love and justice.[65]

People of faith have a responsibility to offer a moral conscience and vision to our society that more closely aligns with God's vision of a thriving world.

Just as the imperatives of our faiths call upon us to take measures to prevent the spread of disease—to treat others as we wish to be treated by them—so too do they implore us to take action on a wider scale. None of us wish to be denied medical care, food, shelter, or employment; none of us wish to be subjected to violence, discrimination, and intolerance. Yet these are the conditions under which many Americans are forced to live year after year, and which threaten health and wellbeing as deeply as does the coronavirus. These

63. Barber, "In Times Like These."

64. Roll and Grinstein-Weiss, "Did CARES Act Benefits Reach Vulnerable Americans?"

65. Theoharis, "Plagues Expose the Foundations of Injustice"

same factors, too, fuel the spread of COVID-19 through our communities. We have the freedom and the capacity to alleviate suffering and promote well-being far more broadly through our society; that, therefore, creates a moral responsibility to do so. While we wait in social distance, let us use this time to free our moral imaginations to envision and build a world in keeping with God's vision of a beloved and loving community.

Bibliography

Aldoff, Frank. "Religion during and after Coronavirus: Individualism or Inclusive Solidarity?" *Berkley Forum*, April 22, 2020. https://berkleycenter.georgetown.edu/responses/religion-during-and-after-coronavirus-individualism-or-inclusive-solidarity.

Anderson, Gerard F., et al. "It's Still The Prices, Stupid: Why The US Spends So Much on Health Care, and a Tribute to Uwe Reinhardt." *Health Affairs* 38.1 (2019) 87–95. https://doi.org/10.1377/hlthaff.2018.05144.

Anti-Defamation League. "Reports of Anti-Asian Assaults, Harassment and Hate Crimes Rise as Coronavirus Spreads." https://www.adl.org/blog/reports-of-anti-asian-assaults-harassment-and-hate-crimes-rise-as-coronavirus-spreads.

Arango, Tim, and Brenda Ann Kenneally. "'Just Because I Have a Car Doesn't Mean I Have Enough Money to Buy Food.'" *The New York Times*, September 4, 2020. https://www.nytimes.com/2020/09/03/us/food-pantries-hunger-us.html.

Asante-Muhammad, Dedrick, et al. "White Supremacy Is the Preexisting Condition: Eight Solutions to Ensure Economic Recovery Reduces the Racial Wealth Divide." https://ips-dc.org/white-supremacy-preexisting-condition-eight-solutions-economic-recovery-racial-wealth-divide/.

Axelrod, Tal. "Pelosi: Trump Not Wearing a Mask Is 'Cowardly.'" *The Hill*, June 26, 2020. https://thehill.com/homenews/house/504813-pelosi-trump-not-wearing-a-mask-is-cowardly.

Barber, William James, II. "In Times Like These." *Repairers of the Breach* (blog), March 14, 2020. https://www.breachrepairers.org/blogs/in-times-like-these.

Bellazzi, Francesca, and Konrad v Boyneburgk. "COVID-19 Calls for Virtue Ethics." *Journal of Law and the Biosciences* 7.1 (2020) 1–8. https://doi.org/10.1093/jlb/lsaa056.

Bhargava, Vibha, and Jung Sun Lee. "Food Insecurity and Health Care Utilization among Older Adults in the United States." *Journal of Nutrition in Gerontology and Geriatrics* 35.3 (2016) 177–92. https://doi.org/10.1080/21551197.2016.1200334.

Bogel-Burroughs, Nicholas. "What We Know about the Alleged Plot to Kidnap Michigan's Governor." *The New York Times*, October 9, 2020. https://www.nytimes.com/2020/10/09/us/michigan-militia-whitmer.html.

Bonhoeffer, Dietrich. *Ethics*. Edited by Clifford J. Green. Vol. 6. Minneapolis: Fortress, 2005.

Burke, Daniel. "Second Pastor Charged with Violating Public Orders Says Church Doors Will Still Be Open on Sunday." *CNN*, April 1, 2020. https://www.cnn.com/2020/03/31/us/louisiana-pastor-arrest-tony-spell/index.html.

Carrega, Christina, and Lakeia Brown. "'Sorrowful': Black Clergy Members and Churches Reeling from COVID-19 Losses." *ABC News*, May 21, 2020. https://abcnews.go.com/US/sorrowful-black-clergy-members-churches-reeling-covid-19/story?id=70434181.

Carroll, Aaron E., and Austin Frakt. "It Saves Lives. It Can Save Money. So Why Aren't We Spending More on Public Health?" *The New York Times*, May 28, 2018. https://www.nytimes.com/2018/05/28/upshot/it-saves-lives-it-can-save-money-so-why-arent-we-spending-more-on-public-health.html.

Censky, Abigail. "Heavily Armed Protesters Gather again at Michigan Capitol to Decry Stay-at-Home Order." *NPR*, May 14, 2020. https://www.npr.org/2020/05/14/855918852/heavily-armed-protesters-gather-again-at-michigans-capitol-denouncing-home-order.

Centers for Disease Control and Prevention. "Communities, Schools, Workplaces, & Events." https://www.cdc.gov/coronavirus/2019-ncov/community/organizations/meat-poultry-processing-workers-employers.html.

———. "COVID-19 Hospitalization and Death by Race/Ethnicity." https://www.cdc.gov/coronavirus/2019-ncov/covid-data/investigations-discovery/hospitalization-death-by-race-ethnicity.html.

Coury, Sarah, et al. "Women in the Workplace 2020." https://www.mckinsey.com/featured-insights/diversity-and-inclusion/women-in-the-workplace.

Dey, Matthew, et al. "Ability to Work from Home: Evidence from Two Surveys and Implications for the Labor Market in the COVID-19 Pandemic." *Monthly Labor Review* (2020) 1–19. https://doi.org/10.21916/mlr.2020.14.

Donaghue, Erin. "2,120 Hate Incidents against Asian Americans Reported during Coronavirus Pandemic." *CBS News*, July 2, 2020. https://www.cbsnews.com/news/anti-asian-american-hate-incidents-up-racism/.

The Editors. "Buddhist Response to COVID-19." *Tricycle: The Buddhist Review*, Fall 2020. https://tricycle.org/magazine/buddhist-response-to-covid/.

The Editors. "New Report Finds Religious People Are More Likely to Donate." *Philanthropy Daily*, October 25, 2017. https://www.philanthropydaily.com/religious-philanthropy-faith/.

Gecewicz, Claire. "Few Americans Say Their House of Worship Is Open, but a Quarter Say Their Faith Has Grown amid Pandemic." *Pew Research Center*, April 30, 2020. https://www.pewresearch.org/fact-tank/2020/04/30/few-americans-say-their-house-of-worship-is-open-but-a-quarter-say-their-religious-faith-has-grown-amid-pandemic/.

Godoy, Maria. "What Do Coronavirus Racial Disparities Look Like State by State?" *NPR*, May 30, 2020. https://www.npr.org/sections/health-shots/2020/05/30/865413079/what-do-coronavirus-racial-disparities-look-like-state-by-state.

Gonzalez, Dulce, et al. "Almost Half of Adults in Families Losing Work during the Pandemic Avoided Health Care Because of Costs or COVID-19 Concerns." *Urban Institute*, July 10, 2020. https://www.urban.org/research/publication/almost-half-adults-families-losing-work-during-pandemic-avoided-health-care-because-costs-or-covid-19-concerns.

———. "Parents Are Struggling to Provide for Their Families during the Pandemic." *RWJF*, May 21, 2020. https://www.rwjf.org/en/library/research/2020/05/parents-are-struggling-to-provide-for-their-families-during-the-pandemic.html.

Goodman, Bryan. "Faith in a Time of Crisis." *APA*, May 11, 2020. https://www.apa.org/topics/covid-19/faith-crisis.

Goodman, Jane, and Claire Conway. "Poor Health: When Poverty Becomes Disease." *UC San Francisco News*, January 6, 2016. https://www.ucsf.edu/news/2016/01/401251/poor-health-when-poverty-becomes-disease.

Goodwyn, Wayne. "Texas Governor Faces Lawsuit, under Fire over Contact Tracing Deal, Mask Order." *NPR*, August 7, 2020. https://www.npr.org/2020/08/07/900279650/texas-governor-faces-lawsuit-under-fire-over-contact-tracing-deal-mask-order.

Goodyear, Sheena. "Ohio Pastor Calls on Governor to Shut down Church Services during Pandemic." *CBC*, April 7, 2020. https://www.cbc.ca/radio/asithappens/as-it-happens-the-tuesday-edition-1.5524929/ohio-pastor-calls-on-governor-to-shut-down-church-services-during-pandemic-1.5524935.

Goshen-Gottstein, Alon. "Coronavirus—A Spiritual Message from Brooklyn." *The Times of Israel*, March 20, 2020. https://blogs.timesofisrael.com/coronavirus-a-spiritual-message-from-brooklyn/.

Gould, Elise, and Valerie Wilson. "Black Workers Face Two of the Most Lethal Preexisting Conditions for Coronavirus—Racism and Economic Inequality." Washington, DC: Economic Policy Institute, June 1, 2020.

Hess, Amanda. "The Medical Mask Becomes a Protest Symbol." *The New York Times*, June 2, 2020. https://www.nytimes.com/2020/06/02/arts/virus-mask-trump.html.

Hill, Terrence D., et al. "The Blood of Christ Compels Them: State Religiosity and State Population Mobility during the Coronavirus (COVID-19) Pandemic." *Journal of Religion and Health* 59.5 (2020) 2229–42. https://doi.org/10.1007/s10943-020-01058-9.

Himmelstein, Kathryn E. W., and Atheendar S. Venkataramani. "Economic Vulnerability among US Female Health Care Workers: Potential Impact of a $15-per-Hour Minimum Wage." *American Journal of Public Health* 109.2 (2019) 198–205. https://doi.org/10.2105/AJPH.2018.304801.

Kelly, Jack. "The Rich Are Getting Richer during The Pandemic." *Forbes*, July 22, 2020. https://www.forbes.com/sites/jackkelly/2020/07/22/the-rich-are-getting-richer-during-the-pandemic/.

KFF. "Health Insurance Coverage of the Total Population." https://www.kff.org/other/state-indicator/total-population/.

Khurana, Mansee. "The Right to Worship: Church and State Clash over Religious Services in the Coronavirus Era." *NBC News*, May 9, 2020. https://www.nbcnews.com/politics/politics-news/right-worship-church-state-clash-over-religious-services-coronavirus-era-n1201626.

Kinder, Molly. "Essential but Undervalued: Millions of Health Care Workers Aren't Getting the Pay or Respect They Deserve in the COVID-19 Pandemic." *Brookings*, May 28, 2020. https://www.brookings.edu/research/essential-but-undervalued-millions-of-health-care-workers-arent-getting-the-pay-or-respect-they-deserve-in-the-covid-19-pandemic/.

Koeze, Ella. "6 Months after Coronavirus Shutdowns, the Shape(s) of the Economic Crisis." *The New York Times*, October 5, 2020. https://www.nytimes.com/interactive/2020/10/05/business/economy/coronavirus-unemployment-recovery.html.

Kutty, Shaikh Ahmad, and Faisal Kutty. "Practicing Islam in the Time of COVID-19." *The Star*, March 26, 2020. https://www.thestar.com/opinion/contributors/2020/03/26/practicing-islam-in-the-time-of-covid-19.html.

Leonhardt, David, and Lauren Leatherby. "Where the Virus Is Growing Most: Countries with 'Illiberal Populist' Leaders." *The New York Times*, June 2, 2020. https://www.nytimes.com/2020/06/02/briefing/coronavirus-populist-leaders.html.

Lucas, Amelia. "CDC Says 9% of Meatpacking Plant Workers Have Been Diagnosed with COVID-19." *CNBC*, July 7, 2020. https://www.cnbc.com/2020/07/07/cdc-says-9percent-of-meatpacking-plant-workers-have-been-diagnosed-with-covid-19.html.

"Mark Urquiza—Obituary." *The Arizona Republic*, July 6, 2020. https://www.legacy.com/amp/obituaries/azcentral/196459145.

Marshall, William F., III. "Coronavirus Infection by Race: What's behind the Health Disparities?" *Mayo Clinic*, August 13, 2020. https://www.mayoclinic.org/diseases-conditions/coronavirus/expert-answers/coronavirus-infection-by-race/faq-20488802.

Olson, Jeremy. "COVID-19 Surveys Halted in Minnesota amid Racism, Intimidation." *Star Tribune*, September 25, 2020. https://www.startribune.com/covid-surveys-halted-in-minn-amid-racism-intimidation/572535141/.

Orthodox Union. "Orthodox Union Guidance Regarding COVID-19." https://www.ou.org/covid19/.

Pietsch, Bryan. "Coronavirus Survey Halted after Workers Faced Racial Slurs, Officials Say." *The New York Times*, October 12, 2020. https://www.nytimes.com/2020/09/25/us/minnesota-coronavirus-racial-slurs.html.

Pitt, David. "CDC: Minorities Affected Much More in Meatpacking Outbreaks." *Washington Post*, July 8, 2020. https://www.washingtonpost.com/health/cdc-minorities-affected-much-more-in-meatpacking-outbreaks/2020/07/08/9b208a7e-c156-11ea-8908-68a2b9eae9e0_story.html.

Roll, Stephen, and Michal Grinstein-Weiss. "Did CARES Act Benefits Reach Vulnerable Americans? Evidence from a National Survey." *Brookings*, August 25, 2020. https://www.brookings.edu/research/did-cares-act-benefits-reach-vulnerable-americans-evidence-from-a-national-survey/.

Romo, Vanessa. "Governor Drops Lawsuit against Atlanta Mayor over Masks, but Fight May Not Be Over." *NPR*, August 13, 2020. https://www.npr.org/sections/coronavirus-live-updates/2020/08/13/902347003/governor-drops-lawsuit-against-atlanta-mayor-over-masks-but-fight-may-not-be-ove.

Ruiz, Neil G., et al. "Many Black, Asian Americans Say They Have Experienced Discrimination amid Coronavirus." *Pew Research Center*, July 1, 2020. https://www.pewsocialtrends.org/2020/07/01/many-black-and-asian-americans-say-they-have-experienced-discrimination-amid-the-covid-19-outbreak/.

Schaeffer, Katherine. "6 Facts about Economic Inequality in the U.S." *Pew Research Center*, February 7, 2020. https://www.pewresearch.org/fact-tank/2020/02/07/6-facts-about-economic-inequality-in-the-u-s/.

Schneider, Avie. "Enough Already: Multiple Demands Causing Women to Abandon Workforce." *NPR*, October 2, 2020. https://www.npr.org/sections/coronavirus-live-updates/2020/10/02/919517914/enough-already-multiple-demands-causing-women-to-abandon-workforce.

Sekhsaria, Kavita Pallod. "How Hindu Spiritual Practices Can Help Manage Your COVID-19 Anxiety." *Hindu American Foundation*, March 21, 2020. https://www.hinduamerican.org/blog/hindu-spiritual-practices-manage-anxiety-covid.

Stack, Liam. "Backlash Grows in Orthodox Jewish Areas over Virus Crackdown by Cuomo." *The New York Times*, October 8, 2020. https://www.nytimes.com/2020/10/07/nyregion/orthodox-jews-nyc-coronavirus.html.

Theoharis, Liz. "Plagues Expose the Foundations of Injustice." *Sojourners*, March 18, 2020. https://sojo.net/articles/plagues-expose-foundations-injustice.

Townes, Emilie M. *Womanist Ethics and the Cultural Production of Evil*. New York: Palgrave Macmillan, 2007.

United States Census Bureau. "Measuring Household Experiences during the Coronavirus Pandemic." https://www.census.gov/householdpulsedata.

————. "Parents Juggle Work and Child Care during Pandemic." The United States Census Bureau. Accessed October 14, 2020. https://www.census.gov/library/stories/2020/08/parents-juggle-work-and-child-care-during-pandemic.html.

————. "Poverty Rates for Blacks and Hispanics Reached Historic Lows in 2019." https://www.census.gov/library/stories/2020/09/poverty-rates-for-blacks-and-hispanics-reached-historic-lows-in-2019.html.

Vatican News. "Pope Celebrates Passion of the Lord, as Papal Preacher Reflects on Covid-19 Pandemic." *Vatican News*, April 10, 2020. https://www.vaticannews.va/en/pope/news/2020-04/pope-francis-passion-of-the-lord-cantalamessa-sermon-coronavirus.html.

Waxman, Rabbi Deborah. "When the Threat Is Random, the Jewish Response Is Compassion." *The New York Jewish Week*, March 22, 2020. https://jewishweek.timesofisrael.com/when-the-threat-is-random-the-jewish-response-is-compassion/.

World Health Organization. *Pandemic Influenza Preparedness and Response: A WHO Guidance Document*. Geneva: World Health Organization, 2009. https://www.ncbi.nlm.nih.gov/books/NBK143067/.

5

Reimagining the Human

How Shall We Be for Each Other?

—Eleazar Fernandez

It was not in my wildest dreams that I would experience a pandemic of this catastrophic magnitude that would last this long. When COVID-19 came, I was entertaining the idea that it would pass quickly and we would return to "normal" as we knew it. But, as the trend continues, it seems that it is not going to go away soon, and I must learn to deal with it and understand how to live with the virus, which is not easy.

Even though there were warnings, none of us were really prepared for the pandemic. This is not surprising. We are not even prepared for our own death even though we know it is just around the bend. It is like the story of the Titanic—the most famous sea disaster of our times. Overly confident of its size and make, despite several warnings of the presence of icebergs, the ship continued to sail toward its destination at full speed until it struck an iceberg that brought it down to the bottom of the Atlantic Ocean. There are other examples that I do not need to mention of the catastrophic consequences of ignoring critical warnings. Those who give the warnings are, oftentimes, labeled as alarmist, misguided, insane, and, in many cases, silenced. A statement ascribed to Friedrich Nietzsche is on target: "People don't really want to hear the truth, because they don't want their illusions destroyed."

Given the havoc that the pandemic has wrought on our lives, it should send us thinking about life in general and about being human in particular. What can the pandemic teach us about ourselves and how we dwell together? What is it revealing about us and our situation? Who are we and what are we becoming in relation to the pandemic? How shall we dwell together?

Revelations: What Is Our Plight?

"Unprecedented" has become a popular word in this time of pandemic. We have used it to describe the qualitatively novel character of the coronavirus. Yes, novel and "unprecedented" in many ways, but we should be clear on this, the coronavirus did not come out of thin air or in a vacuum. This "unprecedented" virus and how it has affected us has "precedents." We have helped pave the way for it. This is the wreckage of the train that has been careening down the rickety track for years.

As the coronavirus continues to take its toll, a revelation is happening. By revelation I do not mean that a body of truths from another world is disclosed, but an event of worldly un-concealment or unveiling. The pandemic has opened our eyes and brought us to an acute realization that the "health crisis" is an "economic crisis," and the economic crisis is a "political crisis." Moreover, the coronavirus, which was initially thought of as politically non-partisan and non-ideological, has been weaponized for political purposes. Using an apocalyptic lens, the coronavirus pandemic has only revealed or unveiled the destructive path we have taken for quite some time and, if we continue with business-as-usual, worse catastrophic socio-political and ecological unraveling is to be expected.

The Essentials Are the "Sacrificials"

The pandemic has exposed the fault lines in our healthcare, political, and economic systems, systems driven by the pursuit of the "bottom line"— profits. When we allow the "bottom line" to take the driver's seat, we should not be surprised to know how unprepared we are to serve the needs of all, except for those who can afford to pay. When profit becomes god, deciding what matters and who will live or die, the "essentials" will be the "sacrificials" and the "frontliners" as well as the "backliners" will be cannibalized by the vulture-like, carcass-hungry "bottom-liners."

What is happening to the frontliners and essential workers is not a surprise. Let us remember, an idol demands sacrifice. It feeds on the flesh of others, especially the most vulnerable. Among the frontliners and essential workers, the most vulnerable and the "sacrificials" are the migrants, the working poor, and racial minorities. COVID-19 infections and deaths among frontliners has disproportionately affected racialized minorities, new immigrants, and migrant workers. This is particularly true of workers from large agribusinesses, such as meat-packing industries, which are heavily made up of migrant labor.

Highfalutin paean for our essential and frontline workers is everywhere, but how are we really treating our frontliners and essentials workers? We may call them "heroes" because they, indeed, perform "heroic" acts. But, when we do that, our rhetoric may be contributing to the harm: it makes us think that the essential workers have voluntarily signed-up for the "altar of sacrifice" and it makes us oblivious of their real plight.

Are We on the Same Boat?

Words of consolation have been uttered here and there, like, "we are on the same boat." Yes, if we mean we are sailing on the same "boat" we call earth. The coronavirus global pandemic has made us all the more acutely aware of this fact. The rapid spread of the border-defying virus has made us realize that there is no space or corner of our boat that is beyond the aggressive reach of the virulent coronavirus. This virus does not have a "facial-recognition technology," nor does it conduct "credit score" test to discriminate a famous actor, billionaire, and world leader from a bottom-rank employee, and daily-wage worker. Do you need proof? Even the rich and famous are not spared: Tom Hanks, Boris Johnson, Prince Charles, Donald Trump, and many more.

Yet, if we are familiar with sailing passenger ships, especially cruise ships, I do not have to belabor the point that our situation on that same boat is not exactly the same. Some passengers may have first class and tourist class accommodations, while others are in the economy class, or whatever categories you have (cruise cabins, ocean-view cabins, inside cabins, etc.). Our experience on this same boat is shaped by the amount we pay. Short of the final denouement when no one can get out of this world (boat) alive, there may be more lifeboats on the first-class deck than on the economy class.

Maybe the metaphor of being on the same boat is not accurate. Or, maybe there is a better metaphor to describe our situation in this time of pandemic. How about if we say that we are facing the same storm, but we are on different ships. Some of us may be riding out the storm on a luxurious ocean liner, private yacht, or recreational sort of boat, while many are in much smaller rickety boats.

Relating this to the pandemic, I say that our encounter and experience of the pandemic is not exactly the same, and we should stop ignoring that significant difference. Power-differentials affect how we encounter, experience, respond, get treatment, recover, or die as a result of the pandemic and its fallout. The generic language of being on "the same boat" and that "we are in this together" does not reveal the painful reality of our different experiences of the pandemic.

Questions That Must Be Asked to Examine Our Situation

Significant questions must be asked and not evaded as we continue to face the pandemic. Here are some questions for us to seriously consider.

What is "staying home and staying safe" for those who do not have homes or those who are living on streets, beside railroad tracks, under dark bridges (so called "bat people" of Manila), underbelly of the overhead highway, cemeteries, mountains of garbage, steep mountain slopes, and mosquito infested swamps?

What is "sheltering-in-place" for those who are living in refugee tents, hastily constructed shelters made of rusty corrugated metals, sheets of plastic, and cardboard boxes in crowded slums, and those whose shelters are under flyovers, atop stagnant water choked with litter and refuse, and floating shacks on brackish water just offshore?

What is "working home" for the front liners who have no choice but to go to work, the street-vendors, laborers, and farmers who produce essential goods? And, how about those who do not have regular full-time work, which means no-work, no pay, and those whose homes are not even safe places of work?

What is lockdown for those who have been locked-up in prison cells and victims of human trafficking who are hidden behind locked doors in brothels and factories? And, how about the Palestinians and those in the Gaza Strip who have suffered lockdown for several years now?

What is social distancing for those who have been victimized by cultures of exploitation and discrimination, such as casteism, racism, classism, xenophobia, those in crowded prison cells where prisoners must learn to take turns sleeping? And, how about those whom we want to distance ourselves from by sending them back to their "shithole countries"?

What does this idea of "flattening the curve" mean for the victims of our systems and practices that "widen the gap," and for those who are working to "close the gap" of social inequities to whom we have turned a deaf ear or whom we have silenced? And, how about those who died and are dying before their time because we have not done enough to "close the gap," pandemic or none?

An honest answer to these questions reveals what is truly happening in our society. Although coronavirus, as virus, does not discriminate, social injustice does. There is a significant difference between the one who complies with the "shelter-in-place" mandate in a luxury mansion in an exclusive village and the one who does it in a small shanty in an overcrowded village.

COVID-19 and Other Pandemics: Interlocking Connections

In spite of criticism because of his outright racist rhetoric, Donald Trump, the President of the "land of the free and home of the brave," who wants to "Make America Great Again," continues to call COVID-19 the "China virus." In fact, rather than toning down his racist speech, he has raised it to feverish pitch. "You can call it many different things—from China virus—I don't want to go through all the names because some people may get insulted but that's the way it is," Trump said. In a rally in Tulsa, Oklahoma (June 20, 2020), he used the slur "kung flu." Three days later, at another rally in Phoenix, Arizona, Trump repeated the slur with his audience "cheering."[1] As someone said on Twitter, this mob crowd may have thought of Trump as a toddler who "makes pee pee" in the toilet for the first time. Everyone cheered.

Can you imagine a great crowd cheering its leader for using a racial slur? What kind of people would cheer a leader for using a racial slur? It tells us not only about Trump, it tells us about what we have become as a nation or as a people. I think we should also put our focus here, instead of just shooting at the visible symptom and a much easier target of our frustrations.

George Packer in *The Atlantic*, said, "Trump doesn't create anything new—he amplifies existing bigotry and vulgarity by getting rid of taboos. He takes language that's already popular at the level of talk radio, reality TV, social media, and sports bars, and uses it at the highest level of power." "Trump isn't the kind of strongman who orders his followers to commit acts of violence," as we normally think. *"He's like a boy who starts tossing matches near a gasoline spill to see what happens.* He rouses ugly emotions and lets the chips fall, in the belief that he'll come out on top."[2]

We have observed that as the identification of the coronavirus with Asia, particularly China, intensified, attacks against China have also intensified and the US pivot in the Asia-Pacific has become more pronounced. Along with the heightening of the coronavirus rhetoric against China, the US has also flexed its military muscles by conducting military exercises in the Asia-Pacific region. For those who have eyes to see, and ears to hear, this tells us that the coronavirus is not just a health issue, it is a geopolitical issue, or it has at the very least become a part of US geopolitics. If this is only a health issue, why escalate and intensify geopolitical conflict?

1. Nakamura, "Trump Sparks Backlash."
2. Packer, "The Left Needs a Language."

Any conflict or adversarial relations with nation-states abroad will have a corresponding effect on how the US relates to its ethnic minorities within. If the conflict is with Arab nations, Arab Americans would likely face discrimination and hate crimes. If the conflict is with an Asian country, Asian Americans would likely face discrimination and hate crimes. The Chinese Exclusion Act is one such example. Another example was at the onset of World War II when Japanese Americans were routed and placed in internment camps. It did not matter if they were US citizens.

While COVID-19 may be unprecedented, discrimination against Asians, which is often triggered by certain events, is not new and, therefore, not surprising. More particularly, it is not true that this is the first time that a disease or epidemic has been used against Asians. More than 100 years ago, the whites of North America (including Canada) had labeled Chinese people as "dangerous to the whites." They were consistently accused of being carriers of infectious diseases, such as syphilis, leprosy, and smallpox. For many years the recurring smallpox epidemics were erroneously blamed on Chinese.[3] The language of disease has been used effectively in North America as a tool of racism, discrimination, and global domination.

Given our highly racialized climate and the naming of the virus as a "Chinese virus," it is not a surprise that we are witnessing the heightening of discrimination against Asians in general and of Chinese in particular. If COVID-19 is an "Asian virus," a "kung flu," we should not be surprised that discrimination, racism, hate crime, and physical assault against Asians and Asian Americans are spiking in the US.

As if the not-so-novel coronavirus pandemic were not enough, recent events have only heightened our awareness of a pandemic that has been with us for a long time, a pandemic that has destroyed many lives over the years. Many have said that we are facing a double pandemic: COVID-19 and racism, which is undergirded by the ideology of white supremacy. This can be expressed in many ways: "There's COVID-19 and there's COVID-1619— the year when slavery came to America." Or, "corona is the virus, racism is the pandemic." I would like to add a third moniker, suggested by many, to make it a trinity of pandemics: the pandemic of stupidity. This "pandemic of stupidity" according to Dietrich Bonhoeffer, a theologian who participated in the assassination plot against Hitler, "is a more dangerous enemy of the good than malice. . . . Against stupidity we are defenseless."[4]

Exposing the longtime pandemic of white supremacy has triggered social upheaval that has raged like fire across the "land of the free and

---

3. Larsson, "Anti-Asian Racism during Coronavirus."

4. Bonhoeffer, "An Account," 43.

home of the brave." The social action has even been felt on foreign shores, including New Zealand, Australia, Great Britain, Canada, and Israel-Palestine. This is a mass movement whose fire is fueled by a long and haunting history of dehumanization and subjugation of black people, which has taken form most recently and prominently under the banner of Black Lives Matter. As a movement, Black Lives Matter gained impetus and momentum in recent months due to a spate of killings of blacks. In the few weeks following the killing of George Floyd, protests came in waves across the US and beyond, and smoke from burning buildings could be seen across the skies of the proud cities of our groaning and bleeding land. Along with the burning came rioting and looting.

What is disconcerting and troubling are the obstinate and vociferous voices of those who are focused on the manner of walking or method of protests, but have not really joined the protests, nor cared enough to listen well to the deep pain and suffering beneath the ocean of raging storms and waves. In the walking (social actions) we may sometimes miss the mark of our socio-moral ideals, but it is another matter entirely for critical self-satisfied onlookers to demand decency and politeness from people who have suffered for so long, when their social/racial status have given them the privilege of choosing whether or not to deal with the issue or pain.

Yes, there is rioting and looting, but we should not be distracted from addressing the deep roots of this social unraveling and uprising. I do not want to exhume the "skeletons in the closets" of "the land of the free and home of the brave," but I must remind us that the rioting is a symptom of centuries of oppression. The rioting did not come out of thin air. It emerged from the soil fertilized by a long history of systematized looting of the fruits of black labors and institutionalized racism. America has been suffering from the pandemic of white supremacy and racism long before this novel coronavirus pandemic.

The Pandemic and Ecological Connections

Beyond unveiling our precarious socio-economic and political situation, the pandemic has also unveiled our relationship with our ecosystem. Viruses of various kinds have always been in existence. They were here before us and will continue to exist after us. We cannot simply wish them away. Why at times they seem to emerge, become active and aggressive, and cause harm to human beings is something worth pondering.

Viruses of various kinds are a part of our earthly habitat. We share the same earth and for generations we have lived together in ways that allow us to flourish together. Yet, as part of our recorded history, we have known of times when the encounters between human beings and certain viruses had been lethal. Human intrusion and destruction of the natural habitats, oftentimes in the name of development and progress, may help explain the unleashing or spillover of the viruses from their natural habitat into a human population that does not have the natural defenses to fight it. As humans continue their activities through logging, mining, dam and road construction, the likelihood of contact between human populations and wildlife increases. Tropical forest edges are a major launch-pad for the encounter. When 25 percent of the original forest cover is lost, encounters between wildlife and human populations heightens.[5] While many of the viruses may not be harmful to other species of mammals, they may have lethal effects on human hosts. When this happens, an epidemic or pandemic is just waiting to happen.

Global trade for wildlife, both legal and illegal, is another phenomenon that must be considered when we think of the relationship between pandemics and the ecosystem. Some of the animals, such as bats, pangolin, civet, lizards, birds, snakes, etc., may end up in cages and on the dining tables of humans. Demands for exotic pets have created a lucrative industry. Although it may be a luxury for others, in some places bushmeat is one of the main sources of protein. To maintain tradition and market demand for alternative sources of protein, China has an extensive wildlife farming industry.[6] The way these animals are transported, the lack of health screening, the unsanitary warehouse conditions, and the lack of health protocols related to how these animals are distributed to the consumers all contribute to the spreading of viruses and diseases. Zoonotic diseases are, therefore, not a surprise.

Re-orienting Ourselves: What Is Our Compass and Ballast

Even though denial has continued, a rupture in the fabric of our lives is happening. I really hope that we look deeper into ourselves so we may know where we are and what has become of us. It is high time to find our compass and ballast so we may find our bearings and direction. Most of us are familiar with a compass, which helps us find our position and direction, but less so with ballast. Ballast is a heavy material that is placed in the hold of a ship or the gondola of a hot air balloon to enhance stability. Without good ballast, a ship could tip over. A fluorescent lamp also uses ballast to limit or

5. Dobson et al., "Ecology and Economics," 379–81.
6. Dobson et al., "Ecology and Economics," 379–81.

regulate the flow of electric current, which would otherwise be destructive. In short, ballast is for stability.

Without direction our lives would be like flotsam and jetsam in the ocean of history, floating willy-nilly wherever the ocean currents take us. "If one does not know to which port one is sailing, no wind is favorable," a saying attributed to the philosopher Seneca. No wind is favorable, indeed, for those who do not know their destination. Experienced sailors can help us find our location and direction; they can teach us how to use the compass to find our true north and destination. Those familiar with ship travel across the ocean, especially in stormy weather, will agree with this advice: find a spot where you can see out, such as on a deck with a view or through a porthole, and extend your sight to the horizon to get a wider perspective and a sense of balance.

I hope that we will use this time of crisis, along with Pope Francis, as "a time of choosing," and that people will use this as an opportunity to "choose what matters and what passes away, a time to separate what is necessary from what is not."[7] I hope we will make use of this opportunity for a soul-searching reflection about our lives. It is time to take personal stock about ourselves: who we are, where we have been, and where we are heading. We need to ask existential questions: What does the coronavirus reveal of our depths as human beings? What does the coronavirus pandemic say about who we are and what we ought to be? What threatens us and what gives us life and joy? What is it that should truly matter to us? What is it that we should truly care about?

No doubt, the pandemic has upended or turned our world upside down. Life, as we knew it, has come to a screeching or grinding halt. Important schedules got cancelled. If there was one thing that was never cancelled though, it was death. Some people we know or who were close to our hearts lost their lives, many, but not all, due to COVID-19. We could have wished for God to be gracious enough not to let the death of loved ones or friends happen during the pandemic, especially when we cannot gather for the wake nights to grieve, say our goodbyes, and celebrate the life of someone we cared about.

Suddenly we have come to the rude awakening of our vulnerability and the fragility of our lives. The coronavirus has reminded us of our impermanence and that we are not the masters of our lives and destiny. Much as we would like to chart a solid plan for our next steps, it is not within our power to predict and control everything, not even the length of our numbered days. When we are busy trying to accomplish what is in our

7. Giangravé, "Pope Francis Says."

next to-do-list, everything seems long except time. And, without noticing it, time tracks us down like a running grave.

I would like us to adopt David Brooks's questions, a *New York Times* columnist: Are you living for your résumé or for your eulogy? Are you spending so much time building your résumé virtues or eulogy virtues?[8]

Résumé virtues are career driven. They are the ambitious side of us. We need them in order to boost our credentials and our marketability. They help us find a job. Eulogy virtues, on the other hand, are the legacy virtues. As we think about meaning and reason for being in the universe, we think about eulogy virtues. As we think about how fleeting life is and what we would like to leave behind for the next generation, we think of eulogy virtues. They are the eternal virtues that can withstand the passage of time. They are the virtues that cannot be lost in a shipwreck. Now, I encourage us to make a personal inventory of our eulogy virtues.

Life is short and our days are numbered. In the words attributed to Mae West, "We only live once, but if we do it right, once is enough." We must learn to measure life not simply by the number of years that we have accumulated, but by the quality of our lives. Or, as someone said, "Life is not measured by the number of breaths, but by those moments that take your breath away." It is not that we are not aware of what truly matters, but we often postpone or reserve for the future—the beyond—that which truly counts. We make the future the repository of our noble impulses, while we busy ourselves today with "building more barns to house our bountiful harvest" (Luke 12:16–21). Instead of "getting a life" now, we are consumed by one dimension of life: by "what we do" (work and official function) rather than by "what we are" (kind, compassionate, generous, caring, etc.). To quote Joan Chittister, "What we *are* is reserved for the obituary. What we *do* determines the way we're identified now. Such a pity. It means that one part of us has consumed the rest of us—to the point where, far too often, we ourselves confuse the two and lose sight of the dimensions of our lives that really count."[9]

"Fool," the parable in Luke 12:16–21 rebukes the man who was consumed with building more barns to store his wealth, "this very night your soul will be required of you." All your accumulations will be nothing; you cannot bring them to your grave. It is basically saying, "make your priorities right." I could hear the parable saying, "Don't postpone what is important; don't postpone living; live abundantly, now!" If we have chosen our

---

8. Mead, "David Brooks's Search for Meaning"; Preece, "Resume Virtues vs. Eulogy Virtues."

9. Chittister, *Between the Dark and the Daylight*, 44–45.

priorities right, while always attentive to the mundane and daily chores, when our souls will be required of us, Martin Copenhaver said it well, "we will discover that we did not build all the barns we could have, but, with God's help, we did build an abundant life."[10] Building an abundant life is what really counts as the most meaningful and fulfilling life.

Are we living our lives fully, truly, and boldly? What have we done with our one wild and precious life? Are we losing our life so as to find it? We owe an answer to ourselves. We owe an answer to the generations who were here before us; we owe an answer to the generations who are coming after us. Our responsibility lies with how we live our lives in the present.

Who Are We?

If there is one important lesson that the coronavirus has taught us, it is that we must see ourselves in relation to others and to the world around us in a much richer way. It is teaching us of our deep connections. It is informing us that our fundamental attribute is not rationality, but relationality. What happens to us affects other human beings and nature. What happens to nature happens to humans. Our lives are intertwined even if we often behave as if we are isolated selves.

No matter how we deny it, resist it, or violate it, our fundamental reality is that we are interdependent. It is not that we are independent first and, in relationship, we become interdependent. It is not that we are individuals first, and community second. On the contrary, our fundamental reality is that we are a "community of interdependent beings." There is no life, no self, and no individual without this interdependence. It is only in the context of the web of life, which is characterized by interdependence, that we live, exist, flourish, or perish.

Relationship is constitutive of who we are and what we can become. Relationship, not rationality, is decisive to our humanity. Not all individuals have the ability to reason (at least in the way we commonly construe reason), as in the case of total mental disability, but we all relate to the web of life. René Descartes's human being, defined primarily in terms of thinking (*Cogito ergo sum*), must be transmuted into *Cognatus ergo sum* (I am related, therefore I am) and *Cognatus ergo summus* (I relate, therefore we are).[11]

Cognatus ergo summus finds resonance in the Bantu cultures of Africa in the phrase *umuntu ngamuntu ngabantu* (I am because we are, and because we are, I am). Desmund Tutu's "ubuntu" theology is rooted in the proverbial

10. Copenhaver, *Room to Grow*, 8.

11. Gonzalez, *Out of Every Tribe and Nation*, 74.

Xhosa expression *ubuntu ungamntu ngabanye abantu* (roughly translated, "each individual's humanity is ideally expressed in relationship with others").[12] These sayings from various cultures make the point that we can only be human through relationship with other human communities.

We must, however, extend this relationship to other species and the whole ecosystem. The Lakota phrase *mitakouye oyasin* ("for all my relations") articulates in a profound way the intrinsic relationship of all creatures. The relationship is not simply extrinsic but intrinsic: the wellbeing of the ecosystem is our well-being because our very being is intrinsically one with it. When we say we are because of our relationship, we should not forget, as George Tinker reminds us, our relationships beyond the two-leggeds, which includes the "four-leggeds, the wingeds, and the living-moving-things."[13]

If being in relation is what constitutes who we are, then it is also what makes us truly an image of God. Relationship is the primary lens through which we interpret the notion of the image of God. We see the image God most profoundly when our relationship reflects life-giving relations. Conversely, the image of God construed in a relational framework presupposes what God is like: The very essence of God is "to be in relation." God is the web of life-giving relation. This recognition that God's very being is "to be in relation" challenges us to rethink seriously about the relations not only of human beings, but all of reality.

We can find our humanity only in the context of relationship, not outside of it. If relationship makes us, it also breaks us. In this case, relationship as such is not a sufficient category. Many expressions of relationship are destructive—not life-giving. This is especially so under the present condition of unjust social ordering, which is hierarchical, anthropocentric, androcentric, classist, sexist, and racist. Insights from eco-justice perspectives tell us that the dominant way of construing the human is not congruent with the web of life.

We must articulate the gestalt or shape of relationship that makes us truly human. What is the gestalt or shape of the relationship that makes us truly human?

Broadly, relationship must take the shape of harmony, justice, and mutuality among intrinsically interdependent beings. The *Kanaka Maoli* (native Hawaiian) word *pono* conveys profoundly the meaning of harmony: justice, righteousness, balance, and right relation. Harmony exists when there is justice or righteousness and mutuality (balanced relation) among creatures. Following Hawaii's state motto: "The life of the land is perpetuated

---

12. Battle, *Reconciliation*, 39.

13. Tinker, "An American Indian Theological Response to Ecojustice," 158.

in righteousness" (*Ua Mau ke Ea o ka Ai Aina ka Pono*). Justice and mutuality are critical hermeneutical lenses through which we must view and evaluate harmony and order in a social context.

If we are to pursue this matter further, we must ask, what does mutuality and order look like? What is harmonious mutual relationship among intrinsically interdependent beings?

Mutuality is characterized by mutual giving and receiving of self. This giving and receiving happens only in an atmosphere of openness, an openness to the gift of the other. In a mutual interaction, both participants come out affirmed and nourished. The individuality of each participant thrives in the process of mutual interaction. Each one becomes fully alive in the interactive process. Mutuality sustains life in a biocratic cosmos. Taking the gestalt of harmony, justice, and mutuality, we can say that the relationship among beings in the web of life can be summed up as one right/just relation. Well-being and shared flourishing happen only as right relationship exists within the web of life.

Given the fundamental reality of our intrinsic interdependence within the web of life, I would like to pose these questions: How are we exercising our self-agency as individuals and our collective agency as a people in relation to our fragile and interdependent world, or in relation to the "web of life" into which we all are woven? Does our exercise of self-agency as an independent nation contribute to our "shared flourishing?" Are we exercising our national self-agency in the direction of "common good," not only within our national borders or our tribe, but also across the seas to other lands with people whose hearts are beating with hopes and dreams as true and high as ours? With the threat of the coronavirus in mind and our vision of shared flourishing, I suggest that we reframe our question from, "How shall we exercise our freedom unhampered?" to the question, "How are we for and with each other in our highly globalized, interdependent, and vulnerable world?" "*What is the most loving and caring thing to do?*"

Practices for Becoming the Better Versions of Ourselves

Understanding who we are, our plight, and how we are responding to our situation, especially in a moment of crisis, such as the coronavirus pandemic, is critical as we imagine moving forward to become the better versions of ourselves. What follows are some of my thoughts, which I hope will be helpful in guiding us in our journey.

Gratitude

Gratitude is a fundamental stance in life that we need to assume to chart our way to our desired new tomorrow and in becoming the better versions of ourselves. It is not easy to speak of gratitude in this time of pandemic because gratitude is often associated with having received something delightful. It is not easy to speak of gratitude at a time when some feel they are more loved by God and more blessed for having been spared from the deadly virus while others have become unfortunate casualties.

Do we know how to be grateful without feeling "spiritually high" or privileged at the expense of others who are suffering, grieving, and mourning?

Whatever our situation is, coronavirus or none, life is an instance of grace, yes, sheer divine grace. Our very existence is an instance of grace. It has been there long before we have asked for it, long before we have invoked it.

What is the most fitting response to grace? There is no other most fitting response to grace than gratitude. Like sky and earth, grace and gratitude are intertwined. The theologian Karl Barth wrote that grace and gratitude "belong together like heaven and earth. Grace evokes gratitude like the voice of an echo. Gratitude follows grace like thunder [follows] lightning."[14]

Gratitude makes a difference in how we see life in relation to others. Christine Pohl said it well: "When our lives are shaped by gratitude, we're more likely to notice the goodness and beauty in everyday things. We are content; we feel blessed and are eager to confer blessing. We are able to delight in the very existence of another human being."[15] Our failure to appreciate and delight in the gifts of others is what Pohl calls "spiritual pornography." "Spiritual pornography takes many forms," says Pohl, "but its saddest results are the incapacity to appreciate small gifts and the tendency to trample fragile expressions of beauty and goodness."[16]

Gratitude changes the way we see and relate to the world around us. It helps us see the dawn even as the darkness still hovers the horizon. Gratitude helps us hear its arrival even before we see it. It helps us to be more receptive, first to the slight tweets of birds and then to the increasing melody of their chirps and peeps. "The birds know, as we sometimes do," says Mary Jo Leddy, "that the light does not dawn because of our singing. We sing

---

14. Barth, *CD* 4/1:41–42.

15. Pohl, *Living into Community*, 22.

16. Pohl, *Living into Community*, 22.

because the dawn appears as grace."[17] The presence of grace in our lives makes us sing even as the daybreak is still in the distant horizon.

Do we want to be joyful? We must practice gratitude. It is gratitude that makes us joyful. In the order of being, it is not joy that makes us grateful; rather, it is gratitude that makes us joyful. When grace makes us sing while waiting for the dawn, we can say that joy has found a dwelling place in us. More than happiness, joy is our ability to smile and sing even through our tears, even as dark clouds still hover above us.

Joanna Macy and Chris Johnstone speak of the four attributes of gratitude: (1) promotes a sense of well-being, (2) builds trust and generosity, (3) antidote to consumerism, and (4) motivates us to act for the world.[18] When our lives are shaped by gratitude, we are more likely to notice the gifts of others and delight in fragile expressions of goodness and beauty. When we are truly grateful, we are more likely to confer blessings on others and offer extravagant generosity. And, when we are grateful, we are more likely to give back to the world in as many ways as we can for its well-being.

Naming and Honoring Our Pain

Naming and honoring our pain is crucial for our journey toward a new and better tomorrow. Without the courage to name and honor our pain, we are without words to articulate our deepest joys and soaring hopes. To move forward is not to forget, but to remember the dismembered and exhume the skeletons in our closets so we can be accountable and responsible. There is no healing without naming and honoring our pain. There is no joy without raising our laments to the heavens. Conscious or unconscious, denial of our pain fosters a sense of futility and only mires us deeper into our miserable condition. It throws us into the role of helpless victims, which robs us of our power to proactively respond to the situation.[19]

When the Zen master, Thich Nhat Hanh, was asked what we need to do to save the world, his reply was simple yet profound: "What we most need to do is to hear within us the sounds of the Earth crying."[20] When we welcome the pains of the world into our lives and experience them, the *world will be feeling through us*. Moreover, "when we think of ourselves as interconnected

17. Leddy, *Radical Gratitude*, 39.
18. Macy and Johnstone, *Active Hope*, 43–56.
19. Macy and Brown, *Coming Back to Life*, 34.
20. Quoted in Macy and Brown, *Coming Back to Life*, 91.

parts of a larger web of life, just as we may feel the Earth crying within us, perhaps we can experience the *Earth dreaming within us too.*"[21]

As we see and feel the plight of the people, especially the least among us, and that of our fragile ecosystem, I would be surprised if we would not be heartbroken. What we see and hear will break our heart. But what "breaks our heart" does not have to be fatal. When we honor our pain for the world, we will be brokenhearted, but not necessarily "broken apart." Instead of being "broken apart," our hearts will be "broken open."[22] When our hearts are broken open our capacity to receive the world's pain is expanded and deepened.

With ears wide open, our hearts will be broken open and claimed by the groaning and sighing of our suffering people. Not only will we develop large ears, but we will also acquire large hearts, hearts as large as the world, and hearts that break down the walls of divisions and hostilities. And, with hearts as large as the world, we cannot help but be claimed by the misery that has befallen our people, and we cannot prevent the deluge of tears from rumbling down our face. We would be like Jeremiah of the Hebrew Bible, who, if his "head were a spring of water" and his "eyes a fountain of tears," he would weep day and night for the slain of his people (Jer 9:1).

Like Jesus who shed tears at the beginning of his ministry, we too, have to shed tears because of the many deaths that humanity has to die: a death to a false understanding of power and authority, a death to false methods and means, a death to false goals and measurements of success, and a death to false expectations and hopes.[23] As Jesus wept and shed tears, we too, are to weep and let our tears flow with those who labor so much and yet get so little, weep and shed tears for the failure of our world to nurture peace. When the world's cry and ours become one, we are learning the heart of compassion.

Learning and Practicing Compassion

Literally, the word compassion means, "to suffer from the bowels." It is an expression that comes out of our depth. It also suggests space. In reference to God, it suggests the spaciousness of God's heart or the breadth of divine love. To exercise compassion is to say, "There is a space in myself for you." My heart is spacious enough to welcome your fears, your hopes,

---

21. Macy and Johnstone, *Active Hope*, 175.

22. Palmer, *Healing the Heart of Democracy*, 1–27.

23. Hunter, *Desert Hearts and Healing Fountains*, 67.

and dreams. My heart is deep and wide enough to embrace your pain and your deluge of tears.

Compassion is at the heart of the major religious traditions of the world. Jews, Christians, and Muslims share this main tenet.[24]

We cannot claim Christ-like faithfulness with authenticity without manifesting compassion. Compassion is a crucial mark of what it means to be Christlike, the one who defied the gods of indifference and power in the tradition of Prometheus who, upon seeing the plight of humans, took some fire from the altar of heaven and brought it down to the human race that they might be enlightened and warmed. When Zeus found out that Prometheus had shown compassion, he was punished and chained to a rock with vultures eating endlessly at his insides.[25]

To be Christlike is to be compassionate, as Jesus was. Compassion is at the core of our Christian faith. When Jesus saw a large crowd following him, harassed and helpless like sheep without shepherd, he had *compassion on them* (Matt 9:36). When, after his retreat, he went ashore and saw a great crowd, he had *compassion and cured their sick and gave them food to eat* (Matt 14:13–21). When two blind men sitting by the roadside in Jericho begged for mercy and recovery of their sight, Jesus, *moved with compassion, touched their eyes and they regained their sight* (Matt 20:34).

If compassion is at the core of the Christian faith, the same is true of other major religious traditions. Compassion is ecumenical and interfaith. This is not a surprise because compassion is at the heart of our humanity. There is nothing more ecumenical than what we share as human beings. "Love and compassion are necessities, not luxuries. Without them humanity cannot survive," says Dalai Lama. Compassion is not only the test of true religiosity; *it is what brings us to the presence of the Divine.* When we lose our compassion, we lose our humanity; finding compassion is finding our humanity. Compassion is one of the attributes of Allah, says the Quran. To exercise compassion is to be in the presence of God. It is compassion that brings us to Nirvana, says the Buddha. We may ask, why? Because when we become compassionate, we dethrone ourselves from the center of our world and put the other person there. And when we are liberated from our ego, our eyes will begin to see the Divine.[26]

You may be familiar with this story from "The Iliad," an epic poem attributed to the Greek poet Homer, which recounts some of the significant events of the final days of the Trojan War and the Greek's siege of the

---

24. Armstrong, "My Wish."

25. Claypool, *Stories Jesus Still Tells*, 106.

26. Armstrong, "My Wish."

city of Troy. In the war, a Trojan prince, Hector, killed Patroclus, Achilles's best friend. Achilles, the famous Greek warrior, went mad with grief, rage, and revenge. He killed Hector and mutilated his body and refused to give his body back to the family for burial which, in the Greek world, would mean that Hector's soul would continue to wander, eternally lost. Then one night, the elderly king of Troy, Priam, came to the Greek camp incognito and made his way to Achille's tent to ask for the body of his son—Hector. Everyone was shocked as the old man took off his head cover. Achilles looked at him intently and thought of his father. Then he started to weep. Priam, the king of Troy, looked at the man who murdered so many of his sons and people and he, too, began to weep. *And the sound of their weeping filled the whole tent.* (The Greeks believe that weeping together creates a bond between people.) Then Achilles took the body of Hector and he handed it tenderly to the father, and the two men looked at each other, and *they saw the Divine in each other.*[27]

Do you want to see God? Exercise compassion. Be compassionate. Do you want to know God? Do justice, love kindness, and act compassionately.

It is not easy to be compassionate; it is much easier to be self-righteous and express pity for the misfortunes of others. A colleague of mine posted something on Facebook, which is both painful and humorous. It says, "Don't tell your problems to people; eighty percent don't care; and the other twenty percent are glad you have them." We can change the ratio and add a certain percentage for those who really care. But, without stretching it far, there is the tendency for people to feel good when others are in trouble because it allows them to feel more blessed than those who are suffering. Then they express pity for them. When we pity others, we feel good with ourselves.

Pity is not the simple equivalence of compassion. In compassion, the pain of the other is internally ours because we are fundamentally and internally related. We cannot say to our tooth, I do not care if you are aching, because it is not I who is aching. The pain of others is our pain. The delight of others is our delight.

What does compassion look like? To appropriate the lines attributed to St. Augustine, "It has the hands to help others. It has the feet to hasten to the poor and needy. It has eyes to see misery and want. It has the ears to hear the sighs and sorrows of [humanity and creation]. That is what [compassion] looks like."[28]

But there is also another face of compassion. Contrary to common and superficial perceptions, acting compassionately demands prophetic boldness.

27. Armstrong, "My Wish."
28. Cited in Ramos, "Saint Augustine's 'Confessions.'"

Do we want to be compassionately caring? If so, we must be prophetically bold. Do we want to be boldly prophetic? We must be compassionately caring. Without compassion, prophetic boldness is *arrogant self-righteousness.* Without prophetic boldness, compassion is *oppressive niceness.*

We must exercise our prophetic boldness and compassionate presence with the larger public in mind. Speaking to a gathered group Dr. Yvonne Delk said: "You *are not just a pastor to your congregation; you are a pastor to your community. . . . Your church pays you to be a pastor to the community. They don't know it yet, so you have to teach that to them!*"[29]

In the context of oppression, acting compassionately demands that we speak and act with prophetic boldness. In the face of continuing violation and systemic oppression, loving boldly and prophetically takes the form of social justice. "Never forget," philosopher-activist Cornel West reminds us, "that justice is what *love looks like* in public." Compassion demands more than charity in the face of systemic oppression. "Faith-based charity provides crumbs from the table; faith-based justice offers a place at the table," says Bill Moyers.[30]

Choosing the way of compassion can be threatening, but it is a path worth taking if we are to rekindle the fire that will illuminate the dark, purgatorial night that leads to the daybreak of our new tomorrow. It can be threatening because it demands speaking truth to power and exposing its death-dealing schemes. Choosing the path of compassion can be threatening because it is subversive. It is subversive because it is a seedbed of a new tomorrow. When we honor our pain for the world, it claims our whole being and calls us to imagine a different world, one that is just and compassionate. When we let the pain and the groaning make a claim on us, we cannot help but muster all the creative energies that we have to give birth to a new and better tomorrow. Compassion allows us to face the painful reality lovingly, but it refuses to be imprisoned by the painful and ugly reality. Rather, it sees the world from the perspective of beauty, possibility, and life-giving in the midst of a precarious situation.

Embracing the Gift of Vulnerability

Contrary to common misconception, acceptance of our vulnerability is not a sign of weakness but a mark of strength. But it can only be a sign of strength or a gift if it is befriended. It requires strength and courage to befriend vulnerability. When not befriended, vulnerability can be dangerous

---

29. Cited in Premawardhana, "Public Ministry in a World of Many Faiths," 164.
30. Moyers, Foreword to Wallis, *Faith Works*, xvii.

and it can easily slide into the slope of paralyzing fear. When we are fearful, worse things are likely to happen. When we are afraid, our default is self-protection. When we are uncertain and afraid, hearts constrict and moral imagination shrinks. We construct walls of fear and division. We convert instruments of peace into instruments of war.

In times when people are feeling scared, we need to be extra alert. Fear makes people feel extremely vulnerable and their fears can easily be manipulated for hideous purposes. Some politicians have learned the art of stoking fears among the already scared populace, weaponizing fear to their advantage. If you can keep people afraid and give them an enemy to scapegoat, they would be more than willing to do almost anything. They would be willing to surrender their rights in the name of security. After all, as it has been argued, "what are human rights if you don't have human life." This is a common playbook of authoritarian regimes around the world.

We cannot trust without being vulnerable. If we are not vulnerable, there is no real trust. As Brené Brown puts it, "We need trust to be vulnerable, and we need to be vulnerable to trust."[31] To trust is to put ourselves in a vulnerable situation. Vulnerability tempts us to embrace hollow and deceptive forms of security. In Luke 9:3, we have Jesus instructing his disciples to "take nothing for the journey." This is an exercise in vulnerability as well as of trust and dependence. The beauty of vulnerability and insecurity is that we are called to relearn trust and dependence on God. If God provides for the sparrows and the lilies of the field, God will do the same for humans and other creatures. Moreover, vulnerability challenges us to relearn trust and dependence upon each other.

Befriending vulnerability strengthens our ability to care, not only for ourselves, but for others as well. When we befriend it, we learn to relate to others not always from the standpoint of power and privilege, but from the understanding that we could one day be the receiver of care. When we embrace the posture that we could be the receiver of care, we are more likely to help create and advocate fiercely for a system in which the most vulnerable members of our society receive the care that they need.[32]

Uncertainty and Intentionality

Compounding our sense of vulnerability is the sense of uncertainty. It is difficult to live with uncertainty. We want certainty so we can control and predict outcomes. This, we think, is the road to a comfortable life. If we

31. Brown, *Dare to Lead*, 30.
32. Fernandez, *Burning Center, Porous Borders*, 279.

really pursue this path, I can only imagine how un-exciting this life would be. "What if," along with Lissa Rankin, "living a meaningful, fulfilling life is about recognizing that there is something beyond comfort and certainty, that uncertainty is the gateway to possibility?"[33]

Preparing for what is uncertain is a challenge because it is a moving target, but something positive can also come out of us when we are in this situation. Let us take the following example: If we watch a basketball game and the score of our team is so far ahead of the other team that we can already predict the winner, we would likely not pay much attention to the game anymore. In fact, as we have observed watching basketball games, those in the stadium would start leaving even before the game is over. What is it that keeps our eyes glued to the ball when watching a closely matched basketball game? It is *uncertainty*. It is a toss-up!

Uncertainty wakes us up and engages our full attention. When there is uncertainty and unpredictability, we observe our surroundings keenly. Uncertainty makes us alert and attentive. All our senses are maximized to support our full attention. We can learn from the martial artists: the elegant poise of a martial artist expresses a state of readiness.

Having befriended vulnerability, given disciplined attention to what is before us even in the midst of uncertainty, and in light of our dreams and longings, we are adding "intentionality" to our decisions and actions. Attention, guided by our dream of a new and better tomorrow, leads to "intentional actions" that seek to transform a given reality into a new reality. Intentional actions that have honored the pain of the past and are lured by the promise of a new tomorrow, do not simply accept a given reality as it is or as the way things are. Something may not exist in the present picture, but it does not mean that the possibility is not there.[34]

To use the famous lines of George Bernard Shaw, "You see things and you say why? But I dream things that never were; and I say, why not?" Another way of putting it, to adopt William Lee Miller's lines, "high politics is *not* the art of the possible; it is the art of enlarging what is possible and making what has heretofore been impossible come in the range of what can be considered [possible]."[35]

Active intentionality sees the bleak reality of how things are now, but does not end there. The choices we make influence what happens next based on our vision. Our vision of a new world will not arrive by a simple wishing upon a star, but it is the result of our "intentional" as well "connectional"

33. Rankin, *The Anatomy of a Calling*, 152.
34. Macy and Johnstone, *Active Hope*, 8.
35. Quoted in Hessel, *Social Ministry*, 163.

actions of transformation. Together—through our connections—we can accomplish even more and make a difference.

Bibliography

Armstrong, Karen. "My Wish: The Charter for Compassion." *TED*, February 2008. https://www.ted.com/talks/karen_armstrong_my_wish_the_charter_for_compassion?language=en.

Barth, Karl. *Church Dogmatics*. 4/1: *The Doctrine of Reconciliation*. Edited G. W. Bromiley. Edinburgh: T. & T. Clark, 1956.

Battle, Michael. *Reconciliation: The Ubuntu Theology of Desmond Tutu*. Cleveland: Pilgrim, 1997.

Bonhoeffer, Dietrich. "An Account at the Turn of the Year 1942–1943." In vol. 8 of *Letters and Papers from Prison*, edited by John W. de Gruchy, 37–52. Minneapolis: Fortress, 2010.

Brown, Brené. *Dare to Lead: Brave Work, Tough Conversations, Whole Hearts*. New York: Random House, 2018.

Chittister, Joan. *Between the Dark and the Daylight: Embracing the Contradictions of Life*. New York: Image, 2015.

Claypool, John. *Stories Jesus Still Tells: The Parables*. Boston: Cowley, 2000.

Copenhaver, Martin. *Room to Grow: Meditations on Trying to Live as a Christian*. Grand Rapids: Eerdmans, 2015.

Dobson, Andrew P., et al. "Ecology and Economics for Pandemic Prevention." *Science* 369.6502 (2020) 379–81. https://www.science.org/doi/full/10.1126/science.abc3189.

Fernandez, Eleazar. *Burning Center, Porous Borders: The Church in a Globalized World*. Eugene, OR: Wipf & Stock, 2011.

Giangravé, Claire. "Pope Francis Says 'We Are All in the Same Boat,' during Urbi et Orbi Ceremony." *Religion News Service*, March 27, 2020. https://religionnews.com/2020/03/27/pope-francis-only-together-we-can-do-this-during-extraordinary-indulgence-ceremony/.

Gonzalez, Justo. *Out of Every Tribe and Nation: Christian Theology at the Ethnic Roundtable*. Nashville: Abingdon, 1992.

Hall, Douglas John. *Why Christian? For Those on the Edge of Faith*. Minneapolis: Fortress, 1998.

Hessel, Dieter. *Social Ministry*. Rev. ed. Philadelphia: Westminster, 1992.

Hunter, Victor. *Desert Hearts and Healing Fountains: Gaining Pastoral Vocational Clarity*. Cleveland: Pilgrim, 2003.

Larsson, Paula. "Anti-Asian Racism during Coronavirus: How the Language of Disease Produces Hate and Violence." *The Conversation*, March 31, 2020. https://theconversation.com/anti-asian-racism-during-coronavirus-how-the-language-of-disease-produces-hate-and-violence-134496.

Leddy, Mary Jo. *Radical Gratitude*. Maryknoll, NY: Orbis, 2002.

Macy, Joanna, and Molly Young Brown, *Coming Back to Life: Practices to Reconnect Our Lives, Our World*. Gabriola Island: New Society, 1998.

Macy, Joanna, and Chris Johnstone. *Active Hope: How to Face the Mess We're in without Going Crazy*. Novato, CA: New World Library, 2012.

Mead, Rebecca. "David Brooks's Search for Meaning." *New Yorker*, May 27, 2015. https://www.newyorker.com/culture/cultural-comment/david-brookss-search-for-meaning.

Moltmann, Jürgen. *The Source of Life: The Holy Spirit and the Theology of Life.* Translated by Margaret Kohl. Minneapolis: Fortress, 1997.

Nakamura, David. "With 'Kung Flu,' Trump Sparks Backlash over Racist Language—And a Rallying Cry for Supporters." *Washington Post*, June 24, 2020. https://www.washingtonpost.com/politics/with-kung-flu-trump-sparks-backlash-over-racist-language--and-a-rallying-cry-for-supporters/2020/06/24/485d151e-b620-11ea-aca5-ebb63d27e1ff_story.html.

Packer, George. "The Left Needs a Language Potent Enough to Counter Trump." *The Atlantic*, August 6, 2019. https://www.theatlantic.com/ideas/archive/2019/08/language-trump-era/595570/.

Palmer, Parker. *Healing the Heart of Democracy: The Courage to Create a Politics Worthy of the Human Spirit.* San Francisco: Jossey-Bass, 2011.

Pohl, Christine D. *Living into Community: Cultivating Practices That Sustain Us.* Grand Rapids: Eerdmans, 2012.

Preece, David. "Resume Virtues vs. Eulogy Virtues." *YouTube*, January 6, 2020. https://www.youtube.com/watch?v=gQNqlvKYYME.

Premawardhana, Shanta. "Public Ministry in a World of Many Faiths." In *Teaching in a Multifaith World*, edited by Eleazar S. Fernandez, 163–78. Eugene, OR: Pickwick Publications, 2017.

Ramos, Silvana. "Saint Augustine's 'Confessions': 11 Essential Quotes on the Christian Life." https://catholic-link.org/11-quotes-saint-augustine-essential-for-our-christian-life/.

Rankin, Lissa. *The Anatomy of a Calling: A Doctor's Journey from the Head to the Heart and a Prescription for Finding Your Life's Purpose.* New York: Rodale, 2015.

Tinker, George E. "An American Indian Theological Response to Ecojustice." In *Defending Mother Earth: Native American Perspectives on Environmental Justice*, edited by Jace Weaver, 153–76. Maryknoll, NY: Orbis, 1996.

Wallis, Jim. *Faith Works: Lessons from the Life of an Activist Preacher.* New York: Random House, 2000.

Web Editors. "Voice of the Day: Bill Moyers." *Sojourners*, May 21, 2009. https://sojo.net/articles/voice-day-bill-moyers.

6

COVID-19 and Traumatic Stress

—AHYUN LEE AND ROLF R. NOLASCO JR.

THE PIVOT TO EMERGENCY remote learning because of COVID-19 has catapulted us as faculty into unfamiliar territory. The glaring opportunity to exercise theological imagination has been eclipsed by the urgency to provide a different kind of presence and pedagogy amidst fear and uncertainty that enveloped the world at the height of the pandemic. The affective labor exacted from this abrupt shift had to be suspended in favor of recalibrating how courses are delivered. In a way, we have operated on "survival mode," a typical response upon exposure to a traumatizing event. With the tumult of the Spring semester on our rearview, we are now confronted with the trauma residue that was momentarily deferred.

And all this came to a head very early on in the Fall semester. With the rhythm of a new academic year in full display, an unremitting sense of anxiety followed me a like shadow. Having woken up from a restless sleep the previous night, which has become a common occurrence these days, I laid in the bed almost immobilized, disoriented and awash in sadness and grief. The psychological hazard brought by the pandemic of COVID-19 has finally hit me with such intensity, and the shadow of fear and anxiety continues to loom large, casting doubt and uncertainty of a better tomorrow and a return to the familiar.

I remember vividly a faculty meeting where I was asked to pray for my family and friends when the COVID virus rapidly spread in Asia around the middle of January. At that time, nobody imagined that the COVID virus would spread over the Pacific Ocean, would impact them, or that they would experience the threat of a pandemic virus around the globe. Everything shifted so quickly after the World Health Organization (WHO) officially declared the novel coronavirus (COVID-19) a pandemic on March 11, 2020. In a month, the total number of the COVID-19 cases was almost over two million with over 120,000 deaths globally.[1] There was a rapid shift of everyday life interaction because of fear of catching the virus and the uncertainty of "being back to normal."

I am sure by the time you read this, and in varying degrees, we all have been impacted by the devastating effects of COVID-19. Many lives have been lost or sacrificed, and many more lives are teetering along or have already suffered from unemployment, financial hardships, food insecurity, and unresolved and complicated grief. Given that our body, mind, and spirit are intricately woven, what ails in the physical realm as a result of this pandemic evokes psychological and mental reactions that can take a life of its own, and often for the worse, if not attended to.

This short event reveals that the COVID-19 outbreak has become a traumatic experience, and persons and communities experiencing traumatic stress are neither sick nor bad but injured.[2] Lenore Terr, a child psychiatrist, explains that trauma occurs "when a sudden, unexpected, overwhelming, intense emotional blow or a series of blows assaults the person from outside. Traumatic events are external, but they quickly become incorporated into the mind."[3] People experience psychological trauma when it is too much to deal with and it is hard to address, identify and process. Judith Herman, a pioneering researcher of trauma, says "traumatic events . . . overwhelm the ordinary human adaptations to life."[4] Simply, trauma is not merely about an overwhelming event that is considered outside the range of human experience. Its salience lies in its impact on self and others that is often described as totalizing. Our care, connection, and meaning-making system are all shattered into pieces, rendering us more precarious and vulnerable to further psychic and collective injury. At the same time, trauma's immediate impact is on our material and physical body, hence, any intervention or healing pathways must start with the body.[5]

But before we discuss this any further, it is important to lift up the "politics of trauma" that often underlie and remain unspoken in trauma discourse. That is, the deployment and reception of trauma narratives are often locked within an existing power relation.[6] This means that some trauma narratives

1. Dong et al., "An Interactive Web-Based Dashboard."
2. Bloom, *Restoring Sanctuary*, 5.
3. Terr, *Too Scared to Cry*, 8.
4. Herman, *Trauma and Recovery*, 33.
5. Menakem, *My Grandmother's Hands*, 39.
6. Pratt, "Filipino Migrant Stories and Trauma," 84.

are headline worthy, evoking strong empathic reception, and, in the process, make judgments about whose lives and traumas are worth intervening in or grieving while others are silenced, even thrown into oblivion.[7] When the pandemic reached its peak, it was common knowledge that COVID-19 was infecting and killing Americans, but data on social inequality and economic disparities experienced directly by communities of color during this critical time was not considered "headline worthy."

This only drives home the point that trauma discourse is situated within personal and collective histories of oppression and injury, such that the high rates of COVID deaths among Black and Hispanic communities are directly related to a history of socio-economic inequities and inequalities in this country. Hence, the unremitting assault towards marginalized bodies, whose lives and traumas are not considered as grievable and therefore subjected to further subjugation and trauma, is a form of slow social death, a socially sanctioned mechanism for racial extinction.

As well, the deployment of trauma discourse, though a potent medium for dialogue and collective action, carries certain risks. That is, there is a tendency to go by familiar patterns of who tells and receives stories of trauma, which can re-inscribe and forge further hierarchies of privilege and marginalization.[8] The privileged listen and empathize and the marginalized or subjugated experience and tell.[9] In this manner, empathic connection may not be what we are aiming for but "empathic unsettlement,"[10] as a way to express solidarity and action with those "othered" because of marked difference. With that as a backdrop, understanding the COVID-19 outbreak as a traumatic experience brings to our attention the psychological responses to this abrupt and uncertain event. Trauma involves three parts, including what a traumatic event is, how persons and communities experience the event as threatening and damaging, and how their trauma reactions affect the daily function and interactions. The Substance Abuse and Mental Health Services Administration (SAMHSA) provides the following definition of trauma.

> Individual trauma results from an event, series of events, or set of circumstances that is experienced by an individual as physically or emotionally harmful or life-threatening, and that has lasting adverse effects on the individual's functioning and mental, physical, social, emotional, or spiritual well-being.[11]

7. Butler, *Precarious Life*, 20.

8. Pratt, "Filipino Migrant Stories and Trauma," 84.

9. Pedwell, *Affective Relations*, 10.

10. Pedwell, *Affective Relations*, 15.

11. SAMHSA, "Concept of Trauma," 7.

This definition, which could very well be extended to communities, highlights the pandemic of the novel coronavirus as a traumatic life event, which leads to all different kinds of psychological symptoms, such as anxiety and stress, by the overwhelming situations. Ali Jawaid, a researcher on the impact of traumatic events on the brain and other body organs, said, "After COVID-19 emerged, it quickly became evident that it would be a 'global traumatic event' of sorts. Within days of lockdowns, people started reporting all different kinds of psychological symptoms, from sleep disturbances to suicidal ideation."[12] People experience the pandemic of COVID-19 as emotionally and physically threatening event as they handle their fear of catching the virus and uncertainty about how the COVID-19 outbreak will affect them socially, relationally, and economically, as well as how long they will have to deal with this.

The outbreak of COVID-19 is a complex and collective trauma. Jayne Lenard writes about trauma and points out physical and emotional symptoms of trauma in *Medical News Today*.[13] He provides several types of trauma, which include, (1) Acute Trauma as a single stressful or dangerous event, (2) Chronic Trauma as encountering repeated and prolonged exposures to highly stressful events, and (3) Complex Trauma as multiple traumatic events.

The outbreak of COVID-19 is a Complex Trauma. The threat is still unfolding and invisible. At the beginning of the COVID-19 pandemic, people had emotional and psychologically disruptive experiences with this single event. People have since faced prolonged exposure to the threat of virus infections, making COVID-19 a Chronic Trauma. The ongoing battle with COVID-19, and its requirements of quarantine, social distancing, and isolation in the global community impacts all areas of life such as human health, medical systems, the economy, global market, job industry, education, etc. The rate of domestic violence[14] and racial discrimination has risen rapidly[15] during this time of pandemic. People experience trauma as a result of the prolonged struggles of domestic violence, bullying, abuse, poverty, and racism. Thus, the outbreak of COVID-19 becomes a Complex traumatic experience fueled by multiple traumatic events such as social-cultural, political, and intergenerational conflicts, not just a single event. This leads to the accumulation of psychological distress, especially

---

12. Aten, "What to Do about the Mental Health Consequences of COVID-19."
13. Leonard, "What Is Trauma?"
14. Bettinger-Lopez, "A Double Pandemic."
15. Kingsland, "Racial Minorities."

developing Posttraumatic Stress Disorder (PTSD).[16] People feel over-whelmed, helpless, and experience difficulties in processing their traumatic emotions because of the complexity of the trauma.

The Institute of Trauma and Trauma-Informed Care (ITTIC), a part of the Buffalo Center of Social Research and University at Buffalo School of Social Work, articulated the impact of adversity and traumatic events on an individual level, which later was consistently confirmed by numer-ous studies on the psychological sequelae of COVID-19 in the general population.[17] The following is a cursory description of the extent in which COVID-19 impinges upon our daily lives based on ITTIC analytics: (1) impairment in motion regulation (e.g., having difficulty controlling our impulses, or failure to read our own emotional cues and those of others); (2) impairment in cognitive functioning (e.g., difficulty concentrating especially those working from home or doing school online); (3) impair-ment in physical and mental health (e.g., prolonged quarantine renders people, especially those with pre-existing conditions, more vulnerable to various diseases and illnesses, mental health challenges, substance abuse and self-harm behaviors); (4) impairment in perception and beliefs (e.g., becoming more fearful of the future, despairing over the unpredictability of the current situation, losing hope and trust in ourselves and others); and (5) impairment in relationships (e.g., taking out anger on those around us, aggressive in our ways of meeting our needs, and alienating those who may have the capacity to alleviate our situation).

On a neural level, the emotional stress induced by unremitting fear, uncertainty, and anxiety surrounding COVID-19 alters the inner workings of our sympathetic nervous system to a level that is detrimental to our phys-ical and psychological well-being.[18] The body's alarm system goes into high gear and never lets up, especially when exposed repeatedly to traumatizing events. Hence, we find persons constantly on high alert, disquieted, tense, and afraid. The physical body gets flooded with cortisol, a stress hormone, resulting in various physical ailments (e.g., increased blood pressure, com-promised immune system) and psychological maladies (e.g., depression, anxiety, substance abuse), as discussed below.

The outbreak of COVID-19 is also a Collective Trauma. Collective Trauma refers not only to its sudden influence on individuals but to the

16. Posttraumatic Stress Disorder means "a psychiatric disorder that can occur in people who have experienced or witnessed a traumatic event such as a natural disaster, a serious accident, a terrorist act, war/combat, rape or other violent personal assault." See APA, "What Is Posttraumatic Stress Disorder?"

17. See, e.g., Serafini et al., "The Psychological Impact of COVID-19," 531–37.

18. Bremner, "Traumatic Stress," 445.

serious and negative effects on entire communities and societies.[19] Richard Mollica, the author of the book, *Healing Invisible Wounds: Paths to Hope and Recovery in a Violent World*, writes about COVID-19 as a shared Collective Trauma that impacts all living beings.[20] Collective Trauma keeps impacting the self and others, the community people live in, and the world to which people relate. The Collective Trauma experienced with the outbreak of COVID-19 impacts the personal understanding of the self and changes relational experiences with others. Also, it challenges policies and governmental processes, alters society functions, and even shifts the social and cultural norms of safety.[21] This leads to having long-term effects on people's well-being. Complex and Collective Trauma reveal that people experience the outbreak of COVID-19 to be associated with singular, multiple, and enduring traumatic events. It means that trauma by the pandemic outbreak is a process encountering an event of COVID-19 or series of the COVID-19 related events and involving the individual and community's levels of vulnerability and resiliency.

The world breakout of COVID-19 as a Complex and Collective Trauma causes people to deal with mental health challenges because it affects their usual daily activities and their routines and everyday living with people and in the community. A study conducted in the US "investigated more than ten million Google searches and assessed the changes in mental health search queries after stay-at-home measures. Topics related to anxiety, negative thoughts, sleep disturbances, and suicidal ideation increased dramatically before stay-at-home orders with a leveling of the curve after implementation."[22] The traumatic stressors of the pandemic outbreak lead to an increase in cases of mental health concerns, including depression, suicide, substance uses, and self-harm, apart from other symptoms reported globally due to COVID-19.[23] How do people cope with or react to the threat of a pandemic outbreak as Complex and Collective Trauma? Although all mental challenges people experience will be different and subjective, there are some common survival mechanisms and psychological reactions, including the emotional, behavioral, cognitive, developmental, as well as cultural and social responses.

19. Erikson, *Everything in Its Path*, 154.

20. Mollicas, *Healing Invisible Wounds*.

21. Chang, "Living with Vulnerability and Resiliency."

22. Brooks et al., "The Psychological Impact of Quarantine."

23. Yao et al., "Patients with Mental Health Disorders."

Emotional

Fear and anxiety about a new virus such as COVID-19 and what could happen can be overwhelming and cause intense psychological distress. Traumatic stress from the outbreak of COVID-19 can evoke two emotional extremes between being overwhelmed and numbing. These are both natural emotional reactions to traumatic stress and anxiety. People may experience difficulty in regulating their emotions. People can feel a wide and ambiguous range of emotional responses to the pandemic outbreak. Immediate emotional reactions can include anger, anxiety, or severe fear, sadness, feeling unreal, feeling out of control, denial, and feeling overwhelmed.[24] It is possible for people to even encounter difficulty in recognizing and identifying any of these feelings.[25]

With long-term traumatic stress, people may find delayed emotional reactions, including irritability and/or hostility, depression, hopelessness, instability, anxiety, grief, shame, guilt, feelings of fragility, and vulnerability. A cross-sectional study of health-care workers conducted across several sites in China have found "that 50.4% of the sample reported symptoms of depression, 44.6% anxiety, 71.5% general distress, and 34.0% insomnia; prevalence estimates were elevated among frontline workers in Wuhan, China."[26] In the context of increasing total cases and deaths from COVID-19, feeling depressed, helpless, and numbness can also increase the risk of poor mental health.

Thus, clinical treatment of emotional reactions to the pandemic outbreak needs to help people recognize their emotional struggles as a natural response to stress and to regulate difficult emotions. So, people can learn new coping skills to tolerate emotional distress and disturbances.

Behavioral

People often engage in behaviors to manage the emotional intensity or distress aspect of the traumatic experiences of the COVID-19 outbreak. Bessel A. Van der Kolk writes on the relation of trauma to behavior: "Traumatized people chronically feel unsafe inside their bodies: The past is alive in the form of gnawing interior discomfort. Their bodies are constantly bombarded by visceral warning signs, and, in an attempt to control these processes, they often become expert at ignoring their gut feelings and in numbing awareness

---

24. Roth et al., "Complex PTSD in Victims."
25. SAMHSA, "Trauma-Informed Care," xvi–xix.
26. Lai et al., "Factors Associated with Mental Health Outcomes."

of what is played out inside. They learn to hide from their selves."[27] People tend to decrease the emotional tension and stress through avoidance behaviors, self-medicating through substance use of alcohol or drugs, compulsive behaviors such as overeating or obsessive cleaning, self-harm or self-destructive injurious behaviors like suicidal ideation. A systematic review of the mental health effects with the behavioral response found the increased use of alcohol and tobacco during the pandemic time.[28]

Also, because of the prolonged stress from continuously emphasizing handwashing, wearing masks, and social distancing, people may show maladaptive behaviors to mitigate coronavirus infections. People may show withdrawal, experience social relationship disturbances, and decreased activity level as the avoidance behaviors. M. A. Cava et al. researched the long-term behavioral changes after the quarantine period, such as vigilant handwashing and avoidance of crowds, and, for some, the return to normality was delayed by many months.[29] These avoidance behaviors relate to the anxiety and fear of catching the virus and lead to a behavioral need to avoid. People often shape their behavioral reactions from traumatic experiences. The clinical response to the behavioral reactions from the trauma of the COVID-19 outbreak is to learn the history of the traumatic stress and to recognize behavior reaction patterns. Then, it is crucial to take the step of unlearning the behavioral reactions through externalizing the consequences of behavioral changes and separating them from the associated behavioral symptoms.

Cognitive

Collective and Complex Trauma can affect cognitive responses to everyday life. The immediate cognitive reactions to the trauma of the COVID-19 outbreak can be difficulty concentrating, racing thoughts, distortion of time and space, and confusion in getting appropriate information. Also, there are possible delayed cognitive responses with post quarantine and prolonged social distancing practices. People tend to be preoccupied with traumatic events and experience difficulty in making decisions. People experience stress because of inadequate and poor information from public health authorities. Insufficient clear guidelines for protection lead to confusion about the rationale and the purpose of quarantines and wearing

27. Bessel, *The Body Keeps the Score*, 97.
28. Wu et al., "Alcohol Abuse/Dependence Symptoms."
29. Cava et al., "The Experience of Quarantine."

masks.[30] It causes people to fear the worst and affects cognition about the world or life assumptions that provide cognitive navigation to daily life.[31] The pandemic outbreak affects and alters belief, the world, and people. When you leave the house in the morning, you now think that the outside is not safe and that people are dangerous because some people may be infected, which could cause you to catch the virus. The belief you hold to take care of yourself and others is challenged. It can become confusing to believe that your efforts and intentions cannot protect yourself and your family from the virus which increases personal vulnerability. When people feel disempowered to respond to a serious threat, they experience a loss of agency and encounter a sense of powerlessness.

With the prolonged time of dealing with COVID-19, people's perception of safety has shifted and been challenged. This can lead to compensating behaviors (e.g., obsessive handwashing, withdrawal of social interactions, etc.) from traumatic experiences. The difficulty of the pandemic outbreak is the uncertainty of restoring and returning to the previous belief system after the pandemic outbreak, which may lead to a worldview that life and people are unsafe.

A. T. Beck et al. offers a cognitive triad model explaining three main cognitive patterns as a reaction of traumatic experiences:[32] (1) thoughts about the self, (2) the world (others/environment), and (3) the future. For example, people come to see themselves as damaged or powerless to protect themselves and others. It challenges their belief that others are safe people and the world is safe. Therefore, people see the future as hopeless because the virus is not going to disappear suddenly and will continue to be out there. So, the future will be dark. The three cognitive processes can greatly influence how people understand who they are. It can limit their ability to use their internal coping resources and seek external support from others and the world. These cognitive reactions to COVID-19 may become sustained and contribute to the development of depression and anxiety symptoms even after the pandemic outbreak ends. Understanding this cognitive pattern can be helpful protecting against debilitating psychological symptoms and reconstructing alternative and accessible cognitive patterns during and after the pandemic outbreak.

---

30. Brooks et al., "The Psychological Impact of Quarantine," 916.

31. Janoff-Bulman, *Shattered Assumptions*, 86.

32. Beck et al., *Cognitive Therapy of Depression*, 11.

Developmental

People respond to the stress of a pandemic such as the COVID-19 outbreak differently and uniquely. The COVID-19 outbreak brings attention to high-risk levels with the elderly. Also, with the various shifts of the COVID-19 symptoms, children are at high risk. The ways of responding to a traumatic experience are different, depending on the developmental stages.

Children before school age may display heightened arousal and confusion, generalized anxiety, nightmares, and physical symptoms, including stomachaches or headaches. At this age, children express traumatic stress through physical reactions.[33] School-aged children may exhibit physical, emotional, and cognitive reactions, including aggressive behavior and anger, regression of behavior, lack of concentration, and disturbed and worst academic performance in the online learning context.[34]

Adolescents may show some levels of depression and relational withdrawal. With the confusion and fears, they may display rebellion and increased risky activities such as sexual acting out or sleeping and eating disturbances.[35] Adults, including young and middle adults, may show sleep disturbances, increased agitation, isolation or withdrawal, depression, and the increased use of alcohol or drugs. Lastly, the elderly may experience increased withdrawal and isolation, loneliness, reluctance to leave home, worsening of chronic illnesses, confusion, depression, and fear.[36] Especially, social distancing and the quarantine increase the feelings of loneliness in settings like nursing care, hospice, or nursing homes, which quickly lead to high-risk factors for depression, anxiety disorders, and suicide.[37]

Social/Interpersonal

The pandemic outbreak of COVID-19 is Collective Trauma. It profoundly impacts all races, gender, class, health, etc. In interpersonal experiences, the fear of COVID-19 challenges us to discern whether someone can protect us or not. It leads to difficulty in connecting with people. People have to deal with the feeling that someone can be an asymptomatic person and precautions do not protect you. Fear of catching the virus can negatively affect supportive relationships during this time.

33. SAMHSA, "Trauma-Informed Care," xxviii.
34. Bartlett et al., "Resources for Supporting Children's Emotional Well-Being."
35. Hamblen, *PTSD in Children and Adolescents*.
36. Banerjee, "The Impact of COVID-19 Pandemic," 1–2.
37. CDC, "Coping with Stress."

On the other hand, there is the danger of social stigma and isolation. Even though someone has been in contact with a person with COVID-19 or is at risk, they are reluctant to get tested because of stigma. They are scared that they will be blamed or isolated from their neighbors or family. It often causes people not to seek appropriate support for their mental health challenges. Also, in the context of increasing access to online content, social media exposure increases fear, anxiety, and stress through the abundance of rumors and misinformation, which have not been proven or verified.[38] Feelings of isolation and lack of social interaction can increase the risk of poor mental health. Further, the fear in interpersonal experiences leads to the increased development of hate crimes, discrimination, and incidents against marginalized groups.

The outbreak of COVID-19 also severely affected the global economy and financial markets. Joseph Zeballos-Rorig, in an article in *Business Insider*, reported that more than ten million people applied for unemployment benefits during the last two weeks of March alone, and pointed out the struggle of state governments to respond to unemployment due to the massive surge of laid-off workers filing for benefits.[39] With a rise in the unemployment rate, Connor Perrett shared that the Department of Labor reported over 701,000 jobs had been lost between March and April. Of the unemployment rate, about 60 percent of those job losses were experienced by women according to the Institute for Women's Policy Research.[40] Under the global economic challenges and the threat of financial instability, women stand in a vulnerable position along with teenagers and the elderly.[41]

All racial, ethnic, gender and socioeconomic groups are differently impacted by the pandemic outbreak. Erin Einhorn, of NBC News, reported the higher risk of death of African Americans in Chicago, Milwaukee, Philadelphia, Detroit, and other cities. From Einhorn's report, 70 percent of people who died from COVID-19 in Chicago were black, even though the city›s population is just 30 percent Black. In Milwaukee County, which is 27 percent Black, the figure is 81 percent.[42] The death rate by COVID-19 is higher for nonwhites as they are vulnerable population.

Kat Stafford et al. shares:

> the AP nationwide report of COVID-19 related to racial breakdown analyzed with the gathering data from eight states, six

38. Denckla et al., "REACH for Mental Health," 2.

39. Zeballos-Rorig, "Here's Why Millions of Americans Are Struggling."

40. Perrett, "Nearly 60% of People."

41. Perrett, "Nearly 60% of People."

42. Einhorn, "African Americans May be Dying."

major U.S. cities, including New York City and the District of Columbia, and six of Florida's largest counties. The data collected ranges from New York to Illinois to Alabama to San Diego, California, and covers an area that represents 82 million Americans, nearly 43% of whom are nonwhite. Other minority groups' cases and deaths are fairly in line with their demographics, although those among Hispanic individuals in some hot spots are still high.[43]

The Henry J. Kaiser Family Foundation (2008), found that

> Minority Americans are much less likely to have health insurance offered through their jobs, and even after accounting for work status, minority Americans are still more likely than Whites to be uninsured. (At least 1 in 3 nonelderly Latinos (36%) and American Indian/Alaska Native (33%) are uninsured, as compared with 22% of African Americans, 17% of Asian and Pacific Islanders, and 13% of Whites.).[44]

The outbreak of COVID-19 shows the systemic problems of racial disparities and inequity in access to health care and economic opportunities in the United States, especially for people of color.

Lastly, racial minority groups, especially Asian American and African Americans, encounter COVID-19 related discrimination. According to NBC News, the online reporting forum *Stop AAPI Hate* said that since its inception on March 18, it has received more than 650 direct reports of discrimination, primarily targeting Asian Americans.[45] Anti-Chinese rhetoric like "Chinese virus" or "Kung Fu Virus" stirred up hate crimes, racism and discrimination, as well as xenophobia against Asians and the spread of misinformation.[46] COVID-19-related discrimination became overt in interpersonal experiences. Feeling discriminated against and targeted as the origin of the COVID-19 virus leads Asian Americans to experience high stress and anxiety. Even wearing a mask as a way of protecting themselves and others becomes a stressor by stereotyping Asian Americans as the origin for bringing COVID-19 to the community. James Kingsland said, "feeling discriminated against was associated with subsequent reports of mental distress."[47] Along with concerns of disease spread, social distancing, and financial stress,

---

43. Stafford et al., "Coronavirus."
44. KFF, "Eliminating Racial/Ethnic Disparities in Health Care."
45. See "Asian Americans Report."
46. Chung, "Asian Americans Report."
47. Kingsland, "Racial Minorities."

COVID-19-related discrimination negatively affects and increases the risk of mental health challenges such as anxiety and depression.

Our embodied lives, intertwined with other bodies, register and hold all sorts of affects crying out for release, acknowledgment, and sensitive accompaniment. A trauma-informed care may provide a soothing and creative burst that our bodies need and hunger for right now. At its fundamental level, trauma-informed care is about creating conditions for persons and communities to be aware, knowledgeable and have the practical wisdom regarding the prevalence and impact of trauma upon our life together.[48] The first line of intervention is taking a "universal precaution"[49] approach, which means assuming that all individuals, and more particularly those subjected to various forms of dehumanizing oppression, carry with them in their bodies and relations a history of unprocessed trauma, which then calls everyone to glove-up—to prioritize the well-being of each other—in order to reduce the possibility of triggering or re-traumatizing others. The challenge before us is how best to glove-up without re-inscribing hierarchy of power and privilege and pathologizing those dehumanized by this same hierarchy.

Anchoring ourselves in the five values and principles,[50] which guide trauma-informed care work on a communal or organizational level may provide the kind of enriched environment necessary for the protection and recovery of those injured by traumatic events. These five values or principles include, (1) safety, (2) trustworthiness, (3) choice, (4) collaboration, (5) and empowerment.

(1) Safety is about the provision of physical and emotional safety of all persons in our community. Ensuring physical safety is paramount given the transmissibility of COVID-19. Emotional safety is equally important. This means being attentive to signs of discomfort, to assess them in a trauma-informed manner, and to proactively check-in with them and provide psychological support as indicated. The attitude of non-judgment, hospitality, curiosity, and compassionate engagement and care also helps in creating this enriched environment.

(2) Trustworthiness is about striving to provide clear information and clarity about rules and expectations and processes. This also means ensuring and maintaining healthy, respectful, and professional boundaries, prioritizing and protecting privacy and confidentiality and follow-through on agreed plan of action.

---

48. ITTIC, "Trauma-Informed Organizational Change Manual," 24.

49. Bloom, *Restoring Sanctuary*, 29.

50. Harris and Fallot, *Using Trauma Theory*, 3–20.

(3) Choice involves ensuring that everyone has a voice, especially when determining actions that will impact people's lives and providing everyone clear and appropriate messages about rights and responsibilities. Trauma takes away orientation and control and giving people choice is critical to trauma recovery and healing.

(4) Collaboration is about creating conditions of doing and being with rather than doing to or for someone. This is about giving individuals and communities a pivotal role in planning and evaluating their care needs and conveying the message that they have agency and authorship in their own lives.

And lastly, (5) Empowerment, which pertains to acknowledging and building on individual and communal strengths and skills, of encouraging collective community organizing and power analysis so that in the process and mirroring Fanon's commitments to social liberation, we can release ourselves to become "collective political subjects" that work to destroy conditions that induce traumatic experiences.

As mentioned earlier, stress and anxiety are normal reactions to perceived and actual threat to bodily, relational, and social integrity. One of the ill-effects of COVID-19 is the pervasive sense of anxiety, of worrying about our health and those of our loved ones, of getting rattled by unemployment and financial insecurity, of being anxious around this new normal that feels rather unfamiliar and unsettling for many of us. This anxiety is a normal reaction to this unprecedented health crisis.

Bombarded by a never-ending news cycle of deaths and infections, this anxiety lingers and becomes a loud noise that intrudes into our daily living and then renders us almost paralyzed, on high alert, and on survival mode. This emotional state hijacks our ability to be calm, rational, and mindful in our responses to this health crisis. Worse, it compromises and weakens our immune system, signaling a fight-and-flight response that can induce deleterious effects on our way of being.

One of the ways to take back control (and which we have control over) is to listen to our body and pay attention to what it is saying to us. These moments of heightened anxiety are characterized by increased heart rate, rapid breathing, headache, sleep issues, fatigue, muscle tension, sweating, digestive troubles, which are often linked with catastrophizing thoughts and negative emotional valence.

When we experience this, I suggest the following intervention using the mnemonic BREATHE. B stands for breathing deeply, slowly, and calmly. This simple act of mindful breathing can activate our parasympathetic nervous system responsible for making us calm, present, and grounded. R is for remembering our own strength and resilience or source of hope and comfort that has and will carry us through this difficult and uncertain time. E is for equanimity or maintaining a sense of calmness and balance as we go through the ebb and flow of this new normal. This means having a mind that neither over-reacts nor in denial but is open to whatever emotions this crisis brings to the fore without getting lost in them. Letter A stands for affect or emotional regulation. Related to equanimity, when varied emotions are shored up, treat them not as enemies to fight or resist against but as guests bearing gifts of awareness, exploration, action. Cry if we must, express fear in words or images, or display gratitude to those who are toiling night and day to care for those sick with the virus. T is for time-out. Take a time-out from our screens or from gobbling up COVID-19 related news. Cut the noise and focus on what is in front of us and make space to reconnect with ourselves and with those around us. H is for Home. This means staying or sheltering at home, literally. Take this opportunity to stay connected to or inhabit through imagination a "sacred space" that evokes feelings of security, comfort, and peace. This shelter-in-place could also be an opportunity to shelter-in-God who is our refuge and strength. Lastly, E or exhale. As best as we can, let us exhale all the unnecessary and debilitating fears that clutter our ability to be clear-minded and inhale those that enlivens and gives us courage amidst this uncertain time.

In conclusion, this chapter explores why the pandemic outbreak of COVID-19 can be understood as Complex and Collective Trauma and how its traumatic experiences affect psychological symptoms. The COVID-19 pandemic is unpredictable, uncontrollable, and has the threat of death or serious injury. Those three characteristics are related to traumatic experiences as described in ICD-11 (the International Classification of Diseases) and DSM-5 (Diagnostic and Statistical Manual of Mental Disorders) diagnostic criteria.[51] When a person experiences trauma and feels disempowered to the threat of trauma from COVID-19, people engage in emotional, behavioral, cognitive, developmental, and social/interpersonal survival psychological reactions. Traumatic stress and anxiety by the pandemic outbreak of COVID-19 brings a sense of loss, including a loss of agency, a loss of relational intimacy, a loss of social functions, a loss of profound sense of power, etc. The prolonged traumatic experiences of the pandemic outbreak keep increasing the risk of mental health issues. The pandemic of COVID-19 deeply and widely affects the sense of being, the sense of others, and the sense of the community and the world. This chapter ends with a few suggestions on how to mitigate the psychological hazards of COVID-19 both from a communal and personal level.

51. Denckla et al., "REACH for Mental Health," 1.

Bibliography

American Psychiatric Association. "What Is Posttraumatic Stress Disorder?" https://www.psychiatry.org/patients-families/ptsd/what-is-ptsd.

"Asian Americans Report More Than 650 Racist Acts over Last Week, New Data Says." *NBC News*, March 26, 2020. https://www.nbcnewyork.com/news/national-international/asian-americans-report-racist-acts-data/2346256/.

Aten, Jamie D. "What to Do about the Mental Health Consequences of COVID-19: Interview with Dr. Ali Jawaid on the Short- and Long-Term Effects of COVID-19." *Psychology Today*, July 23, 2020. https://www.psychologytoday.com/us/blog/hope-resilience/202007/what-do-about-the-mental-health-consequences-covid-19.

Banerjee, Bebanjan. "The Impact of COVID-19 Pandemic on Elderly Mental Health." *International Journal of Geriatric Psychiatry* 35.12 (2020) 1446–47.

Bartlett, Jessica Dym, et al. "Resources for Supporting Children's Emotional Well-Being during the COVID-19 Pandemic." *Child Trends*, March 19, 2020. https://www.childtrends.org/publications/resources-for-supporting-childrens-emotional-well-being-during-the-covid-19-pandemic.

Beck, Aaon, et al. *Cognitive Therapy of Depression*. New York: Guilford, 1979.

Bettinger-Lopez, Caroline. "A Double Pandemic: Domestic Violence in the Age of COVID-19." *Council on Foreign Relations*, May 13, 2020. https://www.cfr.org/in-brief/double-pandemic-domestic-violence-age-covid-19.

Bloom, Sandra. *Restoring Sanctuary: A New Operating System for Trauma Informed Systems of Care*. Oxford: Oxford University Press, 2013.

Bremner, J. Douglas. "Traumatic Stress: Effects on the Brain." *Dialogues Clin Neurosci* 8.4 (2006) 445–61. doi:10.31887/DCNS.2006.8.4/jbremner/

Brooks, Samantha, et al. "The Psychological Impact of Quarantine and How to Reduce It: Rapid Review of the Evidence." *The Lancet* 395.10227 (2020) 912–20. https://doi.org/10.1016/S0140-6736(20)30460-8.

Butler, Judy. *Precarious Life: The Powers of Mourning and Violence*. New York: Verso, 2006.

Cava, Maureen A., et al. "The Experience of Quarantine for Individuals Affected by SARS in Toronto." *Public Health Nurse* 22.5 (2005) 398–406.

Centers for Disease Control and Prevention. "Coping with Stress." https://www.cdc.gov/coronavirus/2019-ncov/daily-life-coping/managing-stress-anxiety.html?cdc_aa_refval=https%3a%2f%2fwww.cdc.gov%2fcoronavirus%2f2019-ncov%2fprepare%2fmanaging-stress-anxiety.html.

Chang, Kay. "Living with Vulnerability and Resiliency: The Psychological Experience of Collective Trauma." *Acta Psychopathology* 3 (2017). https://www.primescholars.com/articles/living-with-vulnerability-and-resiliency-the-psychological-experience-of-collective-trauma-104272.html.

Chung, May. "Asian Americans Report Increase in Racism, Xenophobia during Coronavirus Pandemic." https://www.clickorlando.com/inside-edition/2020/03/25/asian-americans-report-increase-in-racism-xenophobia-during-coronavirus-pandemic/.

Denckla, Christy A., et al. "REACH for Mental Health in the COVID-19 Pandemic: An Urgent Call for Public Health Action." *European Journal of Psychotraumatology* 11 (2020) 1–4. https://doi.org/10.1080/20008198.2020.1762995.

Dong, Ensheng, et al. "An Interactive Web Based Dashboard to Track COVID-19 in Real Time." *The Lancet* 20.5 (2020) 533–34. https://doi.org/10.1016/S1473-3099(20)30120-1.

Einhorn, Erin. "African Americans May Be Dying from COVID-19 at a Higher Rate. Better Data Is Essential, Experts Say." *NBC News,* April 7, 2020. https://www.nbcnews.com/news/nbcblk/african-americans-may-be-dying-covid-19-higher-rate-better-n1178011.

Erikson, Kai T. *Everything in Its Path: Destruction of Community in the Buffalo Creek Flood.* New York: Simon and Schuster, 1978.

Hamblen, Jennifer. *PTSD in Children and Adolescents: A National Center for PTSD Fact Sheet.* Washington, DC: National Center for PTSD, 2001. https://www.ptsd.va.gov/professional/treat/specific/ptsd_child_teens.asp.

Harris, Maxine, and Roger Fallot. *Using Trauma Theory to Design Service Systems: New Directions for Mental Health Services.* Hoboken, NJ: Jossey-Bass, 2001.

Herman, Judith. *Trauma and Recovery: The Aftermath of Violence—From Domestic Abuse to Political Terror.* New York: Basic, 2015.

Institute of Trauma and Trauma-Informed Care. "Trauma-Informed Organizational Change Manual." http://socialwork.buffalo.edu/social-research/institutes-centers/institute-on-trauma-and-trauma-informed-care/Trauma-Informed-Organizational-Change-Manualo.html.

Janoff-Bulman, Ronnie. *Shattered Assumptions: Towards a New Psychology of Trauma.* New York: Free, 1992.

Kaiser Family Foundation. "Eliminating Racial/Ethnic Disparities in Health Care: What Are the Options?" https://www.kff.org/disparities-policy/issue-brief/eliminating-racialethnic-disparities-in-health-care-what/#back10.

Kingsland, James. "Racial Minorities Experience Higher COVID-19-Related Discrimination." *Medical News Today,* July 10, 2020. https://www.medicalnewstoday.com/articles/racial-minorities-experience-higher-covid-19-related-discrimination.

Lai, Jianbo, et al. "Factors Associated with Mental Health Outcomes among Health Care Workers Exposed to Coronavirus Disease 2019." *JAMA Network Open* 3.3 (2020) e203976. https://jamanetwork.com/journals/jamanetworkopen/fullarticle/2763229.

Leonard, Jayne. "What Is Trauma? What to Know." *Medical News Today,* June 3, 2020. https://www.medicalnewstoday.com/articles/trauma.

Menakem, Resmaa. *My Grandmother's Hands: Racialized Trauma and the Pathway to Mending Our Hearts and Bodies.* Las Vegas: Central Recovery, 2017.

Mollicas, Richard F. *Healing Invisible Wounds: Paths to Hope and Recovery in a Violent World.* Nashville: Vanderbilt University Press, 2006.

Pedwell, Carolyn. *Affective Relations: The Transnational Politics of Empathy.* London: Palgrave Mcmillan, 2014.

Perrett, Connor. "Nearly 60% of People Who Have Lost Their Jobs Due to the Coronavirus Pandemic Are Women according to Report." *Business Insider,* April, 8, 2020. https://www.businessinsider.com/coronavirus-unemployment-women-60-percent-2020-4.

Pratt, Geraldine, et al. "Filipino Migrant Stories and Trauma in the Transnational Field." *Emotion, Space, and Society* 24 (2017) 83–92. https://doi.org/10.1016/j.emospa.2015.09.002.

Roth, Susan, et al. "Complex PTSD in Victims Exposed to Sexual and Physical Abuse: Results from the DSM-IV Field Trial for Posttraumatic Stress Disorder." *Journal of Traumatic Stress* 10 (1997) 539–55.

Serafini, Gianluca, et al. "The Psychological Impact of COVID-19 on the Mental Health in the General Population." *QJM: An International Journal of Medicine* 113.8 (2020) 531–37. https://doi.org/10.1093/qjmed/hcaa201.

Substance Abuse and Mental Health Services Administration (SAMHSA). "Trauma-Informed Care in Behavioral Health Services." https://store.samhsa.gov/sites/default/files/d7/priv/sma14-4816.pdf.

———. "SAMHSA's Concept of Trauma and Guidance for a Trauma-Informed Approach." https://cantasd.acf.hhs.gov/wp-content/uploads/SAMHSAConceptof Trauma.pdf.

Stafford, Kat, et al. "Coronavirus: Racial Disparities Cause Concern among Health Experts." *Mercury News*, April 8, 2020. https://www.mercurynews.com/2020/04/08/coronavirus-racial-disparities-cause-concern-among-health-experts/.

Terr, Lenore. *Too Scared to Cry: Psychic Trauma in Childhood.* New York: Harper and Row, 1990.

Van der Kolk, Bessel A. *The Body Keeps the Score: Brain, Mind, and Body in the Healing of Trauma.* New York: Penguin, 2015.

Wu, Ping, et al. "Alcohol Abuse/Dependence Symptoms among Hospital Employees Exposed to a SARS Outbreak." *Alcohol and Alcoholism* 43.6 (2008) 706–12. https://doi.org/10.1093/alcalc/agn073.

Yao, Hao, et al. "Patients with Mental Health Disorders in the COVID-19 Epidemic." *The Lancet* 7.4 (2020) e21. https://doi. org/10.1016/S2215-0366(20)30090-0.

Zeballos-Rorig, Joseph. "Here's Why Millions of Americans Are Struggling to File for Unemployment Benefits at a Time When They've Never Been More Generous." *Business Insider*, April 7, 2020. https://www.businessinsider.com/unemployment-benefits-insurance-workers-furlough-coronavirus-economy-states-2020-4.

7

Pastoral Care for Grief and Loss
in Pandemics

—TRINA ARMSTRONG

Introduction

IN DECEMBER OF 2019, COVID-19 became the latest influenza pandemic to wreak havoc on our lives and livelihoods. As of this writing, over one million people across the globe have died, a number that is certainly going to rise before it is controlled and eradicated. Pandemics are one-time, sudden and sometimes persistent global outbreaks of an infectious disease. They are pointedly marked throughout history by the swift, astronomical, and indescribable loss of human life. Most notably from 1346–53, the Black Death pandemic killed fifty million people across Asia, North Africa, and Europe. In just one year the 1918 Spanish Flu pandemic claimed over fifty million lives.[1] Others like smallpox and the persistent pandemics of tuberculosis and HIV/AIDS have also infected and claimed millions of lives across the globe. Pandemics are akin to disasters like earthquakes, fires, tsunamis, flood, and tornadoes, because their crisis nature severely overwhelms and disrupts the everyday lives and initial coping capacities and resources of individuals, families, and communities.[2] Influenza pandemics are the most common and are the focus of this chapter with some reference to the HIV/AIDS pandemic. As history attests, they are the deadliest due to their high transmissibility. As Nancy Bristow notes in *American Pandemic*, influenza pandemics are not selective in their victims, belying notions of gender, class,

---

1. Hays, *Epidemics and Pandemics*, 385.
2. Roberts and Ashley, *Disaster Spiritual Care*, xv.

and race, and all markers of difference.[3] Though infections and death are the most obvious markers of a pandemic, the spiritual, emotional, financial, physical, and ecological disruption creates other losses that produces a ripple effect of untold and unacknowledged suffering that can linger far beyond the immediate impact of the pandemic. These losses and pastoral care responses to them are the focus of this chapter.

Lived Experiences of Pandemics

"And then COVID hit!" I hear this statement often in the recounting of plans, hopes, and dreams that were affected because of the pandemic as indicative of the way COVID-19 ushered in fear, uncertainty, worry, disappointment, loss, and grief. Weddings, travel plans, plans for starting or continuing education, visiting family and friends, graduations, birthday celebrations, and employment all fell victim to the pandemic. These suspended life events capture the interrelated experience of living through a pandemic that has altered millions of lives. In this vein a pandemic is a public health crisis and a social occurrence that quickly disrupts our lives. Initially, this disruption is fueled by a sense of urgency to understand, track, contain, and prevent transmission of the virus until a vaccine is developed. Then uncertainty looms, especially in the beginning of a pandemic, because we want to know how many people have been infected and died, how it is transmitted, who is at risk, and when the pandemic will be truly over.

The onset of an influenza pandemic is accompanied by safety measures like quarantine, social distancing, and wearing masks. In addition, fear, worry, and confusion are common psychological responses. These emotions permeate questions about human connection and moving safely in the world. The high transmissibility rate renders all of us susceptible for infection and, depending on comorbidity, some are more vulnerable than others. With COVID-19, older adults and persons with pre-existing medical conditions like diabetes, obesity, heart disease, and cancer are among high-risk conditions. Other vulnerable persons who are also susceptible to infection and death include African Americans, Latinos, Indigenous persons, homeless persons and others who live in close proximity or in densely populated areas. Unfortunately, persons of color and marginalized populations are among the highest percentage of the daily heartbreaking death reports used to measure the scope and scale of pandemics. Unfortunately, measuring pandemics in this way reduces their lives to a mere number. In all instances casualties of pandemics are wives, husbands, mothers, fathers, beloved grandmothers and

3. Bristow, *American Pandemic*, 42.

grandfathers, aunts, uncles, cousin, sisters, and brothers—real people with families, friends, hopes, dreams and aspirations.

In a poignant, expansive, and captivating exposé titled *An Incalculable Loss*, published by the New York Times when COVID-19 deaths in the United States hit the grim milestone of one hundred thousand deaths (one thousand per day), the brief multilayered and diverse narratives of one thousand victims where shared.[4] Their names, ages, occupations, and personal stories were drawn from various media sources, and reminded us that the incessant and numbing daily reporting of victims does not tell the whole story. Among them was a loyal and generous friend, a nurse planning for retirement, a thirty-three-year-old recent immigrant to America, a middle-aged police detective, veterans who proudly served in the military, clergy who dedicated their lives to ministry and their congregations, entertainers, a founder of a food pantry, beloved public school teachers, artists, doctors, nurses, and other health care workers, cancer survivors, business owners and entrepreneurs, survivors of other human tragedies, persons with a passion for social justice, newly released felons hoping for new life, and many more lives. They are disproportionally Black, Latino, and elderly.

The author, Dan Barry, noted that *An Incalculable Loss* "is intended to help us reckon with what was lost while reminding us that a number is an 'imperfect measure when applied to the human condition. Numbers provide an answer to how many, but can never convey the individual arcs of life, the 100,000 ways of greeting the morning and saying good night. That each number represents someone who was among us yesterday.'"[5] He adds "Some died alone in jam-packed hospitals without a final goodbye from families, others in nursing homes, some were too sick or scared to go to a hospital because their closest relative was a half-world away.[6] Dan also noted that the broader impact of the pandemic prevented many from mourning in usual and customary ways, suppressing our nature as social creatures, for fear that we might infect or be infected.

> Among the many indignities, it has denied us the grace of being present for a loved one's last moments. Age-old customs that lend meaning to existence have been upended, including the sacred rituals of how we mourn. Before, we came together in halls and bars and places of worship to remember and honor the dead. We recited prayers or raised glasses or retold familiar stories so funny they left us nodding and crying through our

4. Barry, "U.S. Deaths Near 100,000."
5. Barry, "U.S. Deaths Near 100,000."
6. Barry, "U.S. Deaths Near 100,000."

laughter. . . . In these vital moments of communion, it could feel as though the departed were with us one last time, briefly resurrected by the sheer power of our collective love, to share that closing prayer, that parting glass, that final hug. Even I in the horrible times of wars and hurricanes and terrorist attacks that seemed to crumble the ground beneath our feet, we at least had time-tested ways of grieving that helped us take the first hesitant step forward. . . . Not now.[7]

In addition to COVID-19 deaths, many families were deprived of the opportunity to physically comfort relatives who died from illnesses unrelated to the virus. For example, a son who had to self-quarantine because he was exposed to the virus, was devastated when he was not allowed to enter the facility where his mother was dying of cancer to comfort her. He shared that watching a video of her surrounded by masked strangers in her last moments was painful. In another instance, the wife of a COVID-19 patient described being isolated without family and friends in the aftermath of her husband's death. While she connected to family and friends over phone and email, she said she missed the presence of people who made the time to bear witness and share her loss. Given the magnitude of death over the history of pandemics, there are undoubtedly many more untold heartbreaking stories of loss and grief.

The true extent of the grief and loss may never fully be known because to control and end an influenza pandemic, politicians and public health officials must temporarily close and limit non-essential gathering places. These decisions impact everything from schools, businesses, restaurants, sports, entertainment, and religious communities. Specific examples of these losses include students who no longer saw friends or could play outside when they moved to online learning; parents who adjusted their lives to accommodate their children; teachers who pivoted to virtual classes; and senior trips, proms, graduations, and all commemorative celebrations that were altered or canceled, leaving students across all educational spectrums without rituals of celebrations experienced by countless students before them. One student lamented, "When my college moved online, I didn't say a single goodbye. Everyone rushed home—leaving behind our belongings, our plans, our jobs, and our friends."[8]

Mandated social distancing and masked faces are stark reminders of human disconnection in pandemics. In a four-part news series on the impact of COVID-19 on a local youth organization, a student lamented that

7. Barry, "U.S. Deaths Near 100,000."
8. Cupcakes and Cashmere, "Short Stories."

social distancing, "separated us from other parts of society. This has made me feel very much disconnected from my friends."[9] Another student shared:

> This is my last year being around people I have spent four years watching grow and growing with; friends who have become family, friends and people who I love that I cannot dap up or hug or have face-to-face interaction or conversation. This disconnect from people is heartbreaking and hard to say the least. This year is supposed to be the year where I live it out with these people who are so close to me because I don't know when I will see these friends again after I graduate.[10]

Due to mandated quarantines, non-essential workers from restaurants, recreation, and entertainment lost jobs or were furloughed in ways that they would never have prepared for, especially those on the precipice of living without savings or a safety net. Long held and new family businesses were no longer afforded the walk-ins and reservations that were their lifeline. According to the National Restaurant Association, the industry lost billions of dollars, five to seven million jobs, and tens of thousands of restaurants closed.[11] One new entrepreneur shared:

> We are entering our second year of business and were really getting our stride when I suddenly had to shutter the store. As a business [that] relies primarily on foot traffic to make money, this was of course terrifying. On top of that, I have a team of 12 women whom I suddenly had to figure out how to keep paying and carry 75+ independent brands who also rely on our sales to make their living. I know I am not unique in feeling the immense strain and stress that small businesses around the world are feeling.[12]

Along with restaurants and bars, entertainment venues, movies, theatres, concerts and gyms are also temporarily impacted. Athletic seasons and sporting events across all levels of competition are postponed, adjusted, and cancelled. The professional conference and educational industries are also impacted as conferences are canceled, postponed, or moved online. This means more job loss and reductions in hotel occupancy and restaurant traffic. This list is not exhaustive because many other sectors of society and the lives that are intricately linked to them are impacted. To this end, Margaret Kornfeld reminds us that for many of us, work is a significant experience in

9. Model D, "How Has COVID-19 Affected You?"

10. Model D, "How Has COVID-19 Affected You?"

11. Klein, "Restaurant Industry Has Already Lost $120 Billion."

12. Cupcakes and Cashmere, "Short Stories."

our lives, an anchor to which our self-esteem, identity, friendships, and sense of purpose is tied. While people need to work to make money to live, many believe work is more than their means of survival—it is a way they express themselves and how they spend a sizeable portion of their lives.[13]

Many people work on the frontlines as doctors, nurses, health aides and other health services, bus drivers, police, firefighters, grocery workers, waste collectors, drivers, and delivery persons who risk their health without the assurance of safety and security in encounters with patients and strangers. Healthcare workers, especially those caring for victims of the virus, contend with sick and dying patients in the shadows of public doubt and denial. They often work without assurances of safety or as was the case in the beginning of COVID-19, proper equipment and sufficient resources to meet the demands of testing and care that converges on hospitals and clinics. Stories abound about the scarcity of ventilators, personal protective equipment (PPE), and other necessary healthcare supplies to treat the most severe cases. They also watch people suffering behind protective gear, without the presence of loved ones, including themselves, directly and indirectly grieving. Physician and health journalist Amitha Kalaichandran, warns:

> COVID-19 will leave behind a complicated form of grief that will linger—potentially for many years after the immediate crisis has abated. Patients are dying and much like during the Ebola crisis in West Africa, fears of contagion have interfered with families' ability to mourn. . . . All of this damage is occurring while people are still dying from other causes, too—and when grieving people are being discouraged from even going outside, much less seeking solace from their loved ones. Making matters worse, the current crisis has put enormous stress on the healing professions that, in normal times, help families deal with loss and bereavement. Our society is ill-prepared for the kind of grief the coronavirus is visiting upon so many people during so short a span.[14]

I believe pastoral caregivers in all settings are essential and they are among those on the frontlines who can respond to Kalaichandran's concerns. Like other professionals in pandemics, pastoral caregivers, pastors, chaplains and faith-based communities are already providing ministry for ongoing cares and concerns. At the beginning of the COVID-19 pandemic, many churches stopped in-person worship because gatherings of people in close proximity to one another pose a risk for transmission of influenza

---

13. Kornfeld, *Cultivating Wholeness*, 194.

14. Kalaichandran, "We're Not Ready for This Kind of Grief."

viruses. Unlike previous pandemics, the presence of technology and social media helped many communities quickly move their ministries to virtual settings. While this helps religious communities connect, the social support gained from in-person fellowship and rituals like funerals and communion are significant losses. No doubt the individual and collective losses of pre-pandemic ministry impact all religious communities. Acknowledging and caring for this loss and grief is one of the most crucial roles for religious communities in pandemics. As one pastor notes:

> We as a society are dealing with a lot of grief and loss right now. Woe to us, the church, if we don't recognize and live into our crucial and unique role in this situation. In particular, I see two important but largely neglected roles for the church: public lament and grief shepherding. These two things are not identical but definitely related.
>
> Churches are very familiar with grief, and our sacred texts have the language for lament. But do we recognize how needed that is right now? People are getting pummeled mentally and spiritually. Our world needs the language of public lament and needs to be shepherded through this wide-ranging and public grief. Unfortunately, the grief and lament aspect of this is easy to miss, even for the church. . . . The collective and public anger, denial, and depression we are experiencing is normal and valid, but some of its expressions have been unhealthy. This is where the church is desperately needed. The public needs us to shepherd our communities through this grief, which involves both recognizing what it is as well as teaching and modeling healthy expression.[15]

Loss and Grief in Pandemics

Pastoral caregivers who understand the magnitude of loss and grief can offer more empathetic and compassionate responses in their ministry contexts by bearing witness to the depths of loss and grief that will likely outlive the pandemic. Loss is universally understood as losing something or someone. It can be physical or symbolic and tangible or intangible. Death and loss of a material item that has special significance are examples of physical and tangible losses. Losses like divorce, retirement, a chronic illness, or shattered dream are examples of symbolic or intangible losses.[16] Other ways

15. Fields, "Public Lament and Grief Shepherding."
16. Rando, *Grief, Dying, and Death*, 16.

of delineating loss are material, relational, intrapsychic, role, systemic, and functional.[17] Material losses are meaningful objects like a house, favorite toy, or family heirloom; a relational loss is the end of emotional and physical intimacy with another person; intrapsychic loss is the loss of an internal self-image or possibilities of what might have been, the abandonment of future plans, or a dying dream; a functional loss is a part of the body that no longer functions as intended; role loss is the loss of a social role or accustomed place in a social network; and systemic loss occurs when an important person leaves a family or organization effectively changing how it functions. Losses are experienced individually or interdependently as a primary loss, or as a secondary loss that develops from the primary loss.[18]

All of these forms of loss are evident in pandemics. For example, death is a primary relational loss that is accompanied by role loss in the system with the death of a husband, wife, mother, father, grandmother, grandfather, or other family member. These deaths can evoke losses of dreams and hopes of living life together. Additionally, millions of people experience primary, psychosocial, and material losses when they lose jobs that result in secondary losses of financial security, health insurance, and homes. Others may experience an intrapsychic loss of a significant image of oneself as an employee or business owner or an image of oneself defined by a vocation. One may experience a functional loss with lingering complications from the virus. The extent of this for survivors of COVID-19 is not well known, but persons living with HIV/AIDS who are benefiting from antiretroviral therapy no longer face the imminent threat of death, though they do contend with physical side effects that impact bodily functioning.

Other examples of loss common to influenza pandemics stem from quarantine and social distancing that close churches, schools, and other communal gatherings resulting in a psychosocial loss or the loss of opportunities to connect with family and friends. These losses are also evident in the postponement of weddings, canceled or altered birthday celebrations, graduation ceremonies, and limited gatherings at funerals. Containment measures also restrict movement leading to primary psychosocial losses of freedom to travel, which can then lead to secondary losses of relationships, recreation, social support, reduced emotional and physical intimacy and possible dissolution of intimate relationships involving partners, family, and friends.[19] Even though technology creates opportunities for virtual connections, for many, not being in the same physical space

17. Mitchell and Anderson, *All Our Losses*, 36–45.
18. Rando, *Treatment of Complicated Mourning*, 20.
19. Zhai and Du, "Loss and Grief amidst COVID-19," 80.

with friends, family, and church communities can result in secondary losses of isolation and loneliness.

Some pandemic losses are ambiguous because they are uncertain, complex, confusing, and occur without closure.[20] There is often little clarity and conflicting information, which makes us vulnerable to loss of security, safety, normalcy, and fear of infection or that friends and family may be infected. Some families have experienced ambiguous loss from not being present with loved ones who died in isolation. There is also much uncertainty when pandemic protocols force students, teachers, and parents into remote learning, losing access to classrooms and classmates without the certainty of when in-person classes will resume. Parents can experience ambiguity in not knowing how long they need to accommodate their children for remote learning. Employees who are not accustomed to working from home live with ambiguity as a result of blurred boundaries between home and work, uncertain when or if they will return. And young people can experience ambiguous loss when they do not know when they will return to school or play with their friends.

For religious communities, loss can emerge from shifting how one practices ministry, disruption of services, limited contact with members, preaching in unfamiliar settings, an empty church, or from their homes, losing control over planning and directing services by yielding to political leaders and public health officials that restrict funerals, baptisms, and weddings. Another loss could be from unconventional celebrations of liturgical holidays without knowing what those gatherings will look like when they and their congregations can return. Unfortunately, these losses are seldom recognized by society as generating feelings that require processing.[21] One reason the significance of non-death related losses is not commonly recognized is because death is finite, it has an end. Non-finite losses like material, relational, and functional losses are life-altering events, but they have an ongoing physical and psychological presence.[22] Holding this expansive understanding of death and non-death related loss affirms Mitchell and Anderson's claim that loss is a normative metaphor for understanding life experiences that produce grief.[23]

---

20. Boss, *Ambiguous Loss*, 6.

21. Rando, *Treatment of Complicated Mourning*, 20.

22. Harris and Gorman, "Grief from a Broader Perspective," 2.

23. Mitchell and Anderson, *All Our Losses*, 54.

Grief, Bereavement, and Mourning Losses in Pandemics

Grief is the normal human response to loss. Grief, as one expression of loss, is used interchangeably with bereavement, and mourning; however, each is distinct in its expression of a loss. Grief is the emotional response to loss; bereavement is the objective situation of losing someone significant; and mourning is the action and manner of expressing grief, often reflecting the mourning practices of one's culture.[24] Alternatively, grief is "great sorrow or sadness associated with loss,"[25] or simply a response to an important loss.[26] The latter definitions better account for grief that accompanies all forms of loss in pandemics.

For some, experiences of loss yield feelings of shock, sadness, depression, numbness, irritability, denial, guilt, and/or anger. Grief can also manifest as physically as fatigue, tightening in the chest, headaches, problems concentrating, and in behaviors, like sleep disturbances, excessive eating, or loss of appetite. Though these are common manifestations of grief, no two people will be affected by a loss and grieve in the same way. Doka notes:

> Some people have profoundly debilitating reactions to a loss, while others have more muted or resilient reactions. Some reactions, such as sadness and tears, we may clearly identify as part of grieving. Yet other reactions, such as irritability, an inability to concentrate, or even physical pain, may be less identifiable as stemming from grief, and so cause concern and confusion. The truth is that loss can affect every dimension of our being, so grief can express itself in our emotions, behavior, and thought processes. Grief can also manifest itself physically and spiritually.[27]

The act of grief involves processing the thoughts, feelings, and behaviors associated with loss. Ideally this can occur in a space where the thoughts and feelings aroused by the loss are acknowledged and expressed so the grieving person can discover and express emotions that are common consequences of loss.[28]

Three other forms of grief are present in a pandemic: anticipatory, disenfranchised, and complex. Most manifestations of grief occur in the aftermath of an unexpected loss, one that while not welcomed, has already occurred. Grief can also occur in anticipation of a loss. This grief can manifest

---

24. Stroebe et al., *Handbook of Bereavement*, 5.

25. Doka, *Grief Is a Journey*, 39.

26. Kelley, *Grief*, 9.

27. Doka, *Grief Is a Journey*, 39.

28. Mitchell and Anderson, *All Our Losses*, 95.

with such intensity that one grieves as if the object were already lost.[29] The presence of anticipatory grief in pandemics can occur with anticipated closures when the virus continues to spread or when deaths and infections decrease, but the waves of the virus push us back to curfews and quarantine. As the virus rages on, anticipatory grief can emerge with fear of friends and family acquiring or dying from the virus, uncertainty about future plans, anticipating significant life events that may not happen as hoped, or knowing that more people jobs will lose jobs.

Though death is the most acknowledged form of loss in pandemics, other experiences of loss can be just as prevalent but impact us in different ways. When grief is expressed and acknowledged after the death of a loved one, it elicits support from others and is accompanied by formal rituals like funerals and memorial services, expressions of condolences, and offers of prayers. These structured ways of mourning and sharing with others who knew the deceased are helpful ways of coping. However, loss outside of death does not offer similar ritualistic opportunities. And since there is a general lack of awareness of other types of losses that people may be grieving, this grief is disenfranchised. This means that persons are grieving but their grief is not acknowledged, socially validated or publicly mourned. This can be due to the way a person grieves, the nature of the loss, or the nature of the relationship.[30]

Disenfranchised grief is important because the swift pace of pandemic infections, deaths, and changes are often overshadowed by the sense of urgency to return to normal. In *American Pandemic*, Nancy Bristow noted that in the aftermath of the 1918 influenza pandemic, the public response to finite and non-finite losses was denial. As the country moved on when the virus subsided, erasing the painful memories many Americans held in their hearts from public discourse, many were left to suffer privately, exacerbating the tragedy of the epidemic.[31] Disenfranchised grief was also evident at the height of the HIV/AIDS pandemic when it was initially labeled as a gay man's disease. Unfortunately, many infected gay men who died were stigmatized and rejected by some segments of society, family, and religious communities. The grief that accompanied the many losses they experienced was disenfranchised, as well as the grief experienced by surviving friends and the many communities that were decimated by the many deaths that occurred during this time and over the course of the pandemic.[32]

---

29. Mitchell and Anderson, *All Our Losses*, 58.

30. Doka, *Disenfranchised Grief*, 5.

31. Bristow, *American Pandemic*, 36.

32. Klein, *Heavenly Hurts*, 49.

Melissa Kelley offers an important description of disenfranchised grief, grief born of injustice or preventable events. This is unnecessary grief that is not part of the "natural order," that is caused by unjust structures and actions or inactions of individuals, groups, and systems.[33] This type of grief can emerge in a pandemic as a result of the uneven political and public health responses to pandemics that slow the process of developing a vaccine or public health guidelines that can slow and contain transmissions through behaviors. When the HIV/AIDS virus burgeoned in the United States, with gay men experiencing the highest infections and deaths, it was politicized as a gay disease and interpreted by prominent religious leaders as the consequences of sin, thus slowing public health responses. There were similar responses in Africa where it began and where it spiraled out of control.[34] The end result was many lost lives, many orphaned children, and countless grieving friends and family.

In pandemics, it is essential for pastoral caregivers to recognize the process of grieving and the impediments that make grieving complex. Although grief is a normal reaction to loss, some persons will experience complicated grief. Complicated grief is characterized by the length, intensity, and impact of the loss on one's thoughts, emotions, life, work, and relationship behaviors. Five models of grief that help us understand the process of grief in pandemics are the five-stage model, four-stage model, and phase model, and the six "R's" of grief model. All these models were developed in the context of death and dying, but they can also help us understand the broader experience of grieving losses in pandemics. The most common model of grief is the five-stage model developed by Elisabeth Kubler-Ross of denial, anger, bargaining, depression, and acceptance.[35] William Worden, like Kubler-Ross, says we experience grief through the four tasks of mourning: accepting the reality of the loss, processing the pain of grief, adjusting to the world without the deceased, and remembering the deceased while moving on with the rest of one's life.[36] Rando acknowledges that thinking of the grieving process in stages can feel like we need to complete one task before we move to the next. Instead, she sees grief as a process of recognizing the loss, reacting to the separation, reexperiencing the person who died, releasing attachment to the deceased and the old assumptive world, readjusting to the world without forgetting the old, and reinvesting energy in new things

33. Kelley, *Grief*, 15.
34. McMillen, *Pandemics*, 107–9.
35. Kübler-Ross, *On Death and Dying*, 38–112.
36. Worden, *Grief Counseling and Grief Therapy*, 43–51.

and new people.[37] However, stages theories were long misinterpreted as a linear process. Kubler-Ross clarified this misconception in her later work where she described the stages of grief as a framework that makes up our learning to live with the loss, tools to help us frame and identify our feelings rather than seeing them as stops on a timeline in grief, and finally, recognizing that not everyone goes through all the stages of grief in a prescribed order.[38] Kelley highlights this in her mosaic model of grief, noting that emotional and behavioral responses to grief exist, but each person's experience of grief is particular and formed by the unique interplay of past, relationships, ways of making meaning, experience of the Divine, history of losses, sense of community, and cultural perspectives.[39]

Many agree that there is an end to the grieving process, whether acceptance, moving on, or reinvesting energy and emotions in new things and new people. When this does not happen, grief becomes complicated. Complicated grief is prolonged grief or the absence of normal grief reactions. In pandemics many are susceptible to complicated grief by the sheer fact that a pandemic is a highly stressful public health crisis that impacts many areas of life with fear, worry, uncertainty, sadness, anger, and guilt. The possibility of disenfranchised and complex grief is even more possible for people who are already suffering from chronic health issues and mental health challenges like anxiety and depression. The circumstance of death and loss is certainly a significant factor in how one copes with grief. As with the 1918 influenza and COVID-19 pandemics, death was and is swift and many died or will die alone or after agonizing stints in intensive care without the comfort of family and friends. For some surviving friends and family, guilt could complicate the grieving process when a loved one dies because of an infected a family member or friend, hosted a gathering where people became infected, or were in close proximity to infected persons. These scenarios can evoke complex feelings, deep remorse, and impact one's ability to adjust to and accommodate the loss—all complex layers to the grieving process.[40]

Coping and Meaning Making in Pandemics

How a person copes with loss and grief is related to one's attachment to what was lost and how one makes meaning out of the loss. According to attachment theory, an attachment is an important aspect of the relationship

37. Rando, *Treatment of Complicated Mourning*, 45–46.
38. Kübler-Ross and Kessler, *On Grief and Grieving*, 7.
39. Kelley, *Grief*, 5–6.
40. Roos, *Chronic Sorrow*, 26.

between a child and primary caregiver that ensures the child feels safe, se-cure and protected.[41] This relationship provides a secure base for the child, especially as a form of comfort when the child is distressed or separated from the primary caregiver. Over time, the attachments we form are integral for our survival and continue throughout life as "working models" of ourselves and others who can meet our needs for safety and security.[42] These working models become embedded in the mind, body, environment, material pos-sessions, home, work, and interactions with other persons, forming the basis of our assumptive world—everything we know or think we know, including our interpretation of the past and expectations for future plans.[43]

Our assumptive world also includes beliefs that ground, secure, ori-ent us, and provide a sense of reality, meaning, or purpose.[44] Some beliefs guide our view of others and their intentions, how we believe the world should work, and how we view ourselves.[45] In the face of loss, these beliefs can be shattered along with any illusions of what we thought the world to be. This results in a profound sense of loss, so much so that we often need to rethink our beliefs while also grieving what no longer works. Thus, pandemics can profoundly alter our assumptions and beliefs about safety, security, predictability, control, and freedom. Rando explains when this happens, a mourner can lose a view of the world and the countless feel-ings, thoughts, behaviors, interaction patterns, hopes, wishes, fantasies, dreams, assumptions and beliefs that required the loved one's presence or the presence of our object of attachment.[46]

For some, life through a pandemic is a profoundly spiritual experi-ence, and many will draw on their spiritual and religious resources to cope and make meaning of their losses. Religion is a system of explanations about the meaning of human life or creeds, rules or codes that govern everyday behavior, and rituals to act out the understandings expressed in creeds and codes. These creeds and codes are expressed in communities, groups of people either formally or informally bound together by these shared creeds, codes, and rituals.[47] Spirituality is a person's path to finding meaning in their life experiences, in light of a relationship to the God.[48]

---

41. Bowlby, *Attachment*, 178–82.

42. Bowlby, *Attachment*, 354.

43. Parkes, "Psycho-social Transitions," 103.

44. Kauffman, "Introduction," 1.

45. Janoff-Bulman, *Shattered Assumptions*, 6.

46. Rando, *Treatment of Complicated Mourning*, 21.

47. Albanese, *America, Religions, and Religion*, 7–10.

48. Roberts and Ashley, *Disaster Spiritual Care*, xvii.

Making sense of suffering in a pandemic helps to create order, sense, and purpose out of experiences and events like pandemics that could otherwise seem random, nonsensical, disordered, or chaotic."[49]

To make sense of this, some find meaning in science and the psychology of human behaviors, while many Christians find meaning in Old and New Testament Bible passages that describe plagues, pestilences, and natural disasters as God's judgement and call for the repentance of a sinful humanity. The latter was certainly the case in the early stages of the HIV/AIDS pandemic, when many believed it was sent by God to punish gay men. Because pandemic renders us vulnerable, accounts like these can make the seemingly meaningless event more palatable. As grief expert Darcy Harris asserts:

> Searching for meaning in what seems to be a meaningless event is how human beings attempt to re-establish a sense of order and security in their world and to minimize the high degree of vulnerability that occurs after basic assumptions are shattered. Thus, it can be said that meaning-making is the primary task involved in rebuilding the assumptive world after it has been shattered by significant loss experiences; the process of meaning-making and the grief response are intricately entwined.[50]

In a pandemic, some will experience God as a secure base, a source of safety and comfort, and the foundation of their orienting system. An orienting system is a way of being in the world through one's habits, values, relationships, generalized beliefs, and personality. An orienting system contains both resources and burdens that function as a reservoir one draws on during hard times, a frame of reference, and a blueprint of oneself and the world used to anticipate and come to terms with life events and away from others.[51] Beliefs about God's presence or absence in pandemics are among the ways many employ spiritual, material, physical, and social resource in a crisis. Some resources come from prior experiences with a particular stressor, social supports, problem solving skills, and seeing crisis and adversity as an opportunity for growth or to achieve a goal.[52] Burdens of coping are real material, physical, psychological, social, and spiritual liabilities and deficits like a history of failure, a physical handicap, destructive family, personality problem, financial debt, or dysfunctional beliefs about oneself or others.[53]

---

49. Kelley, *Grief*, 78.
50. Harris, *Non-death Loss and Grief*, 13–14.
51. Pargament, *The Psychology of Religion and Coping*, 100.
52. Pargament, *The Psychology of Religion and Coping*, 101.
53. Pargament, *The Psychology of Religion and Coping*, 101.

According to Pargament, those who experience a greater loss of resources in a crisis are more likely to encounter more distress, and, he adds, that how one taps into their remaining resources at this time is one of the key tasks of coping.[54] Many draw on religious resources like prayer and sacred texts to cope because they are immediately available in the absence of other resources and they are compelling for those who are more aware of the limitations of the human condition.[55]

Pastoral Care for Loss and Grief in Pandemics

Pastoral care for loss and grief in pandemics simultaneously attends to persons, families, and communities by enfranchising grief as a normal response to death and non-death related losses. It also helps people adapt to short-lived and prolonged crises without the certainty of when or if life will return to some semblance of normal. The enfranchisement process for pastoral care in pandemics starts by acknowledging the breadth of loss in the wider society. Pastoral caregivers recognize that grief is a normal response to loss and the sudden and universal impact of pandemics, like natural disasters, creates intersecting losses that can result in complicated individual and collective grief responses. Pastoral caregivers create opportunities to grieve primarily through the ministry of presence or the act of listening deeply to empathize with, validate, comfort, and ritualize the pain of others. This is as a hallmark of pastoral care and an important aspect of ministry for helping persons, families, and communities process grief. In the context of COVID-19, physical presence is not always an option, so pastoral care givers have created virtual practices of care using technology and social media to provide grief support. Options include telephone prayer, conference calls for groups, video technology like Zoom, Skype and Facetime on phones, tablets, and computers, and Facebook groups, all of which are providing support for grief.

Enfranchising pandemic grief is helped by rituals that center the practice of lament. Rituals respond to transition and change in order to help manage the powerful feelings aroused by the loss.[56] Lament is an expression of these powerful feelings or repeated cry of pain, rage, sorrow, and grief.[57] In pandemics, lament gives voice to grief by humanizing the lives of the deceased, families and friends left behind, and all who have been impacted.

54. Pargament, *The Psychology of Religion and Coping*, 102.
55. Pargament, *The Psychology of Religion and Coping*, 147.
56. Mitchell and Anderson, *All Our Losses*, 140.
57. Swinton, *Raging with Compassion*, 104.

It is also a way for survivors to wrestle with deep spiritual questions that are necessary for rebuilding pre-pandemic assumptions and worldviews that are no longer viable. Rituals like funerals commemorate endings and provide hope for the future. They need be frank and straightforward to enhance the process of grieving.

> A ritual of ending is a part of the grieving process; therefore, it should say seriously and realistically that an end has been reached and should symbolize that end; encourage the expression of feelings related to that end; and enhance the remembering of what has been lost. A ritual of ending exists for the sake of those who have undergone the loss; therefore, their needs should supersede most other needs, but the existence of a larger community that shares in the loss should be recognized.[58]

Public support for pandemic grief occurs through candlelight vigils, prayer vigils, and moments of remembrance. The *New York Times* article mentioned earlier is a public form of remembrance. The most notable pandemic memorial is the NAMES Project AIDS Memorial Quilt conceived by HIV/AIDS activist Cleve Jones.[59] It was a traveling memorial where each of the quilt panels was inscribed the names of persons who died of AIDS. "Today, the AIDS Memorial Quilt is an epic 54-ton tapestry that includes more than 48,000 panels dedicated to more than 105,000 individuals. It is the premiere symbol of the AIDS pandemic, a living memorial to a generation lost to AIDS and an important HIV prevention education tool."[60] The quilt was a global phenomenon and a model of attending to pandemic grief that gives people from all walks of life the opportunity to grieve, remember, and hope.

Bibliography

Albanese, Catherine L. *America, Religions, and Religion*. 5th ed. Belmont, CA: Thomson/ Wadsworth, 2013.

Barry, Dan, et al. "U.S. Deaths Near 100,000, an Incalculable Loss: National Desk." *The New York Times*, May 24, 2020.

Boss, Pauline. *Ambiguous Loss: Learning to Live with Unresolved Grief*. Cambridge: Harvard University Press, 1999.

Bowlby, John. *Attachment and Loss*. Vol. 1, *Attachment*. 2nd ed. New York: Basic, 1969.

Bristow, Nancy K. *American Pandemic: The Lost Worlds of the 1918 Influenza Epidemic*. New York: Oxford University Press, 2012.

58. Mitchell and Anderson, *All Our Losses*, 148.

59. Jones and Dawson, *Stitching a Revolution*, 1.

60. National AIDS Memorial, "The History of the Quilt."

Cupcakes and Cashmere. "Short Stories: How COVID-19 Has Been Impacting Your Lives." https://cupcakesandcashmere.com/lifestyle/short-stories-how-covid-19-has-been-impacting-your-lives.

Doka, Kenneth J. *Disenfranchised Grief: New Directions, Challenges, and Strategies for Practice*. Champaign, IL: Research, 2002.

———. *Grief Is a Journey: Finding Your Path through Loss*. New York: Atria, 2016.

Fields, Corey. "Public Lament and Grief Shepherding: Neglected Roles of the Church in these Times." *The Christian Citizen*, June 10, 2020. https://christiancitizen.us/public-lament-and-grief-shepherding-neglected-roles-of-the-church-in-these-times/.

Harris, Darcy. *Non-death Loss and Grief: Context and Clinical Implications*. New York: Routledge, 2020.

Harris, Darcy, and Eunice Gorman. "Grief from a Broader Perspective: Nonfinite Loss, Ambiguous Loss, and Chronic Sorrow." In *Counting Our Losses: Reflecting on Change, Loss, and Transition in Everyday Life*, edited by Darcy Harris, 1–13. New York: Routledge Taylor & Francis Group, 2011.

Hays, J. N. *Epidemics and Pandemics: Their Impacts on Human History*. Santa Barbara, CA: Abc-Clio, 2005.

Janoff-Bulman, Ronnie. *Shattered Assumptions: Towards a New Psychology of Trauma*. New York: Free, 1992.

Jones, Cleve, and Jeff Dawson. *Stitching a Revolution: The Making of an Activist*. San Francisco: HarperSanFrancisco, 2000.

Kalaichandran, Amitha "We're Not Ready for This Kind of Grief: The Coronavirus Pandemic Will Leave Lasting Emotional Scars." *The Atlantic*, April 13, 2020. https://www.theatlantic.com/ideas/archive/2020/04/were-not-ready-for-this-kind-of-grief/609856/.

Kauffman, Jeffrey. "Introduction." In *Loss of the Assumptive World: A Theory of Traumatic Loss*, edited by Jeffrey Kauffman, 1–12. London: Routledge, 2014.

Kelley, Melissa M. *Grief: Contemporary Theory and the Practice of Ministry*. Minneapolis: Fortress, 2010.

Klein, Sandra Jacoby. *Heavenly Hurts: Surviving AIDS-related Deaths and Losses*. Amityville, NY: Baywood, 1998.

Klein, Danny. "Restaurant Industry Has Already Lost $120 Billion." *QSR*, June 30, 2020. https://www.qsrmagazine.com/fast-food/restaurant-industry-has-already-lost-120-billion.

Kornfeld, Margaret Zipse. *Cultivating Wholeness: A Guide to Care and Counseling in Faith Communities*. New York: Continuum,1998.

Kübler-Ross, Elisabeth. *On Death and Dying: What the Dying Have to Teach Doctors, Nurses, Clergy, and Their Own Families*. New York: Macmillan, 1969.

Kübler-Ross, Elisabeth, and David Kessler. *On Grief and Grieving: Finding the Meaning of Grief through the Five Stages of Loss*. New York: Scribner, 2005.

McMillen, Christian W. *Pandemics: A Very Short Introduction*. New York: Oxford University Press, 2016.

Mitchell, Kenneth R., and Herbert Anderson. *All Our Losses, All Our Griefs: Resources for Pastoral Care*. Philadelphia: Westminster, 1983.

Model D. "How Has COVID-19 Affected You? Detroit Youths Share Their Stories." https://www.modeldmedia.com/features/youth-essays-covid19.aspx.

National AIDS Memorial. "The History of the Quilt." https://www.aidsmemorial.org/quilt-history.

Pargament, Kenneth I. *The Psychology of Religion and Coping: Theory, Research, Practice.* New York: Guilford, 2001.

Parkes, Colin Murrary. "Psycho-social Transitions: A Field for Study." *Social Science & Medicine* 5.2 (1971) 101–15.

Rando, Therese A. *Grief, Dying, and Death: Clinical Interventions for Caregivers.* Champaign, IL: Research, 1984.

———. *Treatment of Complicated Mourning.* Champaign, IL: Research, 1993.

Roberts, Stephen, and Willard W. C. Ashley. *Disaster Spiritual Care: Practical Clergy Responses to Community, Regional, and National Tragedy.* Woodstock, VT: SkyLight Paths, 2008.

Roos, Susan. *Chronic Sorrow: A Living Loss.* 2nd ed. Milton: Taylor and Francis, 2017.

Stroebe, Margaret S., et al. *Handbook of Bereavement: Theory, Research, and Intervention.* New York: Cambridge University Press, 1993.

Swinton, John. *Raging with Compassion: Pastoral Responses to the Problem of Evil.* Grand Rapids: Eerdmans, 2007.

Worden, J. William. *Grief Counseling and Grief Therapy: A Handbook for the Mental Health Practitioner.* 5th ed. New York: Springer, 2018.

Zhai, Yusen, and Xue Du. "Loss and Grief amidst COVID-19: A Path to Adaptation and Resilience." *Brain, Behavior, and Immunity* 87 (2020) 80–81.

8

Spirituality in an Age of Pandemics

*Breathing with Uncertainty, Isolation, and Pain: Envisioning
a Different World*

—RUBEN L. F. HABITO

WE ARE ALL LIVING in unusual and perilous times, wherever we may be located in this interconnected global society of ours. The coronavirus has ushered in a world of widespread contagion, calling on each and every one of us to be vigilant and alert, at the cost of our very life itself.

As we open our eyes and ears to what is going on around us, three salient features emerge that describe our state of mind and way of being in this age of pandemic. First, there is *uncertainty* in the air. How long will all this last? What will happen to us through all this? This uncertainty breeds anxiety, which can degenerate into fear. Second, we are all enjoined, rather, mandated to maintain social distancing, with restrictive rules of physical contact with others, which leads to more and more *isolation* among human beings. This isolation can put walls of separation between myself and those I care for, making me tend to feel hemmed in and left to my own resources, with a sense of helplessness. Third, we become more and more acutely aware of the *pain and suffering* that is being experienced by our fellow inhabitants of this Earth, pain and suffering that we are all vulnerable to, some more intensely and directly than others, especially those economically less advantaged: the death toll from the coronavirus is highest among the poor of the earth. This pain and suffering weighs us down and can lead many of us to pessimism and despair.

In this context, a question I address in this chapter is: How can spiritual practice make a difference in the way we live through this time of spreading and lingering contagion? Another way of framing the question would be: what spiritual resources are available to us, to enable us to live with this uncertainty, isolation, and pain and suffering, in a way that does not drag us into destructive attitudes and behavior? In short, how may we overcome anxiety and fear, alienation and separation, pessimism and despair and instead be able to muster through this pandemic with the dignity that befits us as human beings and not just survive by the skin of our teeth and come back to our "normal ways," but putatively come out of it with a new vision and a new horizon for our global community?

We will explore ways of tapping into a force that may provide us with the vision and empowerment to live with the uncertainty, isolation, and pain and suffering that the pandemic has wrought upon us as individuals and as a global family, and explore ways in which this pandemic can be seen as an occasion to overcome our self-preoccupied and tribalistic mentalities to enable us to usher in a new world order based on a renewed appreciation of our kinship with one another and with the entire Earth community.

Uncertainty, Isolation, Pain, and Suffering: The Downside

Daily media reports have repeatedly harped upon the heavy toll of the pandemic in our individual and communal lives, in all its dimensions.

The uncertainty surrounding it all is unsettling. Given the dislocation we have all been through, with the restrictions on travel, on our work, in our social life, in our economic activities, in our well-trodden way of going about things, the questions naturally come up: "When do we get back our life again?" "Will it be a few more months? A year, or two?" "Will a vaccine effectively protect us from the virus?" And so on, with so much that remains in the realm of the unknown.

In the midst of this, we can begin to sense the anxiety cropping up, and coming to negatively affect the ways we live and do our daily tasks. Anxiety can easily give way to fear. Fear can paralyze us and render us incapable of doing creative and constructive tasks necessary for us to thrive. The most powerful kind of fear that can lay its grip on us is the fear of death. And with the coronavirus precisely being an agent of death for so many of those who contract it, this fear comes to be felt as a pervasive one as we weave our way through this pandemic.

From a biological point of view, living with fear has negative consequences for our health. Our immune system is weakened, and can result in cardiovascular damage, as well as gastrointestinal problems such as ulcers and irritable bowel syndrome. It can even lead to premature aging and early death. Fear can impair our memory and interrupt brain processes that enable us to regulate our emotional reactions to situations. As a result, we tend to act impulsively and reactively to things, rather than being able to reflect before taking action and make sound ethical decisions.[1]

Fear can also set us apart from one another, and tend to look at other human beings around us with suspicion and doubt, and thus harbor animosity toward them. This animosity will naturally be felt by those against whom we hold these sentiments, and will be returned in kind. This way of living in animosity with those around us will make life unpleasant and unbearable. We tend to recoil and build a protective wall between ourselves and others around us, and relate to others in either aggressive or defensive ways, seeking to protect our own turf from being invaded by others, and thus aggravating the sense of alienation from others. And once fear takes over us, we begin to think, say, and do things that can be destructive for ourselves and for those around us.

Another feature of our life in the age of pandemic that is also connected with the anxiety and fear generated by uncertainty is isolation. Part of the protocol during pandemic times is of course "social distancing," wherein we are enjoined to stay physically apart from others so as not to infect one another with the virus and further its spread. The physical isolation that is required of us for our own safety can aggravate a sense of alienation from others and add another layer to the anxiety and fear already creeping in on our lives.

Even independently of the pandemic, our global community is already wracked by divisiveness, segregation, and fragmentation, along socioeconomic, racial, ethnic, cultural, linguistic, and other lines that tend to separate us from one another. The inequalities that mark our global society tend to be highlighted all the more with the pandemic.

During these times we are hearing an eruption of voices decrying the inequities in our human community, determining in great part who succumbs to the virus and who gets by with little damage. The socioeconomic divide looms large, with tens of millions losing their jobs and their sources of income that provided for themselves and their families, placing countless people in dehumanizing situations of hunger and homelessness and vulnerability. It is evident that those in the lower rungs of the economic scale are the ones most likely to contract the virus and are also more likely to die from it, given all the factors combined.[2]

---

1. See Delagran, "Impact of Fear and Anxiety."
2. Fisher and Bubloa, "As Coronavirus Deepens Inequality."

The racial divide is also one with stark consequences, heightening the inequality and putting communities of color in greater danger. An article from the Center for American Progress notes that "persistent segregation has restricted millions of people of color to some of the most densely populated urban areas in the country; structural and environmental racism has produced extraordinarily high rates of serious chronic health conditions among people of color; and entrenched barriers in the health system continue to prevent people of color from obtaining the care they need."[3]

The racial divide has come to be highlighted in the United States with the senseless killing of George Floyd and a number of others by police officers on duty, setting off an outcry not only in the United States but which also reverberated throughout different parts of the world, with people being empowered to raise their voices against injustice and inequity and against authoritarian cruelty. The persistence of these voices may on the one hand serve to awaken us to take steps toward restructuring our societies for a more equitable, more just social order. On the other hand, rising voices of protest against the injustice and inequity of the system may also incite those in power to exercise more authoritarian measures and quash those voices in the name of "law and order," upholding a socio-political and economic system that only serves to protect the wealthy and maintain those in power in keeping the *status quo*.

Such an outcome will only aggravate the situations of great pain and suffering that many of our contemporaries are already being subjected to. At this writing, increasing numbers are contracting the virus and are in danger of losing their lives, or have been debilitated by it. Besides the physical pain, there is emotional pain: the very thought of the contracting the virus provokes anxiety and fear, depression, anger, and other negative emotions that impact our way of life. There is the pain and suffering of those individuals and families who have been economically displaced, having lost their livelihood, their source of income, their dwelling, and are rendered destitute. Just seeing the countless numbers of people adversely affected in many places across the world through media reports rends our heart and weighs down upon all of us.

In light of the above, the questions placed before us are: (1) How can we live with uncertainty that does not let us succumb to anxiety, and fear? (2) How can we live with the physical isolation in a way that does not lead to our alienation or separation from others, but instead, fosters solidarity and community even in the physical distancing? (3) How can we live with the pain and suffering borne by ourselves and our fellow human beings, in

---

3. Maxwell, "Coronavirus Compounds Inequality."

a way that does not embitter us and further isolate us from one another, but rather open our hearts to one another in compassion?

Exploring avenues of spiritual practice may open ways for us to address these vital questions that pertain to our very lives.

Spiritual Cultivation and Practice: Interfaith Resources

The living religious traditions of the world present different perspectives on what they consider the "spiritual," and a very short overview of some of these may be helpful in our exploration. These are merely encapsulated descriptions that do not do justice to the rich complexities of the traditions described, but our point in laying these out is to underscore the fact that spiritual cultivation is not the monopoly of any one religious tradition, but rather, is an underlying feature that connects the doctrinal message of the particular tradition with the day to day lives of its adherents.

In many indigenous traditions, the notion of a Great Spirit, referred to with different names, such as *Wakan Tanka* (Sioux), *Orenda* (Iroquois), or *Gitchie Manitou* (Algonquian), understood as a unifying life force that flows throughout and connects everything, a pervasive sacredness manifest in everything, is a central feature of their worldviews. Especially chosen individuals come to be regarded as spokespersons that mediate the world of humans with this Great Mystery that surrounds all, to ensure that order is maintained in the cosmos and that humans live in its accordance.[4] Different indigenous traditions have their various customs and practices that serve as ways of connecting with the Great Spirit, so that it comes to be a vibrant reality that informs their day to day lives.

In the Hindu tradition, Ātman is regarded as the underlying reality of all things, the True Self (also rendered as "soul") that makes everything what it is. Ātman is considered to be identical with *Brahman*, the ground and goal of the universe, a timeless and boundless reality in and through which the manifold phenomena we perceive with our senses are merged and experienced as One. Etymologically, the term "Ātman" derives from the word for "breath," as hinted at by the Greek word ατμός, "steam, vapor, fume, air" (as in "atmosphere") or the German verb *atmen*, "to breathe" (=noun, *Die Atmung*). Another word for "breath" in Sanskrit is *prāna*, a life-force directly linked to the Ātman.[5] The practice of yoga (from the

4. For engaging conversations on indigenous spiritualities and how these are approached from different angles, see Irwin, *Native American Spirituality*. For a theologically reflective approach, see O'Murchu, *In the Beginning Was the Spirit*.

5. See Sivaraman, *Hindu Spirituality*.

Sanskrit verb *yuj*, "to unite," "to integrate") with its many stages and intricate prescriptive steps toward traversing those stages, with intentional practices of breathing as an underlying component, is considered a path of spiritual practice that enables the individual human being to come to union with one's True Self, and thus transcend the vicissitudes of this impermanent life in the realm of worldly phenomena.

In Chinese traditions, the *Qi (chi)* is a life breath, a life-sustaining force which runs through the universe, and maintains the living energy that circulates through different channels. The discovery and knowledge these channels through which this life breath flows and their appropriate locations in the intricate human body, is the key to healing in Chinese medicine. It is intimately linked to the *Dao*, the Way of the Universe, the Way of Nature, the principle that sustains the universe. Living in accordance with the *Dao* and in consonance with this *Qi* is the way to peace and harmony.[6]

In the Jewish and Christian traditions, the word "spiritual" refers back to the word for *breath—rūah* in Hebrew, *pneuma* in Greek, *spiritus* in Latin. It is the Divine *rūah* that hovers over the waters and gives everything its form and shape. It is the same *rūah* who leads Israel out of Egypt, gives voice to the prophets to remind the people of their covenant with God, and brings back the people from exile.[7] In the New Testament, the *pneuma* of God, the Holy Spirit, is a creative power that performs mighty acts that reveal God's presence among the people. It is the Power that comes to Mary and enables her to bear a child (Luke 1:35), who is named *Yeshua* ("God saves") or Jesus in English. Jesus is led by the Spirit into the desert, consoled by the same Spirit as he triumphs over temptation, and called forth to proclaim to the multitudes: "The Spirit of the Lord is upon me, and has anointed me, to bring good news to the poor." (Luke 4:18). It is the Spirit that empowers Jesus to do the will of God throughout his life, and it is the Spirit that Jesus gives back to God in total surrender upon the cross (Matt 27:50). It is this Holy Spirit that is poured out on all people, and comes to fill the hearts of the followers of Jesus, opening their eyes to the wonders that God has shown to humankind in Jesus, and empowering them to be messengers of the good news of salvation to the ends of the earth. (Acts 2:1–39).

In Islam, the term *rūh*, which comes from the same root as the Hebrew *rūah*, appears in the Qur'an in connection with the term Ruh al-Qudus, "Holy Spirit," an agent of divine communication or action. *Rūh* as an expression in itself is translatable as "spirit," and can mean a locus or source of divine revelation, as in prophetic pronouncements.

---

6. See Lopez, *Religions of China in Practice*, 96.

7. See Levison, *A Boundless God*.

It must be emphasized at this point that the term "spiritual" as we use in this essay is *not* about a realm distinct from or opposed to the physical, material aspect of our human existence. In short, "spiritual practice" is not about seeking an escape from our concrete existential human situation, to lift us to another realm separate and distinct from our down to earth, material, physical existence. Regrettably, a way of thinking based on a dualistic separation between the spiritual as immortal, infallible, eternal, as opposed to the material-physical as mortal, fallible, ephemeral, subject to decay and death, has been all too prominent in Western culture. This dualistic opposition would value the "spiritual" as good, true, and beautiful and regard the "material" as evil, false, and the ugly aspect of our composite existence as human beings.

In Plato's *Phaedo*, a well-known discourse set in Socrates' final moments, arguments are lined up for immortality of the soul (*psychē*), setting it in clear opposition to the perishable body subject to death and decay. This dualistic mode of thinking has also found its way into Christian thought. Many tend to understand the gist of Christian belief as "doing good in this life to merit an eternal reward in heaven," where immortal souls reside.

In contrast, the Apostle's Creed that Christians regularly recite in liturgical celebrations proclaims the belief not in "the immortality of the soul" but in "the resurrection of the body, and life everlasting." The Nicene Creed proclaims "the resurrection of the dead, and life in the world to come." These proclamations of Christian belief indicate that it is the *whole human person*, and not just the soul as separated from the body, that is lifted up and opened to eternal life.

With the variety of ways the term "spiritual" is understood in the different living religious traditions in the background, we will take our cue from a working definition provided in a multi-volume series on World Spirituality issued by Crossroads Publications, and use this as our reference point. This twenty-two volume series presents the spiritual message of living world religious traditions, including Hindu, Buddhist, Jewish, Christian, Islamic, Indigenous, Confucian, African, and also Secular spirituality, with essays by renowned scholars and practitioners in their respective fields and traditions. A common preface before each of the volumes (authored by the late Catholic theologian Ewert Cousins) distills a consensus by the editors of the series on their understanding of the common theme of "spirituality."

> *The spiritual core is the deepest center of the person. It is here that the person is open to the transcendent; it is here that the person experiences ultimate reality.*

There is another dimension to this "spiritual core" that needs to be highlighted: *it is also here, at the deepest center of the person, where one experiences an intimate interconnectedness with everything that exists.* In short, the "spiritual" is to be understood as a unifying force that integrates our entire being in all its dimensions, which also includes and embraces the bodily, material aspects of our existence in a holistic perspective, while opening us to a dimension that is transcendent and holy, and at the same time also connecting us horizontally to all beings.

In offering a cursory overview of the various ways in which the term "spirit" is used in particular contexts and frameworks in different religious traditions as presented above, what I would like to highlight here is the intimate connection, manifested in particular forms and conceptualizations within each tradition, with this very concrete and palpable aspect of human experience, that is, the *breath*. This living reality we all experience in common, the *breath*, is interpreted and articulated in specific contexts of meaning in the different religions within their respective philosophical and theological frameworks. Here I suggest that *breath*, in the very concrete and palpable way it figures as a dynamic and central feature of our day-to-day human experience, is our direct gateway to that spiritual core, the innermost center of our existence as human beings, which opens us to the transcendent, as it opens us to our intimate interconnectedness with one another and with the entire universe.

Breathing is a basic function of all living beings, whether plant or animal life, but we humans may go about our business from day to day taking this for granted, without realizing its significance, or its immense power. There are moments when we feel overtaken by the hectic pace of life, and find it necessary to "catch our breath," so we can get our bearings again. That is it—"catch our breath," to recover, to reconnect with this power that holds us and connects us with the rest of the universe, to assure us that we are held, we are connected with the source of life. Or perhaps better, let the breath catch up with us. Let us just take a deep breath now, together, in, out. And once more, breathing in, receiving this gift of life, and breathing out, in that outward flow of the breath, giving back ourselves to the world. Receiving this gift of life, giving back with gratitude. Each breath is *just that*—an exchange of Life, receiving, and giving back.

The first practical point I would like to suggest here is this—an invitation to take a deep breath with awareness and intention at various times throughout the day, whenever it comes to us that we need to do so. Going about our daily chores, taking a walk, writing an email, driving a car, caring for the kids, waiting in line at the grocery store—in the midst of all this, taking a deep breath or two or three, with awareness of doing so, brings our busy minds back to the here and now, and reconnects us with our entire bodily being, enabling us to appreciate the gift of *this very moment*, in all that this entails. "Here I am, alive, breathing . . . !" —relishing the moment just as it is.

Or we may be in pain due to an injury, or may be in a hospital bed, or brokenhearted because of something that happened in a relationship. Those are moments when the breath beckons us to come home to itself and find comfort therein. Breathe, take in this gift of new life, and breathe out the pain, breathe out the sorrow, breathe out the heartache . . . and find solace, peace, acceptance, as we allow the breath to take over us, and lift up that little self that is hurting, and bring it to a different level of being, turning it around . . . into what? A wounded healer, capable of opening one's heart to bear the wounds of others, having known what it is to be wounded oneself.

I remember while I was a little child running around in the dirt, in my hometown in the Philippines, and once, I slipped, fell to the ground, hurting myself with a gash on my knee, some blood trickling out. My mother who was nearby immediately came close to me, bent down and blew a gentle breath or two on my wounded knee to assuage its pain. She took me in, washed the wound with a sanitizer, which caused it to hurt a little more, and again blew gently a few times into the gash that was causing me pain. Ah, that was comforting. This is what the breath can do for us—give us comfort, give us some relief, the midst of our pain and suffering. This is the breath that we turn to, with a renewed appreciation, as we live through this uncertainty, isolation, pain and suffering. To repeat, just breathe deeply, throughout the day, as often as we are able, as we notice our mind getting taken up by whatever may be before us, and come back to the full awareness of the here and now, with that deep breath.

The second practical point I would like to suggest, is to be intentional in giving time in our day-to-day lives to open ourselves to this healing power of the breath, even with a few minutes a day, for starters. We begin by finding a posture conducive to stillness, preferably seated, with our back straight so we can breathe easily from our lower abdominal region, called the *hara* in Japanese, where the center of gravity of the body is located, relaxing our shoulder and neck muscles. We put our hands gently on our lap, and sit straight, keeping our eyes slightly open; we then pay attention as we take each breath, breathing in, breathing out, breathing in, breathing out, and just going with that slow rhythm; third, we let the mind to simply rest in the present moment with each breath, breathing in, breathing out, allowing the mind to just be still, right here, right now. For some it may be helpful to count with each outbreath. Or by silently uttering a sacred word that is close to your heart, audible only to yourself, as you breathe out. This is a basic and common format of different kinds of meditative and contemplative practice found in many different religious traditions, but it may also be taken up by anyone without any religious belief system, as long as one has a trusting heart that there is something in this life that is bigger than what I can capture with my senses. Begin with five minutes a day. After a while, extend this to ten minutes.

The intentional practice of finding a posture conducive to outer and inner stillness, breathing with awareness, and allowing the mind to settle in the present moment, coming home to the here and now, are the three key components of Zen practice.[8] We will find similar features as we explore other forms, like Insight meditation, Christian Centering Prayer, secular mindfulness practice, or contemplative practice found in different religious traditions.[9] Taking on such a form of spiritual practice on a regular basis, even starting with a few minutes each day, can make a difference in how we live through these times. In what way?

What happens if we allow ourselves this time in our day-to-day lives to simply entrust ourselves to the breath in this intentional and focused way? We may notice something happening in us. We tend to feel less hectic, less agitated. We are more able to do our tasks with a deeper sense of peace and equanimity that people around us tend to notice perhaps more than we ourselves do. We can taste our food better; we can find little joys and surprises in the little things of day-to-day life. And, also, our hearts tend to be a little more open, to paying attention to those around us, open to welcoming others into our hearts. Our hearts are opened up to be able to see the pain and suffering of others around us as our very own, which helps unleash the power of compassion in us, the capacity to suffer-with. And in doing so, we become less preoccupied with our little egoic projects, my own little needs and wants and preferences, and become more disposed to wanting to help in alleviating the pain and suffering of others. Better disposed to give ourselves back to this wounded world, as an agent of healing, even in our little fumbling ways.

As we find this form of spiritual practice bearing fruit in our lives, of just being still, being aware of the breath, allowing the mind to come home to the present moment, which we call meditation or contemplative

---

8. See Habito, *Healing Breath*.

9. There are many books that offer detailed guidelines on meditation and contemplative practice, as well as video clips available on YouTube. I recommend the long-selling classic by Thich Nhat Hanh, *The Miracle of Mindfulness*, available in different editions by different publishers. A recently published volume which provides concrete guidelines for breathing as spiritual practice in the context of Christian Trinitarian spirituality is by Piccione, *Receiving God and Responding*.

practice, we are inspired and encouraged to give it a little more time, and more regularity and consistency, in our day-to-day lives. From a few minutes, to say, ten minutes, or twenty, twice a day. And this may inspire us to join a weekend, or a weeklong, or a ten-day contemplative retreat, and see where this takes us.

This intentional practice of stopping to return home to the breath, in the various ways it can be undertaken, may open a new horizon that may transform our life. We may understand this practice as connecting with the *Rūah* or *Rūh* of the Holy One, the Holy Spirit sent by the Risen One, the *prāna* or Ātman, or the Great Spirit that is the living source of life and energy in indigenous traditions, or the *Qi* (*Chi*) in Chinese religions. Or we may simply call it "reconnecting with the breath." And as we allow ourselves to come home to this breath, and be immersed in it, and are transformed by it, as more and more of us make this gradual but world-changing turn from a life of self-centered preoccupation and isolation, to one of inner peace and equanimity and solidarity, with a heart open to one another and able to welcome one another in compassion, indeed, what a different world, what a wonderful world this would be! It may not come in a day, but as we welcome each day as a new opportunity to live no longer in that self-preoccupied way, but in a way that is centered on this healing breath, little by little, we may see a new world in the making. Each of us can participate in bringing about this New World, beginning with our little circles of love and widening this to include the entire Earth, the entire universe!

Living with Uncertainty, Isolation, and Pain

Let us again look at the prevailing features that the pandemic has wrought on our individual and collective lives. Uncertainty can breed anxiety and degenerate into fear. Isolation can heighten a sense of alienation, and separation from one another, from those we love, from those with whom our destinies are intricately bound. Pain and suffering abound on all fronts. What can spiritual practice, in particular, the intentional practice of breathing, in the forms briefly described above, offer in this light?

Uncertainty is an unavoidable fact of life especially in these times. But the crucial difference is whether we are able to live with this uncertainty and find inner peace and equanimity in the midst of it, and not allow it to breed anxiety and fear that can become destructive for us and for those around us. If we have already found our way to a practice of cultivating stillness on a regular basis, it is those times of stillness that can open a way to see through this all this, and lead us to a place of peace, right in the midst of the uncertainty, that is, without knowing the answers to those questions about what is to happen next, which tend to preoccupy our minds. Fear and anxiety come about when our insecure mind projects into the future and we imagine a dreaded or unwanted outcome or situation. This practice of sitting in stillness, breathing in and breathing out, allowing the mind to settle in the here and now, to come home to the present moment, opens me to experiencing and appreciating *this present moment as such, as a gift.*

As I come home to this present moment, what happens? As I sit right here, right now, I breathe in, breathe out, my lower abdomen rises and falls, I am aware of sensations throughout my body, from the soles of my feet, my legs, my knees, my lower back, my shoulders, my head kept straight as I keep my eyes open seeing at what is in front of me. I look around the room, I see a table, a chair, a picture hanging from a wall. *Just this!* I look out the window, and I see a tree. I see the sky. I notice a squirrel climbing a tree, going from branch to branch. I see a blue jay perched on a branch then flying away. *Just this!* Each and every thing I see, hear, touch, taste, feel—*Just this!*

This is all-encompassing and all-embracing. If I am truly fully there, there is no future, no past, no fleeting present going into an uncertain future. There is *Just this!* To experience and taste this *Just this!* is our way to inner peace, to equanimity, to an open-hearted and free acceptance of what is, namely, *Just this!*, whatever "this" may be. With this open heart, we are able to take whatever comes, with the same equanimity, inner peace, acceptance, and share that peace and inner freedom with everyone around us. This palpable sense of equanimity allows us to open our eyes to the wonder and beauty of what is around us, and live our lives with joy and gratitude, rather than cowering in anxiety and fear.

Second, the practice of cultivating stillness can enable our social distancing, our condition of physical isolation, to lead us not to a state or feeling of loneliness and alienation, but conversely, to allow us to experience intimacy and deep interconnectedness with everyone around us, with everyone in the world, with all that exists! Going deep into the stillness that this practice opens me to precisely allows me to enter into a place where I realize I am never alone. A Latin verse comes to the fore in this regard: *Numquam minus solus quam cum solus* ("I am least alone when I am alone").[10]

As I look more deeply into things, I realize that this breath is the same breath being received, and given back, by all breathing beings the world around. To realize this very fact connects me directly with everyone who breathes, right here, right now, throughout the world, in their different

10. Often attributed to St. Augustine, but is found among the sayings of the Latin poet Cicero.

contexts and situations. As I go deeper, I am able to taste this intimacy with everyone, and I come to realize that there is no "I" or "me" unless there is everyone, each and everything that makes up this entire universe, that make me who "I am." This intentional practice of entering into stillness enables me to turn my solitude into *solidarity*, and especially in these times, solidarity with all those who are in pain and suffering.

This is the third element that is staring at all of us in the face. Pain and suffering are already in our midst, for some more intensely and directly than for others. All this can make us recoil within ourselves, bring us a sense of powerlessness, and perhaps make us become embittered and pessimistic about it all, seeking to put the blame somewhere. It can aggravate the sense of "us versus them," a tribalistic mentality that generates animosity and even incites violence against others. And yet, it is this very experience of pain and suffering that can turn our hearts around, and open us up to a heart of com-passion. Com-passion means "to suffer with," "to bear pain with" others, and this is a most natural direction our human hearts take when confronted with the realities of pain and suffering. If we do not react with fear and panic and do not allow our egoic defense mechanisms to get the better of us, that is, as we are able to find a place of inner peace and tranquility in our practice of stillness, we are able to open our hearts to bear the pain and suffering of the world as our very own suffering, accepting it within ourselves. This capacity to open our hearts to the pain and suffering of others inspires and empowers us to give ourselves back to the world as a gift of com-passion, to help alleviate the suffering and pain in the world, in whatever little or big way we are able. Each one of us can begin to figure out the most effective way we can contribute to this shared effort toward the alleviation of one another's pain and suffering.

In sum, breathing with *uncertainty* enables us to set aside speculations about what is to come in the near or far future, and instead come back to the certitude of this moment, right here, right now, where I can celebrate *what is, just as it is*, and not be worried about what will unfold from here on, tomorrow, next day, or next month or next year. To simply live my life, right here, right now, and open myself to that infinite gift that each moment offers, and thus be inspired to give back my gift of who I am as I am given to do so, in each moment. Going to the grocery store, just welcoming in our hearts all of those other shoppers instead of thinking, "Oh I better rush to the shelves to get my desired item before anyone else does, and so on." That kind of way of taking the uncertainty as an invitation to living my life right here, right now with my full awareness and confidence.

Breathing with *isolation* is a way of going deeper into our own hearts and connecting ourselves with the wider circle of other beings who are also like me seeking a connectedness and that is a deep, deep, longing in our heart, that connectedness with one another. So, let that be fully unleashed, that sense of connectedness, and see each and every one, each and every thing, as intimately connected with who we are.

Then, as we breathe with the pain and suffering of our fellow beings, not just other humans, but also all sentient beings, we naturally are drawn to open our hearts, and bring forth a heart of compassion that will move us to give ourselves back to the world as a gift, in a way that might, even in some little way, alleviate the suffering of those around us.

Conclusion: Becoming Agents of a New World in the Making

Our global society continues to be plagued by major crises on many fronts. The violence being perpetrated by human beings against one another on the personal, structural, and ecological levels continues to take its toll in countless lives. The disparity between the economically privileged and those who are barely making it through continues to grow. The ecological threat upon our planet, our habitat of life, continues to hover over us and forebode catastrophic scenarios. All this had already been impinging upon us before the Coronavirus came upon the scene.[11] We are in urgent need of a veritable transformation in the way we live our lives together on this Earth, or proceed headlong toward a destructive future.

And now, with the pandemic, an added threat to our individual and communal lives has come to weigh down upon our global society, already in dire straits as it is.

As we look around and survey what is happening, there are two kinds of directions that the pandemic can have as an outcome. We have seen how panic can drive many to rush to the stores to stack up on what they thought they needed—besides food and basic supplies, items like hand sanitizers and toilet paper were soon gone from the shelves. The uncertainty has indeed brought forth anxiety and fear, and panic, to come to the fore in the way many people have behaved. The divisions among us, in economic class, in racial identification, in national boundaries, have come to be more pronounced, aggravating the pain and suffering of many. The isolation has led many to recoil and put protective walls for themselves, watching out only for their own interests, separating them further from others. The pain and suffering have, indeed, led

---

11. For a detailed analytic look at our global situation, with prescriptive recommendations for addressing these, see Sheppard, *Ten Years to Midnight*. For a shorter account, see Habito, "Spiritual Practice and Formation."

to despair and pessimism among countless numbers of our contemporaries. These are facts that we cannot make light of.

And yet, and yet, on the other hand, we also are invited to open our eyes to new horizons that the pandemic can open, to those with a heart willing to listen to our basic humanity from the depths of our being. It is very significant to note that in the midst of our common plight, random acts of compassion, neighborliness, generosity, sacrifice, solidarity, are being witnessed and reported on so many fronts.[12] In this regard, a comment by astronaut Scott Kelly, who spent nearly a year in a space station, strikes home to us.

> Seen from space, the Earth has no borders. The spread of the coronavirus is showing us that what we share is much more powerful than what keeps us apart, for better or for worse. All people are inescapably interconnected, and the more we can come together to solve our problems, the better off we will all be.[13]

To see the Earth from outer space is a privilege only a small handful of individuals have been given. But to behold the Earth, and all things therein, living and non-living, from *inner space*, that is, from that perspective of the deepest center of our being which the intentional practice of being still and being aware of the breath, is available to anyone with a willingness to turn one's gaze in this direction. We can call spiritual practice the art of learning to view things from *inner space*. And from this perspective, we will also be able to proclaim, with as much, or even much stronger emphasis, that we are all "inescapably interconnected."

The pandemic has brought us to a fork in the road in our historical journey, and the direction we choose to go will impact our collective future. This critical situation we are all in can either bring out the worst, or the best in us as human beings, depending on how we react or respond to the situation before us. In this light, the intentional practice of being aware of our breathing, and finding time to immerse ourselves in stillness, to be able to come home to the deepest center of our being, to our spiritual core, can be the crucial factor that determines our collective future.

As we take on this intentional practice, and experientially realize our inescapable interconnectedness, that is, *intimate kinship* with one another,

12. See, e.g., the concrete instances of such acts that give us all a sense of hope in humanity and how the pandemic is "bringing out the best in all of us": Tester, "Coronavirus Impact"; Polly, "Can a Pandemic Bring Out the Best in Us?"; Taylor, ""How Bad Times Bring out the Best in People"; Bregman, "Disasters and Crises Bring out the Best in Us."

13. Kelly, "I Spent a Year in Space."

we will be able to reach out to one another across our differences, and be able to join hands and work together to dismantle the current global system that breeds economic, racial, and other kinds of inequity, disparity, oppression, and ecological destruction that are blights on our life together on this Earth.

We may thus be able to envision and work toward bringing about a different world from our current one, a world that would be more equitable, more just, more accepting of our differences, and more conducive to the well-being of all. This is a world wherein we are able to go beyond our self-preoccupied and tribalistic ways of thinking and, instead, grounded in inner peace and equanimity, a deeply felt sense of solidarity and active compassion, celebrate our mutual *kinship* as breathing beings together on this Earth whose destinies are intricately bound with one another. In this way we may we be able to usher in a "more beautiful world our hearts know is possible."[14]

Bibliography

Bregman, Rutger. "Disasters and Crises Bring out the Best in Us." *TED*, March 20, 2020. https://ideas.ted.com/disasters-and-crises-bring-out-the-best-in-us/.

Delagran, Louise. "Impact of Fear and Anxiety." https://www.takingcharge.csh.umn.edu/impact-fear-and-anxiety.

Eisenstein, Charles. *The More Beautiful World Our Hearts Know Is Possible*. Berkeley: North Atlantic, 2013.

Fisher, Max, and Emma Bubloa. "As Coronavirus Deepens Inequality, Inequality Worsens Its Spread." *New York Times*, March 15, 2020. https://www.nytimes.com/2020/03/15/world/europe/coronavirus-inequality.html. Accessed July 5, 2020.

Habito, Ruben L. F. *Healing Breath: Zen for Christians and Buddhists in a Wounded World*. Boston: Wisdom, 2006.

———. "Spiritual Practice and Formation in a World of Violent Extremism." In *Teaching in a World of Violent Extremism*, edited by Eleazar Fernandez, 208–34. Eugene, OR: Pickwick Publications, 2021.

Hanh, Thich Nhat. *The Miracle of Mindfulness: An Introduction to the Practice of Meditation*. Boston: Beacon, 1999.

Irwin, Lee, *Native American Spirituality: A Critical Reader*. Omaha: University of Nebraska Press, 2000.

Kelly, Scott. "I Spent a Year in Space, and I Have Tips on Isolation to Share." *New York Times*, March 21, 2020. https://www.nytimes.com/2020/03/21/opinion/scott-kelly-coronavirus-isolation.html.

Levison, Jack. *A Boundless God: The Spirit according to the Old Testament*. Grand Rapids: Baker Academic, 2020.

14. Eisenstein, *The More Beautiful World*.

Lopez, Donald, Jr., ed. *Religions of China in Practice*. Princeton Readings in Religion. Princeton: Princeton University Press, 1996.

Maxwell, Connor. "Coronavirus Compounds Inequality and Endangers Communities of Color." *CAP*, March 27, 2020. https://www.americanprogress.org/article/coronavirus-compounds-inequality-endangers-communities-color/.

O'Murchu, Diarmuid. *In the Beginning was the Spirit: Science, Religion, and Indigenous Spirituality*. Maryknoll, NY: Orbis, 2012.

Piccione, Joseph J. *Receiving God and Responding, in Breath Meditation: Praying at the Intersection of Christian Trinitarian Spirituality and the Breath Practice of Zen and Mindfulness*. New York: Herder & Herder, 2020.

Polly, Shannon. "Can a Pandemic Bring Out the Best in Us?" https://www.shannonpolly.com/can-a-pandemic-bring-out-the-best-in-us/.

Sheppard, Blair. *Ten Years to Midnight: Four Urgent Global Crises and Their Strategic Solutions*. San Francisco: Berrett-Koehler, 2020.

Sivaraman, Krishna. *Hindu Spirituality: Vedas through Vedānta*. New York: Crossroad, 1989.

Taylor, Bill. "How Bad Times Bring out the Best in People." *Harvard Business Review*, March 20, 2020. https://hbr.org/2020/03/how-bad-times-bring-out-the-best-in-people.

Tester, Hank. "Coronavirus Impact: Pandemic Bringing out the Best in People." *CBS Miami*, April 24, 2020. https://miami.cbslocal.com/2020/04/24/coronavirus-bringing-out-best-in-people/.

9

Mission and Ministry in the Age of Pandemics

—JONATHAN BARNES

DURING THESE UNCERTAIN DAYS, as the numbers of global infections and deaths from COVID-19 continue to rise, it is important to remember that God's mission of love, forgiveness, reconciliation, and justice (the *missio Dei*) in our world is both perennial and contextual. In referring to God's mission in the world as perennial, we are saying that God has been, continues to be, and will always be working in and through the world to bring *shalom*. One helpful way of thinking about this God of constant and eternal mission is by saying that "God . . . might best be described as a *verb*, not a noun. . . . God is a Movement, an Embrace, a Flow—more personal than we can ever image—who is always and everywhere present in God's creation."[1] In referring to God's mission as contextual, we are saying that mission must be, by necessity, received, understood, and embodied in the real lives, cultures, and circumstances of people. While those of faith may rely on sacred texts and tradition for guidance, these texts and traditions must be interpreted in ways that speak to people in the concrete realties of their lives. In seeking to be a part of making God's perennial mission visible in the specific contexts in which we find ourselves, we are invited to join this "flow" by discerning, as best we can, what God is doing in the world and then participating in it.

Our current context is one marked by liminality. The word "liminal" comes from the Latin word *limen*, referring to a threshold, such as a doorway, between two spaces. Just as crossing through a doorway can move one from inside a house, with its walls, ceilings, and artificial light, to a yard that

---

1. Bevans and Schroeder, *Prophetic Dialogue*, 9.

is carpeted with grass and open to the sky, liminal times of life are spaces between one way of living or engaging the world that is comfortable (or at least familiar) to another that is new and often unfamiliar and undefined. At times we enter liminal space of our own volition, such as going on a retreat where we intentionally leave our normal, day-to-day existence and create time for silence, reflection, discernment, and rest. In my own life, most notably just after a near-death experience a few years ago, entering intentionally into liminal spaces of retreat and reflection were life-giving as I tried to discern what life looked like going forward. Other times, however, we are thrown into liminal spaces by circumstances that are completely out of our control. The loss of a job and secure income, the death of a spouse or child, or facing our own mortality through the diagnosis of terminal illness are just a few examples that many of us or those we love have experienced. In these liminal spaces of life our old way of living and experiencing the world ends, the walls that gave us structure, security, and meaning crashing down around us. And in the darkness, confusion, and uncertainty, the "what's next" of a new normal is not clear.

In this time of global pandemic, we have all been flung into a liminal space not of our own choosing. Whatever our nationality, language, culture, or religion, the signposts and maps we formerly used to navigate our lives in the world are at best outdated and, in many cases, obsolete. This fact became viscerally apparent on my first trip to the grocery store after "stay-at-home" orders had been instituted in mid-March. As I walked down an aisle, I noticed someone walking towards me. As we approached one another, my immediate thoughts were "Is this person a danger to me?" and "Am I a danger to this person?" I tried to take as wide a berth as possible in the aisle, not knowing if either of us had been exposed to the disease and could possibly endanger the other. It was an unnatural and jarring experience that simply being near another human could be potentially dangerous to one or both of us. This was our new reality, not just in my local community but globally as well. While at this point these precautions have been in place for a number of months, we are still living in unfamiliar territory and, at least as I sit here and write this chapter, there are few answers. How long will we have to practice social distancing? What about those who, due to conditions beyond their control, are not able to be socially distant and are most at risk? Will hospitals be able to handle future waves of the pandemic and what about those who are not able to access medical care? What about those who have lost jobs and the security of a paycheck? And, even with the welcome news that vaccines are on the way, when will this end? However, despite this new and unwelcome global context, our calling as people of faith to join God in what God is doing, to participate in the *missio*

Dei, has not changed. During this liminal time, mission and ministry must continue to be contextually relevant.

Because liminal spaces are times of uncertainty and confusion with no clear path forward, what can be said about mission and ministry in these days? Remembering that any idea put forward must be tentative, I would like to suggest a few general directions for those seeking to participate in what God is doing in the world. First, this time can help us realize our shared humanity and connection to God's wider creation. We are experiencing this pandemic together as COVID-19 has affected all areas of the world; not one nation or group has been unaffected. In addition, as travel and industry have shut down, we are seeing small signs of creation's healing and can begin to understand just how interdependent we are with the natural world. Second, while we may be connected through this shared experience, our connections often do not lead to community. While all are affected, not all are affected equally and we must acknowledge and face the great disparities that exist between people, both locally and around the world, that this disease is making newly apparent. Finally, mission in a time of pandemic demands at least three mission motifs: mission as lament, as we recognize the deep suffering and social dislocation a pandemic causes; mission as dialogue, as we understand that all peoples are affected and all have gifts to share; and mission as a witness to life, as this "great pause" offers the chance to rethink how we structure our lives and societies to be in harmony with God's economy.

A Reminder That We Are All Connected

One thing that is abundantly clear during this pandemic is how connected we are as a global community. While some political leaders in the United States labeled the disease as a "foreign" or "Chinese" virus, pandemics do not recognize national borders or discriminate based on nationality, language, ethnicity, or culture. Notably, the spread of the virus, both in its speed and intensity, speak to the global connections that are a reality in our world. Due to satellite communications and internet connections, people around the world could watch the spread of the disease as it happened, each day bringing updates as to the impacts on the worst affected communities in China, Italy, Iran, Spain, and the United States. Countries around the world closed schools, stopped receiving international flights, and went into various levels of lockdown.

During these days, we continue to be connected in both our collective sorrow as well as in our capacity to show love and care to others. In communities across the world, stories of overwhelmed hospitals, grieving families, stores running out of basic necessities, and millions losing employment and the security of income continue to dominate the news cycles. At the same time, we have seen images of healthcare workers serving tirelessly, many having to quarantine away from family and friends due to possible exposure to the virus. Nurses have held the hands of dying patients or connected families virtually to be with loved ones in their final moments of life. There have been videos of people in Italy going to their balconies each evening to sing together, truces between rival gang members in South Africa as they work together in church food distribution centers, and celebrations in the US as COVID-19 survivors are released from hospitals. One of the most popular YouTube videos during the early days of the pandemic was SGN (Some Good News), produced by actor John Krasinski. Krasinski began the SGN series in early April, seeking to bring stories of hope and community to a global audience, and by the time he produced the eighth and final installment in mid-May, similar videos were being created in places like India, Vietnam, Nepal and Canada. We are also able to recognize that our connections go beyond humanity to all of creation as the shutdown in the normal activities of work and travel led to lower pollution levels, wildlife roaming freely, and the earth actually vibrating less!

When one looks at the history of mission work, especially in its Western manifestations, it is easy to critique the church's ties to colonialism and the spread of so-called "modern" civilization. There are, however, many examples that show recognizing our connectedness and common humanity is not new for people of faith who have sought to participate in God's mission. At the Edinburgh World Missionary Conference in 1910, V. S. Azariah, the first ordained Indian bishop in the Anglican Communion, addressed issues of missionary paternalism, asking for a qualitatively different relationship: "Through all the ages to come the Indian Church will rise up in gratitude to attest the heroism and self-denying labours of the missionary body. You have given your goods to feed the poor. You have given your bodies to be burned. We also ask for *love*. Give us friends!"[2] Over the years, through organizations like the World Student Christian Federation and the YMCA, leaders like Azariah, John Mott, Sherwood Eddy, K. T. Paul, and C. Y. Cheng sought to bring people together cross-culturally, believing that their common faith was a bond that bridged any differences of ethnicity, culture or language.[3] Following World War II, the establishment of the

---

2. World Missionary Conference, *History and Records*, 309.

3. For more on cross-cultural friendship as a missional motif, see Robert, "Cross-Cultural Friendship."

World Council of Churches in 1948 led to a formal, worldwide ecumenical movement that, recognizing our shared humanity as well as our shared destiny on planet Earth, sought to bring people together to face issues such as violence, racism, women's rights, and economic and environmental justice that affect all people, regardless of nationality or faith tradition. In the second half of the twentieth century the terminology of "friendship" was replaced by that of "partnership." While the practice of "partnership" has been problematic,[4] the ethos of connecting individuals and communities into a global family of faith has continued.

People of faith recognizing our common humanity and connectedness continues today, and not just within the Christian tradition. Churches, mosques, gwardas, synagogues, and temples have all had to shut down in-person worship and other gatherings for the safety of their communities. Adjustments have had to be made to the way holy times such as Christmas, Ramadan and Yom Kippur are observed. Many churches in the US and around the world have moved to online worship and virtual times of fellowship, recognizing the importance of protecting members, especially those that are older and have underlying health conditions. In Jamaica, congregations associated with the United Church in Jamaica and the Cayman Islands have organized care packages for those most in need and organized weekly, nationwide times of prayer for all who are suffering. The Zimbabwean Council of Churches, in coordination with ecumenical partners, is providing protective clothing and sanitizer to affected communities. And the Middle East Council of Churches has asked people of all faiths to take time for prayer, fasting, and acts of charity, seeing this liminal time as a "new opportunity to confirm that 'human fraternity' stems from our brotherhood in Christ and that spiritual solidarity can be lived through prayer and fasting."[5] Along with these, many other examples could be shared as to how faith communities, recognizing our connectedness in this shared context of pandemic, are seeking to participate in God's mission.

But Our Connections Do not Necessarily Lead to Community

While this pandemic is making our connections more apparent, it is also revealing the deep disparities among us, both within the US and around the world. While it has been said that we live in a "global village," the late

4. For an analysis of how the term "partnership" in mission originated and developed over time, see Barnes, *Power and Partnership*.

5. Global Ministries, "MECC."

South African scholar Steve DeGruchy noted that "this is a [global] village that has a chief, a headmen, and favoured families, and poor families, and women who collect the water and the firewood, and beggars living on the scraps on the edge of the town; and lepers who aren't allowed in town. And the price of having a stall in the market is too high for some families to trade their goods."[6] Disparities among communities and people in our world are not new. In May, the murder of George Floyd by a white police officer in Minneapolis, another tragedy in a long list of African Americans killed at the hands of police, sparked protest around the country and world. Systemic racism, sexism, homophobia, and the exploitation of the poor, along with the threat of militant white nationalism, are part and parcel of the daily experience of millions. This pandemic and its resultant misery, however, are revealing these realities in new ways as study after study is showing that multidimensional factors such as race, gender, education, income level, and access to health care are highly accurate indicators of one's ability to cope with its affects.[7] In the US, the wealth gap and race are inextricably connected. African American and Hispanic communities are far more exposed to financial insecurity during this pandemic. It has been estimated that even before the pandemic began, "almost 30 percent of Black college-educated households, and 20 percent of Latinx college-educated households, would not be able to afford to pay all of their bills after a $400 emergency expense."[8] For households without a college-educated individual, those percentages increase to 60 percent for African Americans and 50 for Hispanics. The devastating impacts of the virus on the economy are difficult on all, but they are being disproportionally felt in communities of color. The stay-at-home orders being issued in countries around the world have led to increased confinement, leading to higher rates of gender-based violence, restricted access to family planning services, and disproportionate economic impacts. In many countries like Kenya, India, Brazil and South Africa, large informal settlements, where hundreds of thousands of people live in makeshift housing, practicing social distancing and accessing adequate healthcare are almost impossible. While noting that social distancing is effective in slowing the spread of COVID-19, South African pastor Rev. Sindiso Jele addressed the class issues inherent in who can realistically practice social distancing and who cannot, writing that these policies "seems to be designed with certain people in mind. For the people in informal settlements it does not

---

6. DeGruchy, "Being Connected," 1.

7. Kneebone and Reeves, "Multidimensional Poverty."

8. Solomon and Hamilton, "Pandemic and Racial Wealth Gap."

make sense."[9] Food insecurity is not a new phenomenon in our world, but during this pandemic, millions who live on the margins even in the best of times are forced to depend to an even greater degree on handouts and charity. The devastating effects of COVID-19 on indigenous peoples, such as the Navajo in the US southwest, is apparent as a combination of poverty, lack of adequate healthcare, and a high percentage of individuals living with underlying health issues is causing infection rates that rival those of large urban areas. In addition to the exacerbation of inequalities listed above, those of us living in the US have increasingly seen our divided nation grow even more so as people retreat into their respective political camps. For many politicians, the response to the pandemic seems to be driven not by science but by political expediency. While we may all be connected in this pandemic, our connections have not overcome the deep divides that separate us as communities and individuals.

While we have looked at examples of how involvement in mission has served to connect peoples across divides of culture, race, and language, we must admit that seeking to participate in God's mission has, at times, intensified preexisting inequalities in our world. And if we are honest, those inequalities are often the result of not only a sense of Western superiority but also a concomitant view of white privilege. Despite efforts at cross-cultural friendship and partnership, paternalistic and patronizing mission relationships have mitigated much of what could have been accomplished over the years in converting our connections into genuine community. Henry Venn, secretary of the Church Mission Society in England from 1841 to 1873 and one of the most important leaders and thinkers in the modern Protestant mission movement, shared a story about a conversation he had with a merchant from Sierra Leone, illustrating the problem of paternalism in mission relationships. As the merchant shared about his extensive travels, Venn asked him, "'Now if you can afford to spend money on travelling for your pleasure, why don't you contribute something to the support of your own clergy, instead of leaving it all to us in England?' The merchant replied, 'Mr. Venn, treat us like men, and we will behave like men; but so long as you treat us like children, we shall behave like children. Let us manage our own Church affairs, and we shall pay our own clergy.'"[10]

Whether mission was framed as friendship or partnership, over the decades these relationships have been fraught with difficulties, including debates of a moratorium on sending mission personnel and the sharing of resources, especially finances. As J. Andrew Kirk has noted, "partnership is a

9. Jele, "Choosing between Death and Life."
10. Warren, *To Apply the Gospel*, 26–27.

wonderful idea; pity the practice!"[11] Throughout mission history, the struggle of participating in God's mission in ways that bring about genuine relationships of equality and love over against ways of relating that are aligned with the normativity of Western values and white superiority have made turning our connectedness into community incredibly difficult and, at times, impossible. Our inability to realize this goal is being felt by marginalized communities today as they face the brunt of the pandemic.

Three Missional Motifs

When thinking about what contextually relevant participation in God's mission might look like in these days of pandemic, at least three directions for mission arise. First, in the midst of suffering, death, and a very pervasive unease about the future, involvement in God's mission needs to leave room for lament as we grieve deeply for ourselves and for each other. Second, in recognizing the dignity of all people, communities, and cultures, we need to seek God's mission in dialogue with others, understanding that we all have gifts and insights to share as well as much to learn. Finally, in a world racked with inequality, oppression, and hatred towards the "other," participation in God's mission requires us to take stands as we witness to life. While each motif will be considered briefly, my hope is that the following discussion will help spur further reflection on these as well as other possible directions for seeking to participate in God's mission in this liminal time.

An important insight from the late South African scholar David Bosch can help us frame these three motifs: the need to engage in mission with "bold humility." In explaining what this phrase means in relation to our participation in God's mission, Bosch notes that "we know only in part, but we do know. And we believe that the faith we profess is both true and just, and should be proclaimed. We do this, however, not as judges or lawyers, but as witnesses; not as soldiers, but as envoys of peace; not as high pressure salespersons, but as ambassadors of the Servant Lord."[12] Unfortunately, too much of our past mission engagement has tended to emphasize the first part of Bosch's phrase to the exclusion of the latter. In this liminal time of communal suffering, joining in God's mission necessitates an adjustment in our way of engagement to intentionally emphasize the second word in Bosch's phrase, "humility."

---

11. Kirk, *What Is Mission?*, 191.
12. Bosch, *Transforming Mission*, 489.

Mission as Lament

There have been few times in history when we as a global community have experienced an event of this magnitude corporately. As mentioned earlier, while some nations and peoples have been affected to a greater degree than others, no part of the world has been untouched. Regardless of our nationality, ethnicity, language, culture, or religion, we are all grieving. We are grieving the loss of so many lives, numbering well over one million worldwide. We are grieving that while these numbers are difficult to comprehend, we know that each one has died has a name, a history, and loved ones who are now facing life without them. We are grieving the millions who may have recovered from the virus but will continue to face health issues, such as chronic lung damage, because of the infection. We are grieving the staggering loss of employment and livelihoods as people, many who were living financially on the edge already, face the uncertainty of how to pay for the basic necessities of life: food, shelter, education, and adequate healthcare to name a few. We are grieving the need to isolate from family and friends, knowing that it is necessary for the care and protection of others but desperately missing being in community with those we love. We are grieving the loss of our old ways of life, not knowing when things will normalize or what a new normal will even look like. We are grieving.

One response to grief is lament, a crying out to God in the midst of suffering, pain, and loss. According to scholar Emmanuel Katongole, lament is "a way of dwelling in the ruins."[13] Since grief, suffering, and mourning are part of our human condition, one can find many references to lament in the Bible. In the Hebrew scriptures, the book of Lamentations recounts the cries of the Israelites after the siege and destruction of Jerusalem and the temple in 587 BCE. In 2 Samuel, David laments for Saul and Jonathan after their deaths, and almost two thirds of the Psalms are prayers of lament. In the New Testament, Matthew quotes a lament from the book of Jeremiah in response to the killing of the innocents in Bethlehem and, prior to being raised from the dead by Jesus, Jairus' family mourns the death of his daughter. Even Jesus lamented at the death of his friend, Lazarus, as well as during his crucifixion.

In our current context, we see many Christians ready to move past the pandemic and resultant suffering and death. The internet is full of stories of churches seeking to reopen, blaming governments for overstepping their bounds in restricting access to church buildings and desiring a return to normalcy, even at the risk of congregants. We also see Christians who seem

13. Katongole, *Born from Lament*, 19.

confident that they know or can identify what God is doing or what God may be trying to teach through this time. However, instead of trying to move past this time of suffering, I would contend that taking time to lament is not only helpful but necessary and part of our calling as people of faith.

In speaking to the importance of lament in our faith journey, Katongole writes that "the cry of lament is not only emotionally, psychologically, and physiologically important; it is every bit as crucial and theologically significant in the context of suffering as anything we can physically do."[14] He goes on to note that "the cry of lament is a dynamic and generative cry whose potential is to create a community of solidarity and compassionate advocacy . . . It is a call for God's action on behalf of God's people."[15] During a time of pandemic, there are countless opportunities to reach out to others in love. People are involved in caring for the sick, working at food banks, teaching students online, checking in on elderly neighbors, donating goods or money, and making masks for those on the front lines. One can see any of these and many others as ways to join God in mission today. We cannot, however, overlook that we might be called by God to the action of contemplation, simply being present with ourselves and others in our collective grief. In response to the question "How long, O God, will you hide your face?" (Ps 13:1), one of the best ways to engage in mission during these days might be to sit on the metaphorical ash heap with one another, rending our clothes, and crying out to a God whose response may seem to be silence. For those of us who are accustomed to seeing mission as "doing" something with or for another, the idea of "sitting on an ash heap" may not resonate. However, as Katongole notes, participating in lament is both dynamic and generative. It allows us, in the midst of our grief, to cry out for God's strength and direction in reimagining a new future. Suffering is not a new phenomenon in our world and much of it, as we have noted earlier, is systemic in nature. Participating in lament offers us a space to grieve and at the same time begin the process of rethinking how to structure our lives and world going forward. Lament also allows us to question our presuppositions about God and to be open to new ways of knowing and experiencing the Holy. In liminal times such as these, the ways we have understood God may not hold. Our faith can be changed as we are challenged to envision God's work in the world and our participation in it in fresh ways. Participation in lament also allows us to be in solidarity with the pain being felt in these days, our own and the worlds, and especially that of those who have been pushed even further to the margins of society.

14. Katongole, *Born from Lament*, 52.
15. Katongole, *Born from Lament*, 52.

As Katongole notes, "the cry of lament is not simply a prayer but a social ethic—a passionate, pastoral, and practical engagement on behalf of the crucified of history."[16] In a time of pandemic, the work of simply being present in lament, in solidarity with others and with God in the midst of intense suffering and grief, may be one of the most profound ways to participate in God's work of healing, love and justice.

Mission as Dialogue

At the seminary where I studied, all students were required to take classes in Christian spirituality. During one of our sessions, the professor, Dr. Glenn Hinson, asked us to imagine that the whiteboard in the front of the room represented God. The room was quite large and the whiteboard spanned the entire front space. Dr. Hinson then turned to the whiteboard and drew a small, black square. From where I sat, it actually looked like a tiny dot. He then turned to us and said "If this whiteboard represents God, in all of God's totality and mystery, then this square represents what you understand. Please, when you are serving in ministry and say, 'Thus says the Lord,' remember to have some humility. There is much more that we can't say about the deep mystery and love of God than that which we can."

When looking at the history of Christian mission, there has been a strong emphasis on the first part of Bosch's phrase, sharing the gospel with boldness (which, at times, has bordered on arrogance) and acting as if our small square actually encompasses the entire board. Theologically speaking, this boldness comes from an affirmative or *kataphatic* perspective. *Kataphatic* can be translated as "according to symbols" and relies on metaphors and images to describe God, expressing our understanding of the Holy. Examples include speaking of God as lover, rock, fortress, mighty wind, and as savior. However, while we do need words and images to share the Good News of God's love, mission in a time of pandemic just might help us with a much needed corrective, incorporating an emphasis on the second word in Bosch's phrase, humility, and drawing us towards the rich springs of negative or *apophatic* theology. *Apophatic* means "without symbols" and is the admission that, whatever words and images we find to describe God, they fall utterly short in seeking to understand and name the ineffable. *Apophatic* theology has long been part of the Christian tradition, especially in the Roman Catholic and Orthodox branches. Theologians like Pseudo-Dionysius, Gregory of Nyssa, Meister Eckhart, Julian of Norwich, John of the Cross, and the anonymous author of *The Cloud of Unknowing* are just a few of the great Christian

16. Katongole, *Born from Lament*, 120.

thinkers and who have explored the mystery and unknowability of God in their writings. Even Augustine, known as one of the theological giants in the history of the church, admitted that "if you have understood, then it is not God. If you were able to understand, then you understood something else instead of God. If you were able to understand even partially, then you have deceived yourself with your own thoughts."[17]

Unfortunately, when one studies mission history, especially in its Protestant forms, there is little doubt that the emphasis has been on bold proclamation: humility has had little place in Western Christianity's mission efforts. William Carey, known as the "father of modern missions," helped found the Baptist Missionary Society in 1792. In a famous essay entitled *An Enquiry into the Obligations of Christians to Use Means for the Conversion of the Heathens*, Carey noted the importance of Matthew 28:18–20 as a text undergirding the call on Christians to engage in mission: "And Jesus came and said to them, 'All authority in heaven and on earth has been given to me. Go therefore and make disciples of all nations, baptizing them in the name of the Father and the Son and the Holy Spirit, and teaching them to obey everything that I have commanded you.'"[18] The idea of going out into the world, armed with the truth of the Gospel (as they understood it), led to the creation of literally dozens of voluntary societies that supported thousands of missionaries. This great era of mission activity took place concomitantly with the Age of Humanitarianism as like-minded people banded together to fight for justice, including the ending of slavery and child labor, and for the enfranchisement of women. While there is little doubt that these efforts had positive effects on vulnerable peoples, one result was that the assurance Christians felt about the superiority of their faith was wed to the assurance they felt about the superiority of Western cultures. These feelings only increased after the 1880s as the era of high colonialism enabled European powers to expand their power and influence around the globe.

In recent years, there has been an emphasis on dialogue in mission with many noting the need for humility to replace the certainty of earlier mission efforts. Catholic scholars Stephen Bevans and Roger Schroeder have written about the need for what they have termed as "prophetic dialogue" in mission efforts today, noting:

> [no] longer can we conceive of mission in terms of church expansion or the salvation of souls; no longer can we conceive of mission as supporting the outreach of colonial powers; no

17. Augustine, *Sermo 52*, C. vi, n., quoted in Lane, *The Solace of Fierce Landscapes*, 68.

18. Carey, *Enquiry into the Obligations*, 7–12.

longer can we understand missionary activity as providing the blessings of Western civilization to "underdeveloped" or "developing" peoples or cultures; no longer can we conceive of mission as originating from a Christianized North and moving toward a non-Christian or a religiously underdeveloped South.[19]

Recent scholarship on interfaith relationships has also focused on the importance of dialogue in the effort to experience genuine community. When relating to those of other faith traditions, S. Wesley Ariarajah notes that "both as churches and as individual Christians we live a kind of double life. We seek community with people of other faiths in many spheres of life, but we won't have anything to do with the faith by which they live. . . . We are ready to teach them but are unwilling to learn from them. In other words, we go on seeking community and at the same time deny community."[20]

We are experiencing this pandemic as a global community of different beliefs, religions, and cultures, and we have much to learn from each other if we are willing to engage in dialogue, both sharing *and* listening. While mission has been primarily driven in the past by feelings of certainty that our beliefs about God, as well as the language and symbols we use to describe God, are true, this pandemic is a reminder that those of faith must admit that the God we proclaim is ultimately a God of mystery. While we still hold to faith in a God of love and believe that God's mission continues during these days, an *apophatic* humility, knowing that we may hold some truth but that no one fully comprehends all truth, can lead us further into dialogue with others. This, in turn, can help enable us to be more open to the surprising ways that God may call us to participate in mission and who our friends and partners in mission may be. Humbly acknowledging that we do not know the entire white board but only know the small square (and even that imperfectly!) is a critical missional learning from this communal experience of pandemic.

Mission as a Witness to Life

As we try to move through this time of pandemic, one of the biggest debates within the US and around the world continues to center on how and when to restart economies as the health crisis has turned into an economic crisis. Along with the suffering caused by the millions of people being infected and hundreds of thousands dying, the economic effects of the pandemic have

19. Bevans and Schroeder, *Constants in Context*, 284.

20. Ariarajah, *Strangers or Co-pilgrims*, 25.

been and will continue to be staggering. In the early days of the pandemic, over one hundred countries closed their borders and with the loss of trade and tourism, millions of people either lost their jobs or were in danger of doing so. While projections for 2020 economic growth were set at 2.5 percent prior to the outbreak, economists believe now that a global economic contraction of over 1.2 percent is probable.[21] Those employed in jobs related to the service sector such as hospitality, tourism, restaurants, and travel continue to be hit especially hard. While vaccines have been approved and will soon become available, the damage caused by this pandemic will ripple through the world economy for years to come. And as mentioned earlier, the systemic nature of oppression will leave people of color, women, and those with less formal education most at risk.

In response to these very real issues, some in power have seemingly separated the connection of physical health and wellbeing from economic health. Calls to ease shelter-in-place restrictions and to reopening the economy, at whatever cost, have become talking points for numerous politicians, including in the US. Along with these calls from some politicians, there have been gatherings of protesters at state capitals across the country who believe that their rights are being taken away and demanding the re-opening of the economy and a return to our pre-pandemic lives. What began as a health crisis that called for guidance from scientists and health experts has become a political issue with people retreating into their own camps.

For those seeking to discern how to join in God's mission during these divided and partisan times, it is important to remember that God's mission is ultimately about giving and supporting the flourishing of all life, both human and non-human. The separating of physical health and well-being from economic health is a false dichotomy as the work of mission should seek to address the integrated nature of all aspects of life. One way that may be helpful to think about this is to consider the roots of the word "economy." Our English word "economy" comes from two Greek roots: *oikos*, which means "household," and *nomos*, which refers to the rules used to govern. Our economy is the how we order our household. Should the rules of how we run our household lead us to sacrifice the lives of our loved ones? Should they lead us to sacrificing the most vulnerable among us, including communities of color, the elderly, and the materially poor, all of whom are disproportionately affected by the pandemic and are dying at higher rates?

While admitting the very real suffering this pandemic has caused to both physical and financial health, part of joining in God's mission in our day may be using this opportunity, what some are calling a "great

21. UN, "COVID-19."

pause," to rethink the rules that order the way we run our household. This is not a new calling on those involved in mission. As mentioned earlier, the modern mission movement began during the era when people of faith were concerned about humanitarianism and sought to address, or at least relieve, the causes of human suffering. After World War II, talk of humanitarianism was replaced by that of development and over a number of decades, mission agencies were involved in providing aid as large sums of money, as well as experts in various fields of development such as agricultural, water, and education, sought to address systemic issues related to economic and social development.

One critique of these efforts today is that while there is little doubt that some good came as a result, the larger economic system into which people were being integrated (the same system which some say needs to restart today and which dominates our economic lives to the detriment of millions of people and the natural world) was largely taken for granted. Involvement in God's mission may call for us to use this "great pause" in our lives to rethink how we relate to one another and what rules we need to run our house as we witness to a life-giving God. For many, especially those in the Western world, this will necessitate a rethinking of what we deem as "needs" and how we define success. According to environmentalist Bill McKibben, one insight that is helpful is to realize that as humans, we have the gift of restraint: "We can destroy, but . . . we can decide not to destroy. . . . We're the only creature who can decide *not* to do something we're capable of doing. That's our superpower, even if we exercise it rarely."[22] Theologically, restraint of this kind, deciding *not* to do something, is closely tied to the biblical concept of *kenosis*, which can be translated as "self-emptying." In Philippians 2:7 the concept of *kenosis* is used to describe Jesus' actions on the cross as he "emptied himself, taking the form of a slave," willingly suffering and dying. Jesus self-emptying involved the practice of restraint, putting God's calling above his own desires and wants, even to the point of hanging on a cross. Instead of demanding a return to the life we knew, God's calling may be for us to take up our own cross as we wrestle with our culture's demons of greed, materialism, and conspicuous consumerism, seeking to learn how to restrain ourselves for the health and well-being of all.

Conclusion

We are living in uncertain times. Past ways of being and relating in our world are no more, and a future new normal is not yet clear. As we journey

22. McKibben, *Falter*, 254.

through this liminal time, Rev. Brian Robertson reminds us that "thresh-olds can be periods of great discomfort. The more we can discipline our-selves to be content with being present in the world and ourselves in this state of becoming, the more we can peacefully and freely follow the Spirit's leading."[23] Regardless of how uncertain these times are, we can be assured that the God who has called the faithful to follow in past times continues to call us today. Our response to this call, however, cannot be to simply continue in old forms and patterns. Specifically, in the face of such great suffering, any response to God's calling needs to be undertaken with great humility as we seek to grieve and lament, engage in dialogue, and witness to the need for ways of relating in human community that are life-giving. Today we can be sure that God continues to call us to mission: the "flow" continues. Let us humbly join in.

Bibliography

Ariarajah, S. Wesley. *Strangers or Co-pilgrims: The Impact of Interfaith Dialogue on Christian Faith and Practice*. Minneapolis: Fortress, 2017.

Bevans, Stephen B. and Roger P. Schroder. *Constants in Context: A Theology of Mission for Today*. Maryknoll, NY: Orbis, 2005.

———. *Prophetic Dialogue: Reflections on Christian Mission Today*. Maryknoll, NY: Orbis, 2011.

Bosch, David. *Transforming Mission: Paradigm Shifts in Theology of Mission*. Maryknoll, NY: Orbis, 1991.

Carey, William. *An Enquiry into the Obligations of Christians to Use Means for the Conversion of the Heathens*. London: Button and Son, 1818.

DeGruchy, Steve. "Being Connected: Engaging in Effective World Mission." Address delivered at "Everyone, Everywhere" Episcopal Conference, Baltimore, MD, June 5, 2008.

Global Ministries. "MECC: Let Us Pray Together as Christians and Muslims!" https://www.globalministries.org/mecc_let_us_pray_together_as_christians_and_muslims/.

Jele, Sindiso. "Choosing between Death and Life: A COVID-19 Reflection." https://www.globalministries.org/choosing_between_death_and_death_a_covid_19_reflection.

Katongole, Emmanuel. *Born from Lament: The Theology and Politics of Hope in Africa*. Grand Rapids: Eerdmans, 2017.

Kirk, J. Andrew. *What Is Mission? Theological Explorations*. Minneapolis: Fortress, 2000.

Kneebone, Elizabeth, and Richard V. Reeves. "The Intersection of Race, Place, and Multidimensional Poverty." *Brookings*, April 21, 2016. https://www.brookings.edu/research/the-intersection-of-race-place-and-multidimensional-poverty/.

Lane, Belden C. *The Solace of Fierce Landscapes: Exploring Desert and Mountain Spirituality*. Oxford: Oxford University Press, 1998.

23. Robertson, "On the Threshold of Tomorrow," 60.

McKibben, Bill. *Falter: Has the Human Game Begun to Play Itself Out?* New York: Holt, 2019.

Robert, Dana. "Cross-Cultural Friendship in the Creation of the Twentieth-Century World Christianity." *International Bulletin of Missionary Research* 35.2 (2011) 100–107.

Robertson, Brandan. "On the Threshold of Tomorrow." *Oneing: An Alternative Orthodoxy* 8.1 (2020) 57–60.

Solomon, Danyelle, and Darrick Hamilton. "The Coronavirus Pandemic and the Racial Wealth Gap." *CAP*, March 19, 2020. https://www.americanprogress.org/article/coronavirus-pandemic-racial-wealth-gap/.

United Nations. "COVID-19." https://www.un.org/en/desa/covid-19.

Warren, Max. *To Apply the Gospel: Selections from the Writings of Henry Venn.* Grand Rapids: Eerdmans, 1971.

World Missionary Conference. *The History and Records of the Conference together with Addresses Delivered at the Evenings Meetings.* Edinburgh: Oliphant, Anderson & Ferrier, 1910.

10

Being and Doing Church in the Age of Pandemics

—Neal D. Presa

> He has told you, O mortal, what is good;
> and what does the Lord require of you
> but to do justice, and to love kindness,
> and to walk humbly with your God?
>
> —Micah 6:8

> Gimli: "Never thought I'd die fighting side by side with an Elf."
>
> Legolas: "What about side by side with a friend?"[1]

THE GREAT NINETEENTH CENTURY novel *A Tale of Two Cities* by Charles Dickens opened with these lines describing the state of affairs before and after the French Revolution:

> It was the best of times, it was the worst of times, it was the age of wisdom, it was the age of foolishness, it was the epoch of belief, it was the epoch of incredulity, it was the season of Light, it was the season of Darkness, it was the spring of hope, it was the winter of despair, we had everything before us, we had nothing before us, we were all going direct to Heaven, we were all going direct the other way—in short, the period was so far like the present period, that some of its noisiest authorities insisted on

---

1. This quote is from the film adaptation of J. R. R. Tolkien's *The Lord of the Rings: The Return of the King,* directed by Peter Jackson.

233

its being received, for good or for evil, in the superlative degree of comparison only.[2]

Such a macabre image can be applied to many moments of upheaval in human history, no less than the current global pandemic we face with the COVID-19 coronavirus. The pandemic we face as a global human community has upended our livelihoods in ways not experienced for more than a century since the great influenza pandemic of 1918. Physical distancing, facial protective masks, and shelter-in-place quarantine, together with testing, tracing, and treatment are the orders of the day and for the foreseeable future as we all await an efficacious vaccine. For us in the United States, where the total confirmed cases of infection as of August 22, 2020 stands at a little over 5.6 million (of the total global cases of just over 23 million) and over 176,000 deaths (of the total global deaths of 801,000),[3] this has resulted in unemployment and economic numbers not seen since the Great Depression of the 1920s and 1930s.

With these present realities, the churches all over the world are doing ministry in creative ways. Because in-person worship is not possible, churches have had to employ digital resources for pre-recorded worship services or live-streamed resources broadcast via the Web or social media. Church and educational institutions have had to conduct meetings and learning through on-line platforms such as Zoom, Cisco WebEx, GoTo Meeting, or Google Hangout. The common adage, "I'm Zoomed out," expresses our collective fatigue of having to engage with one another through computer screens, a sacrifice that is being made for the sake of the health of the wider community. As of this writing, the two main political parties in the United States are holding their respective presidential nominating conventions through virtual means, and in my own ecclesiastical polity—the Presbyterian Church (U.S.A.)—we had our biennial General Assembly this past June in a historic virtual meeting that convened more than seven hundred commissioners, advisory delegates, and corresponding members, a feat never before attempted in the 224 years of American Presbyterianism.

This health pandemic has unmasked the wide inequities and inequalities that had been endemic in our society. The number of infections and deaths has affected disproportionately communities of color in the United States, which already suffered from deficient educational and health infrastructures before the coronavirus. Healthcare costs were already beyond the reach of many and are exacerbated when people's jobs are terminated or furloughed.

2. Dickens, *A Tale of Two Cities*, 3.

3. Johns Hopkins University, "COVID-19 Dashboard." Accessed August 22, 2020.

In the midst of this pandemic, the endemic of racial inequality and racial inequity has been put in the forefront, and rightly so. The killings of African Americans such as Breonna Taylor, Ahmaud Arbery, and George Floyd, have galvanized a national and global movement for reckoning with the truth of the pernicious evils of white supremacy, white nationalism, and racial bias, particularly against Black communities, African diasporic communities, Asian and Asian American communities, and Latinx communities.

In these times, and, indeed, in any given time, the church of Jesus Christ is still called to be a community of hope. How is the church to respond? Or rather, what does it mean to be the church of Jesus Christ in this time of a global health pandemic? But I would add this as well: while the COVID-19 coronavirus will have a vaccine hopefully soon, the work towards full racial equality and racial equity is a long and arduous journey that will take generations where reckoning with the truth, confession, repentance, reparations, and, finally, reconciliation will require a sustained, multi-pronged approach; thus, racial injustice is endemic to who we are as a human civilization, to which the church of Jesus Christ has much to say and much to do to shine the hope and possibilities that are in the Gospel.

In this chapter, I wish to humbly address the following question: what does it mean to be the church of Jesus Christ in this age of a health pandemic and the endemic of racial injustice? From my own biographical and professional contexts as a Filipino American pastoral liturgical theologian ecumenist (this is a long way of saying: as a Filipino American I love the church, the church's worship, the church's engagement with God, and the unity of the visible church with all its differences), I will approach this task by engaging two seminal confessions of faith in the Reformed theological traditions: the Belhar Confession (1986)[4] from South Africa and the Accra Confession (2004)[5] from the then World Alliance of Reformed Churches's 25th General Council. These confessions have much to say from global contexts with respect to our health pandemic and racial endemic. The conversation partners of these statements of faith will be two convergence documents from the World Council of Churches's 10th Assembly in 2013: *Towards a Common Vision* (TCV)[6] and *Together Towards Life* (TTL).[7] Where the former describes ecclesiologies for the twenty-first century, the latter describes

---

4. Presbyterian Church, *Constitution*, 299–306.
5. World Communion of Reformed Churches, *Accra Confession*.
6. WCC, *Towards a Common Vision*.
7. WCC, *Together Towards Life*.

how the church in global contexts is living into the witness of the Holy Spirit in communities at the margins of societies.

The Belhar Confession

South Africa was colonized by Dutch and British settlers. The period of colonization in the nineteenth century included importation of workers from India and Malaysia. Thus, the colonized South Africa consisted of indigenous Afrikaans, Indians, Malays, and white settlers. A series of policy moves on the part of colonial powers led to apartheid, the Afrikaans term for "apart-ness" in the Dutch Reformed family, this led to ecclesiastical divisions based on race: the Dutch Reformed Mission Church for "colored" people, the Dutch Reformed Church in Africa for "black" people, and the Reformed Church in Africa for "Indian" people. The Dutch Reformed Mission Church wrote and adopted the Belhar Confession in 1982. In 1994, the Dutch Reformed Mission Church (colored church) and the Dutch Reformed Church in Africa (the "black" church) united to form the Uniting Reformed Church in Southern Africa (URCSA).

In the white populations of the Dutch Reformed family, they also formed two main groupings: Netherdutch Reformed Church of Africa (NHK), which was suspended by the World Alliance of Reformed Churches in 1982 and remained under suspension by the World Communion of Reformed Churches, and the Nederduitse Gereformeedrde Kerk (NGK), which was suspended by the World Alliance of Reformed Churches in 1982 but re-admitted in 1998 after renouncing apartheid.

The situation in South Africa by the mid–twentieth century had deteriorated as the government led violent attacks against protesters. Churches, beginning in 1948, declared there was no Scriptural basis for color-based apartheid, urging the government to "deal with all colored groups in our country in a Christian manner."[8] The World Council of Churches called for a major consultation in 1961 in Cottesloe, then in 1977, the Lutheran World Federation meeting in Dar es Salaam urged for a *status confessionis*.

In 1982, the General Council of the World Alliance of Reformed Churches meeting in Ottawa, the Alliance declared a *status confessionis* over apartheid, renouncing it as sin. A *status confessionis* is a rarely used

---

8. The following summary of the ecclesial, historical, theological, and textual contexts of the Belhar Confession are from the author's unpublished presentation, "Presentation Statement to the Presbytery of Scioto Valley Relative to Confession of Belhar and Accompanying Letter," delivered May 17, 2011, at the First Presbyterian Church in Grove City, Ohio.

declaration by churches, the last one being during Nazi Germany when the German Confessing Churches declared a *status confessionis*, leading to the Theological Declaration of Barmen. A *status confessionis* is a declaration "that Christians, or a church, feel that a 'moment of truth' has arrived, that a situation has developed in which the gospel itself is at stake."[9] The *status confessionis* declared by the World Alliance of Reformed Churches in Ottawa was received and accepted by the Dutch Reformed Mission Church in 1982, the same year that Dr. Allan Boesak, a South African theologian, was elected president of the Alliance. The Dutch Reformed Mission Church synod appointed five members to draft the Confession. The Confession was written within a few days, the draft approved and sent out to congregations, and then finally approved four years later.

How did apartheid get rooted in South Africa? European colonizers had three theological factors that provided a theological justification for apartheid: the theology of nineteenth century German missiologist Gustav Warneck, the theology of nineteenth century Dutch theologian Abraham Kuyper, and the Pietist movement of the Scottish church.

First, Gustav Warneck undertook a careful exegesis of the so-called Great Commission text of Matthew 28:16–20, "Go ye therefore and make disciples of all nations." The phrase "nations" in our Bibles, in Greek *ta ethne*, was rendered by Warneck as "peoples." Warneck saw that the great goal of mission was to Christianize people groups, ethnic groups. What Warneck did was to collapse the results of mission—people becoming Christian—with the method. This led to the notion that mission was used for cultural propaganda.

Second, Abraham Kuyper affirmed the Reformed theological belief that God is sovereign over the entire creation. The question for him was, "How is God's sovereignty exercised and in what places?" Kuyper brought forth the notion of common grace that infiltrates all of creation, with the Holy Spirit bringing about the physicality of that divine essence out of creation. This led to Kuyper's structured notion of pluriformity— multiple existences of grace with particular characteristics. In other words, we all are different, and we discover our true essences, the common grace, as the Holy Spirit works with our particular differences. So, the key, Kuyper averred, was to remain separated so that we can develop and evolve, discovering the grace in us and among us as we participate in the grace given to us in our spheres. Out of this came Kuyper's schema of hierarchies of development, where various nations and civilizations had varying degrees of being

9. Smit, "A Time for Confession?," 416.

affected by grace, with the nations of North America and Europe as having experienced greater degrees of special grace.

Third, the Pietist movement in Scotland. Because of the need for ministers, the Dutch Reformed Church family called clergymen, first from the Netherlands, and eventually from the more theologically conservative Scotland. In Scotland, the nineteenth century Pietist movement was present, which emphasized personal holiness and the plain reading of Scripture, decrying historical-critical methods of interpreting Scripture. This led to an unchallenged attitude towards the prevalent way of interpreting Scripture. It created a vacuum that followers of Warneck and Kuyper used to justify their own hermeneutical lenses of Scripture and of the Gospel itself. The Pietist movement imported into South Africa prevented critical and self-critical perspectives from challenging the dominant approaches to understanding Scripture. Thus, apartheid gained theological justification allied with the ecclesiastical and political mechanisms to take root in the South African soil.

The Dutch Reformed Mission Church drafted the Belhar Confession in 1982 and then adopted it as an official confession of faith in 1986. The Church did so under dire circumstances of political pressure, where ecclesiastical action against the prevailing political, cultural, and economic order would put the Church squarely at odds with the governing powers and principalities. The Confession of Belhar must always be read with the Accompanying Letter, the communique to the congregations of the Dutch Reformed Mission Church that summarized the substance of the actual Confession and laid out the reasons for issuing the Confession. The first paragraph of the Letter tells of the seriousness of the situation that prompted the Confession:

> We are aware that such an act of confession is not lightly undertaken, but only if it is considered that the heart of the gospel is so threatened as to be at stake. In our judgment, the present church and political situation in our country and particularly within the Dutch Reformed church family calls for such a decision. Accordingly, we make this confession not as a contribution to a theological debate nor as a new summary of our beliefs, but as a cry from the heart, as something we are obliged to do for the sake of the gospel in view of the times in which we stand.[10]

The second paragraph of the Letter speaks about the authority, motive, and subject of the Confession. The authority is the Bible, the written Word of God. The motive is to protect the Gospel and the credibility of the church's

10. Presbyterian Church, *Constitution*, 305.

witness. The subject is "we," referring to the church. The third paragraph of the Letter is the object (to "whom" or to "what") of the Confession. The Confession addresses the false doctrine of apartheid, even though the word apartheid is never used. The Confession addresses a false doctrine that has become an ideology, and which has been perpetuated. This is followed by a plea for reconciliation and humility. The fourth paragraph of the Letter points to the implications of the Confession, namely a call for repentance and conversation of all, an invitation to journey together towards reconciliation and justice, and calls for the dismantling of unjust church and social structures.

The Confession itself consists of six sections. Sections three, four, and five begin with "We believe" followed by a corresponding "Therefore, we reject any doctrine." Sections one, two, and six establish the corporate doxological affirmations with respect to God and the church's worship of God.

- Sections one and six open and close with doxology to the Triune God: "We believe in the triune God, Father, Son and Holy Spirit . . ."[11]

- Section two describes the signs of the church by linking the church to the Nicene and Apostles' creeds, and thereby the linkage of the Dutch Reformed Mission Church to the wider Christian community: "We believe in one holy, universal Christian church, the communion of saints called from the entire human family."[12]

- Section three asserts that the church is a reconciled community who have been reconciled by God, and therefore is to work for reconciliation as "gift and obligation."[13]

- Section four asserts that the church has been entrusted with the message of reconciliation

- Section five asserts that God is the One who restores justice, and the church is an agent of God's justice

- Section six offers the church's confession and "to do all these things, even though the authorities and human laws might forbid them and punishment and suffering be the consequence. Jesus is Lord."[14]

Sections three, four, and five contain both affirmations and doctrinal rejections. The doctrinal proscriptions challenge any doctrine "which

---

11. Presbyterian Church, *Constitution*, 301.

12. Presbyterian Church, *Constitution*, 301.

13. Presbyterian Church, *Constitution*, 301.

14. Presbyterian Church, *Constitution*, 305.

absolutizes either natural diversity or the sinful separation of people"[15] or any doctrine "which, in such a situation sanctions in the name of the gospel or of the will of God the forced separation of people on the grounds of race and color and thereby in advance obstructs and weakens the ministry and experience of reconciliation in Christ."[16] These assertions of faith and rejection of false doctrine, and, consequently, false practice and ecclesiastical and civic policies, were reminiscent of the Theological Declaration of Barmen's outright challenge to Nazism and Martin Luther King Jr.'s *Letter from Birmingham*. What the Dutch Reformed Mission Church did was effectively put its life squarely in front of the political hegemons as well as the all-white Dutch churches which supported the apartheid regime. That act of mission leadership for the sake of the Gospel requires Spirit-filled courage, determination, and resilience in the midst of crisis and challenge that is anchored to who the church is and what God in Jesus Christ through the Spirit has called the church to be about in all time and in every place. Our siblings in the South Africa context during the apartheid regime powerfully demonstrated a witness where they discerned that the Gospel was at stake and that to remain silent was not an option.

Recently, Christian educator Rodger Nishioka, executive associate pastor at the Village Community Presbyterian Church in Prairie Village, Kansas, spoke of the critical difference between interruption and disruption.[17] Nishioka proposed that interruption involves a pivotal event that temporarily stops an action, and when that event is dealt with, the action continues on its course. A disruption, on the other hand, involves an event that likewise temporarily halts an action, but when the event is dealt with, the action continues in such a way that is markedly different from how it was prior to the pivotal event. Nishioka has asked whether the responses of churches to the health pandemic and to the racial justice endemic is regarded as an interruption or as a disruption: will churches choose to continue to a status quo, or will there be marked transformation and change in how the church is to live out Christ's calling in the world moving forward?

Tod Bolsinger, vice president for leadership formation at Fuller Theological Seminary, has written extensively on leadership in the midst of disruptive challenge.[18] He observed the following:

> Adaptive leadership is what is needed at moments like that: when you find yourself without a map and recognizing that you

15. Presbyterian Church, *Constitution*, 302.
16. Presbyterian Church, *Constitution*, 303.
17. Nishioka, "Congregational Formation in a Pandemic."
18. See Bolsinger, *Canoeing the Mountains*.

have to lead your people into a reality where the world in front of you is nothing like the world behind you. There is no clear plan, no map to follow, no past expertise to give confidence to both the leader and followers. Instead the leader must calmly and courageously tell the truth about their condition, and when asked, "What do we do?"[19]

To that critical question, Bolsinger proposed this:

In these disruptive moments, the leader will be less a grand visionary or star figure that gathers individuals for inspiration and exhortation and more a convener and equipper of people who together will be transformed as they participate in God's transforming work in the world. To that end, I offer this definition of leadership: Leadership is energizing a community of people toward their own transformation in order to accomplish a shared mission in the face of a changing world.[20]

For the white majority of Christians in America and in the Global North, the racial injustice endemic appears as an interruption that gained traction following the highly publicized deaths of Breonna Taylor, Ahmaud Arbery, and George Floyd. But, communities of color, particularly Black communities, are acutely engaged with the realities of the endemic of racism, racial prejudice, white supremacy, and white nationalism as a daily part of our existence. For us who are persons of color, racial injustice endemic is not a change, it is reality. The question, then, is, "How will the church be disrupted for transformative change?"

For our siblings in the Global South context of South Africa, they responded to the apartheid endemic with protests, one of which took shape in the form of the Belhar Confession. In my present congregational context that is a largely white affluent community, I have received numerous questions from church leaders as to why I would be involved in street protests against racial injustice and why can't the focus be on reconciliation rather than highlighting the differences that divide us. This is the identical question that our South African siblings addressed in the Belhar Confession and which Black Americans in the Civil Rights movement in the 1960s in the United States addressed. In a time of health pandemic that magnifies the racial injustice endemic, the church's response ought to be similar to our South African siblings: reconciliation cannot occur unless and until there is a reckoning with the truth of the evils of the endemic, the unmasking of

---

19. Bolsinger, *Leadership for a Time of Pandemic*, 9.
20. Bolsinger, *Leadership for a Time of Pandemic*, 11–12.

the systemic (theological, cultural, historical, economic, political) structures and foundations that support and perpetuate the endemic, collective confession of complicity and apathy, repentance from that complicity and apathy, reparations towards equity, and then reconciliation. That is why following the end of the apartheid regime, the South African government, in partnership with churches and civic organizations in South Africa, established the Truth and Reconciliation Commission led by Archbishop Desmond Tutu. The Commission could only undertake its work because the country was somewhat ripe and ready to reckon with the ugly truth of apartheid and the pernicious evil of racial injustice.

The Belhar Confession was an act of leadership that was spoken by, spoke to, and spoke with the hearts and lives of South African Christians. The Confession and Accompanying Letter were acts of ecclesiastical and ecclesial leadership as our South African siblings leaned into their collective discernment of who God is, who Christ is, and who they were as the church of Jesus Christ. It was on that basis of ecclesial identity grounded on Christ's constitutive calling that enabled and empowered the Dutch Reformed Mission Church to do what it did. It should be noted that when the World Alliance of Reformed Churches took decisive action in 1982 to declare that apartheid was a sin and to call for a *status confessionis* on that reality, that declaration and assertion of ecumenical solidarity on the part of the global church for South African Christians powerfully demonstrated the voice of the church to speak and act in unity against an endemic. When I traveled to South Africa as part of my work with the World Alliance of Reformed Churches, I had the sacred opportunity to stand in the sanctuary of the congregation at Belhar, the site of the synod meeting where the Belhar Confession was drafted and subsequently adopted. That drive to Belhar was preceded by meetings I had with Professors Dirk Smit and Allan Boesak. Smit was one of the principal authors of the Confession and Boesak had been elected unanimously as president of WARC at the General Council that declared apartheid as a sin, an action that had been taken when Boesak presented the motion. Those who were present at that Belhar synod shared how they felt the weight on their shoulders, the sacredness of the moment, and the high stakes of putting the church on record of challenging the apartheid regime. Such disruptive courage is what the church is to be and do in this time of health pandemic and racial injustice endemic.

The Accra Confession

The Accra Confession was the first statement of faith in the Reformed theological tradition that explicitly addressed economic injustice and environmental/ecological degradation. Adopted at the twenty-fourth General Council of the World Alliance of Reformed in Churches in 2004 held in Accra, Ghana, the Confession was part of the initiative "Covenanting for Justice in the Economy and the Earth."[21] At the turn of the century, Reformed Christians sought to speak prophetically about the adverse impact of globalization on a large segment of the world's population suffering from poverty, commodified for cheap labor, a global climate crisis caused and worsened by industrialized nations which sought monetary gains at the expense of developing nations and the environment. In sum, the Confession critiqued what was regarded as the values of empire and, with it, wealth over and against the poor. Noteworthy is the fact that the location of the General Council was in Accra where the notorious Elmina castle stood in which almost four hundred years prior, at the height of the trans-Atlantic slave trade, millions of Africans were enslaved, kept in dungeons while atop stood a Dutch chapel where colonists and slaveholders would praise the Christian God. At the time of the debate and subsequent adoption of the Accra Confession, Global North delegates, particularly those from European member churches, raised concern over what was viewed as the Confession's explicit critique of the neoliberal economic structure, i.e., capitalism and the military industrial complex, both of which allied to buttress the power of monetary empire. The use of empire is similar to this paper's use of the term "endemic" as the ubiquity and pervasiveness of values so ingrained in the warp and woof of the currency of global human affairs that a critique against the economic, social, and political order was interpreted as a critique or outright rejection of the nations who benefit from that system. Yet, the term "empire" as with the term "endemic" are realities from the perspective of the marginalized, the oppressed, the ones who suffer under the weight of the system, and who, ironically, have contributed greatly to the flourishing of those systems while being subjugated by that very system that they are forced to serve.

In forty-two paragraphs, the Accra Confession exegeted the "signs of the times" through the critical lens of faith. Paragraph six summed up the Confession's concerns:

---

21. For a brief summary of the process leading to the 2004 adoption of the Accra Confession, see Kuo, "The Accra Confession as Dangerous Memory," 6–7.

The signs of the times have become more alarming and must be interpreted. The root causes of massive threats to life are above all the product of an unjust economic system defended and protected by political and military might. Economic systems are a matter of life or death.[22]

Paragraphs seventeen through thirty-one follow a similar pattern as that of the Belhar Confession in an alternating refrain of "We believe" and "Therefore we reject" statements. Paragraphs twenty–eight and twenty–nine are demonstrative:

28. We believe that God calls us to hear the cries of the poor and the groaning of creation and to follow the public mission of Jesus Christ who came so that all may have life and have it in fullness (Jn 10.10). Jesus brings justice to the oppressed and gives bread to the hungry; he frees the prisoner and restores sight to the blind (Lk 4.18); he supports and protects the downtrodden, the stranger, the orphans and the widows.

29. Therefore we reject any church practice or teaching which excludes the poor and care for creation, in its mission; giving comfort to those who come to "steal, kill and destroy" (Jn 10.10) rather than following the "Good Shepherd" who has come for life for all (Jn 10.11).[23]

The concluding paragraphs of the Confession include a confession of complicity and apathy in the values of empire wherein churches have benefited from the fruits of the empire, a commitment to conscientize and equip churches on the Confession's prophetic call and a covenanting to speak and act justly for the flourishing of all of humanity and all of creation.

Sixteen years later, the Confession continues to speak to the crises of our times. Recently, Chinese American scholar Henry Kuo of the Graduate Theological Union linked the Accra Confession to Johann Baptist Metz's concept of "dangerous memory" and how the Confession is an active agent in invoking and provoking past-present realities of peoples often not seen nor heard:

Dangerous memories encourage people today to dare history, to remember a future that confers at least some redemption to the muffled hopelessness and silenced despair of the past by remembering a future where the conditions of hopelessness and despair are liberated with love and joy. Such anamnetic

22. World Communion of Reformed Churches, *Accra Confession*, para. 6.
23. World Communion of Reformed Churches, *Accra Confession*, para. 28–29.

solidarity with the silenced peoples of the past is what dares Christians in the present to imagine new ways of being church, new ways of promoting human flourishing and making communities whole.[24]

He goes on to say how the Accra Confession connects with the crisis of our time, particularly the endemic effects of climate change upon every part of the planet, particularly climate change's catastrophic effects on vulnerable populations who often are disenfranchised or powerless to make policy changes with their governments or economies:

> First, as a confessional statement, the Accra Confession is a doctrinal matrix of dangerous memories that opens possibilities for addressing the ecological crisis as a theological challenge in a variety of contexts. Second, it provides a hermeneutical baseline for the exercise of *caritas* across the Reformed tradition by situating the ground of its expression in the dangerous memories of those who suffer concretely from the negative consequences of the ecological crisis. Finally, the Accra Confession also illuminates the intersectionality of climate justice efforts, providing room not just for theologians but also for scientists, leaders, and other key conversation partners to engage with the quest for environmental justice.[25]

As Kuo rightly points out, the Accra Confession critiqued and exegeted the crises of our times through the lens of faith, grounded in God who is the creator of the world. Because of the universality of the crises, Kuo wisely pointed to the Confession's call for covenanting that necessarily involves an intersectional approach to addressing economic and ecological justice through broad conversations and partnerships across multiple sectors and professional fields, such as the scientific and faith communities, activists, NGOs, governments, businesses/transnational corporations, and farmers, just to name a few.

When the World Alliance of Reformed Churches merged with the Reformed Ecumenical Council to form the World Communion of Reformed Churches in 2010, it occurred as the global economy was rocked by the Great Recession of 2008 in the United States. The Uniting General Council of the World Communion of Reformed Churches was the first full cycle since the previous General Council that adopted the Accra Confession. A colloquium held at Stony Point, New York in 2010 addressed the complementary perspective of both the Accra Confession and the Belhar

24. Kuo, "The Accra Confession as Dangerous Memory," 12.
25. Kuo, "The Accra Confession as Dangerous Memory," 13.

Confession in speaking to the realities of the global economy, and advocated for the new Reformed body to continue the trajectory of the Accra Confession and the "Covenanting for Justice in the Economy and the Earth" initiative. The Colloquium observed:

> Power was seen to be embedded in any consideration of race; repentance, restitution and more just relations in any treatment of reconciliation. Thus Accra was seen to address economic realities implicit in Belhar's justice commitment, as well as realities of power politics that also threaten the church's unity, and hence also call for resistance.[26]

What the Accra and the Belhar Confession both do is speak truth to power by presciently diagnosing the signs of the times through the lens of faith. Both Confessions bear witness in times of pandemic (meaning "all people") and endemic (meaning "in people") because as communities of faith, we know that the Lord sees and knows the heart, the Lord who made heaven and earth is the one who holds all of creation together, who holds the past-present-future, and who moves in and through people to be agents and partners of God's transformative justice in the world. Such prescient truth-telling requires wisdom. It is gravitas, "weight, influence, authority, sobriety, or seriousness."[27] Princeton Seminary president Craig Barnes described gravitas:

> It comes as a result of good responses to hurts, blessings, failures, achievement, boredom and obligations that are all surrendered to their Creator. Some who have the exact same experiences turn instead to cynicism. But souls with gravitas somehow choose to receive their lives, such as they are, with gratitude.[28]

Barnes speaks of pastoral leadership, the role of theological institutions, and especially the formative role of congregations to shape pastors to become wise leaders of gravitas. The church as a living body across generations, whose witness spans millennia, who experience and endure persecution and strife, is Christ's community whose character is gravitas by its very nature. The question is: is how the church engages the current health pandemic and the endemic of racial, economic, and environmental injustices exhibiting the wise gravitas learned from generations of faithful witnesses? The Accra and Belhar confessions are witnesses of faith from the voices, contexts, and

---

26. Colloquium on the Accra Confession, "A Message," para. 3.

27. Corkindale, "In Search of Gravitas."

28. Barnes, "Searching for Gravitas," 269–70. See also my chapter: Presa, "Wisdom in a Wikipedia World."

lives of real communities who face the brunt of powers and principalities that stifle flourishing in God's shalom. The church has many resources in its tradition (NB: from the Latin *tradition* meaning "to bestow"), such as confessions of faith, to empower and inspire present-future witness in times of pandemic and endemic, and in times of none. To remember, to dignify, to internalize, and to live into the "dangerous memory" of what sources like the Accra and Belhar confessions offer to the church requires wise gravitas. It calls forth resilience and courage.

The church has a distinctive witness in a time of a health pandemic and the endemic of racial, economic, and ecological injustice. There is a deep desire in the United States and around the world for the global economy to rebound. One of the key resources in connecting working professionals and students is the seventeen-year-old online company LinkedIn based out of California. LinkedIn provides an online platform, similar to Facebook for social networking, but with a target market for business networking, job boards, sharing of ideas related to one's work, and educational and training modules for professional development. With fifteen thousand employees and with nearly seven hundred million active users across six continents,[29] LinkedIn is the premier site that optimizes digital technology to equip and train working professionals. Recently, to support those looking for employment and to hone the skills needed for key jobs in this time of pandemic and endemic, LinkedIn highlighted the in-demand jobs around the world such as software engineers, software architects, project managers, DevOps Engineer (integrates software development with IT operations), and sales managers, just to name a few. With these profiled jobs, LinkedIn identified the ten most needed skills and for which they are providing the online classes to provide the education and training. The ten skills are: communication, business management, problem solving, data science, data storage technologies, technical support, leadership, project management, digital literacy, and employee learning and development.[30] These technical skills are critical for a vibrant global economy.

Yet, the essential skill needed by all of us human beings which is missing from the list and for which the church is uniquely and distinctly called and qualified to embody and bear witness to is wisdom gravitas allied with courage and resilience. The church's story and history, spanning millennia and born out of persecution and strife, has much to offer our world racked by a health pandemic and the endemic of racial, economic, and ecological injustice. In reflecting upon theological education, but which can be applied

---

29. Aslam, "81 LinkedIn Statistics You Need to Know."

30. Poague, "The Skills Companies Are Hiring For."

more broadly to the church's witness, former Archbishop of Canterbury, Rowan Williams recently offered this wise insight:

> Well, in the broadest possible sense, theological education is learning more about the world that faith creates, or the world that faith trains you to inhabit. That's what I really want to come back to again and again when I talk about theology. It's not about a set of issues or problems, it's about a landscape you move into—the new creation, if you like. You inhabit this new set of relationships, this new set of perspectives. You see differently, you sense differently, you relate differently.

> To do theology is, in some ways, to be taken back to that moment of bewilderment about the newness or the distinctiveness or the strangeness of being in this new Christian framework. So theological education is familiarizing yourself with how people have found their way around that landscape with the perspectives they've occupied and then learning to pitch your own tent, as one might say, in that territory.[31]

What Rowan Williams is speaking of is wisdom, of gravitas. And undergirded with wisdom gravitas, the church faces and engages pandemic and endemic with courage and resilience. That is what the Church needs for all time, and especially in these times.

Two Global Ecumenical Lenses

The Belhar Confession and the Accra Confession emerged from the realities of Global South contexts, raised by the churches in the Reformed theological traditions for global attention. The Belhar Confession speaks to us as courageous witness of resilience in the midst of great strife, when our siblings in South Africa put their lives and limbs on the line to counter the hegemony of apartheid in its political, theological, cultural, and systemic embeddedness. Courage and resilience are what's needed. The Accra Confession offers, among many things, the wise gravitas of rightly reading the signs of the times when, in the early twenty–first century at the time of its adoption, to accurately diagnose and exegete globalization was not popular and was met with doubt and suspicion. Yet, the Global South voices who advocated from their hearts, from their souls, and from their lived realities did so over and against Global North churches, governments, and the business sectors, all the way

---

31. Wayman, "Rowan Williams."

still struggling with the adverse impact of globalization with living faith. Such a confession, such a lived testimony is gravitas; it is wisdom.

Two additional expressions of the faith community come to us from the World Council of Churches (WCC). At the tenth Assembly of the WCC in 2013 held in Busan, South Korea, the Council adopted two convergence documents: from the WCC Commission on Faith and Order came *The Church: Towards a Common Vision* (TCV) and from the WCC Commission on World Mission and Evangelism came *Together Towards Life: Mission and Evangelism in Changing Landscapes* (TTL). The WCC is a fellowship of 350 member churches in 110 countries representing five hundred million Christians from the Orthodox and various Protestant traditions. While the Roman Catholic Church has observer status with the WCC, the Roman Catholic Church is a full voting member of the Commission on Faith and Order. This is all to say that when an ecumenical document achieves "convergence" status, this designates that it is ripe and right for adoption and for reception by member churches because of years of discussion, deliberation, consultation, and communication over many years by various entities representing the wide and diverse interests of the Christian traditions.

TCV builds upon and expands upon the monumental convergence document on ecclesiology, *Baptism, Eucharist, and Ministry* (BEM), which was adopted in 1982 at the Commission on Faith and Order meeting in Lima, Peru.[32] While the BEM sought to find a common denominator among the wide swath of Christian traditions and eventually landed on ecclesiastical and liturgical expressions that privileged those churches with an episcopate (e.g., the emphasis of the three-fold form of church orders of bishop, presbyter, deacon or the high liturgical theologies of the Eucharist found in Orthodox and Roman Catholic contexts), the successive thirty years desired to engage Global South perspectives and voices in ecumenical discussions. At the Plenary Commission of Faith and Order in Kolymbari, Crete in 2009 where the penultimate document antecedent to TCV was discussed and debated, Global South theologians advocated for the inclusion and privileging of Global South realities and stories in the final drafting of the TCV.[33]

The TCV consists of sixty-nine paragraphs discussing various aspects of what it means to be the church of Jesus Christ as a *koinonia*/communion,[34] as the "prophetic, priestly and royal people of God,"[35] as the "Body of Christ

---

32. WCC, *Baptism, Eucharist, and Ministry*. For a summary of the process that led to the 2013 Assembly, see WCC, *The Church*, 41–46.

33. I had the privilege of being the representative of the World Alliance of Reformed Churches at the Plenary Commission.

34. WCC, *The Church*, 10.

35. WCC, *The Church*, 11.

and Temple of the Holy Spirit,"[36] among several descriptors, and how that identity is expressed in the ordained offices of the church and in the variety of worship practices. The TCV noted the diversity of the church's witness: "One challenge for the Church has been how to proclaim the Gospel of Christ in a way that awakens a response in different contexts, languages and cultures of the people who hear that proclamation."[37] This recognition of inculturation in diverse contexts is connected to how the church's witness is expressed with respect to what this volume is discussing: how the church lives out faith and offers compassion and mercy for the hungry, for the sick, for the dying. Paragraph 64 of TCV averred:

> Precisely because of their faith, Christian communities can-
> not stand idly by in the face of natural disasters which affect
> their fellow human beings or threats to health such as the HIV
> and AIDS pandemic. Faith also impels them to work for a just
> social order, in which the goods of this earth may be shared
> equitably, the suffering of the poor eased and absolute destitu-
> tion one day eliminated.[38]

Then it makes this statement:

> Each context will provide its own clues to discern what is the
> appropriate Christian response within any particular set of
> circumstances. Even now, divided Christian communities can
> and do carry out such discernment together and have acted
> jointly to bring relief to suffering human beings and to help
> create a society that fosters human dignity.6 Christians will
> seek to promote the values of the kingdom of God by working
> together with adherents of other religions and even with those
> of no religious belief.[39]

TCV is a monumental expression of ecclesiology for a time of global pandemic and endemic in its recognition and prescription that the Christian
witness necessarily includes collaboration and partnership with people,
communities, and organizations that may not belong to one's church community, let alone, who may likely be outside of the Christian traditions.
TCV describes the on-the-ground realities of churches around the world
who live and serve in contexts where it is not about a sole Christian response to a problem but a human response to which Christians are but

36. WCC, *The Church*, 12.

37. WCC, *The Church*, 7.

38. WCC, *The Church*, 36.

39. WCC, *The Church*, 36.

one among several stakeholders. TCV is a clarion call to churches that faithful responses to addressing the global health pandemic and the endemic of racial, economic, and ecological injustice require interreligious, intersectional analysis and collaboration as we all collectively seek the flourishing of the common good.

TTL is a detailed enhancement of TCV's call for interreligious, intersectional analysis and collaboration. The last global convergence document on ecumenical mission was also in 1982 when the WCC Central Committee adopted *Mission and Evangelism: An Ecumenical Affirmation*. It is strategically intentional that 1982 saw the adoption of both an ecclesiology and a mission and evangelism documents, so did 2013 witness the adoption of TTL and TCV. TTL consists of 112 paragraphs, anchoring the mission affirmation in the triune God by asserting "Mission begins in the heart of the Triune God"[40] and "Life in the Holy Spirit is the essence of mission, the core of why we do what we do and how we live our lives."[41] TTL then acknowledged the changing landscape with this key observation:

> Mission has been understood as a movement taking place from the centre to the periphery, and from the privileged to the marginalized of society. Now people at the margins are claiming their key role as agents of mission and affirming mission as transformation. This reversal of roles in the envisioning of mission has strong biblical foundations because God chose the poor, the foolish, and the powerless (1 Cor. 1:18–31) to further God's mission of justice and peace so that life may flourish. If there is a shift of the mission concept from "mission to the margins" to "mission from the margins," what then is the distinctive contribution of the people from the margins?[42]

This essential recognition, affirmation, and assertion is not only an acknowledgment of new realities from the perspective of the Global North, but an acknowledgment of what has always been the reality in the Global South. That is, God has always been present in every place and the church's witness has been existing for millennia in multiple contexts. The problem is that the historical recognition of that fact and reality was controlled by the powers and principalities concentrated in the Global North. It bears repeating that the work of God in the world was and has never been dependent solely on the church's witness, as TCV; that while the church is a distinct and unique community called out by God to bear witness of God's

40. WCC, *Together Towards Life*, 4.

41. WCC, *Together Towards Life*, 4.

42. WCC, *Together Towards Life*, 5.

love in Christ, God's mission includes but is not bound by the church's action, and certainly not by the church's inaction. TCV de-centered and countervailed the Global North's long-held assumption and presumption of power, authority, and hegemonic determination, and instead humbles the Global North to dignify the Global South as equal partners in the struggle for justice and reconciliation in the world.

TCV's main section headings provide the summary of TCV's pneuma-centered vision:

- Spirit of Mission: Breath of Life[43]
- Spirit of Liberation: Mission from the Margins[44]
- Spirit of Community: Church on the Move[45]
- Spirit of Pentecost: Good News for All[46]
- Feast of Life: Concluding Affirmations[47]

The concluding affirmations assert that "the mission of the church is to prepare the banquet and to invite all people to the feast of life."[48] For God's shalom to be a universal feasting, TCV said this about the essential role of those marginalized and oppressed:

> Marginalized, oppressed, and suffering people have a special gift to distinguish what news is good for them and what news is bad for their endangered life. In order to commit ourselves to God's life-giving mission, we have to listen to the voices from the margins to hear what is life-affirming and what is life-destroying. We must turn our direction of mission to the actions that the marginalized are taking. Justice, solidarity, and inclusivity are key expressions of mission from the margins.[49]

The church in a time of global health pandemic and endemic racial, environmental, and ecological injustice must see itself as one among many agents that is working for the healing and wholeness of the human community. This requires broad based partnerships and collaboration, acknowledging that there is much we need and much to learn from organizations,

---

43. WCC, *Together Towards Life*, 7.
44. WCC, *Together Towards Life*, 14.
45. WCC, *Together Towards Life*, 21.
46. WCC, *Together Towards Life*, 29.
47. WCC, *Together Towards Life*, 37.
48. WCC, *Together Towards Life*, 7.
49. WCC, *Together Towards Life*, 39.

people, and traditions within and outside the church. We recall the prophetic words of Micah: "He has told you, O mortal, what is good; and what does the Lord require of you but to do justice, and to love kindness, and to walk humbly with your God?" (Mic 6:8)

Concluding Thoughts

We are certainly at an inflection point in the world where the COVID-19 coronavirus pandemic has changed the way we relate with one another, how we conduct business, and how we in the church do ministry. The endemic of racial, economic, and ecological injustice requires that we need to change. While the health pandemic will be changed by a medical vaccine, the endemic of injustice will be changed when we as people change. In both instances, the church's call—who we are, what we do, and why we do what we do—has always been grounded on the love of God, the grace of Jesus Christ, and the fellowship of the Holy Spirit; that has not changed. It is on the basis of that core theological affirmation and reality that the robust ecclesiology needed for such a time as this is one gleaned from our courageous and resilient siblings in South Africa who gave to the rest of the church the Belhar Confession, from the wisdom of Global South churches who gave to the rest of the church the Accra Confession, and from the Spirit-inspired voices of the global ecumenical movement in *Towards a Common Vision* and *Together Towards Life*, among many others. Such an ecclesiology is marked by courage, by resilience, by wisdom gravitas, and by humility, kindness, thanksgiving, and love, seeks the Spirit's power to link arms and hearts with all human beings in solidarity for the flourishing of all of humanity in all of God's creation.

Bibliography

Aslam, Salman. "81 LinkedIn Statistics You Need to Know in 2022." *Omnicore*, January 4, 2022. https://www.omnicoreagency.com/linkedin-statistics/.

Barnes, M. Craig. "Searching for Gravitas." In *Schools of Faith: Essays on Theology, Ethics, and Education in Honour of Iain R. Torrance*, edited by David Fergussion and Bruce McCormack, 269–78. London: T. & T. Clark, 2019.

Bolsinger, Tod. *Canoeing the Mountains: Christian Leadership in Uncharted Territory.* Downers Grove, IL: InterVarsity, 2015.

———. *Leadership for a Time of Pandemic.* Downers Grove, IL: InterVarsity, 2020. Kindle.

Colloquium on the Accra Confession. "A Message from the Colloquium on the Accra and Belnar Confessions." https://www.presbyterianmission.org/wp-content/uploads/accrabelharcolloq.pdf.

Dickens, Charles. *A Tale of Two Cities*. Hertfordshire: Wordsworth, 1993.

Jackson, Peter, dir. *The Lord of the Rings: The Return of the King*. New Line Cinema, 2003.

Johns Hopkins University of Medicine Coronavirus Resource Center. "COVID-19 Dashboard by the Center for Systems Science and Engineering." https://coronavirus.jhu.edu/map.html.

Kuo, Henry S. "The Accra Confession as Dangerous Memory: Reformed Ecclesiology, the Ecological Crisis, and the Problem of Catholicity." *Religions* 11.7 (2020) 1–17.

Nishioka, Rodger. "Congregational Formation in a Pandemic." *Facebook*, August 5, 2020. https://www.facebook.com/watch/?v=2720834041533571&extid=0AFII9T B7RwnJKK5.

Presa, Neal D. "Wisdom in a Wikipedia World: Education, Ecumenism, and Leadership in an Age of Globalization." In *Schools of Faith: Essays on Theology, Ethics, and Education in Honour of Iain R. Torrance*, edited by David Fergusson and Bruce McCormack, 279–87. London: T. & T. Clark, 2019.

Smit, Dirk J. "A Time for Confession? On the WARC Project 'Reformed Faith and Economic Justice.'" In *Essays in Public Theology: Collected Essays 1*, edited by Ernst M. Conradie, 399–422. Studies in Religion and Theology 12. Stellenbosch: Sun, 2007.

Poague, Emily. "The Skills Companies Are Hiring For—Right Now." *LinkedIn*, August 17, 2020. https://learning.linkedin.com/blog/advancing-your-career/skills-companies-are-hiring-for-right-now.

Presbyterian Church (U.S.A.). *The Constitution of the Presbyterian Church (U.S.A.), Part 1: Book of Confessions*. Louisville: Office of the General Assembly, 2016.

Wayman, Benjamin. "Rowan Williams: Theological Education Is for Everyone." *Christianity Today*, August 19, 2020. https://www.christianitytoday.com/ct/2020/august-web-only/rowan-williams-theological-education-for-everyone.html.

World Communion of Reformed Churches. *The Accra Confession*. https://wcrc.ch/wp-content/uploads/2015/04/TheAccraConfession-English.pdf.

World Council of Churches. *Baptism, Eucharist, and Ministry*. https://www.oikoumene.org/en/resources/documents/commissions/faith-and-order/i-unity-the-church-and-its-mission/baptism-eucharist-and-ministry-faith-and-order-paper-no-111-the-lima-text.

———. *Together Towards Life: Mission and Evangelism in Changing Landscapes*. https://www.oikoumene.org/resources/documents/together-towards-life-mission-and-evangelism-in-changing-landscapes.

———. *The Church: Towards a Common Vision*. https://www.oikoumene.org/resources/documents/the-church-towards-a-common-vision.

11

God's Passion and the Gospel of Cocooning toward Life's Rising

A Resistance Liturgics Perspective

—FERDINAND ANNO

THE PASSION STORY HAS been a companion to the Filipino people for a long time. Its liturgical and popular observances have effectively communicated to Filipinos across time the *evangelion* of God's presence in trying times. In at least two historical episodes in the country, this gospel has formed a sacramental theology that sees Christ's paschal mystery enacted ritually in the "life-rite" of an empowered people struggling against all odds to bring about a new and just world. Using the concept of the "life-rite" that is appropriated from ritual studies and the Christian rite,[1] this chapter expounds how God's presence is sensed and experienced in the creativity of a ritual process inputted with the God-talk of popular struggles.[2] The struggle for social change seen as a life-rite of passage re-frames, performs, and binds together the story of God's presence and the story of a people's struggle to form a dissident narrative of hope.[3] Once configured, the life-rite of struggle, seen and celebrated as saturated by divine presence, enacts a thoroughly trans-

1. From its original ethnographic context or magico-religious references in the classic works of Gennep, *Rites of Passage*; Turner, *The Ritual Process*.

2. Victor and Edith Turner facilitated this shift of focus from traditional rites of passage to the wider social process involving cultural and social change. See Turner and Turner, *Image and Pilgrimage*, 95.

3. Ricoeur, *Figuring the Sacred*, 243–48.

formative praxis[4] that may serve as a beacon of hope among people in a quarantined and virus(es)-stricken world.

The *Pasyon* of the *Kristo* in the Struggling Masses and God's Presence: Some Historical and Theological Antecedents

The *pasyon* (passion) of Christ: his suffering, death, and resurrection is the popular Filipino idiom of God's radical presence and involvement in human life.[5] This was transmitted chiefly through the liturgy of the Christian church. In the context of colonial Christianity in the Philippines, the liturgical text of the paschal mystery was appropriated by the masses of faithful who were excluded by elitist circles of colonial Catholicism. This appropriation took form in popular paraliturgies that served as the context of the *pabasa* or the sung narration of the *pasyon* narrative.[6] The *pabasa* paraliturgy, a ritual marathon through *semana santa* (holy week) was later contracted[7] and evolved into an anti-establishment language of resistance.

According to the now classic Reynaldo Ileto thesis,[8] the *pasyon* became an occasion for popular interactive catechism that facilitated the merging of the Christ story with the "*Indio*" story.[9] In the *pasyon*'s sung narration, *Hesukristo*'s *pasyon* became the *Indios*' story and the *Indios*' story became core to the *pasyon*'s. It was here that Ileto threw a bombshell on established historiographies from establishment chroniclers, like Zaide, to historians "from below," like Agoncillo, and nationalist and Marxist historians, like Constantino and Guerrero. It was not the writings of Rizal and the propagandists or the republican ideal nor the secularist western liberal "*kalayaan*" (freedom) discourse of revolutionaries that primarily roused the revolutionary imagination and fervor of the illiterate masses but their *pasyon* paraliturgical experiences and performances. In these paraliturgies signifying the "Eucharistic hunger"[10] of the masses, God's solidarity with

---

4. Benford and Hunt, "Dramaturgy and Social Movements," 87.

5. This is a theological restatement of the Ileto thesis in *Pasyon and Revolution*.

6. Ileto, *Pasyon and Revolution*, 16–26; also, Blanco, *Frontier Constitutions*, 117–25.

7. Rafael, *Contracting Colonialism*.

8. Ileto, *Pasyon and Revolution*, 16–26.

9. "*Indios*" was how the indigenous inhabitants of the Philippine archipelago were described and named by the Spanish colonizers—a group at the base of Spanish colonial-era social hierarchy.

10. This is how Blankenhorn describes the "spiritual communion" that is practiced by laity and religious who are without or denied access to the sacraments. See Blankenhorn, "A Short History."

the suffering in the passion of Christ became a wellspring of hope. In turn, this hope generated and formed the *insurecto*'s indomitable revolutionary spirituality. Ileto was not without critics,[11] but he had brought to the surface something that was buried by the deafening noise and cluttered texts of the grand narratives of our country's beginnings. Ileto highlighted the agency of the inarticulate masses in the making of history and re-surfaced a dissident de-colonializing theology from below.

The *pasyon* of the inarticulate Indios formed a faith affirmation and a popular "theology of struggle" that made the existential load of a subjugated people significantly lighter. Deeply felt, God's presence as materially mediated through the *pasyon* para-liturgy enabled the masses to envision an alternative in *kalayaan* or, at the least, gave the secularist discourse of *Ilustrado* agitators a profoundly religious language more indigenous to the masses. More than a miser desperately longing for company in his or her suffering, the *Indio* sees release and historical redemption in God's presence. It was a collective faith that God's participation in Christ's suffering with people is, far from the superficial sadomasochistic suggestions of some popular passion rites like *penitensiya* (self-flagellation) during *Viernes Santo* (Good Friday), a purging of whatever that stands in the way of the new life. The vision of *kalayaan* in the passion-formed revolutionaries corresponded with that stage when *Hesukristo* and the suffering masses rose back to life. Passion plays like the *salubong* or the meeting of Jesus's mother and the risen Christ in popular Catholic Easter rites, articulates this powerful ending to the passion narrative: when the risen Christ takes the veil off the mournful historical underdog in Mary.[12]

A little more than half-a-century later, the *pasyon* theology of God's presence in a people's struggle re-surfaced in a new context, that of an oppressive and repressive neocolonial national security state. This time, it was a theology that emerged out of a circle of church workers, clerics and lay alike who were engaged in an organized resistance against the Marcos dictatorship. A few months following the declaration of martial law in September 1972, a clandestine political organization of Christian activists, the Christians for National Liberation, was formed. Sired by an authoritarian rule, the movement identified at least two challenges as its reason for being: that of *pananampalataya* (faith) and *pakikibaka* (the struggle).[13]

11. One of the more recent was Joseph Scalice who argued against Ileto's "ahistorical" treatment of his source material and on the *pasyon* as a "cross-class and linguistically specific phenomenon." See Scalice, "Reynaldo Ileto's *Pasyon and Revolution* Revisited," 29–58.

12. Fernandez, "Filipino Popular Spirituality," 54.

13. CNL, "CNL 8th National Congress."

The second was the context and the first its text. The second was about the absence of God and the first was on the manifest presence of God. The presence was mediated and sacramental, and it was Christic.[14] It was made manifest not in the center but in the peripheries of established theological imagination. It was a presence celebrated not only in the heroic and more creative non-violent witness of mainstream progressive Christianity that ranged from "critical collaboration" to non-violent resistance; it was a theology of presence that sees God in the vicissitudes of the struggle for justice in the ground among those who knew no resources but their vision, faith, courage, and frail bodies. This theology drew primarily from the same liturgico-theological motif that helped launch the first anti-colonial upheaval in southeast Asia: the passion, death, and resurrection of Jesus Christ as lived in a life-rite of passage involving a "people who suffer but do not struggle" to a "people who suffer and therefore struggle."[15]

The affirmation of God's presence in the *pasyon* is not the simple acclamatory cognizance of both abstract and mundane presence that we do in our bourgeois faith-ing; it is one that is mediated *Kristo*logically in people or even church workers, clerics and lay alike, who break bread with the poor in their suffering and struggle. Consider the untitled poem written for a martyred guerilla priest, Father Zacarias Agatep, who perished in an encounter with government troopers in Ilocos Sur on October 12, 1982.[16] The poem celebrates the presence of an incarnating God even "in farms and villages," in "nipa huts" where people share and pour out their "agony and grief," as well as their "hopes and dreams"—and in their struggle "to build a new world, where no one will die of hunger and terror anymore," to quote some few lines.[17]

This piece may have come from "another context" and others may even dismiss this as an antiquated piece from romantics of a "forgotten" revolutionary era, like Jesus's was to the empire church. But the eulogy to the martyred priest above is a classic literary rendition of how a liturgical

14. Coined by Sathianathan Clarke, the phraseology, "christic presence," has to do with finding some christological structure in non-Christian rites of resistance like the deviant and defiant *Paraiyar* drumming among the Dalits in India. In this essay it means an understanding of God's presence that was shaped from the popular Christian narrative of the passion of Christ and the dramaturgy of passage (from deference to defiance) in the struggle for social change. See Clarke, *Dalits and Christianity*, 56.

15. These lines, "people who suffer but do not struggle" and "people who suffer and therefore struggle" were from Fr. Edicio De la Torre, an SVD priest and activist who was one among those detained the longest by the Marcos dictatorship. See De la Torre, *Touching Ground*.

16. PCPR, *That We May Remember*, 181.

17. PCPR, *That We May Remember*, 181.

or Eucharistic hermeneutic of the struggle affirms and celebrates the presence and participation of God in people's suffering and collective struggle to overcome that suffering.   Other non-establishment media through which this hermeneutic of God's radical presence in the struggle is articulated and depicted are the works of some artists who were able to see irruptions of "christic presence"[18] in the grim and squalor of the everyday life of the poor and the struggling masses. Ed De la Torre, an activist priest whose works in prison have visually articulated his theology, saw much of God's passion in the poor rising up from their oppression;[19] ditto with Emmanuel Garibay whose *Kristological* series has shown how radical and immersive the incarnation of God is when the stigmata was made present even in the most profaned pairs of hands among the lowly and destitute.[20]

What all these say in the context of global pandemic is God in Christ is present where bread is broken and cup is shared with and among those that are being victimized by both viral infection and the "new normal" regimes that envision and hope of none but a transition "back" to what was "normal."

One Virus among Many: "Faith" and "Revolution" Revisited

The pre-COVID-19 period was as difficult for most Filipinos, particularly those in the lower rung of society and those who speak with them and for them. Before the extra-judicial killings (EJK) that came with the Duterte government's war on drugs, there were the unabated political persecution and fascist repression of critical and dissident voices from the time of martial rule under Marcos's "new society" to the regimes of "unsheathed sword" and "strong republic" of succeeding governments.[21] The "social cancer,"[22] as described in pre-pandemic times, or the social viruses of social injustice, poverty, mass marginalization, ecological injustice and their attendant politics of repression and unpeace have never been cured or eliminated as these viruses have never been acknowledged by governments in the first place.

Likewise, "quarantining," is not a new phenomenon and it has its political translation in the national security state and its repressive laws that

18. Clarke, *Dalits and Christianity*, 56.

19. De la Torre, *Touching Ground*.

20. Beller, *Kristology and Radical Communion*.

21. The regimes of "unsheathed sword" and "strong republic" refer to the Corazon Aquino (1986–92) and Gloria Arroyo (2001–10) governments, respectively.

22. "Social Cancer" was the English version of *Noli Me Tangere* written by the nineteenth-century Filipino *ilustrado* reformer and national hero, Jose Rizal. This phraseology was also used by social critics of post-martial law in the Philippines to describe social injustice and the poverty epidemic in the country.

prevent people from collectively articulating their dissenting voices. The response to this social cancer and this political quarantining was varied. Some decided to be quarantined and cocooned and went through the motions of the ritual process that offers none but unimaginative reactionary reincorporation into the existing *body politic*, not unlike what our initiation into the neo-Christendom church does.[23]

Some do find their cocooning or quarantining, and it is gaining currency now, as a time to spawn, sire and act out their fascist ideas within the logic of the "old normal"; whence the alliance between the exponents of the old normal and their fascist siblings in the far right which we see in full display in the US and in the Philippines at present. Some still see quarantining however as a crossing of the *limen* into a new order of life more akin to the Jesus movement idea of regeneration and initiation into a radically new community.[24] This leads to an alternative postcolonial understanding of "cocooning" i.e., living "quarantined" under repressive regimes, as equally a lifeblood of revolutionary change.

Succinctly put, the real global pandemic is a multi-viral infection that resurfaces in very clear terms the expansive ecology of the global pandemic and how this intersects with the socio-economic, the ecological, the cultural and the political, the spiritual and moral viruses that relentlessly afflict the mass of humanity and the planet.

It is in this light that the theology of the presence of God in the passion of Christ, the theological thematic of the theologies and liturgies of resistance, is as relevant as ever amongst people living under multiple quarantining. The God that is being affirmed and celebrated in the communities of resistance is the same God that is present in the quarantined world. There is however a big difference between this God-talk and that of the popular creedal affirmation or pastoral mantra, "God is with us during this pandemic." The second could be reduced into a theological cliché that can be misused and perverted by the religious exponents of the "old normal" to pastor the poor and the restive population into submission. The first is emphatic about the untameable *pasyon* of God in Christ and it refers to a presence manifesting itself not in a life-rite of submission but in a life-rite of resistance.

23. This is in view of van Gennep's and Victor Turner's seminal studies on rites of passages in traditional societies that reincorporate initiants into the very society where they were temporarily "separated" and "marginalized" from. See Gennep, *Rites of Passage*; Turner, *The Ritual Process*.

24. Bobby Alexander's revisiting of Victor Turner's "ritual process" as an opening to a new understanding of ritual as an agent of social change. Alexander, *Victor Turner Revisited*.

Having played "witness" to the active participation of God in the passion of Christ, the two above-mentioned epochs in the Filipino story have definite post-liminal trajectories that actively pursued a qualitatively new life. These meant that God's presence is not a periodic irruption that terminates with any given revelatory moment, but one that unfolds even at points when the ecstatic and the numinous has seemingly waned and the persistent dissident voices have been drowned and silenced.

When seen from the Christian idea of the *pascha*, the talk about God's presence during these pandemic months ceases becoming as fleeting as the *limen* in a cyclical rite of unnecessary suffering. Seen from the *pascha* perspective, the *pasyon* intentionally seeks to find a way when the memories of the "lockdown" are no longer permanently cocooned in the repositories of our nostalgic moments but build up into a spiritual energy that is capable of unleashing a new life form. In other words, the *pasyon*-talk is not co-terminus with any quarantine regime.

Historically, from the experience of people's struggles, the resurrection phase of the *pasyon* story calls for the transformation of the post-liminal moment of reincorporation into a revolutionary resolve committed to breaking free from what is cyclical, whence the anti-colonial and the democratic revolution of 1896 and that of the latter half of the twentieth century rages on to this day.

During this pandemic, a poem went viral in social media. It was claimed to have been penned in 1869 during the Irish potato famine by one Kathleen O'Mara and reprinted during the Spanish Flu outbreak from 1918 to 1919. It was fact-checked by Reuters and turned out to be a false claim.[25] Reuters traced it to Catherine O' Meara's poem entry to her March 16, 2020 blog, *In the Time of Pandemic*. In the poem, O'Meara described the quarantined as "[embracing] new ways of being," "[thinking] differently," "healing the earth fully [even as people healed]," "making new choices," "dreaming new images" and "creating new ways of living."[26]

Whatever the intent is, the mind behind this false claim may have relocated the poem to these mid-nineteenth and early twentieth centuries to prove the vanity of the liminal and to express his or her nihilistic regard of the vain romanticism of the O'Mearas of the present. He or she is lamenting, *ala* Qoheleth, the vanity of everything "new" and imagined under the sun; that like in the past no new "choices [will be] made" or that no "new ways of living [will be] created" or that dreams of "new visions"

---

25. Reuters Staff, "False Claim."
26. Riechers, "A Viral Poem for a Virus Time."

will die with the return to the old normal;[27] that no genuine crossing will be made in the life-rite. The soul of the moment like the one penned by "O'Mara" will be archived in nostalgia. This kind of nihilism however does come more as a critique and a challenge to the "smallness" of our grandiose pandemic God-talk than anything else.[28] It can be a challenge not to leave our current "dreaming" and "making of new choices" to rot with the [would-be] spent cocoon abandoned by life. Rite-wise, the separation and marginalization in the *limen* must graduate not in simple reincorporation to the old normal but towards a new path to transformation.[29] Theologically, God's *pasyon* needs to continue through resurrection in the birthing of a new world and not a simple repeat of false theological claims of God's presence in vain cocooning. At the end of the day all the spiritual, intellectual, psycho-social and moral processes that are happening in our cocooning under quarantine will end up in a spiritual and political resolve whether life at the end of the tunnel can get worse or it can get better; and that it can possibly get better means that our *pasyon* God-talk outgrows, outsizes and outlives the small gods of our feel-good cocooning. God's presence-in-the-passion-of-Christ as *sacramentum* calls for the memory to be translated into a lived reality, into a Christ-like reality and, thus, within the range of what is humanly possible.

In all the above, God's presence is being affirmed in the context of suffering and the continuing struggle to overcome that suffering. The God of the *pasyon* stories is the same God whose radical presence can be sensed as we go through our own *leitourgia* of becoming in the context of and against the regime of the "old normal."

---

27. Late nineteenth century and the whole of twentieth century was a period of much turmoil in the global and national scenes, including the two devastating world wars, civil wars, ideological and "civilizational" clashes, and the nuclear arms race, among others. The great revolutions of the period in terms of transportation, communication, information and space technologies have done more to harm than "heal the earth." Inter-human and inter-national relationships, ironically, widened the already vast chasm that separates the haves from the have-nots.

28. J. B. Phillips' sixty-eight-year-old booklet, *Your God Is Too Small* (1952) may still be a relevant companion to the author of the "false claim" in critiquing the smallness of the chaplain-God of our quarantined living. See Phillips, *Your God Is Too Small*.

29. As suggested in another context by Scandrett-Leatherman as he tried to appropriate van Gennep's anatomy of human rites in activities like religious retreats. See Scandrett-Leatherman, "Ritual and Resistance," 311–31.

Sensing God in Our *Leitourgia* of Becoming

Witnessing to God's presence in our part of the quarantined world is not simply about comforting a physically challenged and spiritually tormented people, or easing people of their anxieties and fears or helping them deal with their loss and emotional difficulties, or helping people cope with and survive the boredom of the old normal or, more importantly, performing the rites that would lend semblance of life to our living in the valley of dry bones. All these may be pastoral and immediate to the quarantined but may constitute not the totality of the gospel of God being "with us." These are, in fact, social benefits that come as gifts to those who sense God's presence in their re-living the passion of God in Christ in a life-rite.

Sensing God's presence during this pandemic is like going through the *leitourgia* of worship. We see in God's reverenced and celebrated presence our ruptured relationships, how we have failed God in our stewardship of life, how vast the chasm that we have built between us and our neighbor is, and how disconnected we have become from the earth and all that dwell therein. It is in acknowledging these "sins" of separation that we have an initial sensing that God, indeed, is with us. Without this realization, we may be talking of another "presence" and not the one we saw in Jesus of the *pasyon* story.

From here, our liturgical witness of God's presence emphasizes our being assured of forgiveness that frees us into imagining new possibilities for life.[30] A presence that is incapable of freeing us from our mania for the old order of life is incongruent to the life and being of the one whose passion for the new order had led him to his death.

The passion of God in Christ is not only the self-flagellating kind of self-denial, but also a life-affirming fast. Physical and spiritual quarantining is meant to prepare oneself for radical engagement. It is one that is nourished by the Word and the sacraments. This may be a straightforwardly liturgiological a thesis, but such is the affirmation in our liturgy's charter story. At this time of pandemic, while we are in the *limen* or in our "forty-day" (quarantine) moment, the new *ordo* of life can be rehearsed. This means that our being assured forgiveness frees us to be challenged in our discernment of what God is saying to us in the liturgy of the Word; on how we are being nourished and empowered to transform our life-together into something better in and around Christ's table; and on how we are being primed for the new life in a

---

30. Jennings amplified the act of confession and the assurance of pardon as one of the highest points in the liturgical experience. It sees this a moment of liberation and a deeply sacramental moment that spills over into the Christian's public work in the world. See Jennings, *Liturgy of Liberation*.

new world in our *leitourgia*. Having gone through this liturgical engagement with God while on quarantine, we have seen our contributions and unwitting participation in making things more difficult for everyone during this pandemic; we have heard God talking to us and saying something to us; we have seen God's presence in the outpouring of love and in the sharing of life, made a covenant to pattern our lives in the ways of Christ and his kin-dom, and now allow ourselves to be seized by the Spirit as we participate in God's work of reconciling the world to godself, i.e., in bringing abundance and fullness to our common life in the earth commune.

God's Presence in Our Blessed Rage for the Healing of Life

The firming of the resolve to pattern our lives in the ways of the *Kristo* and his kin-dom requires a continuum of praxis from our *anamnetic* rites to the life-rite, that is, from our popular narratives of the *pasyon* to its translation in the active narration of our becoming. This proceeds from our *shabbath* cocooning under the old normal.

A hermeneutic of retrieval would bring us back to the "original" accounts of the *Kristo* that are congruent to at least the general plot of Jesus' Seminar's critical reconstruction of Jesus[31] though it extends beyond it to include the more popular post-easter reconstructions of the "risen" messiah of the rebellious *am ha'aretz* and official creedal affirmations of the church.[32] This praxis of active narration is thus a critical retrieval of ancient Christianity's sensing of God's radical presence and participation in the *pasyon* of the *Kristo*. The *pasyon* accounts may start with Jesus's weeping over Jerusalem and his insistence to prophesy and share his vision of the full life even in the most dangerous of situations. This *pasyon* was shown in Jesus' overturning of market stalls in the temple to demonstrate his revulsion over the comprehensive marginalization and exclusion of the poor; it was poured out in Jesus bending down to wash the feet of his friends, a symbolic depiction of what God's presence in the world is about. It was about the passion to serve and to serve unconditionally; it was shown in Jesus' abandonment of himself for the sake of his friends. The Jesus of the *pasyon* announced social reversal, pronounced indictment to injustice, rebuked those who called on him to play it safe. He violated the law in order to fulfill the higher law of love. He exposed the hypocrisy of the religious

31. As read from the works of the seminar's more famous scholars: Crossan, *Jesus*; Borg, *Meeting Jesus Again for the First Time*.

32. As expounded in the old but uniquely approached and interestingly relevant material from Fromm, *The Dogma of Christ*, 7.

establishment and the lies of imperial peace. He defied the empire and announced the coming of a new social order. The passion of God in Christ was seen in Jesus's courage to engage powers and principalities and face its consequences. It was seen in Jesus' willingness to die so that others may live and live life to the full. The passion of God was seen in Jesus's enduring the pain of abandonment, of betrayal, of humiliation, of indifference, of apathy, of violence, and the pain of an excruciating death on a rebel's cross. The passion of God was seen in Jesus' "descending into Hades" and rising back to life to proclaim that death is not the last word in this world and in this life; that our lives however defiled and disfigured are not beyond redemption; that history has not yet ended and hopes for a new, just, and better world for everyone stays ablaze. Our hopes for a new life, for a transformed world and a livable planet have found their solid ground in the fact that Jesus rose from the dead. This passion of God in Jesus is the core of the narrative of our faith and it helps us understand what it means to sense God's radical and incarnated presence and live a Christ-like reality beyond and against the regime of the "old normal".

As the COVID-19 pandemic rages on, God manifests God's presence as one sensed and experienced in Jesus the Christ. God is weeping over humanity for not listening enough, for not caring enough, for not loving enough, for humanity's transformation of God's garden and the human city into a howling moral and geographical wilderness, leaving everyone exposed to the innocent viral emanations of a deeply wounded earth. Nevertheless, God in God's weeping, persists in manifesting divine solidarity with humanity and creation by making us see the necessity of overturning those tables that keep us divided and fragmented, by making us see the value of distributing love in all our human institutions and see greed as ferociously ravaging not only our souls but our planet and the human commune in its totality. The COVID-19 pandemic happens not in a vacuum but in a world afflicted by the virus of unlove and injustice and scandalous separation from one another. God's presence manifests itself in us when we are finally able to see this human tragedy as an opportunity for spiritual and moral rebirth; when we see our present predicament as an opportunity to rebuild our relationships, revise the way we live, and give birth to a new world.

Finally, God's presence is made manifest when we are finally able to see the abandonment of ourselves as key to re-building our common life, when to wash in love the feet of the other becomes our moral compass, and when to love and serve unconditionally and efficaciously becomes the fulcrum of our spirituality. This concrete affirmation of God's presence is the most powerful antidote to the present pandemic; it is the one antidote that calls us to approach the current crisis as one human community destined to share the earth; it is the one antidote that can give birth to a radically ecumenical vision and spirituality necessary for the rebuilding of our global and national communities; it is the one antidote that pushes us into expanding the horizons of our creativity and resourcefulness in terms of medical and social cures to both our physical and social malaise; it is the one antidote that we now see at work in big and small ways by those who, amidst our debilitating fears if not mass hysteria, continue to courageously offer themselves in the service of the weak and vulnerable.

Conclusion

The active narration of our becoming calls us to rage against what Chikoy Pura of the Jerks sings as "the dying of the light" or those social viruses that are the dimming the faint rays of hope that gleam on people living in an ever-darkening tunnel. The passion of the one who broke the cocooning law in order to feed the hungry and heal the sick and "fulfilled" the *shabbath* in the process informs our dwelling in the *limen* as an active cocooning. It is this *shabbath* imperative that generates imagination and hope and calls for an active cocooning that rages for healing and transformation–against the further harming of life and our planet. Cocooning when it becomes a defeatist acquiescence or submission to the god of the old normal is both the *limen* of our life-rite wasted and "God's presence" a false claim exposed. Cocooning within the canopy of divine incarnational presence is meant to unleash a new form of life congruent to the vision of a *pasyon*-framed *leitourgi*cal living and enactment of the life-rite.

We are seeing how the new reality is being spawned by every act of defiant love, and resourceful and creative loving—even as we are being lured back for reincorporation into the old normal. But the path of those undergoing cocooning in the life-rite and in the continuum of people's struggle animated by God's presence is that which underwrites and concludes the *pasyon*: life's defiant rising.

Bibliography

Alexander, Bobby. *Victor Turner Revisited: Ritual as Social Change*. Atlanta: Scholars, 1991.

Beller, Jonathan. *Kristology and Radical Communion*. Quezon City: Sipat, 1999.

Benford, Robert, and Scott Hunt. "Dramaturgy and Social Movements: The Social Construction and Communication of Power." *Sociological Inquiry* 62.1 (1999) 85–109.

Blanco, John. *Frontier Constitutions: Christianity and Colonial Empire in the Nineteenth-Century Philippines*. Quezon City: University of the Philippines Diliman Press, 2009.

Blankenhorn, Bernhard. "A Short History and Theology of Spiritual Communion." *Church Life Journal*, April 8, 2020. https://churchlifejournal.nd.edu/articles/the-theology-and-history-of-spiritual-communion/.

Borg, Marcus. *Meeting Jesus Again for the First Time*. San Francisco: HarperOne, 1995.

Christians for National Liberation. "CNL 8th National Congress: Faith and Struggle." https://liberation.ndfp.org/main-stream/pananampalataya-atsa-pakikibaka/.

Clarke, Sathianathan. *Dalits and Christianity: Subaltern Religion and Liberation Theology in India*. New Delhi: Oxford University Press, 1999.

Crossan, John Dominic. *Jesus: A Revolutionary Biography*. New York: HarperCollins, 1994.

Gennep, Arnold van. *Rites of Passage*. Translated by Monika B. Vizedom and Gabrielle L. Caffee. Chicago: Chicago University Press, 1960.

Fernandez, Eleazar. "Filipino Popular Spirituality." In *Global Christianity*, edited by Mary Farrel Bednarowski and Dennis Janz, 37–60. Minneapolis: Fortress, 2010.

Fromm, Eric. *The Dogma of Christ*. New York: Rinehart and Winston, 1963.

Ileto, Reynaldo. *Pasyon and Revolution: Popular Movements in the Philippines, 1840–1910*. Quezon City: Ateneo de Manila University Press, 1979.

Jennings, Theodore. *Liturgy of Liberation: The Confession and Forgiveness of Sin*. Nashville: Abingdon, 1988.

Phillips, John B. *Your God Is Too Small*. 1952. Reprint, New York: Touchstone, 2004.

Rafael, Vicente. *Contracting Colonialism: Translation and Conversion in Tagalog Society under Early Spanish Rule*. Durham: Duke University Press, 1993.

Reuters Staff. "False Claim: Viral Poem on Social Distancing Was Written in 1869." *Reuters*, April 7, 2020. https://www.reuters.com/article/uk-factcheck-poem-social-distancing-1869/false-claim-viral-poem-on-social-distancing-was-written-in-1869-idUSKBN21P227.

Ricoeur, Paul. *Figuring the Sacred*. Minneapolis: Fortress, 1995.

Riechers, Mark. "A Viral Poem for a Virus Time." https://www.ttbook.org/interview/viral-poem-virus-time.

Scalice, Joseph. "Reynaldo Ileto's *Pasyon and Revolution* Revisited: A Critique." *Sojourn: Journal of Social Issues in Southeast Asia* 33.1 (2018) 29–58.

Scandrett-Leatherman, Craig. "Ritual and Resistance: Communal in a Church Retreat." *Missiology: An International Review* 27.3 (1999) 311–31.

Torre, Edicio de la. *Touching Ground, Taking Root: Theological and Political Reflections on the Philippine Struggle*. Quezon City: Socio-Pastoral Institute, 1986.

Promotion of Church People's Response. *That We May Remember*. Quezon City: Promotion of Church People's Response, 1989.

Turner, Victor. *The Ritual Process*. London: Routledge, 1969.

Turner, Victor, and Edith Turner. *Image and Pilgrimage in Christian Culture*. New York, 1978.

12

Post-COVID-19 Pandemic Futures

The New Normal, Status Quo Ante, and a Just, Green,
and Peaceful Future

—Rey Ty

Introduction

Statement of the Problem

BEFORE THE COVID-19 CRISIS, the world was already exposed to and experiencing an environmental crisis, a climate emergency, and the plague of predatory capitalism. Right before the outbreak of the latest coronavirus, the world economy was already in an economic recession. For the most part of the year 2020, half of the world's population has been in one form of lockdown or another. Millions have lost their jobs, while many other lucky ones were able to keep their jobs and worked from home.

Robert Reich, former US Secretary of Labor and professor of Economics at the University of California, Berkeley, explained that, economically, as the world was locked down, on the one hand, some governments saved select rich corporations and gave the poor pittance during the pandemic. On the other hand, US billionaires especially in monopolies, Big Tech, and Big Pharma, for example, got rich off the pandemic, getting wealthier by $637 billion.[1] To understand the linkage between the economy and the pandemic, we have to follow the money to see how the pandemic positively impacts the already rich and negatively impacts the rest of us.

---

1. Now This Politics, "Robert Reich Explains."

The biggest winners of the COVID-19 pandemic are the 1 percent super rich, including digital platforms such as Amazon, Facebook, and Google on the one hand, and Big Pharma on the other hand. To illustrate, Zuckerberg's wealth increased by 59 percent; Bezos', 39 percent; Walton family, an additional $25 billion. Big Pharma has increased the prices on prescription medication, the majority of which is used in conjunction with COVID-19 treatment. Stock options were distributed to company insiders right before receiving government subsidies during the pandemic, who raked in plump earnings after the increase of stock prices thereafter as a result of insider trading. Giant companies, investors, and billionaires profit off the COVID-19 pandemic, while the majority of the people are suffering economically.[2]

Noted Bernie Sanders: "The real looting in America is 644 billionaires becoming much, much richer during the pandemic, while working families lost their jobs, health care and homes."[3] During the pandemic in 2020, the following 1 percenters earned these additional billions: Jeff Bezos, 91.1 billion; Bill Gates, 20 billion; Mark Zuckerberg, 46.5 billion; Elon Musk, 68.2 billion; Warren Buffett, 13.6 billion; Larry Ellison, 21.3 billion; Steve Ballmer, 22.3 billion; and Larry Page, 19.1 billion.[4]

Reich stressed: "I refuse to tolerate a system that lets billionaires add $792,000,000,000 to their wealth during a pandemic but doesn't raise the $7.25 minimum wage for over a decade."[5]

Becoming more rapacious, predatory capitalism reared its ugly head during the pandemic. Naomi Klein calls this disaster capitalism.[6] This coronavirus does not only have physical health and mental health impacts on us but also economic and social impacts due to lockdowns and quarantines. The biggest losers during the COVID-19 pandemic are small businesses, "disposable" blue-, pink-, and white-collar workers, restaurants, the tourism industry, and the hospitality sector in general.

In terms of exposure to the disease, COVID-19, though neutral as such, is not "equal opportunity," so to speak, as it does not strike everyone equally. In both fiction and non-fiction, Luther, Bocaccio, Camus, and Foucault wrote about pestilence, plagues and epidemics. In non-fiction, Luther responded to the query whether one must flee or stay in the event an epidemic would strike. When asked if people must flee Wittenberg

2. Now This Politics, "Robert Reich Explains."
3. Sanders, "The Real Looting in America."
4. Sanders, "The Real Looting in America."
5. Reich, "Our Rigged-for-the-Rich System Is Intolerable."
6. Klein, *The Shock Doctrine*.

when the Bubonic Plague recurred, Martin Luther declared that people personally take the decision to stay or to flee.[7] He noted that the role of pastors is to provide spiritual care, while the role of parents and children is to take care of each other. Luther stated that the role of paid public officials, such as public administrators and emergency responders, is to ensure the health and safety of all.

In fiction, Camus talked about the role of the medical professional in the time of an epidemic. Camus's novel, *The Plague*, was based on an Algerian city's history of survival after experiencing plagues in past centuries. Here, the medical doctor Dr. Bernard Rieux asserted that he was merely performing his duties to relieve the suffering of those who have fallen victim to the epidemic. When hailed for their heroic acts, medical practitioners in the past and in the present have constantly been saying that they are only doing their job to alleviate the suffering of their patients who contracted the diseases,[8] while one thousand migrant children have contracted the virus.[9] Vaccine nationalism is a potential problem as Big Pharma will most likely raise the price of the vaccine and only the rich countries and individuals can afford to pay, which will further reinforce inequality between the Global North and the Global South as well as between the poor and the rich within each country.[10]

Literature reveals that the rich are always able to quarantine in their luxurious country villas or in their paradise islands, while the poor and people of color bear the brunt of getting the disease and dying. Take for example, the *Decameron*. In Bocaccio's fiction, the Black Death was the time during which ten young aristocrats went to a villa in the countryside outside Florence for ten days to quarantine and escape from the pandemic, recounting one hundred comic, romantic, and erotic stories with one another. The many poor who live in congested and dirty city centers got infected with the pestilence, suffered physical agony, mental anguish, and died. Today, coronavirus infects farm workers in California three times the rate of other workers.

In his work, *Discipline and Punish*, Foucault noted that during the seventeenth century plague, areas were partitioned, houses were closed off, areas inspected, and people had to register. Servants clean up after their masters in their primary residences, while the latter leave for their country villas to quarantine, returning only after their servers sanitize their homes.

7. Luther, "Whether One May Flee from a Deadly Plague."
8. Democracy Now!, "California Farmworkers Infected."
9. Democracy Now!, "Sweeping Lockdown Takes Effect in California."
10. Democracy Now!, "COVID-19 Vaccines Start to Roll Out."

The government established institutions and techniques for the purposes of measuring, quantifying, supervising, disciplining, and controlling the population, especially those who were sick. Supervisory institutions were set up as a protection against the plague. Obedience became the norm, as individuals internalized their fear of being under the watchful eye of the state. Surveillance became eternal. However, draconian measures bring about new social problems. Foucault noted the authoritarian and totalitarian normalization of surveillance as a result of measures instituted during the pandemic. The unwarranted permanent surveillance of individuals outside of an emergency, such as a plague, has grave implications to civil liberties and human rights. We see the use, misuse, and abuse of power in times of plagues.

This overreach of power through the totalitarian surveillance of individuals reminds us of Jeremy Bentham's panopticon and George Orwell's Big Brother. In the *Panopticon*, the prison guards have a 360-degree view that lets them see all the inmates at any point in time. In this case, the panopticon is a metaphor of an all-seeing state. The same idea of an all-knowing state is reflected in Orwell's *Animal Farm* and *1984* in which Big Brother has access to all information about everyone in society.

The pandemic revealed how governments and pharmaceutical companies were not ready to deal with the disease head on. The US, the European Union (EU), Russia, and India were hard hit. In Italy, which was hard hit, many elderly folks were left to die, as resources, which were limited, were used to save younger lives. The EU was an epic failure for not providing for the medical needs in Italy during this health emergency. Back in the US, Dr. Paul Farmer of Harvard University states that hundreds of years of economic inequality laid the foundation upon which the pandemic has caused so much suffering and death, especially among people of color.[11]

Ethically, we human beings do not have to choose between who to save and who are left to die, especially in this day and age during which we have almost unlimited resource for medical preparedness for a pandemic for which current governments and Big Pharma decided not to invest prior to the outbreak. On a positive note, places under the leadership of women seemed to have dealt with the pandemic better than their male counterparts in Aotearoa, New Zealand, Denmark, Finland, Germany, Iceland, Norway, and Taiwan.

The economy is toast. Flattening the curve in the contraction of the coronavirus also flattens the curve in the economy of small businesses, job security, livelihood, food security, and homelessness. More and more people are engaged in insecure jobs in the gig economy where there is

11. Farmer, *Fevers, Feuds, and Diamonds.*

neither tenure nor health benefits. We were walking a tightrope between health and the economy. The pandemic exposes and intensifies the crisis of exploitation and gross economic inequality within countries in particular and in the world as a whole.

There are two ways by which the pandemic will end: (1) the medical end and (2) social end.[12] The medical ending happens when no one else can get sick due to physical distancing, the virus morphs into a less harmful form of the influenza, the disease tapers off, or people become immune or get their vaccination. The social ending takes place when we humans decide we have to learn to live with the disease, manage its spread, not become fearful of the disease anymore, refuse to remain in quarantine, and take the chance of contracting the illness by going on with diurnal living.[13] Note that almost all diseases are not medically eradicated, except for the smallpox. New strains of the virus will emerge, as they always do throughout history. The World Health Organization (WHO) cautioned that vaccine alone will not eradicate the virus; we need to make permanent changes in our every-day life to lower the level of virus spread.[14]

This is the time during which we must reflect on and reconfigure the future direction of our human society, including the systems of economic and political power as well as the patterns of production, consumption, and distribution of goods and services that benefit not only humankind but the natural world as a whole as well, all of which have structural implications. The pandemic has compelled us to reexamine our society. It has pushed our economic, political, and social structures to the brink of collapse. In broad strokes, there are three possible futures already happening simultaneously before our eyes right here right now.

Research Questions

This chapter explores the answers three research queries. One, what are the features of the new normal? Two, what are the divergent and competing models of "back to normal?" Three, what are the elements of the structure of the just, green, and peaceful future that its proponents present?

12. The Infographics Show, "How Pandemic Ends."
13. The Infographics Show, "How Pandemic Ends."
14. Lovelace, "WHO Warns."

Purpose of This Chapter

In response to the research questions, the purpose of this research was to expound on the elements of the new normal, to explicate the contending representations of the status quo ante, as well as to elucidate on the proposed structure of a just, green, and peaceful future.

Theoretical Framework

Interactive Historical and Contextual Analysis guided the conduct of this research, according to which the economic, political and ideological structures of nature and society are interconnected.[15] Nature is the contextual foundation on which human society is situated. Humans use the bounties of nature, such as organic matter, minerals, flora, and fauna for our use, either as such or as processed with our hands, tools, and machineries.

Based on the economic activities and relationships among humans, political structures, such as states, laws, the police, and the military are established to provide peace, order, and security. Culture and ideology likewise prop up the economy and politics. The economy, politics, and ideology are not mechanistically linked but interactive. The economy is determinant, whereas politics and ideology are derivative; however, the latter in turn influences the former.

Methodology

This chapter is a critical review of literature regarding alternative futures. It presented three major futures along with their proponents. These three major clashing futures include (1) the new normal, (2) back to normal, and (3) the construction of a new just, green, and peaceful future. The new normal and the status quo ante are the two mainstream futures in front of us. In broad strokes, transnational corporate and military interests advance the model of the status quo ante, whereas politicians and new media moguls promote the model of the new normal, while I have presented my preferred third path as an alternative to the two dominant models.

There are two key subgroups working under the rubric for a just, green, and peaceful future: the civil libertarians and the progressives, both of which are contraposed to the models of the new normal and the status quo ante. Civil libertarians under the fold of the American Civil Liberties

15. Ty, *Human Rights, Conflict Transformation, and Peacebuilding.*

Union (ACLU)[16] and human rights activists who are members of Amnesty International (AI)[17] reject the violation of our right to privacy which form part of the new normal.

In this chapter, I have laid down and synthesized the ideas, actions, and prescriptions of several philosophers, academics, economists, social activists, social commentators, and politicians from different parts of the world. Culling from a critical survey of the literature, a grounded theory of the most likely near future under the incoming US Joe Biden would look like. The model for a just, green, and peaceful future that I propose was grounded on the thoughts of many social activists, authors, politicians, and organizations, many of whom have shared their visions of the post-pandemic period.

Findings

In this section, I presented the argument according to which three si-multaneous futures are already happening right here, right now. Unlike astrologers who engage in hocus-pocus, social scientists do not engage in predictions. I am not looking at a crystal ball. Rather, I observe the trends, as they happen and formulate the proposition according to which three broad trends are occurring right now. These trends include (1) the new normal, (2) back to normal, and (3) the struggle for a new just, green, and peaceful world. Note, however, that as models, these are abstractions of social reality where there are in fact overlaps. Hence, the models are not mutually exclusive. See figure 12.1 below.

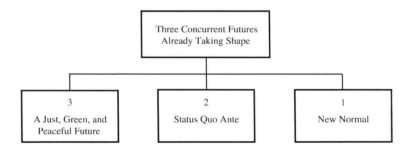

Figure 12.1: Emerging Economic and Political Configurations in the Time of the Coronavirus

16. ACLU, "ACLU, FreedomWorks Launch Multi-State Ad Campaign."
17. AI, "COVID-19, Digital Surveillance and the Threat to Your Rights."

New Normal

The first of the three futures emerging that is presented here is the "new normal." As the world is braced to protect the human population from further infections that lead to disease, incapacity, and death, the anti-pandemic measures, which are put in place at the height of the COVID-19 pandemic, become permanent fixtures. The so-called new normal includes measures such as compulsory wearing of facial protective masks, the use of hand sanitizer, constant and regular washing of hands, physical distancing, and temperature checks as people enter premises.

To avoid contamination and spreading the zoonotic virus, we will not be able to shake hands, embrace, hug, or kiss our family and friends. Children now refrain from visiting their grandparents, while young adults abstain from seeing their parents to protect the elders from getting the virus from the youth who are more resilient to the disease and might not have the typical symptoms, which could be debilitating or even lethal to senior citizens. By physically losing touch literally with one another, we are losing one part of our humanity.

Worse, the temporary measures that were put in place to monitor the spread of COVID-19, such as contact tracing and testing, will become permanent. Politicians and corporations will find justification to make these provisional but intrusive actions, which infringe on our civil liberty to privacy, perpetual and make us get accustomed to constant surveillance. By doing so, we lose our sense of privacy, as we will be under constant surveillance 24/7.

The new normal is very abnormal. There will be more security breaches that impact on privacy issues. Technologists have been talking about the fusion of our physical, biological, and digital identities, which leads to enforced transhumanism in which we lose our privacy altogether. Fighting for our privacy is not a question of whether we have something to hide or not, but a question of maintaining our humanity and our personal autonomy. We need both the right to health and the right to privacy. Pitting health and privacy against each other is an incorrect dichotomy.

As a result of the pandemic and the measures that governments have undertaken, the way in which the world operates has dramatically changed in qualitative terms. Home-based work is on the rise. For those whose employment permits, they go online to perform their work. Office spaces will be less important.

Status Quo Ante

A second possibility in the post-COVID-19 period, which is happening right now, is the return to normalcy, or in the common parlance, "going back to normal." However, do we really want to go back to normal? Is "back to normal" what the world needs now? Can we go back to normal? Should we go back to normal? Can we avoid going back to normal? Robert Reich stressed that we cannot afford to return to "normal" before Trump and his extremely polarizing politics, because the system is rigged for the rich,[18] the middle class was shrinking, income was distributed grossly unequally, and because of corruption, structural racism, and environmental crisis, which in the first place led to the rise of the Trump phenomenon.[19] We need to engage in a fundamental structural change in the economic, political, and social realms, lest the resurgence of a Trump phenomenon will become a recurring reality. Returning to "normal" is not an option. Let me explain below, though, the possible configurations of the elements of what is "back to normal."

There are several sub-types or paradigms within the "back to normal" worldview, namely: (1) reactionary patriotic populism, (2) compassionate conservatism, (3) perpetual war, (4) libertarian neoliberal corporate globalization, (5) predatory capitalism, (6) philanthrocapitalism, and (7) liberal globalism. In a word, the low politics of economic prosperity and the high politics of political power are the ends in view of the status quo ante. See figure 12.2 below.

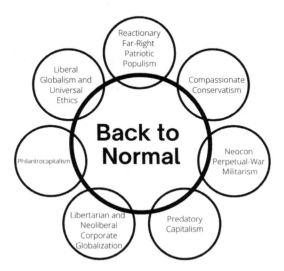

Figure 12.2: Concurrent Competing Scenarios of the Status Quo Ante

18. Reich, "Our Rigged-for-the-Rich System Is Intolerable."
19. Reich, "Why We Can't Go Back to Normal."

Reactionary Patriotic Populism.

Under President Trump, the US was a Banana Republic and an illiberal democracy where an autocratic leader acted whimsically for his personal aggrandizement. Aware that he has violating numerous laws, Trump is even contemplating preemptively pardoning himself. With his "Make America Great Again" (MAGA) tagline, President Trump has egged on the extreme right to intensify their racist rhetoric and racist attacks.[20] Angry white supremacists are anti-immigrant, support voter suppression of African Americans, and fight to keep their white privilege. He insisted on building a wall between the US and Mexico, asserting that Mexico should pay for its construction. He engaged in name calling by giving blanket statements that Mexicans are criminals, rapists, and drug dealers. When journalists asked him on different cases in to condemn violent racist attacks of white supremacists on African Americans and attacks on Jews, with chants, such as the "Jews will not replace us" and riflemen surrounding Beth Israel, he refused to denounce the violent actions of rightwing extremists, saying there are "very fine people on both sides" in Charlottesville, Virginia,[21] Portland, Oregon, and in Wisconsin.[22] Worse, Trump hired people with hate connections to work in the White House[23] who called for a Muslim ban from several countries, the separation of children from parents at the US-Mexican border, as well as for a halt to chain immigration of families of new citizens. After the election results were returned, Trump cried cheating; he and his lackeys tried to orchestrate a coup by different means. His white supremacist base cheered him on and staged protests in different states.

Aside from the Ku Klux Klan and some other long-standing pockets of white supremacist and racist groups, there are now many more openly racist and hate groups emerging all over the US thanks to the populist rhetoric of Trump. They are now emboldened to wreak more havoc, as Trump has left a strong imprint on enabling such groups to spew hate words and terrorist acts against minorities.[24] Unfortunately, hate groups are here to stay, at least for some time, after Trump's departure from the presidential office. Trump set the stage for a reinvigorated white supremacist ultra-right.

20. SBS News, "The Most Memorable Moments of Donald Trump's Presidency."
21. Holan, "In Context."
22. Carvajal et al., "Trump Refuses to Denounce Violent Actions."
23. Hayden, "Trump Official Brought Hate Connections to the White House."
24. SPLC, "Hate Map."

Compassionate Conservativism

Compassionate conservatives are Christian and Muslim conservatives, also known as comcons[25] or theocons[26] who help the poor, the disadvantaged, and people in need through the actions government, charitable institutions, and faith-based organizations[27] with a view to make a dent in the lives of people.[28] George W. Bush is the most recognizable face in compassionate conservatism in the US. Other well-known compassionate conservatives are Theodore Roosevelt, William H. Taft, and Dwight Eisenhower.[29]

Compassionate conservatives are akin to Christian democratic political parties which are social conservatives who call for support of the welfare state for the poor,[30] whereas the majority of the members of the Republican Party are fiscal conservatives who call for tax cuts and oppose government programs that ameliorate the condition of the poor.[31] Within the dominant core of the Republican Party, compassionate conservatives are pejoratively labeled as big-government conservatives.[32] While there are fewer and fewer compassionate conservatives, G. W. Bush has a charitable foundation engaged in charitable work around the world. We will most likely see less impact of compassionate conservative in the coming years.

Perpetual War

The US is militarily the most powerful country in the world today. Politicians who advocate the traditional meaning of security focus on military might, military preparedness, and militarism, for which reason they give rise to timocracy or the rise of a military class who rules the foreign relations of the country, through what Eisenhower called the military industrial complex.[33] The military establishment lobbies for increasing funding for the budget of the department of defense. Defense contractors, politicians in Congress and the White House, and the military have always been collaborating for preparation for war efforts.

25. Magnet, "What Is Compassionate Conservatism?"
26. TheoKonservativ, "Schlüsselwort(e)."
27. Watts, *Dictionary of American Government and Politics*, 30.
28. Bush, "Fact Sheet."
29. Morris, "Conservative Compassion."
30. Kandur, "Christian Democrats and Muslim Democrats."
31. Sullivan, "Is Compassionate Conservatism Dead?"
32. Sullivan, "Is Compassionate Conservatism Dead?"
33. Eisenhower, *The Military-Industrial Complex*.

Neoconservatives, otherwise known as neocons, join the ranks of those who promote perpetual war. Neocons call for the advancement of democracy and foreign interventionism in the international relations of the US. Domestically, George W. Bush was a compassionate conservative, calling for providing welfare for the poor. Internationally, many personalities in George W. Bush's administration were neocons who played prominent roles in the invasion of both Iraq and Afghanistan, ostensibly to promote freedom.[34]

Regardless of which individual politician or which political party is in power, the US has often used war in one form or another for all kinds of reasons to advance its national interest or to resolve conflicts. These wars include the war with Spain in 1898 after which the US gained control of the Philippines, Guam, and Puerto Rico; the First World War, the Second World War, the Cold War, the war on drugs, the War on Terror, and the covert and undeclared wars in Asia, Africa, and Latin America over the years as well as support for counter-revolutionary armed groups in different parts of the world. Based on evidence throughout history, the incoming president will most likely continue to use war as an instrument of national policy. Proponents of the perpetual war perspective seek to increase the quantity and improve the quality of ammunition, weaponry, war material, and the military force.

The US has more than eight hundred military bases dotting the globe. Its military budget is 37 percent of the world's total military expenditure.[35] Reflected Lee Camp: "The corporate media can't stop talking about the exciting 'diversity' of the incoming Biden Administration. It doesn't matter what skin color or gender people are if they all support US empire, US war crimes, and Wall Street-fueled destruction of the world. That's not diversity."[36]

Libertarian Neoliberal Corporate Globalization.

The hallmarks of globalization include the structural adjustment measures which include deregulation, liberalization of trade, and privatization, all of which the US-led World Bank, the International Monetary Fund (IMF), and the World Trade Organization (WTO) support. However, the pandemic dealt a blow to international trade. To add fuel to fire, when Trump came to power, he started to engage in a trade war with China, starting with Huawei, which later snowballed to many other agricultural,

34. Record, *Wanting War.*

35. Vox, "How America Became a Superpower."

36. Lee Camp [Redacted] (@Lee Camp), Twitter, November 24, 2020, 11:47 a.m., https://twitter.com/LeeCamp/status/1331293253849772042.

commercial, and industrial products from China. Giant service and retail companies as well as industrial capitalists were displeased when Trump imposed tariffs on raw materials and goods coming into the US from different countries, which triggered counter-tariffs in other economies as well as when he called for manufacturing to return to the US.

In so many words, the US under Trump called other economies to engage in a trade war with China, including boycotting Huawei electronic products, which the Trump administration claims spies on US citizens on behalf of the Chinese government as well as blaming China for spreading the coronavirus. Trump's trade war with China has spiraled almost out of hand. China retaliated and imposed import tariffs on many US goods the way the US imposed import tariffs on Chinese goods. China engaged in a trade war with Australia, after the latter blamed the former for the spread of the coronavirus.

Transnational corporations support unfettered free trade so that they could get the cheapest raw materials, labor, and products for both import and export in order to make a killing in the production and sale of their products, figuratively speaking. However, everyday cheap prices come with a catch: capitalists pay subsistence wages to workers who have to seek tax-payer paid subsidies elsewhere for their survival. Consumers are given semblances of choices of thousands of different products in different packaging but are all products of a few interrelated conglomerations of giant corporations. Alienation, false consciousness, commodity fetishism, conspicuous consumption, and the concentration of wealth in a very few hands create an army of exploited laborers and the ever-recurring crisis of capitalism.

Other than Trump, most US presidents support unfettered free trade of goods and services. Hence, with his departure from the White House and the arrival of Biden to the President's office, the world shall see a return to a freer flow of commodities and labor. However, as the pandemic has disrupted national economies and supply chains, there is a new trend of bringing factories and manufacturing back to local, national, and regional economies, thus the process of de-globalization has begun. Manufacturing, though, will be more and more mechanized. Jobs, therefore, will be lost both in former host countries and the home countries, due to robotics and artificial intelligence (AI).[37]

What is terrifying is that the director and founder of the World Economic Forum (WEF) sees the pandemic as an opportunity to "reset" for which the 1 percent elite grab the power to decide the best way by which to "build back better" in their own image. Politicians, such as Joe Biden, Justin

37. The Economist, "Will COVID Kill Globalisation?"

Trudeau, Boris Johnson, Prince Charles, and non-governmental organizations are parroting this slogan.[38] Pushing the agenda of neoliberal corporate globalization, the 1 percent of the World Economic Forum meet every winter in posh mountain resorts in Davos, Switzerland, inviting business executives, celebrities, politicians, pop stars, scholars, and media, whose mere presence sanitizes and legitimizes its agenda and platform.

At Davos, there is always noise about how to overcome income inequality, how to deal with the climate emergency, how to fight corruption, and how to promote human rights. The 1 percenters brag about their paternalistic acts of charity to help the poor. Prof. Bregman, who gave a presentation in Davos,[39] loudly proclaims that taxing the rich is the elephant in the room at Davos meetups, after which everyone could hear the pin drop.[40] We the 99 percent, composed of working people, the marginalized, and for whom we care, must ensure that we reset the post-pandemic period on our own terms, not on the 1 percenters' terms.

Predatory Capitalism

Predatory capitalists include executives engaged in finance capital in investment banking, securities, stock markets, investment managements, asset management, prime brokerage, securities underwriting, and other financial services. In this futures trend that is reemerging, we witness the hegemonic power of plutocracy or plutarchy (or the rule of the rich), oligarchy (the rule of the few), corporatocracy (corporate power over the political processes and decision-making through campaign contributions and lobbying), and the mainstream economics of Wall Street (which advances the ethics of self-interest, profit, and greed as well as the debunked trickle-down economics).

The problem with the practice of the "free market" model is that losses are public and socialized, while gains are privatized. In times of economic crisis, the US government, for example, bails out big corporations, letting the taxpayers pay for the losses of monopolies and giant companies. Bernie Sanders calls this socialism for the rich and capitalism for the poor. The so-called free marketers are after the pursuit of self-interest, with the motto of "greed is good." During the pandemic, Walmart, for example, earned $15,600,000,000 in 2020 alone, profiting off the poverty of its workers, as workers are paid starvation wages, who rely on food stamps and Medicaid

38. RT, "'Great Reset' Trends on Twitter."
39. Guardian News, "Rutger Bregman Tells Davos to Talk about Tax."
40. Bregman, *Humankind.*

for their subsistence that taxpayers pay.[41] We must move away from predatory capitalism to a life economy or new economics that promotes the well-
being of nature and people first, not profit and greed.

Philanthrocapitalism

Billionaires avoid paying taxes in so many different ways, among which
are to look for tax cuts, tax loopholes, and tax havens, including setting up
trusts and foundations for tax avoidance. Philanthrocapitalism is fake charity, whose primary interest is to boost the image and prestige of the wealthy
who avoid paying taxes, but appearing to saving the world.[42] The existence
of a few billionaires amidst mass poverty is a sign of the failure of capitalism.
Yet, thousands upon thousands of ordinary folks with bleeding hearts for
the suffering people around the world donate to charities.

Philanthrocapitalism has a dark side. Dr. Henry Jekyll is engaged in
"doing good" and charity work. Mr. Edward Hyde is engaged in all kinds of
investments that maintain the status quo of predatory capitalism. Let me
cite two examples here.

One, shockingly, in one instance, the Red Cross was reported to have
raised half a billion dollars for relief efforts for Haiti but ended up building
only six homes.[43] The Red Cross was also criticized in its relief works for
the survivors of Hurricane Katrina in the US.[44] One can only check how
many more highly reputable and questionable charities earn low-profile
dirty money to fund high-profile "do good" projects.[45]

Two, the investigative reporting of AJ+ français reveals that the Bill
and Melinda Gates Foundation, on the one hand, does "good" work to end
poverty, diseases, and hunger. On the other hand, it does "bad" work, as its
Trust invests in more than 730 biggest global transnational corporations,
including Big Pharma, the petroleum industry, genetically modified organisms (GMOs), and weapons, many of which do harm to nature, the environment, water resources, the climate crisis, social justice, indigenous peoples,
human health, flora and fauna mass extinction, and peace.[46] Some of these
TNCs, which were involved in some scandals, include BASF, BHP, BNP, BP,
Coca Cola, Exxon, Glencore, Goldman Sachs, JP Morgan, Novartis, Pepsi,

41. Brave New Films, "Walmart Profits Off Poverty."
42. BER Staff, "The Merits and Drawbacks of Philanthrocapitalism."
43. Elliott, "How the Red Cross Raised Half a Billion Dollars."
44. Kokalitcheva, "Red Cross Spent Half a Billion Dollars."
45. Charity Navigator, "Advisories."
46. AJ+ français, "Le Système Bill Gates."

Parisbas, McDonald's, Pfizer, Rio Tinto, Total, Unilever, Vale, and Walmart. Many of these corporations are predatory capitalists, practice labor exploitation, were involved in some scandals of major proportion, or engage in dirty industries for which they have received one type of "hall of shame" award or another, as they have caused one type of catastrophe or another in different continents.[47] In 2019 alone, the good work of the Bill and Melinda Gates Foundation benefits from the earnings of its trust from four of the twenty companies that contribute 35 percent of carbon dioxide emission in the world: BHP, Chevron, Exxon Mobil, and Total.[48]

Since its founding in 2000, during which Bill Gates generously left 95 percent of his legacy thereto, the foundation has not lost a single cent but increased his earnings in fact. We are left with the impression that he gave his all to the poor of the world. Contributions first go to a trust which invests in giant corporations, whose earnings fund the charitable work of the foundation. Overtly, the philanthropy of the Foundation works at the service of the environment, health, and social justice as well as in the interest of Bill Gates. But at the end of the day, its philanthropy serves the interests of transnational corporations: this is what Lionel Astruc calls the false generosity of philanthrocapitalism.[49] See figure 12.3 below.

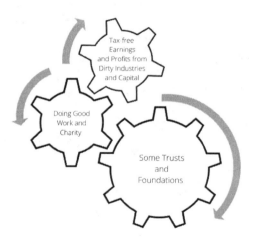

Figure 12.3: An Example of a Model of the False Generosity
of Philanthrocapitalism

47. AJ+ français, "Le Système Bill Gates."
48. AJ+ français, "Le Système Bill Gates."
49. Astruc, L'art de La Fausse Générosité.

In its book, *Gated Development*, Global Justice indicated that the Gates Foundation influences global policies, promotes corporate interests, supports industrial agriculture, and pushes for privatization.[50] Global Justice asserts that the Foundation is not a neutral charity; rather, it serves "to promote neoliberal economic policies and corporate globalization."[51] In an AJ+ français broadcast, Lionel Astruc articulates that the funds of the Foundation goes to the rich countries in the Global North to subsidize, for instance, the work of research laboratories, whereas only 5 percent of the budget for health, for instance, goes to Africa.[52]

Bezos' donation of $100 million to food banks is but 0.07 percent of his net worth, while Zuckerberg's $25 million donation amounts to merely 0.05 percent of his net worth.[53] As a superficial band-aid approach to social problems, philanthrocapitalism does not address poverty, famine, malnutrition, and sickness as a result of stark inequality.[54] AJ+ français cites Vandana Shiva as saying: "Bill Gates is the Christopher Columbus of the modern times," which is far from being a compliment.[55] Philanthrocapitalism masks exploitation and gross inequality in society.

What is needed is justice for people to rise up in societal standing, not paternalistic charity. Bregman calls out the hypocrisy of philanthrocapitalism of billionaires, saying that taxing the rich is the elephant in the room in such pompous gatherings as the World Economic Forum.[56] If billionaires and their TNCs pay their taxes all over the world, we will not need the paternalistic charity of the philathrocapitalists. Governments can rationally and democratically use tax revenues for the social benefits of the people, rather than billionaires giving paternalistic charitable handouts to causes of their choice, which end up serving the TNCs in their home countries.[57] Philanthrocapitalism benefits the super-rich and maintains gross income inequality.[58]

50. Global Justice Now, "Gated Development."
51. Global Justice Now, "Gated Development."
52. AJ+ français, "Le Système Bill Gates."
53. Al Jazeera English, "All Hail the Lockdown."
54. McGoey, *No Such Thing as a Free Gift.*
55. AJ+ français, "Le Système Bill Gates."
56. Bregman, *Utopia for Realists.*
57. AJ+ français, "Le Système Bill Gates."
58. Vallely, "How Philanthropy Benefits the Super-Rich."

Liberal Globalism

Right off the bat, the United States under Trump was a Banana Republic, by which we mean the country and its foreign relations were run by the personality cult, the rule of one man, and the rejection of the rule of law. Instead of progress, Trump turned back the clock to restore the past conditions of racism, bigotry, stereotyping, anti-immigration, sexism, ableism, and other similar discriminatory practices.

Under President Trump, the US has turned inwards, became isolationist, and called for "America First." He has overturned all of the major international agreements of the United States under international law, especially those agreements into which former President Obama enters. Trump pulled out the US from the Paris agreement on climate change. He abrogated the US agreement with Iran and North Korea with respect to the non-development of nuclear weapons. He berated the European Union, the North Atlantic Treaty Organization (NATO), Japan, and South Korea for having a free lunch for US military cover or protection, distancing himself from traditional US allies. He became close to controversial leaders, such as North Korean Supreme Leader Kim Jong-un, Russian President Putin, the Philippine President Duterte, Brazilian President Bolsonaro, and other similar leaders. Furthermore, he also threatened to stop funding the World Health Organization (WHO), as he was more concerned about the stock market than with protection the people from contracting the coronavirus. Aside from moving the US Embassy to Jerusalem, he decided to have a peace accord with Israel without the participation of Palestine. All of these acts were based on his whims and not on the rule of law.

At least one positive "return to normalcy" is the return to the rule of law. Liberal globalists call for the rule of law through adopting, respecting, and applying multilateral international norms and standards, to which most or all states adhere and accept. They are institutionalists who support international regimes, regional organizations, international organizations, and international standards, international instruments, and international law. When the new president steps into the Oval Office, Biden will reverse most of the reactionary policies and actions of Trump, with a few exceptions, as both Trump and Biden openly and strongly support Israel, unlike other past US presidents who at least try to maintain a semblance of neutrality between Israel and Palestine and calling for peace talks.

A Just, Green, and Peaceful Future

The third future prospect already in the making is the struggle for a just, green, and peaceful future of progressives and radicals. Choosing hope over fear, adherents to this model of economic, political, and environmental development are variably called the woke left, progressive democrats, social democrats, democratic socialists, and radicals. Individuals and groups who propose a just, green, and peaceful future are the following: (1) the civil libertarians and (2) the social activists of the progressive and radical movements and politicians. See figure 12.4 below.

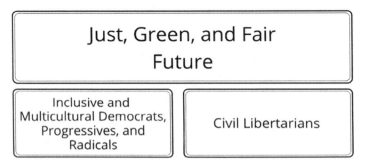

Figure 12.4: Struggle for a Just, Green, and Peaceful Future

Civil Libertarians

Civil libertarians include such groups as the American Civil Liberties Union (ACLU), Amnesty International (AI), and Human Rights Watch (HRW) voice their demands to dominant policy institutions and processes. These groups serve as the conscience of society, speaking truth to power when the liberties and rights of people are violated. With the increased use of state surveillance, especially during the pandemic, as well as of artificial intelligence, we need to appreciate the work of civil libertarians who stand up for the rights of individuals and groups.

The American Civil Liberties Union seeks to make the US government ensure that the provisions of the Constitution are guaranteed and expanded. The civil liberties issues with which ACLU is concerned include: capital punishment, criminal justice, disability rights, free speech, HIV, human rights, immigration, juvenile justice, LGBTQ rights, national security, prisoners' rights, racial justice, religious liberty, reproductive rights, security and privacy, smart justice, voting rights, and women's rights.[59]

Amnesty International works globally and presents its reports to the United Nations.[60] It deals with the whole gamut of economic, social, cultural, civil, and political rights as understood under international law.[61] Amnesty International's research, advocacy, lobbying, campaigns, and actions deal with armed conflict, arms control, climate change, corporate accountability, death penalty, detention, disappearances, discrimination, freedom of expression, indigenous peoples, international justice, living in dignity, police violence, refugees, asylum-seekers, and migrants, sexual and reproductive rights, and torture.[62]

As with Amnesty International, Human Rights Watch (HRW) operates globally to defend human rights. HRW investigates and exposes abuses of human rights around the world with a view to change policies, enforce laws, and serve justice.[63] HRW presents its reports to the United Nations.[64] Among its concerns include: arms, business, children's rights, crisis and conflict, disability rights, environment, free speech, health, international justice, LGBT rights, migrants, refugee rights, technology and rights, terrorism and counterterrorism, torture, and women's rights.

Inclusive and Multicultural Democrats, Progressives, and Radicals

Inclusive and multicultural democrats, progressives, and radicals endorse environmental and climate justice. Inclusive and multicultural democrats, including most Democrats, such as Obama and Biden, accept corporate money, which taints their efforts to work for worker's rights as well as environmental and climate justice. Progressives such as Sanders and Ocasio-Cortez refuse to accept corporate money, as they do not want corporate interests to control their agenda for change. Left radicals will not even think of corporate funding to begin with.

Promoting the Ecocene, proponents of environmentalism and climate justice question and critique the Anthropocene and Capitalocene in the development of the world, after Holocene.[65] Holocene was the period of

59. ACLU, "American Civil Liberties Union."
60. AI, "United Nations (UN)."
61. AI, "Universal Declaration of Human Rights."
62. AI, "What We Do."
63. HRW, "About Us."
64. HRW, "United Nations."
65. Boehnert, *Design, Ecology, Politics.*

12,000 years during which stable climate led to the rise of agriculture, human settlements, and civilizations.[66] Natural scientists concur that we now live in the Anthropocene period during which human-induced actions shape the Earth, including high levels of carbon dioxide in the atmosphere, the rise of sea level, and holes in the ozone layer.[67] Jason W. Moore coined the term Capitalocene, which is a concept that critiques the concept of Anthropocene as a speciesistic term that puts the blame of environmental destruction on the human species in general.[68] The concept of Capitalocene places the blame of climate crisis not on the human species in general but on the role of rapacious capitalism specifically with its quest for greed, power, and wealth at the expense of people and nature.[69] See figure 12.5 below.

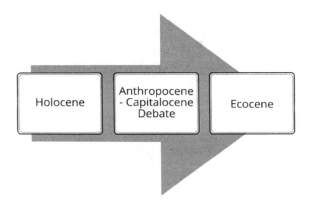

Figure 12.5: Epochs in the History of the Earth

Proponents of this third trend reject predatory capitalism and disaster capitalism. While the second futures trend focuses on Wall Street, this third futures trend gives emphasis on the Main Street in urban, suburban, exurban, and rural areas. Champions of New Economics call for change from below and to struggle for change at the top[70] that will benefit the planet, build a more equal society in which everyone has a say in the administration of the economy.[71] While greed and profit guide free marketers, the common

66. Steffen et al., *Global Change and the Earth System*.

67. Crutzen, "Have We Entered the 'Anthropocene'?"

68. Moore, *Antropocene or Capitalocene?*

69. Moore, "Capitalocene."

70. NEF, "Together We Can Change the Rules."

71. NEF, "New Economics Foundation."

good guides the progressives and radicals who support labor unions, labor rights, decent living wages, workers' cooperatives, Black Lives Matter, free college education, the cancellation of student debts, and universal basic income. The extreme right gives prominence to white privilege and patriarchy, whereas progressives and radicals recognize and honor women empowerment, indigenous rights, and all people regardless of their ethnicity, color, gender, religion, abilities, and other differences.

Robert Reich claimed that free market does not exist anymore for the most part, as big corporations consolidate leading to the emergence of monopolies, which crushes small businesses.[72] Calling for the rejection of disaster capitalism, Žižek insists that locally, the active role of the state must be reinvigorated and globally, the world must engage in effective international cooperation, boldly proclaiming, "communism or barbarism."[73] The adherents of this model for the future champion economic justice, social justice, political justice, cultural justice, gender justice, environmental justice, and climate justice.

If we truly want a just, green, and peaceful world, we must likewise address the questions of sustainable food,[74] clothing,[75] shelter,[76] and travel.[77] We need to engage in the politics of action[78] and act together here and now.[79] Support creative civil disobedience.[80] For this, we need to support local farmers and small businesses. Eat local. Reject fast fashion. Wear ethical clothes. And yes, dare I say, go vegan in one fell swoop.[81] Lest they be sued, no environmental NGO talks about the carbon emission of animal factory farms, which the United Nations declares emits a huge amount of greenhouse gas in the world.[82] The Food and Agriculture Organization of the UN claims that animal factory farms produce 18 percent of all human-produced greenhouse gas emissions, which includes 37 percent of methane and 65 percent of nitrous oxide.[83] The United Nations panel on climate change asserts that we

72. Reich, *Saving Capitalism*.

73. Žižek, *Pandemic!*, 99.

74. Astruc, *Perspectives Durables*.

75. Astruc and d'Erm, *Voyages Aux Sources de La Mode Éthique*.

76. Astruc, *Echappées vertes*.

77. Astruc, *Echappées vertes*.

78. Astruc et al., *(R)Évolutions*.

79. Hopkins and Astruc, *Le pouvoir d'agir ensemble*.

80. Shiva and Astruc, *Vandana Shiva*.

81. Kuhn and Andersen, *Cowspiracy*.

82. Farm Sanctuary, "The Environment."

83. EcoWatch, "How Factory Farming Contributes to Global Warming."

must radically change the way in which we produce food and manage land in order to avert catastrophic climate change.[84]

There are now three general types of social movements in action today. The classical movement is composed of the grassroots working class and peasant class. The "new" social movement is composed of middle-class folks who started initially working for various causes, such as democracy, anti-imperialism, human rights, women's rights, gay rights, and the rights of people of colors, ethnic, religious, cultural, linguistic, and other differences. Today, the leaderless non-hierarchical youth around the world stage the latest type of social movement. All these three types of social movements go hand in hand, promoting, fighting, and working for a comprehensive agenda for a just, green, and peaceful world.

Economic, political, and social crises engender upheavals.[85] In a word, people around the world struggle against greed and terror[86] as well as tyranny and fascism.[87] In 2019 alone, countless protests, mostly leaderless and non-hierarchical that mostly the youth activists have organically organized and mobilized, were held around the globe, demanding for the construction of a fair, green, and peaceful world. Some of the major protest actions involve anti-austerity, anti-corporate globalization, progressive taxation for the rich, climate justice, same-sex marriage, Black Lives Matter, migrant rights, Occupy Wall Street, Friday for the Future, Extinction Rebellion, decent living wages, and universal basic income.[88] The pandemic in 2020 kept countless protests and mass actions at bay for a short period. But the social volcano erupted once again in France, Chile, Ecuador, Thailand, and in many other countries in the same year. The year 2021 and beyond will be no different.

Doom and gloom? The future is a mixed bag. We make it what it will be. If we leave the future to politicians, we shall see the replication of the status quo ante and the imposition of a total-surveillance global society under the new normal. Dare to dream and work for a totally different and new world in our terms, not in the elite's. Radically reimagine and work for a more inclusive, just, and green post-pandemic tomorrow here and now.

From the classical social movements, the new social movements, and the latest leaderless social movements, we see the comprehensive agenda for social change. To peasants, workers, scientists, the youth, students, women, indigenous peoples, minorities, outcasts, the marginalized,

---

84. Hersher and Aubrey, "To Slow Global Warming."
85. Sison, *Crisis Generates Resistance.*
86. Sison, *People's Resistance to Greed and Terror.*
87. Sison, *Struggle against Terrorism and Tyranny.*
88. Jobin-Leeds, *When We Fight, We Win.*

people of faith, atheists, and all forces of progress and peace: Let us pinch ourselves out of this nightmare. We have to speak up and to speak out. Speak on behalf of those who cannot speak for themselves due to being outcast, marginalized, or repressed. Let us build a better future together with jobs, joy, health, and rights. Love with total abandon. Break barriers. Respect the human rights of all.

In no particular order, the agenda for a just, green, and peaceful future is manifold. We need to move:

1. from hate, fascism,[89] bigotry, xenophobia, racism,[90] casteism, and discrimination to respect, love, compassion, human rights, social justice,[91] and racial justice;[92]

2. from fear, selfish power, and competition to equality, cooperation, solidarity,[93] and justice;

3. from profit and greed first to nature and people first;[94]

4. from corporate handouts to universal basic income;

5. from socialism for the rich to socialism for the poor;

6. from profit-seeking health care to health care as public goods and human rights;[95]

7. from big profits for Big Pharm to free mass vaccination for all;

8. from elite power to people power;[96]

9. from elite democracy to grassroots democracy;[97]

10. from a linear economy to a circular economy;

11. from dominion to eco-centrism; from dirty petroleum energy to clean and green energy;[98]

12. from reuse, reduce, and recycle to rethink, refuse, repair, repurpose, re-wild, replant, and reforest;

89. Giroux, *America at War with Itself.*

90. Alexander, *The New Jim Crow.*

91. Chomsky and Foucault, *Chomsky-Foucault Debate.*

92. Davis and Barat, *Freedom Is a Constant Struggle.*

93. Galeano, *Children of the Days.*

94. Chomsky, *Profit over People.*

95. Farmer, *Pathologies of Power.*

96. Foucault, *Power/Knowledge.*

97. West, *Democracy Matters.*

98. Brown et al., *The Great Transition.*

13. from despair to hope; from superstition to science;

14. from misogyny to women empowerment, equal pay for equal work, leadership, and the right to control their bodies;[99]

15. from surveillance capitalism, disaster capitalism, philanthrocapitalism, and gig economy to renewed labor rights and strengthened labor unions; from consumerism to the protection of consumer rights[100] as well as prosumerism in which households produce the basic products we need;

16. from perpetual war to durable peace; from empire building,[101] Orientalism, and imperialism to self-determination[102] and liberation;[103]

17. from traditional national security to human security;

18. from patriotism to international solidarity; from the power of the elite to the power of the people; from alienation to happiness;[104]

19. from predatory capitalism and philanthrocapitalism to a just and sustainable economy;

20. from free trade to fair trade; from exploitation, unpaid labor, unpaid overtime work, and work beyond the job description to shorter work weeks and decent living wages for all workers, including documented and undocumented migrant workers, refugees, and stateless people;

21. from almost no taxes for the rich to taxes for all, including progressive taxation for the rich;[105]

22. from authoritarianism and illiberal democracy to grassroots and participatory democracy;

23. from reactionary ultra-right populism to radical transformation of society;

24. from personality cult to international rule of law;[106]

---

99. Beauvoir, *Le Deuxième Sexe.*
100. Nader, *Told You So.*
101. Amin, *Only People Make Their Own History.*
102. Sartre, *Plaidoyer Pour Les Intellectuels.*
103. Said, *Orientalism.*
104. Maté, *In the Realm of Hungry Ghosts.*
105. Piketty, *Capital in the Twenty-First Century.*
106. Falk, *Palestine.*

25. from Big Farm and agribusiness controlling the production and distribution of food to empowering local farmers and communities to grow our own food;[107]

26. from genetically modified organisms (GMOs) to organic food;[108]

27. from fast food to slow food and clean food;[109]

28. from big business to small and local businesses and farms;

29. from fast fashion to fashion justice;

30. yes, from carnivorism [my neologism] to veganism;[110]

31. from reproducing the normality of the status quo ante to opposing it as well as proposing positive comprehensive structural changes.

Status Quo Ante? Evolution? Revolution? Or Extinction!

Conclusion

In a Nutshell

In summary, three concurrent trends are emerging during the pandemic: (1) the new normal, (2) the status quo ante, and (3) the struggle for a just, green, and peaceful future. Note that the three major perspectives are not mutually exclusive. The dominant model will be the different variants of the (1) status quo ante, while elements of the (2) new normal will be adds-on. The struggle for (3) a just, green, and peaceful future will be an uphill struggle in which progressives of different hues shall continue to be engaged. See figure 12.6 below.

107. George, *How the Other Half Dies.*
108. Astruc, *Vandana Shiva.*
109. Pollan, *In Defense of Food.*
110. Lappé, *Diet for a Small Planet.*

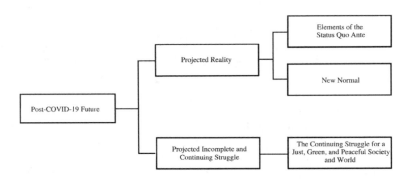

Figure 12.6: The Projected Configuration of
the Post-COVID-19 World under Biden's Presidency

Quo Vadis?

Let us take Joe Biden's presidency as an illustration. Based on his past track record and the track record of US current history, what would be Biden presidency look like? Biden has a lot of house cleaning to do. Note of caution, though: Biden extends his arms to both the Republicans and the Democrats, stating that he will be a president for all Americans, not only for one side and against the other. His words sound conciliatory and he is known for reaching out to both sides of the aisle in Congress. However, US Senators Mitch McConnell and Lindsey Graham have track records of opposing most things, if not everything, the Democrats seek to achieve. They will be in Biden's way.

In addition, while Biden seeks to engage in dialogue and compromise with the right, including the extreme right, valid questions remain. Is a Kumbaya moment of unity possible? Is the chasm within society so deep that the antagonisms and contradictions in society are irreconcilable? The extreme right and white supremacists have avowed African Americans, Jews, and Mexicans as not only beneath them but have actually started verbally and physically harass them and, in some instances, kill them, and not the other way around. The diehard intolerance and bigotry are one way. There is wisdom in the paradox of tolerance: "We should therefore claim, in the name of tolerance, the right not to tolerate the intolerant."[111]

111. Popper, *The Open Society and Its Enemies*, 581.

The road ahead for Biden is paved not in gold but in sand, sticks, gravel, pebbles, stones, rocks, and boulders.

To be sure, aside from steering the US "back to normal," Biden will bring back civility, grace, politesse, and refinement to the White House, in contrast to his predecessor who is characterized by incivility, rudeness, uncouthness, and vulgarity. But if bringing back the US back to normal and returning social graces and good manners back to the White House alone make you happy, then that is quite a low bar. Biden's prim and proper behavior unites him with Wall Street bankers whom the government bailed out during the 2008 financial crisis. These same bankers repossessed the homes of the middle class who were not able to pay their mortgages. Metaphorically, Biden sleeps in bed with the bankers who bankrolled his campaign. Corporate democrats, such as Biden and Obama, talk about supporting the middle class, but do not make mention of the poor, unlike progressives such as Bernie Sanders and Alexandria Ocasio-Cortez.

Paradoxically, the rash, brazen, foul-mouthed, and politically incorrect Trump, however, is able to connect with the common people who are dissatisfied with the status quo under predatory capitalism, and Democrats do not want to rock the boat, unlike Sanders and Ocasio-Cortez who do.[112] Unfortunately, though, while Trump in his 2016 campaign promised to drain the swamp and keep the predators out, he in fact chose which predators stay in his swamp, including his family, his lackeys, and Washington lobbyists, all of whom are out of touch with the lives of Jane, Tom, Dick, and Harry.

The policies and actions of Joe Biden will be a hodgepodge of the three perspectives: (1) back to normal, (2) the new normal, and (3) the struggle for a just, green, and peaceful future. Let me explain. Based on his track record, he surely embodies many facets of the status quo ante. Likewise, he will implement the requirements of the new normal in order to manage and control the further spread of the coronavirus. Most likely, that will include further deepening the mass surveillance of people, making them more permanent, instead of emergency measures only. Surely, the American Civil Liberties Union, Amnesty International, Human Rights Watch are already keeping a watchful eye on the invasion to the right to privacy and will campaign vigorously for defending the right to privacy. Biden will surely recognize and respect the rights of people of different backgrounds, religions, gender, ethnicity, and class, which makes him an inclusive and multicultural democrat.

---

112. Varoufakis, "Hoping for a Return to Normal after Trump?"

Not planning to be a transformational president, Biden asserts that he is only a transitional president[113] and will not make major changes, which is a strong hint of what is to come, which is not to upset the apple cart. Nevertheless, Biden will overturn most of the policy actions of Trump which were based on quirks and simply destroying Obama's legacy. For example, he will treat COVID-19 with utmost seriousness, quite the opposite of Trump. While Trump tried to dump Obamacare, but did not present an alternative plan, Biden will maintain Obamacare. Moreover, he has already stated that he has a Biden Green Deal of sorts, which is not as radical as Ocasio-Cortez's Green New Deal. I am afraid Biden's Green Deal will most likely accept corporate lobbying and money, which will water down the environmental and climate crisis mitigation efforts of the US. However, on a positive note, he already declared that the US will return to the Paris agreement on climate, from which Trump has rescinded.

As he claims he will not be a clone of Obama,[114] Biden's next steps regarding China, Iran, and Russia remain to be seen. The longstanding policy and actions of all US presidents since Nixon was one-China policy, except Trump, who warmed up to Taiwan with arms sales and military exercises, that raised the ire of China. If Biden were to restore US longstanding policy and practice, he will return to the one-China policy.

Many conflicts are brewing all over the world, which could be a flashpoint for a world war: Armenia-Azerbaijan, Ethiopia, Nigeria, South China Sea, Sudan, Yemen, and elsewhere. I am afraid perpetual war will remain perpetual. Just like all US presidents in current history, Biden will most likely support the perpetual war efforts of the military-industrial complex and of the neocons. Yet, all indications show that he will most likely renegotiate nuclear arms control and disarmament with Iran and North Korea, which he will most likely be under the watch of the International Atomic Energy Agency (IAEA).

Today, the US under Trump on the one hand and China on the other hand are vying for the position of the world's hegemon. Trump banned Huawei in the name of national security but the fact is China is way ahead of the US and all countries in 5G technology. China is now in 6G.[115] Note that all internet related gadgets, including cellphones, be they Chinese, US, Korean, European, or otherwise, can and do spy on our online lives. Under different pretexts, both China and the US want to be the regional hegemon in the Asian Pacific region. The South China Sea is a flashpoint for a potential World War III. The US has the Atlantic Alliance, Australia, Japan, and South Korea on its side, while China has Russia, Iran, and seemingly

113. RT, "That's the Spirit!"
114. Fenenbock, "Joe Biden Is Not Barack Obama."
115. BBC, "China Sends 'World's First 6G' Test Satellite into Orbit."

President Duterte's Philippines on its side. India is now at odds with China with respect to the new border clashes.

Biden will halt Trump's isolationism by rekindling and renewing ties with the European Union (EU), the North Atlantic Treaty Organization (NATO), the World Health Organizations (WHO). He already signified his intention to return to the Paris Climate Accord. In this sense, Biden will promote liberal globalism, institutionalism, and appeal to international law. In this sense, he will be a globalist. Furthermore, Biden will most likely continue the international trade policies and practices of all past US presidents in recent history, except for Trump, which makes Biden a supporter of neoliberal corporate globalization.

Obama sowed the seed of Cold War 2.0 with his animosity toward Putin but sought a peaceful solution to the nuclear scare vis-à-vis Iran through international agreements under the watch of the International Atomic Energy Agency. Trump sowed his own seed of discord with China and Iran but befriended North Korea and Taiwan. Biden has to pick up from where Trump has left a whole lot of mess. The Democrats seemed to be toying with Cold War 2.0 with Russia though, as they claimed that Russia helped Trump win the presidency in 2016 through the spread of fake news in cyberspace. What Biden will do remains to be seen.

In a word, the future of the United States and of the world, as the US is the world hegemon that impacts the rest of humanity, depends on the ideologies that Biden brings to his presidency. He will put in place the new normal necessities. Biden is not a reactionary patriotic ultra-right white supremacist. He is more than a compassionate conservative, as he is an inclusive and multicultural democrat who supports most civil liberties. He is a liberal globalist who subscribes to international law and international organizations.

At the same time, Biden, who is transactional,[116] will support predatory capitalism, as all US presidents do. Both Trump and Biden have very warm relations with Israel, at the expense of Palestine, unlike Carter and Clinton who tried to be neutral mediators between the two. Unlike Trump, who imposed tariffs, engaged in trade wars, and is opposed to unconstrained free trade under neoliberal corporate globalization, Biden will be the opposite and support unfettered free trade, as all the recent past US presidents do, except for Trump.

That is how the world will look like in the next four years under Biden's White House. All in all, Biden's policies and actions will be to the left of Trump but to the right of Bernie Sanders and Alexandria Ocasio-Cortez: nothing earth-shaking, just steering US economy, politics, and culture "back to normal" more or less with the addition of "new normal"

116. Smith, "Like Trump, Biden Is Transactional."

precautions. Wrote Varoufakis: "Without a readiness to confront the greatest concentration of corporate power in the history of the United States, even the most amiable of presidents will fail to deliver either social justice or serious climate change mitigation. At least Trump wasn't hypocritical, his supporters might say."[117]

His success or failure does not only depend on his vision but also the reception of the Republic Party bigwigs of his proposed policies. But make no mistake: he's no revolutionary. He supports electoral democracy; but Sanders and Ocasio-Cortez would go one step further, promoting direct grassroots participatory democracy. He will seek to heal the divide. But is unity possible? Will Republicans McConnell and Graham take him for a ride? Surely, the embittered Trump will provide background noise which will worsen the political climate, as he will incite the extreme right and the news media will pick up the sound bites, which will increase their audience share and subsequently their advertising revenues.

Who knows what would happen? We might be in for a few surprises. Still, with the social ending of the COVID-19 pandemic, the world will still be recognizable, as it will mostly be a mirror image of the status quo ante, but with a certain degree of de-globalization, as economists learn about the problem with the supply chain in the event a pandemic strikes again. See figure 12.7 below.

Yes to	No to
•Civil Liberties	•"Alternative Facts"
•Climate Science	• Anti-Immigration
•Corporate Interests	•AOC's Green New Deal
•Disaster Capitalism	•Climate Change Denial
•Finance Capital	•Conspiracy Theories
•Inclusion and Multicultualism	•Fake News
•Liberal Globalism	•Fascist Groups
• Medicare	• Isolationism
•Neoliberal Corporate Globalization	• Racism
•New Normal	•Reactionary Ultra-Right White Supremacy
•Perpetual War	•Rudeness, Incivility
• Philanthrocapitalism	• Supremacy
•Politesse, Civility, and Grace	•Trade Wars
• Science	•Voter Suppression
	•White Privilege

Figure 12.7: Rey Ty's Grounded Theory of the Near Future in the US
and in the World under Biden's Presidency

117. Varoufakis, "Hoping for a Return to Normal after Trump?"

Bibliography

AJ+ français. "Le Système Bill Gates." *Facebook*, November 20, 2020. https://www.facebook.com/ajplusfrancais/videos/3464055340298751.

Al Jazeera English. "All Hail The Lockdown." *Facebook*, November 20, 2020. https://web.facebook.com/aljazeera/videos/151345386690383/.

Alexander, Michelle. *The New Jim Crow: Mass Incarceration in the Age of Colorblindness.* New York: New, 2020.

American Civil Liberties Union. "ACLU, FreedomWorks Launch Multi-State Ad Campaign to Reform Surveillance Laws." https://www.aclu.org/press-releases/aclu-freedomworks-launch-multi-state-ad-campaign-reform-surveillance-laws.

———. "American Civil Liberties Union." https://www.aclu.org/.

Amin, Samir. *Only People Make Their Own History: Writings on Capitalism, Imperialism, and Revolution.* New York: Monthly Review, 2019.

Amnesty International. "COVID-19, Digital Surveillance, and the Threat to Your Rights." https://www.amnesty.org/en/latest/news/2020/04/covid-19-surveillance-threat-to-your-rights/.

———. "United Nations (UN)." https://www.amnesty.org/en/what-we-do/united-nations/.

———. "Universal Declaration of Human Rights." https://www.amnesty.org/en/what-we-do/universal-declaration-of-human-rights/.

———. "What We Do." https://www.amnesty.org/en/what-we-do/.

Astruc, Lionel. *Echappées vertes: Propositions de vacances écologiques.* Mens: Terre vivante, 2009.

———. *L'art de La Fausse Générosité: La Fondation Bill et Melinda Gates (Récits d'investigation).* Arles: Actes Sud, 2019.

———. *Perspectives Durables.* Paris: Archipress, 2012.

———. *Vandana Shiva: victoires d'une indienne contre le pillage de la biodiversité.* Mens: Terre Vivante, 2011.

Astruc, Lionel, and Pascale d'Erm. *Voyages Aux Sources de La Mode Éthique.* Les Nouvelles Utopies. Paris: Ulmer, 2009.

Astruc, Lionel, et al., eds. *(R)Évolutions: Pour Une Politique En Actes.* Domaine Du Possible. Arles: Actes Sud, 2012.

BBC. "China Sends 'World's First 6G' Test Satellite into Orbit." *BBC*, November 7, 2020. https://www.bbc.com/news/av/world-asia-china-54852131.

Beauvoir, Simone de. *Le Deuxième Sexe.* Paris: Gallimard, 2017.

Bentham, Jeremy. *Panopticon: Or the Inspection House.* CreateSpace, 2017.

BER Staff. "The Merits and Drawbacks of Philanthrocapitalism." *Berkeley Economic Review*, March 14, 2019. https://econreview.berkeley.edu/the-merits-and-drawbacks-of-philanthrocapitalism/.

Bocaccio, Giovanni. *Decameron.* Translated by G. H. McWilliam. London: Penguin Classics, 2003.

Boehnert, Joanna. *Design, Ecology, Politics: Towards the Ecocene.* London: Bloomsbury Academic, 2018.

Brave New Films. "Walmart Profits Off Poverty and Foots US Taxpayers the Bill." *Facebook*, November 25, 2020. https://web.facebook.com/bravenewfilms/videos/388085322629471.

Bregman, Rutger. *Humankind: A Hopeful History*. Translated by Erica Moore and Elizabeth Manton. New York: Little, Brown and Company, 2020.

———. *Utopia for Realists: How We Can Build the Ideal World*. Translated by Elizabeth Manton. New York: Little, Brown and Company, 2017.

Brown, Lester R., et al. *The Great Transition: Shifting from Fossil Fuels to Solar and Wind Energy*. New York: Norton, 2015.

Bush, George W. "Fact Sheet: Compassionate Conservatism." https://georgewbush-whitehouse.archives.gov/news/releases/2002/04/20020430.html.

Camus, Albert. *La Peste*. Paris: Gallimard, 1947.

Carvajal, Nikki, et al. "Trump Refuses to Denounce Violent Actions by Right-Wing Agitators." *CNN*, August 31, 2020. https://www.cnn.com/2020/08/31/politics/trump-supporters-violence/index.html.

Charity Navigator. "Advisories." http://www.charitynavigator.org/index.cfm?bay=search.cnadvisories.

Chomsky, Noam. *Profit over People: Neoliberalism & Global Order*. New York: Seven Stories, 1999.

Chomsky, Noam, and Michel Foucault. *Chomsky-Foucault Debate: On Human Nature*. New York: New, 2006.

Crutzen, Paul J. "Have We Entered the 'Anthropocene'?" *IGBP*, October 31, 2010. http://www.igbp.net/news/opinion/opinion/haveweenteredtheanthropocene.5.d8b4c3c12bf3be638a8000578.html.

Davis, Angela Y., and Frank Barat. *Freedom Is a Constant Struggle: Ferguson, Palestine, and the Foundations of a Movement*. Chicago: Haymarket, 2016.

Democracy Now! "California Farmworkers Infected by Coronavirus at Three Times the Rate of Other Workers." *Democracy Now!*, December 4, 2020. https://www.democracynow.org/2020/12/4/headlines/california_farmworkers_infected_by_coronavirus_at_three_times_the_rate_of_other_workers.

———. "COVID-19 Vaccines Start to Roll Out as U.N. Warns of Disparities in Distribution." *Democracy Now!*, December 12, 2020. https://www.democracynow.org/2020/12/7/headlines/covid_19_vaccines_start_to_roll_out_as_un_warns_of_disparities_in_distribution.

———. "Sweeping Lockdown Takes Effect in California; Data Shows 1,000 Migrant Kids Have Contracted COVID-19." *Democracy Now!*, December 7, 2020. https://www.democracynow.org/2020/12/7/headlines/sweeping_lockdown_takes_effect_in_california_data_shows_1_000_migrant_kids_have_contracted_covid_19.

The Economist. "Will COVID Kill Globalisation?" *Facebook*, November 26, 2020. https://web.facebook.com/TheEconomist/videos/684826758901707.

EcoWatch. "How Factory Farming Contributes to Global Warming." *EcoWatch*, January 21, 2013. https://www.ecowatch.com/how-factory-farming-contributes-to-global-warming-1881690535.html.

Eisenhower, Dwight D. *The Military-Industrial Complex*. https://avalon.law.yale.edu/20th_century/eisenhower001.asp.

Elliott, Justin. "How the Red Cross Raised Half a Billion Dollars for Haiti and Built Six Homes." *ProPublica*, June 3, 2015. https://www.propublica.org/article/how-the-red-cross-raised-half-a-billion-dollars-for-haiti-and-built-6-homes.

Farm Sanctuary. "The Environment." https://www.farmsanctuary.org/issue/environment/.

Falk, Richard. *Palestine: The Legitimacy of Hope*. Charlottesville, VA: Just World 2014.

Farmer, Paul. *Fevers, Feuds, and Diamonds: Ebola and the Ravages of History*. New York: Farrar, Straus and Giroux, 2020.

———. *Pathologies of Power: Health, Human Rights, and the New War on the Poor*. California Series in Public Anthropology 4. Berkeley: University of California Press, 2005.

Fenenbock, Michael. "Joe Biden Is Not Barack Obama." *Media Line*, November 29, 2020. https://themedialine.org/news/opinion/joe-biden-is-not-barack-obama/.

Foucault, Michel. *Discipline and Punish: The Birth of the Prison*. New York: Vintage, 1995.

———. *Power/Knowledge: Selected Interviews and Other Writings, 1972–1977*. Edited by Colin Gordon. New York: Vintage, 1980.

Galeano, Eduardo. *Children of the Days: A Calendar of Human History*. Translated by Mark Fried. New York: Nation, 2013.

George, Susan. *How the Other Half Dies: The Real Reasons for World Hunger*. Montclair, NJ: Allanheld, Osmun, 1977.

Giroux, Henry A. *America at War with Itself*. San Francisco: City Lights, 2017.

Global Justice Now. "Gated Development—Is the Gates Foundation Always a Force for Good?" *Global Justice Now*, January 20, 2016. https://www.globaljustice.org.uk/resources/gated-development-gates-foundation-always-force-good.

———. *Gated Development: Is the Gates Foundation Always a Force for Good?* https://www.globaljustice.org.uk/sites/default/files/files/resources/gjn_gates_report_june_2016_web_final_version_2.pdf.

Guardian News. "Rutger Bregman Tells Davos to Talk about Tax: "This Is Not Rocket Science." *YouTube*, January 29, 2019. https://www.youtube.com/watch?v=P8ijiLqfXPo&ab_channel=GuardianNews.

Hayden, Michael Edison. "Trump Official Brought Hate Connections to the White House." *Southern Poverty Law Center*, October 21, 2020. https://www.splcenter.org/hatewatch/2020/10/21/trump-official-brought-hate-connections-white-house.

Hersher, Rebecca, and Allison Aubrey. "To Slow Global Warming, U.N. Warns Agriculture Must Change." *NPR*, August 8, 2019. https://www.npr.org/sections/thesalt/2019/08/08/748416223/to-slow-global-warming-u-n-warns-agriculture-must-change.

Holan, Angie Drobnic. "In Context: Donald Trump's 'Very Fine People on Both Sides' Remarks (Transcript)." *Politifact*, April 26, 2019. https://www.politifact.com/article/2019/apr/26/context-trumps-very-fine-people-both-sides-remarks/.

Hopkins, Rob, and Lionel Astruc. *Le pouvoir d'agir ensemble, ici et maintenant: Entretiens*. Arles: Actes Sud, 2015.

Human Rights Watch. "About Us." https://www.hrw.org/about/about-us.

———. "United Nations." https://www.hrw.org/topic/united-nations.

The Infographics Show. "How Pandemic Ends." *Facebook*, August 15, 2020. https://web.facebook.com/TheInfographicsShow/posts/3289689171092366.

Jobin-Leeds, Greg. *When We Fight, We Win: Twenty-First-Century Social Movements and the Activists That Are Transforming Our World*. New York: New, 2016.

Kandur, Jane Louise. "Christian Democrats and Muslim Democrats." *Daily Sabah*, October 7, 2016. https://www.dailysabah.com/feature/2016/10/08/christian-democrats-and-muslim-democrats.

Klein, Naomi. *The Shock Doctrine: The Rise of Disaster Capitalism*. London: Picador, 2008.

Kokalitcheva, Kia. "Red Cross Spent Half a Billion Dollars to Build Six Homes in Haiti." *Time*, June 3, 2015. https://time.com/3908457/red-cross-six-homes-haiti/.

Kuhn, Keegan, and Kip Andersen. *Cowspiracy: The Sustainability Secret*. San Rafael, CA: Earth Aware Editions, 2016.

Lappé, Frances Moore. *Diet for a Small Planet*. New York: Ballantine, 1991.

Lovelace, Berkeley, Jr. "WHO Warns Coronavirus Vaccine Alone Won't End Pandemic: 'We Cannot Go Back to the Way Things Were.'" *CNBC*, August 21, 2020. https://www.cnbc.com/2020/08/21/who-warns-a-coronavirus-vaccine-alone-will-not-end-pandemic.html.

Luther, Martin. "Whether One May Flee from a Deadly Plague: To the Reverend Doctor Johann Hess, Pastor at Breslau, and to His Fellow Servants of the Gospel of Jesus Christ." In *Luther's Works*, edited by Jaroslav Pelikan et al., 43:111–38. Philadelphia: Fortress, 1999.

Magnet, Myron. "What Is Compassionate Conservatism?" *The Wall Street Journal*, February 5, 1999.

Maté, Gabor. *In the Realm of Hungry Ghosts: Close Encounters with Addiction*. Berkeley: North Atlantic, 2010.

McGoey, Linsey. *No Such Thing as a Free Gift: The Gates Foundation and the Price of Philanthropy*. London: Verso, 2016.

Moore, Jason W. *Antropocene or Capitalocene? Nature, History, and the Crisis of Capitalism*. Oakland: PM, 2016.

———. "Capitalocene—Locating the Climate Crisis in the Historical Context of Colonialism, Orientalism, and Extractivism." https://capitalocene.org/.

Morris, Edmund. "Opinion | Conservative Compassion." *The New York Times*, August 17, 2005. https://www.nytimes.com/2005/08/17/opinion/conservative-compassion.html.

Nader, Ralph. *Told You So: The Big Book of Weekly Columns*. New York: Seven Stories, 2013.

New Economics Foundation. "New Economics Foundation." https://web.facebook.com/neweconomics.

———. "Together We Can Change the Rules." https://neweconomics.org/.

Now This Politics. "Robert Reich Explains How Billionaires Are Getting Rich off COVID." *Facebook*, November 22, 2020. https://web.facebook.com/NowThisPolitics/videos/387864195962350.

Orwell, George. *1984: A Novel*. New York: Signet, 2002.

———. *Animal Farm: A Fairy Story*. New York: Signet Classic, 1996.

Piketty, Thomas. *Capital in the Twenty-First Century*. Translated by Arthur Goldhammer. Cambridge, MA: Belknap, 2017.

Pollan, Michael. *In Defense of Food: An Eater's Manifesto*. New York: Penguin, 2008.

Popper, Karl. *The Open Society and Its Enemies*. London: Routledge, 2012.

Record, Jeffrey. *Wanting War: Why the Bush Administration Invaded Iraq*. Sterling, VA: Potomac, 2010.

Reich, Robert. "MSNBC: Why We Can't Go Back to Normal." *Facebook*, November 29, 2019. https://www.facebook.com/watch/?v=811847156038824.

———. "Our Rigged-for-the-Rich System Is Intolerable. Tax the Rich. Raise the Minimum Wage. Organize." *Facebook*, July 15, 2020. https://www.facebook.com/ RBReich/posts/3617464421599461.

———. *Saving Capitalism: For the Many, Not the Few*. New York: Vintage, 2016.

RT. "'Great Reset' Trends on Twitter after Trudeau Speech on Covid-19 Hints It's Not Just a 'Conspiracy Theory.'" *RT*, November 16, 2020. https://www.rt.com/ news/506887-trudeau-great-reset-conspiracy-reveal/.

———. "That's the Spirit! Biden Says He's Just a 'Transition Candidate' to Put 'the Mayor Petes of the World' into Office." *RT*, May 1, 2020. https://web.archive. org/web/20201224073119/https://www.rt.com/usa/487482-biden-transition-democratic-candidate/.

Said, Edward. *Orientalism*. New York: Vintage, 1979.

Sanders, Bernie. "The Real Looting in America Is 644 Billionaires Becoming Much, Much Richer during the Pandemic, while Working Families Lost Their Jobs, Health Care and Homes." *Facebook*, October 26, 2020. https://m.facebook.com/ berniesanders/photos/a.324119347643076/3529107610477551/#_=_.

Sartre, Jean-Paul. *Plaidoyer Pour Les Intellectuels*. Paris: Gallimard, 2020.

SBS News. "The Most Memorable Moments of Donald Trump's Presidency." *Facebook*, November 2, 2020. https://web.facebook.com/watch/?v=658648614821724.

Schwab, Klaus, and Thierry Malleret. *COVID-19: The Great Reset*. Steinhausen: Agentur Schweiz, 2020.

Shiva, Vandana, and Lionel Astruc. *Vandana Shiva: Pour une désobéissance créative: Entretiens*. Arles: Actes Sud, 2017.

Sison, Jose Ma. *People's Struggles against Oppression and Exploitation*. Vol. 1, *Crisis Generates Resistance, 2009–2010*. Utrecht: International Network for Philippine Studies, 2015.

———. *People's Resistance to Greed and Terror: Selected Writings, 2016*. Utrecht: International Network for Philippine Studies, 2018.

———. *Struggle against Terrorism and Tyranny*. Vol. 2, *August–December 2018*. Utrecht: International Network for Philippine Studies, 2019.

Smith, Karl W. "Like Trump, Biden Is Transactional. That's Not a Bad Thing." *Bloomburg Opinion*, November 11, 2020. https://nz.finance.yahoo.com/news/trump-biden-transactional-not-bad-120015916.html.

Southern Poverty Law Center. "Hate Map." https://www.splcenter.org/hate-map.

Steffen, Will, et al. *Global Change and the Earth System: A Planet under Pressure*. New York: Springer, 2005.

Sullivan, Amy. "Is Compassionate Conservatism Dead?" *USA Today*, January 29, 2012. https://www.pressreader.com/usa/usa-today-us-edition/20120130/287079910658283.

TheoKonservativ. "Schlüsselwort(e): Compassionate Conservatism." https://web. archive.org/web/20070929011437/http://www.theocons.de/index.php?s=Compassionate+Conservatism&sentence=AND&submit=Suche.

Ty, R. "Human Rights, Conflict Transformation, and Peacebuilding: The State, NGOs, Social Movements, and Civil Society—The Struggle for Power, Social Justice, and Social Change." EdD diss., Northern Illinois University, 2011.

Vallely, Paul. "How Philanthropy Benefits the Super-Rich." *The Guardian*, September 8, 2020. http://www.theguardian.com/society/2020/sep/08/how-philanthropy-benefits-the-super-rich.

Varoufakis, Yanis. "Hoping for a Return to Normal after Trump? That's the Last Thing We Need." *The Guardian*, November 8, 2020. http://www.theguardian.com/commentisfree/2020/nov/08/hoping-for-a-return-to-normal-after-trump-thats-the-last-thing-we-need.

Vox. "How America Became a Superpower." *Facebook*, January 10, 2020. https://web.facebook.com/Vox/videos/1398269117027353/.

Watts, Duncan. *Dictionary of American Government and Politics*. Edinburgh: Edinburgh University Press, 2010.

West, Cornel. *Democracy Matters: Winning the Fight against Imperialism*. New York: Penguin, 2004.

Žižek, Slavoj. *Pandemic! COVID-19 Shakes the World*. New York: Polity, 2020.

Threshold Dwelling to Make Hope and History Rhyme

Reimagining a Post-pandemic World

—ELEAZAR S. FERNANDEZ

MANY HAVE WRITTEN ABOUT the onslaught of coronavirus in the early months of the pandemic as a "turning point" or a "watershed moment" in history. Sending shockwaves throughout the world, the pandemic has become an event of unveiling and awakening. Some said that the pandemic had brought a loss of innocence and complacency, while others spoke of the end of the romance with market capitalism. The pandemic is forcing us to leave behind the "old normal" and embrace the "new normal," and now we need to clarify what that is. Having been jolted from our complacency we are now more attentive, many have said, to what truly matters. I really hope so. However, as months have progressed, it appears that people have drifted back to their old, if not worse, normal. If there is something we can learn from the coronavirus crisis, it is that we must take this painful opportunity to take personal stock of where we have been and where we are heading.

In and through the Deep Darkness: Seeking Hope

So many lives lost now and the death toll continues to rise. When will our suffering be over? Is there rhyme or reason in this universe? In the midst of immense suffering, we often ask, where is God? Where is divine justice? In the realm of theology, these questions fall under the theme of eschatology. Although eschatology is often referred to as something about the end-times, it is really more about the question of hope. What do we hope for? Or, what can we hope for? The fertile soil that has given birth to eschatology is the presence of suffering. Theodicy (divine justice in the midst of suffering) is the fertile soil or the womb that gives birth to eschatology (the doctrine of hope).

Why hope? What can we hope for? What is the wellspring of hope? It is truly difficult to speak of hope when we are in the midst of a perfect storm and with no end in sight yet. How can we continue to live in hope when signs of hope are few and far between? Are we consigned to cynicism and despair or to the hell of hopelessness? Living without hope is living in hell; it is to experience death long before our physical cessation. It is no accident that when Dante, in his *Inferno*, wanted his readers to understand the depths of evil he pictured the gates of hell with these words written over them: "Abandon hope, all ye who enter here."[1] Without hope, we can only be swallowed by despair.

The temptation for cynicism and despair is stark and strong, but a spark inside me continues to resist the idea that the world has no rhyme or reason. There is still the voice of life that calls me to believe life is greater than senselessness and death. How can I nourish or shelter this seed of hope so it does not whither under the scorching heat of the summer sun, or freeze to death in the long and severe winter? "Because we don't bring this true hope with us from birth, and because our experiences of life may perhaps make us wise but not necessarily hopeful," says Jürgen Moltmann, "we have to go out to learn hope. We learn to love when we say yes to life. So we learn to hope when we say yes to the future."[2]

Yes, we must learn to hope, which only happens when we are threatened on every side by the forces of death and destruction, cynicism and despair. Yes, we must learn to hope, but this learning is possible only in situations when we are in the midst of the threatening darkness. We cannot learn hope outside of the challenges that threaten hope or make a mockery of hope.

The darkness around us is deep, and it appears to be getting deeper still. No doubt the eerie and ghastly darkness of coronavirus is hauntingly pervasive but, I believe, the coronavirus has not overcome the light. Even in the midst of coronavirus, life continues to glow. If only we have the eyes to see and ears to hear, the darkness itself is whispering gently to our distraught souls that there is light, not in spite of, but through the deep and horrifying darkness. Og Mandino's words are timely, "I will love the light for it shows me

1. Cited in Hall, *Why Christian? For Those on the Edge of Faith*, 103.
2. Moltmann, *The Source of Life*, 39.

the way; yet I will endure the darkness because it shows me the star." There is a light in each of us that only the darkness can help to illumine.[3]

I know that coronavirus has darkened our countenance but let us not allow it to wreak any more havoc than it has already done by allowing it to claim what it is not. Deep inside we desire for certainty, I know. But, when we are uncertain of so many things, even our own existence, faith offers a certainty that can withstand the vicissitudes of time and allows us to hope and continue hoping. In the midst of the pandemic, I wrote this poem with the title: "This We Know Deep in Our Hearts."

We don't know when the tempest and storms of COVID-19 will end,
Much as we ache to know;
We don't know when our trials will be over,
For the future is not given to us in advance;
We don't know when the new day will arrive,
Much as we long for it to arrive in haste;
We don't know the answers . . . we don't know.

But this we know deep in our hearts,
The dawn is slowly breaking in the distant horizon,
Spring is coming,
The trees are swaying to the tune of the breeze,
The birds are dancing and singing hopeful melodies,
The crocuses are coming out of the frozen soil
after a long bleak winter,
The earth is saying, "yes," to life, again!

Some may perish; others may survive,
We grieve for our losses; we carry their memories.
Whatever the outcome be,
It matters how we have walked the journey,
It matters how we are for each other,
It matters what we have become because of this passage.

But this we know deep in our hearts,
The light of hope will help us make it through the night,
With rivers of faithful companions, we will make it to the ocean of life,
And our love for each other will see us through.

---

3. Chittister, *Between the Dark and the Daylight*, 19.

Yes, the coronavirus has claimed so many lives, but life is much larger than the coronavirus. Let us not allow the coronavirus to define and reduce our humanity. On the contrary, let us make what is life-giving define who we are in the face of the coronavirus threat. Yes, we have witnessed the surge of many socio-political maladies, but there are also expressions of the best of the human spirit that we should not fail to see, if only we have the eyes to see. Do we have the eyes to see?

I hope this poem that I wrote at the beginning of the pandemic, "When Love, Courage, and Hope Went Viral," will help us see the star through the deep darkness.

Yes, the coronavirus has gone viral,
but so has love.
Yes, fear has gone viral,
but so has courage.
Yes, doubt has gone viral,
but so has faith.
Yes, uncertainty has gone viral,
but so has hope.

If fear cast out love,
love casts out fear.
If fear constrict hearts and moral imagination,
love makes it as wide as the world.
If the fear for our security is the beginning of folly,
love of life is the beginning of wisdom.
If fear leads to walls rising,
love brings down walls of divisions.

Love has the patience to stay home and stay safe,
that we may help "flatten the curve."
Love has the eyes of care and compassion,
that the needs of others are not banished from sight.
Love has the feet and hands of service,
that those in need are given their share.
Love has the drive to muster prophetic courage,
that walls of greed are brought down
and the table of life is made accessible to all.

The Pandemic Crisis: A Portal

Whether we like it or not, end times will come. We are already living daily in its shadow as we speak. There are already tremors and convulsions, if only we have the eyes of the heart to see and the ears of our hearts to listen. How the end times will unfold depends largely on the way we are living our lives today. Prophecy is not fortune telling, far from it, but it simply says that if we continue with business-as-usual, social unraveling is what we are going to get.

We do not need a monstrous pandemic to come to our senses, but it is already here, and we had better learn from it. Before our dreams turn into nightmares, let us wake up! It could be that the dreaded end times may be our chance for a new beginning; it could be that the closure will be an opening; that the deadline will be our lifeline. Our beginning is not behind us or in the past (as in *origin*); our beginning—new beginning—is what lies before us.

An opportunity for a new beginning is unveiling itself before us. The pandemic has provided us an opportunity to rethink or "reimagine the doomsday machine we have built for ourselves," says Arundhati Roy.[4] "Historically," observes Roy, "pandemics have forced humans to break with the past and imagine their world anew. This one is no different. It is a portal, a gateway between one world and the next."[5] A door or a portal is before us.

A poem by Adrienne Rich says something similar. A door is before us, but it makes no promises. It is simply a door. We may enter, we may not. If we do not enter, we will miss a lot. If we do not, we would not know what is waiting for us. Or we would not know how we would react; we would not know what we would make of the situation. There exists, however, if we take the challenge, "the possibility of stepping across a threshold—from helplessness to action, from caution to belief, from ignorance to knowledge."[6] The good news, according to dispatches from previous threshold crossers, is that the doors are constantly opening. If we miss one now, we will find another. The not so good news is that there are many doors and there is no formula for knowing which one is the right door; there is no road map or route that can be mapped step-by-step to our desired destination.

---

4. Global Goals, "The Pandemic Is a Portal."
5. Roy, "The Pandemic Is a Portal."
6. Westley et al., *Getting to Maybe*, 220.

Threshold: Between Beginnings and Endings

In Roman mythology, Janus, who is usually depicted with one face looking backward and another looking forward, may serve well in portraying the idea of threshold. Teetering between the old and the new, the past and the future, the ending and the beginning, Janus is rightly called the god of doors or gates. Doors or gates depict both the opportunity to depart from the old and to enter the new. Others, instead of door or gate, use bridge as a metaphor for threshold. Its weakness, however, is that bridge emphasizes the idea of connection and less so the idea of transition, and does not strongly convey the idea of leaving the old ways and of welcoming the new.

We may not find a single perfect metaphor for threshold, but what threshold depicts is the notion of "liminal space" that underscores the idea of a location between a vanishing past and an emerging present. "Liminal space" is that "transition space" in which the shedding of the old skin is happening simultaneously as new skin is emerging. "Liminal space" is the "chrysalis in our lives: the time we are neither caterpillar nor butterfly."[7]

I know that this is not a comfortable space, because this is a "space of vulnerability." I am reminded of the "wilderness sojourn" in the Exodus narrative. But this "space of vulnerability" is also the "space of creativity," which suggests that vulnerability and creativity intertwine. We cannot have one without the other.

"In this interregnum," says Antonio Gramsci, "a great variety of morbid symptoms appear."[8] A long time ago, Herodotus said: "Diseases always attack [individuals] when they are exposed to change."[9] The interval between the decay of the old and the emergence of the new constitutes a transition period, which is characterized by "uncertainty, confusion, error, and wild and fierce fanaticism."[10] When fear of our vulnerability takes control, hearts constrict, minds narrow, and balls of courage shrink. We construct walls of fear and division instead of building bridges of connections.

From "Dystopia" to "Atopia"

Yes, there is a door, but it does not make any promise that we will arrive at our desired future or desired place, and it does not give us a clear picture of our desired new tomorrow. There is the possibility of a new tomorrow if we dare

7. Schewe, *Habits of Resilience*, 54–55.
8. Cited in Bridges, *Managing Transitions*, 42.
9. Cited in Bridges, *Managing Transitions*, ix.
10. Cited in Bridges, *Managing Transitions*, 42.

to enter and pursue the journey, but it is not a utopia waiting for our arrival. No, there is no utopian world or there is "not a world that is ready for the escapist to occupy."[11] What we have is an "atopia"—an imagined new world that is alluring and life-giving—out of the "dystopias" of the present.[12]

There is no ideal world waiting for our discovery and arrival. Instead, it is a world we must imagine and create out of the pieces of the past, the present, and our longings for a better future. "We are not measured against perfection," so do not worry about it. What we are called to do is "to set out on an exploration to an imagined destination, an imagined good."[13] There are no certainties; no guarantees. This is not an invitation to join into something that is "definitive," but into that which is "generative."[14] Part of our work is to create the conditions under which a new world can be imagined.

Imagination is so significant here. Imagination is often disparaged. We often say, "It's *only* imagination." Perhaps, it is more fitting to say, "It is *always* imagination." To paraphrase a saying attributed to Mark Twain: "Our eyesight is not of much use if our imagination is out of focus." It is difficult for us to imagine a different world because we have been living inside the imagination of others who cannot imagine that people with disabilities and women can be leaders and CEOs, cannot imagine Black people being free, cannot imagine fat girls being sexy, and that one does not need a whitening lotion to make one's dark skin beautiful. We need to unshackle our colonized imagination.

Do we have glimmers and glimpses of this imagined tomorrow? Yes, we have. Deep in our hearts we know what gives us pain and what gives us joy. We have inklings of what matters to us the most, which the pandemic has helped unveil. Deep in our hearts we know that which endures the vicissitudes of time and those values that cannot be lost in a shipwreck. We have a foretaste of the eternal in the momentary and temporal. We know, recalling loosely someone's thoughts, that our lives are not measured by the "number of breaths," but by those "moments that take our breath away." In us is the residual memory of a paradise lost, which is our way of looking back from our present state of "fallenness." And we have intimations of a new paradise projected to the future (eschatology) out of our present precarious plight. We are a "paradise-haunted creature": we come from paradise and we yearn for it.[15] We are not clueless. We have ancient wisdom and the wisdom of

11. Brown, *Emergent Strategy*, 164.
12. McFague, *Body of God*, 198–99.
13. Westley et al., *Getting to Maybe*, 229.
14. Westley et al., *Getting to Maybe*, xiii.
15. McFague, *A New Climate for Theology*, 152–53.

our religious traditions. Yet, we also know that although we have vision and values, we do not have a clear and detailed road map, and we know that our wills and visions suffer distortions.

We know deep in our hearts that we can only live fully in right relation with others, both human beings and other creatures. Our imagined new world must address this fundamental reality: we are intrinsically related even if we often act to the contrary. No matter how we deny or violate it, our fundamental reality is that we are related and interdependent. There is no life, no self, and no individual without this interdependence. If so, our atopic dream is a world in which right relations exist among beings within this web of life.

If relationship is critical to our wellbeing, it is an aspect that we must be attentive to. Our "need to belong" and "need to be accepted" often slam shut other equally important needs or values: openness, curiosity, and intelligence. It is no wonder that sometimes we lose our independent critical minds when we join a group. We get swallowed by "tribal thinking" or "cult thinking." Our conformity and loyalty to a group or tribe has rewards and addresses our need for belonging and acceptance.[16] And, "where all think alike, no one thinks very much."[17] Going down the slippery slope, to use the words of Loretta Ross, one of the co-founders of the SisterSong Women of Color Reproductive Justice Collective, "when people think the same idea and move in the same direction, that's a cult. When people think many different ideas and move in one direction, that's a movement."[18]

Critical in our communal life, and also for our shared flourishing, is a healthy sense of self. A healthy sense of self is important for us to be able to engage in healthy relationship. And this healthy sense of self requires a healthy understanding of boundaries. Boundaries are important in maintaining our integrity, which sets where we stand and sets our parameters for what is acceptable and what is not.[19]

Getting to "Maybe"

The journey to our imagined new world (atopia) is a journey to "maybe." To say that it is a journey to "maybe" would be unsettling to many. We like certainty. But the journey to "maybe" is all that we have. It is not a journey to "neverland," but to "maybe-land." Let us embrace it!

16. Wheatley, *Who Do You Choose to Be?*, 145.

17. Walter Lippman, cited in Bridges, *Managing Transitions*, 52.

18. Brown, *Emergent Strategy*, 248.

19. Brown, *Rising Strong*, 122–23.

"Maybe" underscores uncertainty and unpredictability, for sure. But it has its other side that we are often oblivious about. "Maybe" is a word for the bold, the inventive, and the adventurous. "Maybe" is not a word for the reluctant and the hesitant; it is not a word of "caution" for the "cautious." Rather, "maybe" is a "defiant claim of possibility" in the face of status quo, which we are not willing to accept as the way things are. It is a daring recognition that the outcome is still in the making.[20] "Maybe" is a venture into a new "possibility" that is replete with uncertainties, but with eyes wide open and attentive to the unexpected. "Maybe" balances "intention" and "determination" with "fluidity" and "unpredictability."

There is something we can learn from migrants and from those in desperate situations, which characterize our dystopic life under the banner of business-as-usual. The desperate migrants have learned to see and to seize the "maybe" as a "chance" or "a way out of no-way" in a life lived "between a rock and hard place" or "between a sword and a wall" (*entre espada y pared*).

Given the certainty of hardship, starvation or death, and unfulfilled dreams, uncertainty is chosen over certainty. If the certain is closed, the uncertain is open. Choosing the uncertain which is open is the right choice in this desperate context. One may fail or die without seeing the fruits of one's dream, but at least there is a chance that the uncertain may turn into a possibility—a possibility for a better life. The one with diasporic spirituality takes the risk and gambles on turning uncertainty into a possibility in his or her favor. He or she knows the possibility of failing and is in some ways prepared for it, but she or he gambles and bets on the good fortune. In the Tagalog (Pilipino) language, it is called "*nagmamasakali*," which is a form of betting on good fortune. "Why not try? What if good fortune would be on my side? Who knows (only God knows) what is there for me?" the desperate migrant thinks.

Diasporic spirituality, whose main embodiment is the migrant, gives a non-fatalistic twist to the once popular song by Jay Livingston and Ray Evans' "*Que sera, sera*." The lyric "what will be, will be" is not the passive "come what may," but a resolve to go on and take risks. The "future" though "not ours to see" and, therefore, uncertain, is turned by the migrant into an opening for a new possibility.

---

20. Westley et al., *Getting to Maybe*, xiv.

Taking the Leap of Faith: Dealing with Our "Threshold Guardians"

So, the journey to "maybe" has to be taken, which is always and fundamentally an act, or a leap, of faith. We walk by faith, not only by sight, because the road is not given in advance. Our journey of a thousand miles begins with a single step, which is an act of faith. "Faith," says Mary Jo Leddy, "is like a lantern on a dark path; it shines only far enough to illumine the next step. Only when the next step is taken does the light move on. Our beginning steps do not have to be great and grand. They need only be real."[21]

Without a doubt, our walking to bridge our heavenly longings and earthly realities will face many obstacles, reactions, and resistances. As in the fantasy adventure, *The Lord of the Rings*, when a clear path seems ready, there is always a monster or enemy about to appear which acts as a "threshold guardian." Threshold guardians may have something important to say, so we need to listen to them.[22] But we must also rise above them and not let them imprison us. Like the true adventurer, we must rise to the occasion, using multiple ways, such as confronting, bypassing, or befriending the monster that is blocking the way. Perhaps, befriending the monster serves to confer blessings on us, so we become monsters in the splendid sense of the old French word, *monstre*, a horror, a wonder, a marvel, a thing of God's own making and remaking.[23]

However, while *outside* obstacles and resistance to change are real and pressing, I believe that our greatest obstacle or "threshold guardian" is ourselves or that which lies within ourselves—our own fears of failure or our desires for fame or success. These fears or desires act as obstacles: they make us confuse credit for success, criticism for enemy, public recognition for self-worth, and significance for fame.

Learning to Let Go

I enjoy the sight of the fall season because of its magnificent colors: *feuille morte* (brownish orange or yellowish brown), sepia (brownish tone), russet (reddish brown), amber (dark orange-yellow), gamboge (vivid yellows), scarlet (bright red color), crimson and carmine (deep red), maroon, auburn (goldish and reddish shades of brown), lurid (pale yellow), and carnelian and cornelian (reddish-orange or brownish-red). Who would

21. Leddy, *Radical Gratitude*, 145.
22. Macy and Johnstone, *Active Hope*, 193.
23. Wood, *Chesterton*, 38.

not be enchanted by the colors of the fall season? Who would not be joyful in such a jocund company?

But my great delight does not come unalloyed. Much as I enjoy the season and cherish its beauty, the coming of the fall season also breaks my heart and makes me sad. Why? Because I have to say goodbye to our morning glory that greets me with its morning smile, and say goodbye to our dahlias, marigolds, peonies, daisies, and petunias, among others. Yet, I have no choice, for the fall season cannot wait. And yet, even as I start to welcome and enjoy autumn, in this part of the world, autumn or fall is too short. Again, even before most of the leaves could fall to the ground, a snow storm may come to mark the beginning winter days. Hastily, I have to say goodbye to fall and face the winter season.

There are no beginnings without endings. Every beginning ends something. Beginnings and endings are intertwined, just as welcoming and saying goodbye are intertwined. I know this. But it is not easy. "All changes, even the most longed for, have their melancholy; for what we leave behind is part of ourselves," says Anatole France.[24] And, "nothing is so dear as what you're about to leave."[25] Difficult as it is, "One doesn't discover new lands without consenting to lose sight of the shore for a very long time."[26]

When I observe the transformation of trees throughout the changing season, I have noticed something incredible: they are experts at letting things go. They are experts in the art of transitioning from one form to another: from being no longer in the splendor of their autumn color and not yet in the robust emergence of spring green. How about if we start learning the art of letting go from trees?

From "Outcry" to "Birth-cry": Making "Hope and History Rhyme"[27]

Many have attempted, but we cannot bend and muscle our social environment or the world completely according to our desires. We cannot control and muscle or force it to be the environment we want it to be without it fighting back to our detriment. Even when things go wrong, we oftentimes do not see the connections. We can, however, cooperate with our social environment and tap its nature and processes in such a way that our intentions and circumstances align. When there is an alignment of our circumstances

24. Cited in Bridges, *Managing Transitions*, 24.
25. Jessamyn West, cited in Bridges, *Managing Transitions*, 89.
26. Andre Gide, cited in Bridges, *Managing Transitions*, 39.
27. From Seamus Heaney's poem, "The Cure at Troy."

with our intentions, we can say that "hope and history rhyme." When this happens, we will begin to see our imagined new tomorrow coming and emerging out of the cocoon of life. And then, what seems impossible looking forward, seems almost inevitable looking in hindsight. Even an obdurate world does yield, does change.[28]

Cooperating with our social environment to make hope and history rhyme for the sake of giving birth to our imagined world is possible because we and our social environment are one. We, as well as our social environment, are by our very nature, constantly changing and emerging. As an organism whose very nature is change, we do not adapt to change. Rather, we thrive on change by integrating our social environment into our process as one of our "environmental variables and creating further change."[29]

Without change, we die. Charles Darwin is attributed to have said: "It is not the strongest of the species that survive, nor the most intelligent, but the one most responsive to." The truly resilient are those who are responsive to change and who stay connected with and are attuned to their surroundings. Look at those considered king of the jungles, such as tigers and lions; they are facing the threat of extinction. But, observe the mushrooms: "From dead plant matter to nematodes to bacteria, never underestimate the cleverness of mushrooms to find new food" and thrive.[30]

What we touch, changes. What we touch, changes ourselves. What changes ourselves, changes others. We do not change alone; we change in relation to and with others: in relationship and interaction we change and are changed. And how we perceive and position ourselves in relation to our social environment affects our shared reality. If it is only in change that we survive, if not thrive, and change is relational and communal, it follows that communal connection is critical to our survival. Any talk about resilience and change must attend to our community connections. We cannot change, survive, and thrive alone.

If everything is changing and emerging, we must stop treating our social environment as if it were static and solid, which can easily be predicted from our flowcharts. Instead of an unmovable solid rock, we may start thinking of a mountain that is shifting in relation to our location and perspective. Perhaps it is better to adopt the metaphor of the sea that is always experiencing sea-change. Failure to take this into account, we would be like the "learned" who are prepared for a world that no longer exists,

28. Westley et al., *Getting to Maybe*, viii.
29. Thomas and Brown, *A New Culture of Learning*, 37.
30. Brown, *Emergent Strategy*, 152.

whereas the "learners" are those who will inherit the earth. Only the learners will survive and thrive.

When everything is changing and emerging, it is telling us that there is no single response to a stimulus or to stimuli. In the face of changing and unpredictable seas, the sailor (the social innovator) has to re-calibrate and reposition while not losing his or her goal to "get to maybe." Understanding the complex nature of reality, the social innovator knows that there are multiple responses to the stimulus/stimuli. Water, for example, has more than one way of responding to an obstacle or a rock. It does not just crash head-on into everything that stands in its path but moves with gravity and around the obstacles and wears them down. When there is no way forward because of barriers, such as a dam or long stretch of desert, it crosses to the other side by turning into vapor and clouds and drops to the other side of the divide as rain.[31]

Our survival, if not how we thrive, depends on our ability to see and move in multiple directions while not losing sight of our center and our destination. Yes, we have to be visionary, but we also must be flexible and responsive to the energetic flow of the unpredictable and the unexpected.

One Sunday morning I was on my way to a speaking engagement in Duluth, Minnesota. The snow was pouring heavy that day. Starting from the base of a hill, I attempted to drive straight uphill to where the church was located. Because of traffic light intersections, I could not drive my car at a desired speed. Losing speed and traction on a road covered with snow, my car skidded to the side and got stranded on a hill of snow. Too late, I realized that I should have taken the longer, gradual, and zig-saggy route to reach to the top. But, I did not. I was one-track minded: I tried to go straight to the top arrogantly oblivious of other conditions and variables along the way.

This incident reminded me of crabs. We have negative association of crabs, like when we say, "crab mentality." But have we really observed closely how crabs behave and move? Instead of moving in a direct linear fashion, a crab walks forward, backward, and sideward. When a crab is surrounded, it buries itself in the sand and then comes out at a later time. And, when it is pushed to the corner, it fights back. We can learn something from crabs that is significant for our day-to-day lives. We need to be "crablike" in our approach to obstacles and challenges, because crabs have the instinctive capacity of multi-directionality. Watching how crabs work the sands of sea tides, we have an image of a creature that embodies "serendipitous sagacity." This is a creature with sideways-looking-eyesight (peripheral vision)—not just forward-looking eyesight (frontal vision)—which is an

31. Brown, *Emergent Strategy*, 153.

antidote to statist politics and tunnel vision, and which has the ability to move with the energetic flow of the unexpected in constantly changing terrain, while not losing sight of one's purpose.[32]

How Shall We Get? Living into Our Dreams and Values

Like many of you, I too dream of a post-pandemic world (not a return to the "once normal" that is destructive and non-sustainable) in which, having come to our senses on what truly matters, we would seriously be committed to the well-being of all in the web of life. We cannot, however, leapfrog into that new alluring and delightful world, for the journey itself is constitutive of the destination. To put it differently, we will not arrive at the new world of our heart's longing unless we are striving to embody that desired future in our day-to-day lives, now.

Do we want to wake up to a new and better tomorrow after this night-time of pandemic? That will largely depend on the way we respond now, not after we have survived the pandemic.

Who are we becoming in this time of pandemic? What daily practices are we doing as embodiments of the new world we are anticipating?

We may have grand dreams and values, but we must learn how to op-erationalize them in our individual and corporate lives. Our dreams and values must match. A value is more than a proposition of what we hold dear; it is "*a way of being or believing* that we hold most important."[33] What do we hold dear or important? Brené Brown's advice is that we name that or those which is/are dear to us, which can guide our way in the dark and resonate/s with how we feel who we really are. We need to ask such questions as: Does this define me? Is this who am I at my best? Is this a filter that I use to make difficult decisions? And, having identified what we hold dear, are we living into our values? Are we walking our talk? Do our intentions, words, thoughts, and actions align with our values?[34]

For Such a Time as Ours: Who Do We Choose to Be?

The phrase, "for such a time as this" (Esther 4:13–14) has been tossed around but without much deep reflection. In common usage, it simply means a "momentous time" or "historic time" for an individual or a

32. Lederach, *The Moral Imagination*.

33. Brown, *Dare to Lead*, 186.

34. Brown, *Dare to Lead*, 190.

community. It simply means "our time" and how we relate to it. The phrase includes this, but also so much more. It refers to a critical time of decision making, "who do we choose to be" when a matter of ultimate significance presents itself to us.

Who are we choosing to be? Our daily choice of who we choose to be shapes who we are becoming. Two plants that I am quite familiar with may give us some ideas on who we want to be. I have wrestled with dandelions while trying to keep my lawn green and healthy in Minnesota. I am also getting familiar with wild mushrooms, with the help of an indigenous (Manobo) student at Union Theological Seminary, Philippines. Adept at survival, mushrooms have a way of taking toxic substances and transforming them as food, while dandelions spread and proliferate quickly even against tremendous odds. Mushrooms are "toxin transformer" and dandelions are "communities of healers" waiting to spread.[35] Who are we choosing to be?

I would not say that ours is the most critical and important moment in history, but this is "our time" and "our challenge." Our challenge is to choose to be the better versions of ourselves every day of our lives until our "choices eventually become habits—our convictions thus having chosen us rather than the other way around."[36] When this happens, our habits become expressions of who we really are. These are choices guided by what is life-affirming, otherwise, we will develop habits that are life-negating. "Be careful what you practice; you may get really good at the wrong thing."[37]

It is not by default that we will re-orient ourselves to that which is true, good, and beautiful because the pandemic has turned our world upside down or downside up, rather it requires a conscious or intentional choice to dwell in our imagined post-pandemic world "as if it were already a reality." Our *attention* and *intention* can lead to "intentional actions," which will serve to midwife the birthing of a new tomorrow. Although we do not have full control of the outcome, with the right "mindset" and "skills set," chance and opportunities favor the "prepared mind."[38] The "prepared mind" can see and seize opportunities. Do we want to help give birth to a "new world"—a world not only different from the "old normal" but "fundamentally better"? If so, let us give our disciplined attention to its creation!

For sure, challenges are plenty, coming from both inside and outside forces, the "threshold guardians." It is not easy to maintain openness and commitment simultaneously. In this situation when innocence is drowned, to

35. Brown, *Emergent Strategy*, 9.
36. Wood, *Chesterton*, 36.
37. Tony Blauer, cited in Menakem, *My Grandmother's Hands*, 111.
38. Westley et al., *Getting to Maybe*, 222.

borrow the lines of W. B. Yeats, "the best lack conviction, while the worst/Are full of intensity."[39] Is this our only choice: "intelligence on ice" or "ignorance on fire"? No, it is not. There are many and varied ways of responding to our constantly shifting, changing, and emerging social reality.

We are embarking on a long threshold journey with doors and portals along the way, the road of which is made by walking. In the words of poet Antonio Machado, "*caminante no hay camino. Se hace camino al andar*" (Traveler, there's no road. The road is made by walking).[40] Our walking, which makes the road, is constitutive of our destination into the "maybe" and the "not yet." With longing and faith, we must dare to walk boldly in the direction of our dreams. We cannot leapfrog to our post-pandemic world, much as we want to, but must wrestle with who we are becoming in light of our quest to become the better versions of ourselves.

There is no doubt that the darkness around us is deep. Our challenges are complex and plenty. But with an active hope in God's faithfulness and in the power of the divine light that cannot be extinguished by the most ferocious storm, we can reclaim and transform the darkness. For, in such a time as this, there is also an opportune moment—the moment of new life and new beginning.

Yes, there is darkness . . . deep darkness. But what if the darkness is no longer the darkness of the tomb but the darkness of the womb. What if, through our intentional transformative actions, our labor of love is bearing fruits and now we are experiencing contractions? What if something is waiting to be born and our art of social midwifery is needed?

What does a midwife tell a pregnant woman who is in the delivery process? "Breathe and push, breathe and push." The instruction is to breathe and push until the water breaks. As social midwives, let us breathe and push until we hear the birthing cry of a new and better tomorrow for our land and for our world. Let our social midwifery usher its birthing! Let our prodigal action welcome its coming!

Bibliography

Bridges, William. *Managing Transitions: Making the Most of Change*. Bridges and Associates, 2009.

Brown, Adrienne Maree. *Emergent Strategy: Shaping Change, Changing Worlds*. Chico, CA: AK, 2017.

Brown, Brené. *Dare to Lead: Brave Work, Tough Conversations, Whole Hearts*. New York: Random House, 2018.

39. From W. B. Yeats' poem, "The Second Coming."
40. Machado, "Proverbio 29."

———. *Rising Strong: The Reckoning, the Rumble, the Revolution*. New York: Spiegel & Grau, 2015.

The Global Goals. "The Pandemic Is a Portal by Arundhati Roy—A Future Where the Global Goals Are Achieved." *YouTube*, September 7, 2020. https://www.youtube.com/watch?v=ALN3UkxXA8g.

Hall, Douglas John. *Why Christian? For Those on the Edge of Faith*. Minneapolis: Fortress, 1998.

Lederach, John Paul. *The Moral Imagination: The Art and Soul of Building Peace*. New York: Oxford University Press, 2005.

Leddy, Mary Jo. *Radical Gratitude*. Maryknoll, NY: Orbis, 2002.

Machado, Antonio. "Proverbio 29." https://sen.scot/antonio-machado-campos-de-castilla/.

Macy, Joanna, and Chris Johnstone. *Active Hope: How to Face the Mess We're in without Going Crazy*. Novato, CA: New World Library, 2012.

McFague, Sallie. *The Body of God: An Ecological Theology*. Minneapolis: Fortress, 1993.

———. *A New Climate for Theology: God, the World, and Global Warming*. Minneapolis: Fortress, 2008.

Menakem, Resmaa. *My Grandmother's Hands: Racialized Trauma and the Pathways to Mending Our Hearts and Bodies*. Las Vegas: Central Recovery, 2017.

Moltmann, Jürgen. *The Source of Life: The Holy Spirit and the Theology of Life*. Translated by Margaret Kohl. Minneapolis: Fortress, 1997.

Palmer, Parker J. *Healing the Heart of Democracy: The Courage to Create a Politics Worthy of the Human Spirit*. San Francisco: Jossey-Bass, 2011.

Roy, Arundhati. "The Pandemic Is a Portal." *Financial Times*, April 3, 2020. https://www.ft.com/content/10d8f5e8-74eb-11ea-95fe-fcd274e920ca.

Schewe, Beryl. *Habits of Resilience: Learning to Live Fully in the Midst of Loss*. New London, CT: Twenty Third, 2015.

Thomas, Douglas, and John Seely Brown. *A New Culture of Learning: Cultivating the Imagination for a World of Constant Change*. CreateSpace, 2011.

Westley, Frances, et al. *Getting to Maybe: How the World Is Changed*. Toronto: Vintage Canada, 2007.

Wheatley, Margaret. *Who Do You Choose to Be? Facing Reality, Claiming Leadership, Restoring Sanity*. Oakland: Berrett-Koeller, 2017.

Wood, Ralph C. *Chesterton: The Nightmare Goodness of God*. Waco, TX: Baylor University Press, 2011.